Air Pollutants
and the Leaf Cuticle

NATO ASI Series

Advanced Science Institutes Series

A series presenting the results of activities sponsored by the NATO Science Committee, which aims at the dissemination of advanced scientific and technological knowledge, with a view to strengthening links between scientific communities.

The Series is published by an international board of publishers in conjunction with the NATO Scientific Affairs Division

A Life Sciences	Plenum Publishing Corporation
B Physics	London and New York
C Mathematical and Physical Sciences	Kluwer Academic Publishers Dordrecht, Boston and London
D Behavioural and Social Sciences	
E Applied Sciences	
F Computer and Systems Sciences	Springer-Verlag Berlin Heidelberg New York
G Ecological Sciences	London Paris Tokyo Hong Kong
H Cell Biology	Barcelona Budapest
I Global Environmental Change	

NATO-PCO DATABASE

The electronic index to the NATO ASI Series provides full bibliographical references (with keywords and/or abstracts) to more than 30 000 contributions from international scientists published in all sections of the NATO ASI Series. Access to the NATO-PCO DATABASE compiled by the NATO Publication Coordination Office is possible in two ways:

- via online FILE 128 (NATO-PCO DATABASE) hosted by ESRIN, Via Galileo Galilei, I-00044 Frascati, Italy.

- via CD-ROM "NATO Science & Technology Disk" with user-friendly retrieval software in English, French and German (© WTV GmbH and DATAWARE Technologies Inc. 1992).

The CD-ROM can be ordered through any member of the Board of Publishers or through NATO-PCO, Overijse, Belgium.

Series G: Ecological Sciences, Vol. 36

Air Pollutants
and the Leaf Cuticle

Edited by

Kevin E. Percy

Natural Resources Canada
Canadian Forest Service – Maritimes Region
P. O. Box 4000
Fredericton, New Brunswick
Canada E3B 5P7

J. Neil Cape

Institute of Terrestrial Ecology
Bush Estate
Penicuik, Midlothian EH26 OQB, UK

Richard Jagels

Department of Forest Ecosystem Science
University of Maine
Orono, Maine 04469, USA

Caroline J. Simpson

Natural Resources Canada
Canadian Forest Service – Maritimes Region
P. O. Box 4000
Fredericton, New Brunswick
Canada E3B 5P7

Springer-Verlag
Berlin Heidelberg New York London Paris Tokyo
Hong Kong Barcelona Budapest
Published in cooperation with NATO Scientific Affairs Division

Proceedings of the NATO Advanced Research Workshop on Air Pollutants and the Leaf Cuticle, held at Fredericton, Canada, October 4-8, 1993

ISBN 3-540-58146-4 Springer-Verlag Berlin Heidelberg New York
ISBN 0-387-58146-4 Springer-Verlag New York Berlin Heidelberg

CIP data applied for

© Springer-Verlag Berlin Heidelberg 1994
Printed in Germany

Typesetting: Camera ready by editors
SPIN 10122383   31/3130 - 5 4 3 2 1 0 - Printed on acid-free paper

Preface

Air pollutants are omnipresent in the northern hemisphere. Those of most concern are sulphur dioxide, oxides of nitrogen, tropospheric ozone, and acidic deposition. Ozone alone is responsible for billions of dollars annually in crop losses. Many forests, particularly those growing at higher elevations in Europe and North America, have been declining and air pollutants have been determined to be causal agents or prominent among a complex of inciting factors. Recently, polluted coastal fogs and marine aerosols have caused tree declines in North America and the Mediterranean, respectively. Critical levels of sulphate in cloud water are also being exceeded in many high elevation forests where decline is not yet manifest.

The leaf surface forms the interface between plants and a deteriorating atmospheric environment. It is, therefore, the first point of contact between plants and air pollutants and presents an effective barrier to pollutant entry. Outermost surfaces of leaves are covered by a thin, lipoidal, non-living membrane called a cuticle. Cuticle integrity is essential to plant survival and has many essential functions, including the prevention of excessive water loss, regulation of solute uptake and protection of sensitive underlying photosynthetic tissues agains harmful irradiation such as enhanced UV-B resulting from stratospheric ozone depletion.

The physicochemical properties of the cuticle vary greatly between and within species. They are known to be sensitive to change through natural and anthropogenic influences. One of the major research areas, dating to at least 1924, is air pollutants. There is a large body of international literature on structural changes to epicuticular waxes induced by air pollutants. This is supplemented by a lesser number of reports on consequential effects to leaf physiology and function. At the same time, no evidence exists for cuticle repair mechanisms. This is of importance for long-lived coniferous tree species where needles are retained over successive growing seasons.

Despite renewed interest in the subject of air pollutant effects on leaf surfaces, considerable uncertainty over precise mechanisms of action and biological implications remains. This book comprises contributions made to a NATO-sponsored Advanced Research Workshop "Air Pollutants and the Leaf Cuticle" held October 4-9, 1993 in Fredericton, New Brunswick, Canada. The objective of the ARW was to bring together for the first time international expertise on the subject of air pollutant interactions with the cuticle. In so doing, a high-level scientific exchange of current research findings would occur and future international collaboration would be stimulated.

In order to facilitate a state-of-science review, the ARW was structured around four themes. They were as follows:

1. Cuticular physicochemical characteristics, physiological, regulatory, and protective roles.

2. Effects, mechanisms, and consequences of air pollutant interaction with leaf cuticles.

3. Non-anthropogenic and environmental influences on the cuticle and potential of the cuticle for biomonitoring and critical levels mapping.

4. New developments in experimental methodology and analytical techniques.

This book is divided into several parts beginning with invited review papers from all four ARW themes. These are followed by selected voluntary papers highlighting new areas of research. Section III contains brief voluntary contributions, mostly relating to theme 3. Section IV contains brief rapporteurs' reports, summarizing the six ARW sessions. Salient points for which there was general agreement in the final plenary session are featured in "Recommendations by Participants".

The Director of the workshop was K.E. Percy. The following scientists formed the ARW Organizing Committee:

K.E. Percy, Director
Natural Resources Canada
Canadian Forest Service - Maritimes Region
Fredericton, New Brunswick
Canada

J.N. Cape, Co-Director
Institute of Terrestrial Ecology
Bush Estate
Penicuick
U.K.

R. Jagels, Co-Director
Department of Forest Resources
University of Maine
Orono, Maine
U.S.A.

The Editorial Board comprised the Organizing Committee and C.M. Simpson, Scientific Editor, Natural Resources Canada, Canadian Forest Service - Maritimes Region, Fredericton.

The Organizing Committee wishes to express its gratitude for the very generous workshop support given by the North Atlantic Treaty Organization and the host organization, Natural Resources Canada, Canadian Forest Service. The Organizing Committee also wishes to thank Varian Canada Inc. for its sponsorship at the ARW reception. The outstanding technical/logistical assistance of P. Gaboury, C. Grey, C. McLaughlin, and D. O'Connor of the Canadian Forest Service - Maritimes Region is gratefully acknowledged.

K.E. Percy
J.N. Cape
R. Jagels

December 1993
Fredericton

TABLE OF CONTENTS

SECTION I - REVIEWS

Plant Cuticles: Physicochemical Characteristics and Biosynthesis

Peter J. Holloway
Department of Agricultural Sciences
University of Bristol
AFRC Institute of Arable Crops Research
Long Ashton Research Station
Bristol BS18 9AF UK

Abstract

Cuticles are the thin continuous layers of predominantly lipid material deposited on the outer walls of epidermal cells and, thus, the interface between higher plants and their aerial environment. The main function of this extracellular, non-living layer, commonly referred to as a membrane, is to protect and waterproof the plant surface. Although not structurally or chemically homogeneous, cuticles are usually characterised by two specific classes of lipid substances. The insoluble high molecular weight polyester cutins constitute the framework of the membrane, the monomeric units of which are biosynthesised in the epidermal cells from C_{16} and C_{18} fatty acid precursors. The soluble long-chain wax constituents are also synthesised by these cells and are eventually deposited not only on the cuticular surface but also within the cutin matrix. Epicuticular waxes have a considerable influence on the wettability of a plant surface whereas the presence of intracuticular waxes governs cuticular permeability. The cuticles of some species also contain variable amounts of another aliphatic biopolymer, cutin, which is non-saponifiable and, consequently, extremely resistant to biodegradation. Because the cuticle is an integral part of the epidermal cell wall, polysaccharides and probably, phenolic compounds are also involved in its construction.

The current status of our fundamental knowledge about the structure, chemical composition, and biosynthesis of plant cuticles will be reviewed in order to highlight the nature of potential sites for interaction with air pollutants.

Introduction

Cuticles are the thin continuous layers of predominantly lipid material deposited on the outer walls of plant epidermal cells and are, thus, the interface between plants and their aerial environment (Martin and Juniper, 1970). The main function of this extracellular, non-living layer, usually referred to as a membrane, is to protect and waterproof the plant surface. Although both the structure and chemical composition of cuticles can vary considerably according to species, they are usually characterised by the presence of two specific classes of lipids, soluble waxes and insoluble polyester cutins, both of which are biosynthetic products exclusive to epidermal cells. Because the cuticle is an integral part of the cell wall, polysaccharides and, probably, phenolic compounds are also involved in its construction.

NATO ASI Series, Vol. G 36
Air Pollutants and the Leaf Cuticle
Edited by K. E. Percy et al.
© Springer-Verlag Berlin Heidelberg 1994

The main thrust of fundamental research on the nature and biosynthesis of plant cuticles was during the 1960s and 1970s. The main objectives of this mini-review, therefore, are to summarise and to give an update on our areas of knowledge as well as of ignorance, bearing in mind the renewed interest in the plant cuticle from the viewpoint of its potential physical and chemical interactions with air pollutants.

Surface structure

The microstructure of the cuticle surface is of primary importance for the initial interaction with air-borne pollutants as this has a considerable influence on its wettability and, consequently, on the deposition and retention of moisture (Holloway, 1970). There is much variation in leaf surface roughness not only between plant species but even between the abaxial and adaxial surfaces of the same species. Much depends on the gross topography of the underlying epidermal features, such as the shape and size of the cells, patterns of venation and the presence or absence of modified cells, especially hairs (trichomes). Thus, the contours of the cuticle may be flat, convex or papillose, with a surface which may be relatively smooth, ridged or covered with a microcrys-talline deposit of epicuticular wax; more than one form of roughness may be present. All these features can be revealed in detail by examination in the scanning electron microscope (SEM) (for a recent survey of weed species consult Harr *et al.*, 1991). Waxy and hairy surfaces are the most difficult to wet because they cause air films to become trapped between the cuticle surface and impinging water droplets.

Surface chemistry

The chemical properties of a cuticle surface are essentially governed by the layer of solid epicuticular wax which may be amorphous or crystalline in form. The quantity present may be as little as 5 μg cm^{-2} or as much as 500 μg cm^{-2} in some xerophytic species. Epicuticular waxes are soluble in non-polar organic solvents, such as chloroform and diethyl ether, and, therefore, can be readily isolated for analysis and identification (Holloway, 1984a; Walton, 1990). Wax composition is species specific but it may change during the course of plant development (Baker, 1982). Many different classes of long-chain organic compounds have been identified in plant waxes. The most characteristic components are aliphatic in nature and show either an even- (Table 1) or odd- (Table 2) carbon number preference; these may be accompanied by cyclic constituents (Table 3) in some species. Plant waxes often contain a predominant class of constituent, for example, alkanes in the leaves of *Brassica* sp. and *Pisum sativum* (adaxial surface), alkanals in *Saccharum officinarum*, 1-alkanols in *Pisum sativum* (abaxial surface) and many grasses, ketones in *Allium* sp., secondary alcohols (mainly 10-nonacosanol) in *Papaver* sp. and several conifers, and ß-diketones in *Eucalyptus* and *Dianthus* sp. Fruit waxes are rich sources of triterpenoids, *e.g.*, *Malus pumila* (ursolic acid) and *Vitis vinifera* (oleanolic acid). On certain species, the crystalline form of the epicuticular wax is related to its chemical composition. For example, rodlet-like crystals are often associated with waxes that have a high alkanal content, short tubes with 10-nonacosanol, long tubes with ß-diketones, and small plates with 1-alkanols.

Table 1   Some aliphatic constituents with a predominantly even-carbon number found in plant epicuticular waxes

Class	Homologue range	Most common
n-Alkanals	C_{16} - C_{34}	C_{26}, C_{28} and C_{30}
n-1-Alkanols*	C_{18} - C_{36}	C_{26}, C_{28} and C_{30}
n-Alkanoic acids*	C_{14} - C_{36}	C_{26} and C_{28}
n-Alkyl monesters*	C_{32} - C_{72}	C_{42} - C_{50}

Branched-chain homologues may also occur in some species

Table 2   Some aliphatic constituents with a predominantly odd-carbon number found in plant epicuticular waxes

Class	Homologue range	Most common
n-Alkanes	C_{17} - C_{35}	C_{29} and C_{31}
β-Diketones	C_{29} - C_{33}	C_{31} and C_{33}
Hydroxy-ß-diketones	C_{29} - C_{33}	C_{31}
n-Ketones*	C_{23} - C_{33}	C_{29} and C_{31}
n-Sec. alkanols*	C_{21} - C_{33}	C_{29} and C_{31}

Positional isomerism varies according to species

Table 3   Some cyclic constituents found in plant epicuticular waxes

Class	Most common
Pentacyclic triterpenols	ß-Amyrin
Pentacyclic triterpenoid acids	Ursolic acid
Sterols	ß-Sitosterol

Various monoesters with either n-alkanoic acids or n-1-alkanols may also occur in some species

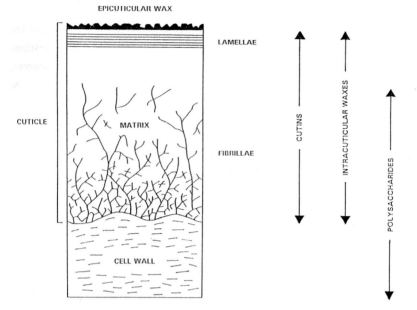

Figure 1   Summary of the main internal ultrastructural and chemical features of plant cuticles (from Holloway, 1993)

Internal structure

Structural and histochemical information about the nature of plant cuticles is obtained by microscopical examination of transverse sections through the outer epidermal wall (Holloway, 1982a; Holloway and Wattendorff, 1987). In the light microscope, the cuticle is usually seen to be sharply delineated from the thickened outer periclinal cell wall but little fine structure is normally visible. Cuticle thickness may vary from <0.1 µm to more than 10 µm in some fruits and xerophytes; a characteristic feature of thicker cuticles are the 'pegs' that penetrate down between adjacent anticlinal cell walls. Cuticles are stained by lipophilic dyes, e.g., sudans, and often show an intense colour reaction with ruthenium red at the junction between the cuticle and the cell wall. The former is ascribed to the presence of cutin, the latter to pectinaceous material.

At the electron microscope level, there is much variation between plant species in cuticle fine structure (Holloway, 1982a). However, in most cuticles the framework is composed of an amorphous matrix of cutin. Within this matrix may be found anastomoses of lamellae and fibrillae (Figure 1), the latter often exhibiting a marked reticulate appearance. Lamellae, when present are of two types, one electron opaque (10-50 nm in thickness), the other translucent (3-10 nm in thickness), and they occur alternately, usually in the outermost region of the cuticle where they form the polylamellate 'cuticle proper' of certain species, *e.g.*, *Agave americana* and *Clivia miniata*. Occasionally, lucent lamellae can also be observed in deeper regions of the cuticle. The precise nature of cuticular lamellae is still unknown. There is some evidence that the opaque lamellae are comprised of cutin, whereas the lucent ones are thought to contain intracuticular waxes. Ultrahistochemical reactions demonstrate that polysaccharides are the principal components of cuticular fibrillae; these often appear to be continuous with the structural elements of the underlying cell wall. Enzyme-gold affinity labelling has recently been used to confirm this identification (Tenberge, 1992).

Thin cuticles may be essentially amorphous (*e.g.*, *Zea mays*) or sometimes entirely lamellate (*e.g.*, *Beta vulgaris*). More substantial cuticles, on the other hand, may be predominantly reticulate (*e.g.*, *Citrus limon*) or possess a two-layered structure either comprising an outer amorphous region with a reticulate inner one (*e.g.*, *Malus pumila*) or a polylamellate outer layer with a reticulate inner zone (*e.g.*, *Agave americana*). Structurally heterogeneous lipid-containing structures of these types provide an effective barrier against desiccation as well as other harmful environmental factors.

Internal composition

For chemical analysis, cuticles can be separated from the epidermal walls of most species by incubating pieces of fresh plant tissue in solutions of pectin - and/or cellulose-dissolving reagents or enzymes (Holloway, 1984b). Thin cuticles are difficult to isolate intact because they are easily fragmented. Waxes embedded within isolated cuticles are often difficult to remove and extraction with hot polar organic solvents may be necessary. These intracuticular waxes usually have compositions different from those found on the surface of the same cuticle; very long-chain alkanoic acids are often the main components of intracuticular waxes (Baker, 1982). Previous reports of the presence of C_{16} and C_{18} acids in such extractives can probably be ascribed to artifacts produced during cuticle isolation with enzymes (Schönherr and Riederer, 1986). The amount of intracuticular wax present in a cuticle may exceed that of epicuticular wax.

Isolated cuticle preparations contain 20-80% by weight of cutin, the quantities on an area basis ranging from 10-30 µg cm^{-2} for thin cuticles, 100-500 µg cm^{-2} for more substantial ones, and up to 1.5 mg cm^{-2} for very thick fruit cuticles. Cutin contents and compositions are determined by depolymerisation of dewaxed cuticles with de-esterifying reagents, such as alcoholic KOH, NaOMe-MeOH and LiAlH$_4$ (Holloway, 1982b; Holloway, 1984b; Walton, 1990). These yield the monomeric units of the original cutin polyester which are usually identified and quantified by gas chromatography and mass spectrometry (Holloway, 1982b); a HPLC method has also been developed recently (Gerard *et al.*, 1992).

Plant cutins are constructed from a unique series of substituted C_{16} (Table 4) and C_{18} (Table 5) alkanoic acids; species differ from one another mainly in the relative proportions of these two groups. Some leaf cutins are exclusively C_{16}, *e.g.*, *Vicia faba* and *Coffea arabica*, others

Table 4   The C_{16} group of cutin acid monomers

Hexadecane-1,16-dioic
16-Hydroxyhexadecanoic
16-Hydroxy-10*-oxohexadecanoic
15-Formyl-9*-hydroxyhexadecanoic
7*-Hydroxyhexadecane-1,16-dioic
10*,16-Dihydroxyhexadecanoic

*Other positional isomers involving the substituents marked * also of common occur-rence, e.g., 9,16-dihydroxyhexadecanoic acid*

Table 5   The C_{18} group of cutin acid monomers

SATURATED
Octadecane-1,18-dioic
18-Hydroxyoctadecanoic
10,18-Dihydroxyoctadecanoic (and other positional isomers)
9,10-Epoxy-18-hydroxyoctadecanoic
9,10,18-Trihydroxyoctadecanoic
9,10-Epoxyoctadecane-1,18-dioic
9,10-Dihydroxyoctadecane-1,18-dioic
9,10,12,13,18-Pentahydroxyoctadecanoic
MONOENOIC
9-Octadecene-1,18-dioic
18-Hydroxyoctadec-9-enoic
9,10-Epoxy-18-hydroxyoctadec-12-enoic
9,10,18-Trihydroxyoctadec-12-enoic
DIENOIC
9,12-Octadecadiene-1,18-dioic
18-Hydroxyoctadec-9,12-dienoic

predominantly C_{18}, *e.g.*, *Spinacia oleracea*. Cutins comprised of monomers of both groups are very common, *e.g.*, leaves of *Malus pumila* and *Clivia miniata*. The most ubiquitous members of the C_{16} group are 9,16- and 10,16-dihydroxyhexadecanoic acids, those of the C_{18} group, 9,10,18-trihydroxyoctadecanoic acid and the corresponding 9,10-epoxide. The presence of the latter group in sectioned cuticular material can be detected using a specific ultrahistochemical reaction (Holloway *et al.*, 1981).

The precise intermolecular structures of cutin biopolymers are still unknown. Obviously, they will differ from species to species because the three-dimensional structure will be governed by the chain-lengths and the numbers and positions of esterifiable groups in the constituent monomers. Hydroxyacids with primary hydroxyl groups can only form a linear polymer, whereas cross-linking of the aliphatic chains is possible with those having secondary hydroxyl groups. After depolymerisation, most cutins show an excess of hydroxyl over carboxyl groups; with C_{16} types of cutin, predepolymerization reactions have demonstrated that these are mainly secondary (Holloway, 1982b). A general representation of the possible structure of cutin is shown in Figure 2.

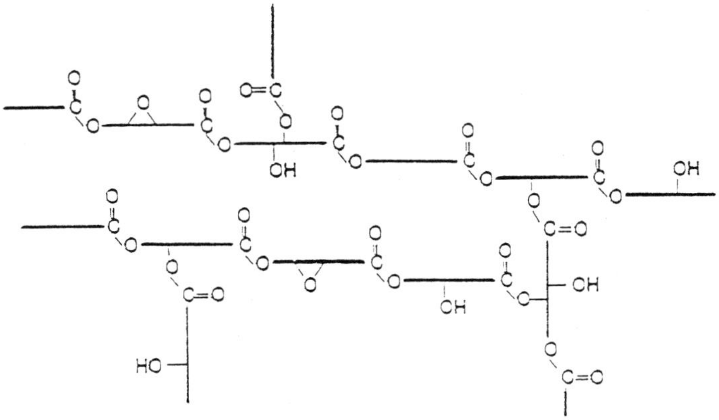

Figure 2   Hypothetical representation of the intermolecular structure of a plant cutin (from Tegelaar, 1990)

After all the wax and cutin components have been removed from an isolated cuticle preparation there is usually some residual material left. For many species, the bulk of this is polysaccharide, mainly cellulose, representing that portion of the epidermal wall that was originally cutinised. However, in some species, the residue is substantial in weight and also contains another type of aliphatic biopolymer, cutan (Nip *et al.*, 1986). Cutans are extremely resistant to chemical

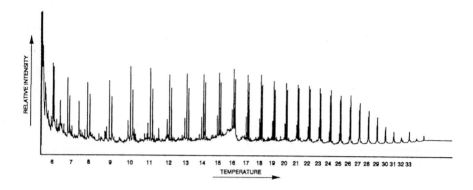

Figure 3   Curie-point (770°C) pyrolysis-gas chromatogram of cutan from leaves of *Agave americana*. The cluster of peaks at each carbon number is comprised of straight-chain alkanes, 1-alkenes and α,ω-alkadienes. Adapted from Tegelaar *et al.* (1989a)

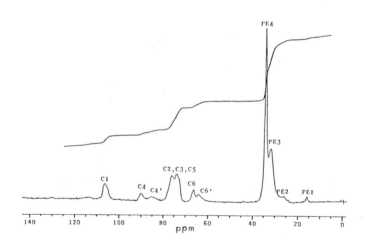

Figure 4   Solid-state magic angle spin-spin decoupled ^{13}C NMR spectrum of cutan from leaves of *Agave americana*. PE = polymethylene signals; C = polysaccharide signals. Adapted from Nip *et al.* (1987)

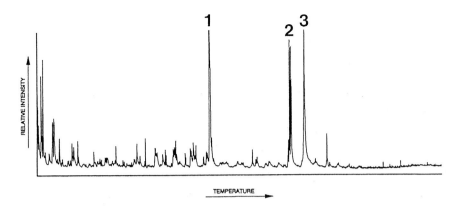

Figure 5   Curie-point (770°C) pyrolysis-gas chromatogram of cutin from fruits of *Lycopers-icon esculentum*. Peak 1 = vinylphenol, probably derived from esterified *p*-coumaric acid; peak 2 = isomeric hexadecadienoic acids, probably derived from fully ester-ified 10,16-dihydroxyhexadecanoic acid; peak 3 = 10-hydroxyhexadecenoic acid, probably derived from partly esterified 10,16-dihydroxyhexadecanoic acid. Adapted from Tegelaar *et al.* (1989b)

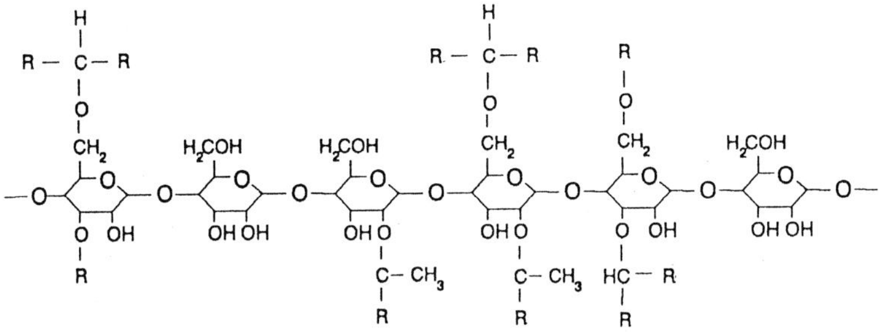

Figure 6   Structure proposed for the cutan from leaves of *Agave americana*. Alkyl groups (R) are covalently bound to the 2,3,6-positions of sugars in the polysaccharide, which is probably cellulose. Adapted from Tegelaar *et al.* (1989a)

degradation and the main evidence for their existence has been obtained from the application of specialised analytical techniques, such as flash pyrolysis (Figure 3) and solid-state NMR (Figure 4). High-temperature pyrolysis of cutans yields a characteristic series of homologous n-alkanes, n-1-alkenes and n-,3-alkadienes ranging from C_5 to C_{35}; this is in marked contrast to the pyrolysis products of a cutin (Figure 5) which are mainly alkenoic and hydroxyalkenoic acids. It would appear that cutan is the predominant biopolymer in the cuticle of *Beta vulgaris* (Nip *et al.*, 1986). The 'non-ester cutin' component found in cuticles of *Clivia* is also probably cutan (Schmidt and Schönherr, 1982).

The solid-state ^{13}C NMR spectra of cutans are relatively simple, showing strong signals for polymethylene groups between 15-40 ppm and weaker signals between 50-75 ppm indicative of cellulose. Again, there are significant differences from the spectra of cutin-containing cuticles recorded using the same technique (Stark *et al.*, 1989). The cross-polarization behaviour of the methylene carbon atoms in cutans is the same as that observed in synthetic polyethylene, showing both amorphous and crystalline regions; polyethylene also gives a pyrolysis profile very similar to that of cutan (Nip *et al*, 1987).

From the pyrolysis and NMR data available, a tentative structure for the cutan from *Agave americana* has been proposed (Figure 6).

Biosynthesis

Research on the biosynthesis of cuticular components has been neglected during the past two decades. Nearly all of our knowledge about wax biosynthesis is based on the pioneer work of Kolattukudy and von Wettstein-Knowles and their respective coworkers, that on cutin monomer and cutin biosynthesis solely from the efforts of the former team of scientists.

It is generally agreed that the epidermal cells are the exclusive sites for the biosynthesis of all the precursors of the cuticular lipids. The various pathways involved in the formation of the common aliphatic epicuticular wax constituents are described succinctly in the elegant paper by Mikkelsen (1978); these are summarized in a simplified form in Table 6. The biosynthesis of wax compounds initially involves *de novo* synthesis of fatty acids, probably from acetate, and their subsequent elongation. At least two separate elongation systems exist, each with complementary decarboxylation, reduction and oxidation systems. One system leads to ß-diketones, hydroxy-ß-diketones and esterified 2-alkanols, the other to alkanes, secondary alkanols and ketones, and, perhaps, to alkanals, 1-alkanols and alkanoic acids as well. The existence of such pathways has been demonstrated in several species by the use of inhibitors for specific steps and by the examination of mutant forms, in which wax composition is altered by intrinsic metabolic blocks. Virtually nothing is known about the mechanism for transport of these long-chain solid

Table 6   Origin of major epicuticular wax classes from the 'fatty acid elongation complex'

Pathway	Principal products
Elongation(s)	Alkanoic acids
Elongation-decarboxylation	Alkanes
	Secondary alcohols
	Ketones
Elongation-reduction	Alkanals
	1-Alkanols
	1-Alkanol esters
ß-Keto fatty acid elongation-decarboxylation	ß-Diketones
	Hydroxy-ß-diketones
	2-Alkanol esters

compounds from the cytoplasm of the epidermal cell, through the wall and onto the surface. Current theories in relation to crystalline waxes are discussed in detail by Baker (1982).

The last state-of-the-art reviews on the biosynthesis of plant cutins were published by Holloway (1982b) and Kolattukudy (1984). Formation of cutin is envisaged as a multienzyme three-stage process involving i) monomer synthesis in the epidermal cell cytoplasm, ii) monomer transport from cytoplasm through the walls and iii) monomer polymerization in the outermost region of the walls. Like waxes, fatty acyls of appropriate chain lengths are the likely precursors for the cutin monomers. A major biosynthetic pathway for the C_{16} cutin acids is hexadecanoic → 16-hydroxyhexadecanoic → 9,16- + 10,16-dihydroxyhexadecanoic, with all monomers eventually becoming esterified into the cutin. Enzymes capable of hydroxylating at the ω- and mid-chain positions, respectively, could be demonstrated in cell-free preparations; both were localized in the endoplasmic reticulum fraction. Biosynthesis of the major C_{18} cutin acids proceeds from the corresponding unsaturated acid, 9-octadecanoic, and the sequence is ω-hydroxylation → epoxidation of double bond → hydration of epoxide. Again, the enzymes responsible for each step have been demonstrated in cell-free preparations. However, unlike those for the C_{16} pathway, these enzymes were found in particulate preparations containing the growing polymer, suggesting, in turn, that the later stages of C_{18} monomer synthesis may be occurring at an extracellular location.

Little is known about the biochemical mechanisms for the transport and polymerisation steps of cutin synthesis. However, particulate enzyme preparations from two species have been shown to catalyse the incorporation of C_{16} cutin monomers into cutins. For hydroxyacyl-CoA: cutin transacylase activity, free hydroxyl groups as acyl acceptors were necessary in the cutin primer; this suggested that cutin was formed mainly by esterification of the carboxyl ends of the incoming monomers. Finally, another factor that is often ignored is the nature of the attachment of cutins to the cell wall which is, presumably, *via* covalent bonding to polysaccharides.

Conclusions

Many gaps still remain in our basic knowledge of plant cuticles and misconceptions and incorrect generalisations about its structure and chemistry are common in the published literature. Probably, one of the biggest mistakes is to treat the cuticle as a separate entity — in reality it is only an integral part of the outer epidermal wall. The current interest in the adverse effects produced by atmospheric pollutants, both inorganic and organic, will surely provide a stimulus for renewed research on plant cuticles, particularly on their biosynthesis *in plants*.

Acknowledgements

The author wishes to thank the organising committee for being given the opportunity to present this paper and to attend their workshop. The substantial contribution made by many colleagues and co-workers over the years to much of the work described is gratefully acknowledged. I am indebted to Mrs C Scott and Mrs J Hynam for production of the manuscript.

References

Baker EA (1982) Chemistry and morphology of plant epicuticular waxes. *In* Cutler DF, Alvin KL, Price CE (*eds*) The plant cuticle. Academic Press London, pp 139-166

Gerard HC, Osman SF, Fett WF, Moreau RA (1992) Separation, identification and quantification of monomers from cutin polymers by high performance liquid chromatography and evaporative light scattering detection. Phytochem Anal 3: 139-144

Harr J, Guggenheim R, Schulke G, Falk RH (1991) The leaf surface of major weeds. Sandoz Agro Ltd, Witterswil, Switzerland

Holloway PJ (1970) Surface factors affecting the wetting of leaves. Pestic Sci 1: 156-163

Holloway PJ (1982a) Structure and histochemistry of plant cuticular membranes: an overview. *In* Cutler DF, Alvin KL, Price CE (*eds*) The plant cuticle. Academic Press, London, *pp* 1-32

Holloway PJ (1982b) The chemical constitution of plant cutins. *In* Cutler DF, Alvin KL, Price CE (*eds*) The plant cuticle. Academic Press, London, *pp* 45-85

Holloway PJ (1984a) Surface lipids of plants and animals. *In* Mangold HK (*ed*) CRC Handbook of chromatography, volume I. CRC Press, Inc, Boca Raton, *pp* 347-380

Holloway PJ (1984b) Cutins and suberins, the polymeric plant lipids. *In* Mangold HK (*ed*) CRC Handbook of chromatography, volume I. CRC Press, Inc, Boca Raton, *pp* 321-345

Holloway PJ (1993) Structure and chemistry of plant cuticles. Pestic Sci 37: 203-206

Holloway PJ, Brown GA, Wattendorff J (1981) Ultrahistochemical detection of epoxides in plant cuticular membranes. J Exp Bot 32: 1051-1066

Holloway PJ, Wattendorff J (1987) Cutinized and suberized cell walls. *In* Vaughn KC (*ed*) CRC Handbook of plant cytochemistry, volume II. CRC Press, Inc, Boca Raton, *pp* 1-35

Kolattukudy PE (1984) Biochemistry and function of cutin and suberin. Can J Bot 62: 2918-2933

Martin JT, Juniper BE (1970) The cuticles of plants. Edward Arnold, London

Mikkelsen JD (1978) The effects of inhibitors on the biosynthesis of the long chain lipids with even carbon numbers in barley spike epicuticular waxes. Carlsberg Res Commun 43: 15-35

Nip M, de Leeuw JW, Holloway PJ, Jensen JPT, Sprenkels JCM, de Pooter M, Sleeckx JJM (1987) Comparison of flash pyrolysis, differential scanning calorimetry, ^{13}C NMR and IR spectroscopy in the analysis of a highly aliphatic biopolymer from plant cuticles. J Anal Appl Pyrolysis 11: 287-295

Nip M, Tegelaar EW, de Leeuw JW, Schenk PA, Holloway PJ (1986) A new non-saponifiable highly aliphatic and resistant biopolymer in plant cuticles. Evidence from pyrolysis and ^{13}C-NMR analysis of present-day and fossil plants. Naturwissenschaften 73: 579-585

Schmidt HW, Schönherr J (1982) Development of plant cuticles: occurrence and role of non-ester bonds in cutin of *Clivia miniata* Reg. leaves. Plants 156: 380-384

Schönherr J, Riederer J (1986) Plant cuticles sorb lipophilic compounds during enzymatic isolation. Plant Cell Environ 9: 459-466

Stark RE, Zlotnik-Mazori T, Ferrantello LM, Garbow JR (1989) Molecular structure and dynamics of intact plant polyesters. Solid-state NMR studies. *In* Lewis NG, Paice MG (*eds*) Plant cell wall polymers. Biogenesis and biodegradation. ACS Symposium series 399, American Chemical Society, Washington DC, *pp* 214-229

Tegelaar EW (1990) Resistant biomacromolecules in morphologically characterized constituents of kerogen: a key to the relationship between biomass and fossil fuels. PhD thesis, University of Utrecht

Tegelaar EW, de Leeuw JW, Largeau C, Derenne S, Schulten H-R, Müller R, Boon JJ, Nip M, Sprenkels JCM (1989a) Scope and limitations of several pyrolysis methods in the structural elucidation of a macromolecular plant constituent in the leaf cuticle of *Agave americana* L. J Anal Appl Pyrolysis 15: 29-54

Tegelaar EW, de Leeuw JW, Holloway PJ (1989b) Some mechanisms of flash pyrolysis of naturally occurring higher plant polyesters. J Anal Appl Pyrolysis 15: 289-295

Tenberge KB (1992) Ultrastructure and development of the outer epidermal wall of spruce (*Picea abies*) needles. Can J Bot 70: 1467-1487

Walton TJ (1990) Waxes, cutin and suberin. *In* Harwood JL, Bowyer JR (*eds*) Lipids, membranes and aspects of photobiology, Methods in plant biochemistry, volume 4. Academic Press London, *pp* 105-158

Modelling Pollutant Deposition to Vegetation: Scaling Down from the Canopy to the Biochemical Level

George E. Taylor Jr.[1] and John V.H. Constable[1]
Department of Environmental and Resource Sciences
University of Nevada-Reno
Reno, Nevada 89512 USA

Abstract

In the atmosphere, pollutants exist in either the gas, particle or liquid (rain and cloud water) phase. The most important gas-phase pollutants from a biological or ecological perspective are oxides of nitrogen (nitrogen dioxide, nitric acid vapor), oxides of sulfur (sulfur dioxide), ammonia, tropospheric ozone and mercury vapor. For liquid or particle phase pollutants, the suite of pollutants is varied and includes hydrogen ion, multiple heavy metals, and select anions. For many of these pollutants, plant canopies are a major sink within continental landscapes, and deposition is highly dependent on the (i) physical form or phase of the pollutant, (ii) meteorological conditions above and within the plant canopy, and (iii) physiological or biochemical properties of the leaf, both on the leaf surface and within the leaf interior. In large measure, the physical and chemical processes controlling deposition at the meteorological and whole-canopy levels are well characterized and have been mathematically modelled. In contrast, the processes operating on the leaf surface and within the leaf interior are not well understood and are largely specific for individual pollutants. The availability of process-level models to estimate deposition is discussed briefly at the canopy and leaf level; however, the majority of effort is devoted to modelling deposition at the leaf surface and leaf interior using the two-layer stagnant film model. This model places a premium on information of a physiological and biochemical nature, and highlights the need to distinguish clearly between the measurements of atmospheric chemistry and the physiologically effective exposure since the two may be very dissimilar. A case study of deposition in the Los Angeles Basin is used to demonstrate the modelling approach, to present the concept of exposure dynamics in the atmospher versus that in the leaf interior, and to document the principle that most forest canopies are exposed to multiple chemical inputs.

Introduction

In the environmental sciences, understanding the deposition of pollutants to terrestrial ecosystems is important for several fundamental reasons. The first is the need to understand the mechanisms underlying air pollution effects on the physiology and growth of vegetation in managed and unmanaged ecosystems. One critical aspect is based in the discipline of physiological ecology and focuses on mechanisms of pollutant transport from the atmosphere to biochemical sites of action, either on the leaf surface or the leaf interior (Hosker and Lindberg, 1982;

---

[1] Biological Sciences Center, Desert Research Institute, P.O. Box 60220, University and Community College System of Nevada, Reno, Nevada 89506 USA

NATO ASI Series, Vol. G 36
Air Pollutants and the Leaf Cuticle
Edited by K. E. Percy et al.
© Springer-Verlag Berlin Heidelberg 1994

Fowler *et al.*, 1989; Taylor and Hanson, 1992). The second addresses the concerns of biogeochemists and recognizes the importance of atmospheric inputs of nutrients (*e.g.*, mercury or Hg) to continental landscapes (Lindberg *et al.*, 1986; Lovett, *in press*). The final reason is the need to investigate the transport and fate of contaminants in the atmosphere in a regional and global context, which is important to environmental toxicologists (Travis and Hester, 1991). In the past, atmospheric processes were thought to be largely responsible for governing the fate of pollutants through scavenging reactions. More recent data indicate that the biosphere is a more important sink for many pollutants (Taylor *et al.*, *in press*).

Within the biosphere, plant canopies of managed and natural landscapes are major sites for deposition of many atmospheric pollutants (Andreae and Schimel, 1989). The effectiveness of plant canopies as a sink can exceed that of most other landscape surfaces for ozone (O_3), nitric acid vapor (HNO_3), nitrogen dioxide (NO_2), ammonia (NH_3), mercury vapor (Hg^0) and sulfur dioxide (SO_2).

The effectiveness of plant canopies as a sink for pollutants in the atmosphere is a consequence of two factors. The first is the high reactivity of plant surfaces for pollutants. Whether the surface onto which deposition occurs is the leaf surface or leaf interior, physical, chemical, and biological features facilitate the transport and reactivity of pollutants, such that assimilation and/or decomposition frequently follows deposition. At low exposure levels, the assimilative capacity appears nearly infinite for most pollutants, resulting in leaves being effective sinks for atmospheric pollutants. The second factor is the array of available deposition surfaces in plant canopies, which exceed that of the subtending land surface by a factor of 2-12, due to a canopy's "layered" architecture. The surfaces for deposition and reaction are greater by an order of magnitude because of the immense area within the leaf interior, which is accessible after the pollutant gas has diffused through the stomata. The effectiveness of plant canopies for scavenging air pollutants is consistent with evolution within the plant kingdom, through which the structure and function of plant surfaces were optimized for the efficient exchange of mass (*e.g.*, carbon dioxide or CO_2, water vapor or water) and momentum (*e.g.*, energy).

Modelling of the atmosphere-canopy exchange of pollutant gases and particles requires a conceptual framework and a mathematical approach, and each must link the disciplines of atmospheric chemistry, meteorology, plant physiology, and biochemistry. This multidisciplinary approach has only recently been promoted in the environmental sciences, and most of the extant modelling methodologies are "top down" approaches from the perspective of the atmospheric sciences or meteorological community (Baldocchi *et al.*, 1991). The development and application of models, either conceptual or mathematical, that extend to the biochemical site(s) of assimilation and action within the leaf interior have not been widely promoted. This last issue (*i.e.*, "scaling down") is the principal focus of this paper.

The objectives are the following:

- discuss some of the principles of modeling atmosphere-canopy and atmosphere-leaf deposition of pollutants;
- discuss some of the available models of deposition beginning at the canopy level and scaling down to the leaf surface and leaf interior;
- discuss the development and application of the two-layer stagnant film model to understand the fate of specific pollutants on the leaf surface and within the leaf interior; and
- discuss some findings relative to atmospheric deposition of pollutant gases and particles based on the application of models.

The approach is largely from the perspective of physiological ecology, with an emphasis on leaf processes operating both on the leaf surface and interior. Other papers offer an analysis that is more oriented from a meteorological or canopy-level perspective (Fowler *et al.*, 1989; Baldocchi *et al.*, 1991). Two additional features of the paper are important. The first is an emphasis on pollutant gas deposition to plant canopies; while other forms of deposition are discussed, pollutant gas transport, deposition, and assimilation are emphasized. The second is a focus on forest canopies, reflecting the research orientation of the ecological community over the last decade.

Atmospheric Processes Controlling Deposition to Plant Canopies

Atmospheric deposition occurs by three processes (Fowler *et al.*, 1989; Lovett, *in press*), and the distinction is important in modelling atmospheric deposition to plant canopies. The first process is wet deposition, which is strictly via precipitation and driven by gravitational settling. The second process is dry deposition, which provides for the input of both particles and gases. This process is accountable to a combination of bulk transport, sedimentation, and diffusion, and the relative importance of each is pollutant dependent. The third process is cloud water deposition, which is defined as deposition from non-precipitating droplets of fog or cloud water; this process is driven by inertial impaction caused by wind turbulence.

The importance of these three processes is site and time dependent, with dry and wet deposition occurring in nearly all landscapes (Lovett, *in press*). Cloud water deposition is restricted primarily to high elevation forests (cloud water impaction) and some seacoast regions. Up until the last decade, the importance of dry and cloud water deposition to terrestrial landscapes was substantially underestimated (Fowler *et al.*, 1989; Johnson and Lindberg, 1992; Lovett, *in press*), and most of the recent focus on modelling (conceptual and mathematical) has addressed these two forms of deposition.

Big Leaf Model

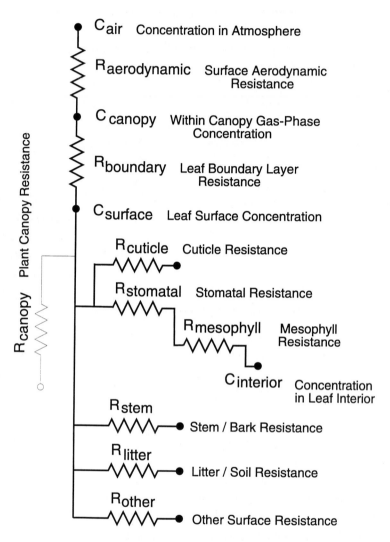

Figure 1   Schematic diagram showing the array of resistances operating within the Big Leaf Model, which is used to simulate pollutant gas deposition to plant canopies (adapted from Baldocchi *et al.*, 1987).

Modelling Pollutant Deposition at the Canopy Level

At the level of the plant canopy, models of deposition estimate an air to surface transfer rate based on a combination of processes governing turbulent transport in the free atmosphere, diffusion on or near the leaf surface in the gas phase and interfacial transport between the gas and either a liquid (cell surface) or solid (cuticle) surface. The turbulent forces operating in the free atmosphere are common to all atmospheric pollutants and are modeled using bulk flow parameters. Conversely, diffusion is a molecular process and is, therefore, specific for both the individual pollutant (*e.g.*, molecular size) and the surface for deposition. Interfacial transport, also governed by molecular processes, determines the ease of pollutant transport across an interface.

One of the most commonly used canopy-level models to simulate the deposition of pollutant gases and particles to forests is the Big Leaf Model (Baldocchi *et al.*, 1987; Hicks *et al.*, 1991). This process-driven code has its origins in modelling the fluxes of mass and momentum in agricultural landscapes and accounts for many of the processes governing deposition at the canopy level (Fig. 1). The model's principal feature is an array of resistances including aerodynamic ($R_{aerodynamic}$), leaf boundary layer ($R_{boundary\ layer}$), soil (R_{soil}), stem (R_{stem}), and a canopy surface ($R_{surface}$) resistance. The last is divided into three resistances operating in series or parallel: cuticular ($R_{cuticle}$), stomata ($R_{stomata}$), and mesophyll ($R_{mesophyll}$). The equations are solved via Ohm's Law and are gas-specific, based on the analogy to H_2O vapor.

The model is parameterized for an individual forest canopy (individual or multiple species) to account for the species-specific features that underlie $R_{surface}$, $R_{boundary\ layer}$, and $R_{aerodynamic}$ and the site's unique environmental conditions (*e.g.*, light, temperature, relative humidity). The most common calculation in the model is deposition (moles $M^{-2}\ h^{-1}$) estimated inferentially as the product of air concentration (mol m^{-3}) and deposition velocity (V_g in units of cm s^{-1}). The v_g differs for each gas and particle and is scaled to account for differences in particle mass. The time step of the model is hourly. The V_g is analogous to the leaf conductance (g_s) parameter used by physiological ecologists, with the distinction being that V_g is a vertically integrated measure through the canopy accounting for all deposition surfaces. Scaling from V_g to g_s is done by dividing by the leaf area index or LAI (Hanson and Lindberg, 1991). The model operates as a single big leaf or as a number of layers, with each layer having a separate input file to account for changes in $R_{aerodynamic}$, $R_{surface}$, and atmospheric concentration of the pollutant gases in the canopy.

Canopy aerodynamic resistance ($R_{aerodynamic}$) is estimated by a combination of meteorological (*e.g.*, wind speed, wind direction) and canopy architecture (*e.g.*, LAI) data. This resistance largely governs V_g for particles/aerosols and highly reactive trace gases (*e.g.*, HNO_3), where $R_{surface}$ approaches zero.

The most significant source of uncertainty in the Big Leaf Model is $R_{surface}$, in general, and $R_{stomata}$, particularly. The prominence of $R_{stomata}$ is most important for pollutant gases whose deposition sites are within the leaf interior (*e.g.*, O_3, SO_2, NO_2, Hg^0). The uncertainty arises from the degree to which $R_{stomata}$ varies as a function of the environment (*e.g.*, light, temperature, vapor pressure, water potential, CO_2) and plant species. The net outcome is that $R_{stomata}$ for a given pollutant at a specific site may range diurnally from ∞ to near zero.

The characterization of $R_{stomata}$ is crucial and must be addressed experimentally at several times during the growing season on a site specific and pollutant specific basis. The manner in which $R_{stomata}$ is parameterized is straightforward. Values for $_{stomata}$ are derived by scaling the maximum $R_{stomata}$ as a function of hourly values for light, air temperature, relative humidity, and plant water status. Each of these must be experimentally derived and numerically coded to match the species, leaf age class and site conditions. Once coded, the model estimates $R_{stomata}$ in units of s cm^{-1} (leaf area basis), and this value is integrated to achieve a landscape-level $R_{stomata}$ using LAI (either for land area as a whole or summed by age class). Subsequently, the estimate of canopy-level $R_{stomata}$ is scaled for each pollutant gas via analogy to H_2O (or experimental data), and the reciprocal value, V_g, is calculated (Hanson and Lindberg, 1991).

An example of a Big Leaf simulation is shown for a representative forest canopy in the semi-arid Southwest, detailing the mean growing season V_g as a function of time of day (Fig. 2) for O_3, NO_2, HNO_3, SO_2, NH_3, and Hg^0. The results show several important features of pollutant deposition to forest canopies. First, all pollutants showed a diurnal pattern of high V_g reached in the early to mid afternoon (1300 - 1400 h) and a substantially lower V_g during the early morning (0100 - 0500 h) and evening (2000 - 2400 h). Second, there are marked differences in V_g among the pollutants; the most notable are the particularly high V_g for HNO_3 and the corresponding low V_g for Hg^0 relative to the other pollutant gases. Of the remaining four pollutants, the V_g was highest for NH_3 followed in order by SO_2, NO_2, and O_3. In general, V_g during daylight hours for HNO_3 approached a maximum of 6 cm s^{-1}, and the average daylight V_g was 3.5 cm s^{-1}; the night time value was uniformly < 1.0 cm s^{-1}. The V_g's for the remaining pollutants were lower by a factor of 5 to 10. The unusually low V_g for Hg^0 is a consequence of a very high $R_{mesophyll}$ that exceeds $R_{stomata}$ by a factor of 2-3 (Lindberg *et al.*, 1992). The $R_{mesophyll}$ appears to be a consequence of biochemical processes that control both Hg^0 transport across the gas-liquid interface and the pollutant's assimilation in the mesophyll tissue (Lindberg *et al.*, 1992).

The distinct diurnal pattern of V_g for all pollutants is a consequence of two processes, one atmospheric and the other biological. The first is greater turbulence and transport of the pollutant to the reactive leaf surfaces during the daylight hours, and this explains the elevated daytime V_g

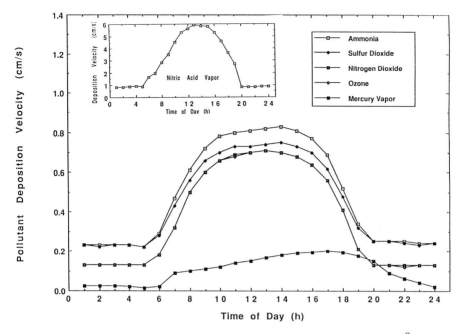

Figure 2. Growing season deposition velocities ($_g$) for HNO3, NO2, SO2, NH3, Hg^0, and O3 for a representative conifer forest in the semi-arid Southwestern United States as simulated using the Big Leaf model.

for HNO3; in essence, the canopy is a perfect sink for the pollutant so that transport to the assimilatory surface is rate limiting (Hanson and Lindberg, 1991). Conversely, the same pattern in the other five pollutant gases largely reflects the accessibility of sites for deposition within the leaf interior, and this accessibility is controlled by stomatal porosity. The role of each is simply a matter of magnitude, since both processes are important to a different degree depending on the pollutant gas being studied.

The model clearly demonstrates the large daily amplitude in the effectiveness of the plant canopy as a sink for gas-phase atmospheric pollutants and that this amplitude reflects both atmospheric and biological controls. Pollutants vary in physical properties that translate to substantial differences in rates of transfer from the atmosphere to plant canopies. Whereas this example illustrates the variability of V_g on a diurnal time step during the growing season, comparable variability in V_g is evident on seasonal or interannual basis, depending on a mix of biological and environmental factors. For example, V_g during the winter is reduced due to parallel declines

Multiple Layer Model

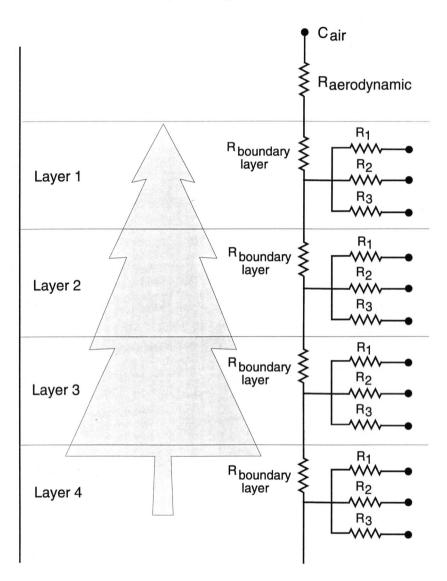

Figure 3 Schematic diagram of the array of resistances used in modeling cloud water deposition at the canopy level (adapted from Lovett *et al.*, 1982).

in $R_{stomata}$ and LAI. Conversely, V_g is higher during periods of abundant rain versus that during extended periods of drought, reflecting a decline in $R_{stomata}$.

Models of cloud water deposition are derived from the same principles used to model pollutant gas deposition (Lovett *et al.*, 1982), although there are some notable differences (Fig. 3). For example, since deposition is solely to the leaf surface, $R_{stomata}$ is not simulated. In addition, transport through the boundary layer proximal to the surface is governed by inertial impaction rather than molecular diffusion, simplifying the simulation (Fowler *et al.*, 1989). Unlike many other kinds of deposition models, cloud water deposition requires estimates of surface area, canopy architecture and within-canopy wind speed, which are commonly simulated in multiple layers within the plant canopy (Fig. 3).

Cloud water deposition models are, therefore, simplified by removing the requirement for diffusion and some of the biological/physiological factors operating on the leaf surface. At the same time, the models require additional parameters (*e.g.*, canopy architecture) that influence cloud water movement and impaction on leaf surfaces.

Modelling Pollutant Deposition at the Individual Leaf Level

Models operating at the canopy level (*e.g.*, Big Leaf) are effective simulators of deposition of gas-phase pollutants to plant canopies. However, their "top-down" approach is unable to investigate the potential fate of pollutants on the leaf surface and within the leaf interior.

Simulation of pollutant fate on biologically active surfaces requires information about reactions with molecules on the cuticular surface (gas/solid interactions) and within the leaf interior, including both gas/liquid and gas/gas interactions.

In "scaling down" from the plant canopy, the first level of organization for which models exist are those that address leaf-level processes. Moving progressively closer to the leaf and into the laminar boundary layer, molecular transport begins to play an increasingly important role, and the models are developed to simulate transport but account for the reactivity of the leaf surface (internal and external) and the unique physical and chemical properties of each pollutant gas.

Leaf architecture and anatomy varies widely (Nobel, 1991) and is beyond the scope of this chapter. However, many surface and internal features have a significant impact on gas transport due to an effect on the laminar boundary layer and leaf interior characteristics (Fig. 4). Nevertheless, leaves of many temperate forest species are similar enough to offer generalizations important in modeling atmosphere-leaf exchange of pollutant gases. These similarities are as follows:

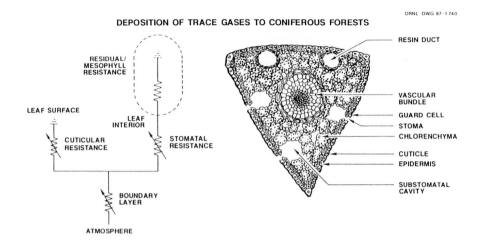

DEPOSITION OF TRACE GASES TO CONIFEROUS FORESTS

ORNL-DWG 87-1740

Figure 4 Schematic diagram of the morphology of a conifer needle (leaf surface and leaf interior) and the associated analog resistance model used to simulate pollutant gas deposition.

- layer of packed palisade parenchyma that is efficient in absorbing gases;
- more loosely organized spongy parenchyma with numerous interconnected intercell-ular air spaces;
- upper and lower epidermis punctuated by stomata;
- internal surface area that exceeds the projected surface area by a factor of 10 to 40 (Nobel, 1991); and
- cuticular covering over the epidermis with a chemistry and structure unique from that of other leaf surfaces (Schönherr, 1982).

As a molecule of a pollutant gas is transported near the leaf, it enters a significantly different physical and chemical environment than that found in the bulk atmosphere, and this chemical environment is best examined at two spatial scales. The first is external to the leaf and occurs in the laminar or unstirred boundary layer, whereas the second occurs in the intercellular air spaces of the leaf interior. At both scales, pollutant gas flux to a surface is controlled by the partial pressure gradient between the gas-phase and the surface, that is determined by a combination of physiochemical and physiological factors. Physiochemical factors are gas specific and include the diffusion coefficient in air and water, reactivity, molecular diameter, and solubility in water (Table 1). Physiological factors are more complex and variable and include diffusivity and solubility in water as modified by interaction with organic molecules and biochemical processes. The most important process is the rate of degradation or scavenging of the pollutant gas on and within the cell. The dynamic nature of leaf physiology and the biochemical interaction with gaseous species diffusing from the atmosphere make the "scaling down" processes difficult to model, either conceptually or mathematically.

Table 1   Relevant physiochemical properties of trace gases that are important in understanding the deposition of gases across a gas to liquid interface in general and the atmosphere-leaf interface specifically (adapted from Taylor *et al.*, 1988).

Trace gas	Molecular Weight (g)	Molecular Diameter (nm)	Water Solubility ($\mu mol\ cm^{-3}$)	Air Diffusion Ratio	Henry's Law Coefficient ($m^3\ \mu atm^{-1}\ \mu mol^{-1}$)	Diffusivity in air ($m^2\ s^{-1}$)	Diffusivity in water ($m^2\ s^{-1}$)
CO_2	44.01	0.378	76.5	0.64	2.99E-2	1.65E-5	1.65E-9
H_2O	18.01	0.225	∞	1.0	NA	2.42E-5	∞
O_2	31.99	0.267	2.18	0.75	NA	2.27E-5	2.27E-9
N_2	28.01	0.260	1.04	0.80	NA	2.31E-5	2.3E-9
HNO_3	63.00	0.427	∞	0.53	7.0E-9	1.18E-5	1.18E-9
O_3	47.99	0.360	21.9	0.61	2.29	1.58E-5	1.58E-9
SO_2	64.05	0.393	3559	0.53	7.88E-4	1.22E-5	1.22E-9
NO_2	45.98	0.366	decompose	0.63	NA	1.84E-5	1.84E-9
NH_3	17.01	0.234	52789	1.03	NA	2.64E-5	2.64E-9

NA, not applicable or not appropriate

Modelling Deposition to the Leaf Surface and Leaf Interior Using the Two-Layer Stagnant Film Model

The two-layer stagnant film model (Liss, 1971; Liss and Slater, 1974) has been used extensively in the environmental sciences to investigate the transport and fate of pollutant gases at the gas-liquid interface, largely in the open ocean. This model is also applicable to understanding the flux of pollutant gases at the atmosphere-leaf interface, and it is proposed that this interface is one of a few natural situations in which the model can clearly be applied.

The two-layer stagnant film model (Fig. 5) provides a conceptual framework for separating physiochemical and physiological factors that control pollutant gas flux at the molecular level and is largely based on modelling the distribution of pollutant gases between a gas and aqueous phase in a system dominated by consecutive stagnant layers (Taylor *et al.*, 1988). The model can estimate flux to a leaf surface and/or interior as modified by the effects of dissolution in the aqueous phase (*e.g.*, the physiochemical sink in the apoplast and symplast).

TWO-LAYER MODEL OF FOLIAR GAS EXCHANGE

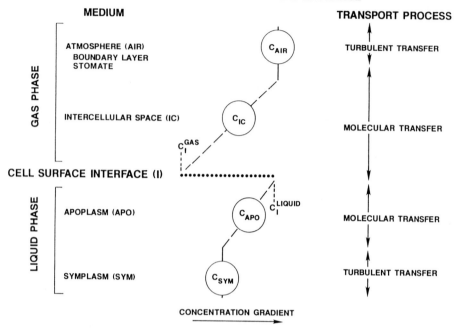

Figure 5   Diagram of the two-layer stagnant film model, showing the spatial relationships among (i) the model's two stagnant layers, (ii) areas of turbulent versus molecular transport, (iii) the gas-liquid interface within the leaf interior, and (iv) the morphology of the leaf.

Pollutant gas flux in the model is calculated based on Fick's first law modified by a Henry's Law coefficient, such that flux ($_p$) is as follows:

$$J_p = (D_w/K_h \cdot h) \cdot (P_a - P_w) \qquad [1]$$

where D_w is the diffusion coefficient in water, K_h is the Henry's Law coefficient, h is the distance across which diffusion is occurring, and P_a and P_w are the partial pressures in air and water, respectively, of the pollutant gas. While the influence of dissolution in the aqueous layer on gaseous flux is accounted for in the model, the effect of sinks due to physiological mechanisms that remove or scavenge hydrated forms of the gas or its derivatives from the aqueous phase is not modelled. Transport of CO_2 and oxygen across the air-water interface can be altered by biological processes (Kanwisher, 1960, 1963; Smith, 1985). Whereas physiological interactions with many pollutant gases and their effect on gas flux are unknown, the model can estimate the physiochemical sink within the leaf based on water solubility and its subsequent effect on gaseous flux into the leaf.

With respect to its application to atmosphere-leaf deposition of pollutant gases, the two-layer stagnant film model has assets and limitations. The principal assets are the following:

- requirements for stagnant air and water layers are satisfied in the boundary layer and the leaf interior due to the lack of turbulent transport;
- water solubility, either on the leaf cuticle or interior, influences the physical partial pressure gradient that drives flux towards the leaf;
- accurate estimation of pollutant gas flux both towards and within the leaf requires an accounting of resistance in both the gas and liquid phases; and
- damaging effects of pollutant gases are mechanistically specific and unique in location and may occur in either gas or aqueous phase of the leaf interior.

While the inclusion of water solubility as a model parameter represents an important step in modelling pollutant flux to the leaf, there are limitations to the application of the two-layer stagnant film model to atmosphere-leaf exchange of pollutant gases. These limitations include the following:

- equilibrium is assumed between the gas and liquid phases that rarely occurs in a dynamic biological system such as the leaf;
- array of physiochemical parameters are required, including D_a, D_w, and H_h, and these are gas specific and unavailable for some exotic chemicals;
- gases interact with effluxing chemicals, including both organic (*e.g.*, hydrocarbons) and inorganic (water) species;
- physiologically mediated reactions that influence the flux rate towards or into the leaf are not accounted for (*e.g.*, stomatal closure, saturation of a surface); and
- water solubility (either on or in the leaf) is explicitly accounted for, whereas the solubility in hydrophobic lipids (on the leaf cuticle or leaf interior) is not.

Table 1 demonstrates the diversity of physiochemical characteristics of several common pollutant gases; these characteristics are reported to control rates of deposition and reaction of pollutants either on the leaf surface or within the leaf interior (Taylor *et al.*, 1988; Hanson and Lindberg, 1991). Solubility in water spans a range of five orders of magnitude, whereas the Henry's Law coefficients extend over nine orders of magnitude.

Although the two-layer stagnant film model does not account for physiological controls over gas flux, the importance of the physiochemical aspects, especially water solubility and reactivity in the gas and liquid phase, should not be underestimated. Hill (1971) demonstrated that pollutant gas absorption by leaves was related to water solubility, and Chameides (1989) concluded that ascorbic acid was a major determinant of the fate of O_3 in the leaf interior.

Application of the Two-Layer Stagnant Film Model: Deposition to the Leaf Surface

As trace gases are transported close to the leaf surface, their movement is increasingly dominated by molecular processes. In the leaf boundary layer, there is a logarithmic decline in turbulent transport and a parallel increase in molecular-dominated transport/diffusion (Inoue, 1963). Modelling of molecular transport within the boundary layer frequently takes the following form:

$$J_i = D_i(Ci_{atm} - Ci_{ls})/h \qquad [2]$$

where flux of species i (J_i) is a function of the diffusivity coefficient (D_i), partial pressure in the atmosphere (Ci_{atm}) and at the leaf surface (Ci_{ls}), and the transport distance (h). This equation over-simplifies transport within the boundary layer by assuming a linear partial pressure gradient between the leaf surface and the atmosphere and negligible interactions with other gases. Whereas this equation estimates pollutant gas transport to the leaf surface, no allowance is made for the physiochemical and physiological reactions that violate the requirement for a linear partial pressure gradient. These reactions can occur either in the gas phase (*e.g.*, components diffusing from the leaf interior) or on the leaf surface with the cuticle or on the cuticle with previously deposited particles or an aqueous H_2O film.

Reactions of influxing pollutant gases with compounds effluxing from the leaf interior can take a range of forms including those with water vapor (McLaughlin and Taylor, 1981), volatile organic compounds including terpenoids (Tingey and Taylor, 1982; Sharkey and Loreto, 1993), NH_3 (Farquhar *et al.*, 1980) or other compounds (*e.g.*, SO_2). The rate at which a gas reacts is determined by physiochemical properties, partial pressure and flux rates of the counter current gases (Taylor *et al.*, 1983).

Leaves intercept a broad range of atmospheric compounds, many of which remain on the leaf surface (Riederer *et al.*, *this volume*). Particles become impacted on the cuticle and form a distinct reactive surface. Rates of particle deposition vary with atmospheric conditions, leaf morphology/anatomy (*e.g.*, pubescence, trichomes, shape) and chemistry (*e.g.*, cuticular composition, exuded substances). Further complexities arise from compounds adsorbed on these particulates or the presence of epifaunal communities (Schreiber and Schönherr, 1993).

Pollutant gases can also cause cuticular degradation (Boyce, *this volume*; Huttunen, *this volume*) or an alteration in cuticle synthesis (Percy *et al.*, *this volume*). Similarly, pollutant gases can also react with underlying mesophyll tissue through lesions in the cuticle. The cuticle is a complex structure composed of multiple layers of differing chemical composition (Schönherr, 1982;

Holloway, *this volume*). The outermost layer is composed of epicuticular wax overlying a wax/cutin matrix overlying the pectic substances of the middle lamella. These layers can be broadly separated into: a soluble fraction (waxes) that is extremely diverse containing fatty acids, fatty alcohols, esters and paraffins (Schönherr, 1982); and an insoluble fraction (cutin and non lipid other compounds including polyuronic acids, phenolic compounds, proteins and cellulose.

The total resistance of the cuticle to gaseous diffusion is determined by individual resistances of the soluble and insoluble fractions acting in series (Lendzian, 1982). A limited number of potential reaction sites on the cuticle has been demonstrated for O_3 (Bennett *et al.*, 1973). These sites may account for the O_3 decomposition noted by Kerstiens and Lendzian (1989); however, some O_3 flux through the cuticle was observed although it was estimated to be a factor of 10^4 lower than that through the stomata. Experiments have determined that O_2 obeys Henry's Law in cuticles (Lendzian, 1982). Therefore, the properties of the cuticle make it susceptible to hydrophobic gases that partition to the epicuticular wax and potentially degrade the cuticle's physical structure. Such partitioning is not currently addressed by the two-layer stagnant film model, but could be incorporated where reaction with epicuticular waxes serves as a pollutant sink.

In contrast to the previous reactions, modeling the effects of surface water from dew fall or precipitation on pollutant gas flux is one of the two-layer stagnant film model's strengths. Surface water represents a strong sink as gases enter solution at a rate governed by the physiochemical properties of the gas. Fowler and Unsworth (1979) determined that deposition of SO_2 was always elevated on leaves with wet surfaces regardless of leaf physiology and that the presence of a water layer may short-circuit pollutant flux through the stomata and into the leaf interior for many atmospheric pollutants (*e.g.*, SO_2, NH_3). The role of surface water in modifying pollutant flux rates to the leaf surface is frequently underestimated but can be explicitly modelled using the two-layer stagnant film model.

Application of the two-layer stagnant film model: deposition to the leaf interior

The distinctive structure of the leaf dictates that pollutant gases enter the leaf through the stomata into a substomatal chamber and subsequently into the intercellular air spaces surrounding the parenchyma cells. Inside the leaf, trace gases are exposed to an environment saturated with water vapor and rich in volatile organic compounds (Tingey and Taylor, 1982). Transport within the highly tortuous intercellular air space is dominated by molecular processes. The combination of molecular transport and the large surface area of the mesophyll cells (which is physiologically dynamic), dictates that the fate of a pollutant gas depends on leaf morphology/anatomy and physiology coupled to the molecular behavior of the gas in a stagnant layer.

Whereas the physical environment inside the leaf shares some similarities with that found in the boundary layer, the critical difference is a physiologically and biochemically dynamic cell surface that can rapidly assimilate many pollutant gases. Leaf physiology controls the development of a steady-state rate of pollutant gas uptake through the ability to deplete the partial pressure of the gas in a liquid media via metabolism or reactivity with cellular compounds.

One of the consequences of the stagnant layer within the leaf interior and the attendant role of molecular processes is that the fate of pollutant gases on the leaf surface and within the intercellular space will differ depending on the physiochemical properties of the gas (Table 2).

Table 2   Predicted sites of deposition for representative pollutant gases at two levels of organization: individual leaf level (leaf surface *versus* leaf interior) and the level of the leaf interior (substomatal cavity *versus* lower palisades *versus* upper palisades). These estimates assume that stomatal resistance is minimal and sites of deposition within the leaf interior are accessible via diffusion.

Pollutant/	Leaf level[a]		Sites of Deposition (% of total) Within leaf interior[b]		
Trace gas	Surface	Interior	Substomatal cavity	Lower palisades	Upper palisades
CO_2	0	100	0	0	0
SO_2	30	70	80	20	0
O_3	20	80	20	20	60
HNO_3	80	20	100	0	0
NO_2	20	80	20	20	60
NH_3	30	70	50	30	20
HgO	10	90	10	20	80

[a] *Distribution is the percentage of the pollutant deposited to either the leaf surface or leaf interior*
[b] *Distribution is the percentage of the total that enters the leaf interior only*

One of the more obvious consequences is that the mean diffusion distance of pollutant gases will vary significantly; gases will have dissimilar sites of deposition and assimilation on leaf surfaces. For example, the mean diffusion distance of water-soluble and reactive gases is short, whereas that of less soluble and non reactive gases is longer (Taylor *et al.*, 1988). The mean diffusion distance for SO_2 is likely to extend only into the substomatal cavity, whereas that of O_3 is nearly three to five times longer, terminating within the palisade tissue (Hanson and Taylor, 1990). In contrast, most of the HNO_3 deposits to the leaf surface and very little diffuses through the stomata and into the leaf interior. One of the consequences of this stagnant layer within the leaf interior is that pollutants will deposit in different tissues resulting in tissue-specific injury. Since many physiological and biochemical processes are segregated by tissue within the leaf interior (*e.g.,*

CO_2 assimilation, phloem loading, stomatal control), pollutants will have dissimilar physiological effects based solely on where they are deposited within the leaf interior.

This understanding of pollutant behavior and effects is not predicted from models operating at higher levels of organization (*i.e.*, whole leaf or canopy level) and simply reflects the emphasis on molecular interactions that is imposed by the two-layer stagnant film model.

Models of photosynthetic carbon dioxide assimilation

While the two-layer stagnant film model focuses attention on molecular aspects of pollutant gases in both the gas and liquid phase in the leaf interior, there have been few efforts to model the processes controlling pollutant flux at this level of organization. Conversely, there have been a number of advances made in understanding the assimilation of CO_2, and these can serve as a framework for modelling pollutant gas flux into the leaf interior, recognizing that the molecular properties of CO_2 and pollutant gases are dissimilar in a number of aspects.

Models for simulating photosynthesis have gone through a significant evolution. The simplest models calculate CO_2 flux into the leaf as in Eq. 1 modified for the physiochemical characteristics of CO_2. Such a treatment solely describes diffusion into the leaf through the stomata based on the CO_2 partial pressure gradient between the atmosphere and the leaf interior. While this allows CO_2 to enter the leaf, it ignores the physiological complexities of stomata and carbon metabolism that control photosynthetic CO_2 demand. More recent efforts have resulted in analog models for simulating CO_2 and H_2O vapor exchange between the leaf interior and the atmosphere. These separate CO_2 flux into a stomatal conductance component that emphasizes diffusion of CO_2 into the leaf through the stomata and an internal component to describe the physiological and biochemical aspects of carbon fixation. Theoretical and mathematical models for estimating carbon gain have been developed by Farquhar and von Caemmerer (1982) in which photosynthesis (A) is expressed as follows:

$$A = (1 - G/C_i) \text{ minimum } (W_c, W_j) - R_d \qquad [3]$$

where G is the CO_2 compensation point, C_i is the intercellular gas space CO_2 partial pressure, W_c and W_j are the rates of carboxylation limited by Rubisco activity and RuBP regeneration respectively, and R_d is the rate of day respiration.

Within this framework, other researchers have accounted for additional physical and metabolic processes. Parkhurst and Mott (1990) included the effects of the variability of the intercellular CO_2 partial pressure and its effect on photosynthesis, whereas Ball (1987) modelled the interaction of CO_2 molecules with effluxing water molecules. Further improvements have incorporated pools of carbon cycle intermediates along with a time lag required for sucrose

synthesis (Laisk and Walker, 1986), carbon cycle intermediates and the activation and inactivation dynamics of Rubisco by light (Gross *et al.*, 1991), linkage between photosynthesis and
stomatal behavior as modified by light intensity, sucrose synthesis pathway and the biochemical
properties of Rubisco (Collatz *et al.*, 1991).

These models combine physiochemical and physiological attributes of the photosynthetic
process into a single entity, joining dynamic leaf physiology/biochemistry with the physiochemical forces controlling CO_2 flux from the atmosphere and solubility in the cell solution. The
increased predictive ability of these models centers on the inclusion of leaf biochemistry that
implicitly accounts for the physiological CO_2 sinks within the leaf. Although the CO_2 sink is
treated as a single process, it is divided into physiochemical and physiological aspects. The
physiochemical aspect represents the dissolution of gaseous intercellular CO_2 into the apoplastic
water film surrounding the cell, hydration and transport to the chloroplast. In contrast, physiological aspects account for respiratory and photorespiratory CO_2 release and interactions with
cellular pH control mechanisms. The dependence of existing photosynthetic models on our
understanding of photosynthetic biochemistry limits their adaptation to pollutant gases for which
physiology/biochemistry is less well known.

In spite of our lack of physiological details of pollutant gas metabolism required to adapt existing
photosynthetic models, physiochemical details can be incorporated by using the two-layer
stagnant film model. This represents an accounting of the water solubility of the gas that can
relate directly to the gas's toxicity. Hill (1971) attributed variations in pollutant deposition to
differences in water solubility. A later study (Taylor *et al.*, 1983) attributed 40-50% of the
variation in deposition to water solubility for a range of sulfur-containing gases; the remainder
of the variation was accountable to molecular size differences among the gases. In an adapted
photosynthetic model physiological realism would be limited, but physiochemical features would
be increased due to incorporation of the two-layer stagnant film model through its effect on the
partial pressure (C_i) of the gas in the intercellular air space.

Whereas one-to-one correspondence between CO_2 flux and that of a pollutant gas does not exist,
it is possible to use the basic format of Farquhar and von Caemmerer's photosynthetic model
(1982) as a template (Eq. 3). In such an adaptation appropriate values would be substituted to
account for the specific properties of the pollutant gas as follows:

$$J_p = (1 - G_p/C_{pg} - C_{pa}) \cdot (W_p) \qquad\qquad [4]$$

in which pollutant flux (J_p) is controlled by the gas "compensation point" (G_p), intercellular
partial pressure (C_{pg}) and a specific physiological sink term (W_p), while the respiratory component is eliminated. The physical effects of pollutant dissolution in the aqueous phase, as modelled
by the two-layer stagnant film model, would be incorporated by subtracting the pollutant partial

pressure entering the aqueous phase (C_{pa}) from the partial pressure of the gas in the gaseous phase (C_{pg}). In effect, C_{pa} controls gas flux into the leaf through its effect on the partial pressure of the gas in the intercellular air space (C_{pg}).

The adaptation of CO_2 assimilation models to simulating the deposition of pollutant gases has some limitations. The first is that the sinks within the leaf interior for most pollutant gases are unknown. The fact that sinks within the leaf interior may be distributed in a gas-specific manner is not accounted for by the model. For example, O_3 decomposition on the plasmalemma and cell wall is reported by Laisk et al. (1989) and attributed to ascorbic acid scavenging in the cell wall (Chameides, 1989). More recently, O_3 scavenging has been extended to the gas-phase and attributed to the presence of reactive hydrocarbons (Tingey and Taylor, 1982; Sharkey and Loreto, 1993) or nitric oxide. The second limitation is the apparent non-zero internal partial pressures of some pollutants due to physiological activity and/or re-emission (Tingey and Taylor, 1982). Non-zero partial pressures for pollutant gases, such as that for NH_3 or NO_2, have been termed "compensation points" by Farquhar et al. (1980) in an analogous sense to that for CO_2. However, for pollutant gases the term is misleading since the biochemical process underlying the non-zero partial pressure is not accountable in a parallel sense to the balancing of assimilation and respiratory functions. The third limitation is the issue of diffusion distance, which is gas dependent and not analogous to that experienced by CO_2 or H_2O vapor.

Therefore, while adaptation of photosynthetic models to simulate pollutant gas deposition and assimilation is not possible, the two-layer stagnant film model allows for the inclusion of pertinent physiochemical/molecular parameters (e.g., water solubility, gas-phase scavenging reactions) that dictate pollutant transport, fate and toxicity in the leaf interior. This is an avenue for pursuing the "scaling down" process and resulting in a linkage between the communities of atmospheric chemistry and plant physiology/biochemistry.

Conclusions

Modelling atmospheric deposition of pollutants to plant canopies has progressed significantly over the several decades, evolving from a base in biometeorology. More recently, this modelling has progressed more along biological lines (i.e., "scaling down") addressing the dynamics of pollutant behavior on plant surfaces and the resulting fate of pollutants either on the leaf surface or within the leaf interior. This evolution is continuing and is beginning to simulate the micro-environmental coupling between the atmosphere and stomatal physiology, capacity of the leaf surfaces to assimilate pollutants at chronic levels and fine-scale aspects of pollutant deposition on leaf surfaces and within the leaf interior.

Based on the evolution of these models, several conclusions are offered from the perspective of physiological ecology. First, pollutants behave differently at the interface between the atmosphere and the deposition surface depending on whether the transport process is one of wet, dry or cloud deposition. The mechanisms controlling each are dissimilar so that different modelling approaches are required.

Second, the modelling process has evolved from a "top down" perspective from the plant canopy level. This approach was initially developed for agricultural crops with homogeneous canopies growing in ideal conditions, and its application to more complex canopies and terrain has required a number of modifications, particularly with respect to forests. A "bottom up" approach from the level of the leaf interior and emphasizing leaf-level morphology and biochemistry is emerging. There are fundamental differences in the processes governing deposition from the "top down" versus the "bottom up" perspective; the two-layer stagnant film model provides a conceptual framework for developing the "bottom up" approach.

Third, there are many processes controlling pollutant deposition that are common among pollutants, and this has fostered the development and application of analog models based on the pathways for water vapor and CO_2. The analogy between CO_2, water vapor and most pollutant gases is not complete, and many pollutants show a very marked divergence due to their unique physiochemical properties. The most notable consequences of these differences are that the sites of pollutant gas deposition may be very different from those of CO_2 assimilation or water evaporation. Some pollutants exhibit an "effective compensation point", and gas-phase and liquid-phase scavenging reactions on the leaf surface and within the leaf interior.

Fourth, pollutant deposition is scale dependent as one moves both vertically within a canopy and horizontally across a landscape. There is a pronounced shift in processes controlling deposition from purely turbulent events to ones based on molecular processes at the gas-liquid interface. Similarly, there is a horizontal scale that affects deposition, such that the form and rate of deposition vary among plant communities.

Acknowledgements

The authors acknowledge with appreciation support from the U.S. Environmental Protection Agency's "Ozone Forest Response Program". The senior author was funded in part during manuscript preparation by the College of Agriculture, University of Nevada-Reno.

References

Andreae MO, Schimel DS (*eds*) (1989) Exchange of trace gases between terrestrial ecosystems and the atmosphere. John Wiley and Sons, New York

Baldocchi DD, Hicks BB, Camara P (1987) A canopy stomatal resistance model for gaseous deposition to vegetated surfaces. Atmos Environ 21: 91-101

Baldocchi DD, Luxmoore RJ, Hatfield JL (1991) Discerning the forest from the trees: an essay on scaling canopy conductance. Agr For Meteor 54: 197-226

Ball JT (1987) Calculations related to gas exchange. *In* Ziegler E, Farquhar GD, Cowen IR (*eds*) Stomatal function. Stanford University Press, Stanford California *pp* 445-476

Bennett JH, Hill AC, Gates DM (1973) A model for gaseous pollutant sorption by leaves. J Air Poll Control Assoc 23: 957-962

Boyce RL (1994) The effect of age, canopy position and elevation on foliar wettability of *Picea rubens* and *Abies balsamea*: implications for pollutant-induced epicuticular wax degradation. *In* Percy KE, Cape JN, Jagels R, Simpson CM (*eds*) Air pollutants and the leaf cuticle. Springer, New York (*this volume, pp*)

Chameides WL (1989) The chemistry of ozone deposition to plant leaves: role of ascorbic acid. Environ Sci Tech 23: 595-600

Collatz GJ, Ball JT, Grivet C, Berry JA (1991) Physiological and environmental regulation of stomatal conductance, photosynthesis and transpiration: a model that includes a laminar boundary layer. Agric For Met 54: 107-136

Farquhar GD, Firth PM, Wetselaar R, Weir B (1980) On the gaseous exchange of ammonia between leaves and the environment: determination of the ammonia compensation point. Plant Phys 66: 710-714

Farquhar GD, von Caemmerer S (1982) Modeling of photosynthetic response to environmental conditions. pp 549-587 *In* Lange OL, Nobel PS, Osmond CB, Zeigler H (*eds*) Physiological plant ecology II. Water relations and carbon assimilation. Encyclopedia of Plant Physiology, New Series Volume 12B Springer-Verlag, Berlin

Fowler D, Unsworth MH (1979) Turbulent transfer of sulphur dioxide to a wheat crop. Quart J Met Soc 105: 767-783

Fowler D, Cape JN, Unsworth MH (1989) Deposition of atmospheric pollutants on forests. Phil Trans Royal Soc Lon B 324: 247-265

Gross LJ, Kirschbaum MUF, Pearcy RW (1991) A dynamic model of photosynthesis in varying light taking account of stomatal conductance, C_3-cycle intermediates, photorespiration and Rubisco activation. Plant Cell Environ 14: 881-893

Hanson PJ, Garten CT (1992) Deposition of $H^{15}NO_3$ vapor to white oak, red maple and loblolly pine foliage: experimental observations and a generalized model. New Phytol 122: 329-337

Hanson PJ, Lindberg SE (1991) Dry deposition of reactive nitrogen compounds: a review of leaf, canopy and nonfoliar measurements. Atmos Environ 25A: 1615-1634

Hanson PJ, Taylor GE Jr (1990) Modeling pollutant gas uptake by leaves: an approach based on physiochemical properties. *In* Dixon RK, Meldahl R, Ruark G, Warren WG (*eds*) Process modeling of forest growth responses to environmental stress. Timber Press Portland Oregon *pp* 351-356

Hanson PJ, Rott K, Taylor GE, Gunderson CA, Lindberg SE (1989) NO_2 deposition to elements of a forest landscape. Atmos Environ 23: 1783-1794

Hicks BB, Hosker RP, Meyers TP, Womack JD (1991) Dry deposition inferential measurement techniques I. Design and tests of a prototype meteorological and chemical system for determining dry deposition. Atmos Environ 25: 2345-2359

Hill AC (1971) Vegetation: a sink for atmospheric pollutants. J Air Poll Control Assoc 21: 341-346

Holloway PJ (1994) Plant cuticles: physiochemical characteristics and biosynthesis. *In* Air pollutants and the leaf cuticle. Percy KE, Cape JN, Jagels R, Simpson CM (*eds*) Springer, New York (*this volume, pp*)

Hosker RP, Lindberg SE (1982) Review article: atmospheric deposition and plant assimilation of airborn gases and particles. Atmos Environ 16: 889-910

Huttunen S (1994) Effects of air pollutants on epicuticular wax structure. *In* Percy KE, Cape JN, Jagels R, Simpson CM (*eds*) Air pollutants and the leaf cuticle. Springer, New York (*this volume, pp*)

Inoue E (1963) On the turbulent structure of airflow within crop canopies. J Met Soc Japan 41: 317-326

Johnson DW, Lindberg SE (*eds*) (1992) Atmospheric deposition and forest nutrient cycling: a synthesis of the integrated forest study. Springer-Verlag New York

Kanwisher J (1960) P_{CO2} in sea water and its effect on the movement of CO_2 in nature. Tellus 12: 209-215

Kanwisher J (1963) On the exchange of gases between the atmosphere and the sea. Deep-Sea Res 10: 195-207

Kerstiens G, Lendzian KJ (1989) Interaction between ozone and plant cuticles. I. ozone decomposition and permeability. New Phytol 112: 13-19

Laisk AC, Walker DA (1986) Control of phosphate turnover as a rate-limiting factor and the possible cause of oscillations in photosynthesis: a mathematical model. Proc. Royal Soc Lond B 227: 281-302

Laisk A, Kull O, Moldau K (1989) Ozone concentration in leaf intercellular air spaces is close to zero. Plant Phys 90: 1163-1167

Lendzian KJ (1982) Gas permeability of plant cuticles. Oxygen permeability. Planta 155: 310-315

Lindberg SE, Lovett GM, Richter DR, Johnson DW (1986) Atmospheric deposition and canopy interaction of major ions in forest. Science 231: 141-145

Lindberg SE, Meyers TP, Taylor GE, Turner RR, Schroeder WH (1992) Atmosphere/surface exchange of mercury in a forest: results of modeling and gradient approaches. J Geophys Res 97: 2519-2528

Liss PS (1971) Exchange of SO_2 between the atmosphere and natural waters. Nature 233: 327-329

Liss PS, Slater PJ (1974) Flux of gases across the air-sea interface. Nature 247: 181-184

Lovett GM (1994) Atmospheric deposition of nutrients and pollutants in North America: an ecological perspective. J Ecol Appl (*in press*)

Lovett GM, Lindberg SE (1984) Dry deposition and canopy exchange in a mixed oak forest as determined by analysis of throughfall. J Appl Ecol 21: 1013-1028

Lovett GM, Reiners WA, Olson RK (1982) Cloud droplet deposition in subalpine balsam fir forests: hydrological and chemical inputs. Science 218: 1303-1304

McLaughlin SB, Taylor GE (1981) Relative humidity: important modifier of pollutant uptake by plants. Science 211: 167-169

Nobel PS (1991) Physiochemical and environmental plant physiology. Academic Press New York

Parkhurst DF, Mott KA (1990) Intercellular limits to CO_2 uptake in leaves. Studies in air and helium. Plant Phys 94: 1024-1032

Percy KE, McQuattie CJ, Rebbeck JA (1994) Effects of air pollutants on epicuticular wax chemical composition. Percy KE, Cape JN, Jagels R, Simpson CM (*eds*) Springer, New York (*this volume, pp* 67-79)

Riederer M, Jetter R, Markstadter C, Schreiber L (1994) Air pollutants and the cuticle: implications for plant physiology. *In* Air pollutants and the leaf cuticle. Percy KE, Cape JN, Jagels R, Simpson, CM (*eds*) Springer, New York (*this volume, pp*)

Schönherr J (1982) Resistances of plant surfaces to water loss: transport properties of cutin, suberin, and associated lipids. *In* Lange OL, Nobel PS, Osmond CB, Zeigler H (*eds*) Physiological plant ecology II. water relations and carbon assimilation. Encyclopedia of Plant Physiology, New Series Volume 12B Springer-Verlag, Berlin *pp* 153-179

Schreiber L, Schönherr J (1993) Determination of foliar uptake of chemicals: influence of leaf surface microflora. Plant Cell Environ 16: 743-748

Sharkey TD, Loreto F (1993) Water stress, temperature, and light effects on the capacity for isoprene emissions and photosynthesis of Kudzu leaves. Oecologia 95: 328-333

Smith SV (1985) Physical, chemical and biological characteristics of CO_2 gas flux across the air-water interface. Plant Cell Environ 8: 387-398

Taylor GE Jr, Hanson PJ (1992) Forest trees and tropospheric ozone: role of canopy deposition and leaf uptake in developing exposure-response relationships. Agr Ecosys Environ 42: 255-273

Taylor GE Jr, Hanson PJ, Baldocchi DD (1988) Pollutant deposition to individual leaves and plant canopies: sites of deposition and relationship to injury. *In* Heck WW, Taylor OC, Tingey DT (*eds*) Assessment of crop loss from air pollutants. Elsevier Publishers London *pp* 227-257

Taylor GE Jr, Johnson DW, Andersen CP (1994) Air pollution and forest ecosystems: a regional to global perspective. J Ecol Appl (*in press*)

Taylor GE JR, McLaughlin SB, Shriner DS, Selvidge WJ (1983) The flux of sulfur-containing gases to vegetation. Atmos Environ 17: 789-796

Tingey DT, Taylor GE Jr (1982) Variation in plant response to ozone: a conceptual model of physiological events. *In* Unsworth MH, Ormrod DP (*eds*) Effects of gaseous air pollutants on agriculture and horticulture. Butterworth Publishers London *pp* 113-138

Travis CC, Hester ST (1991) Global chemical pollution. Environ Sci Tech 25: 814-820.

Air Pollutants and Plant Cuticles:
Mechanisms of Gas and Water Transport, and Effects on Water Permeability

Gerhard Kerstiens
Institute of Environmental and Biological Sciences
Division of Biological Sciences
Lancaster University
Lancaster LA1 4YQ
United Kingdom

Abstract

A short overview of studies carried out by K.J. Lendzian and his group on transport rates of pure pollutant gases across isolated cuticles will be given. They show that the boiling point of a gas is a good predictor of cuticular permeability. Apparently good prediction quality, however, contrasts with a considerable gap between uptake rates determined in stomata-free systems, and rates of dry deposition to whole leaves observed under conditions where stomata should be closed to the maximum extent. Apart from other possible reasons for this difference, examination of cuticular sorption and diffusion characteristics indicates two major problems that may account for inconsistencies to some extent: (1) transport rates of gases in cuticles may be concentration-dependent and (2) interactions in gas mixtures with respect to cuticular transport are possible. Potential mechanisms of transport across cuticles and ways of interaction between gases (including water vapour) will be discussed.

There has long been the notion that air pollutants may affect the water barrier quality of plant cuticles. This hypothesis has been tested in a recent study of effects of a wide range of air pollutants and elevated UV-B radiation on adaxial *in situ*-cuticular water permeability of various broadleaf tree species. No effects were found unless the leaves showed visible signs of stress due to treatment or chamber effects.

Introduction

Two questions are to be answered in this paper. What do we know about mechanisms by which gaseous air pollutants penetrate the cuticular membrane? Does prolonged exposure to air pollutants change the cuticle's effectiveness as a barrier to uncontrolled water loss? Although much is known about certain aspects of transport phenomena in cuticles, we cannot yet explain and predict permeabilities in quantitative terms. Three aspects of gas transport across cuticles will be discussed here: the role of waxes as the main barriers in the membrane; the role of polysaccharides as potential diffusion pathways through the cuticle, and the conclusions which may be drawn from recent findings that gas transport in cuticles is concentration-dependent. Transport of gases such as SO_2 and NO_2 in the ionic form is outside the range of this review.

NATO ASI Series, Vol. G 36
Air Pollutants and the Leaf Cuticle
Edited by K. E. Percy et al.
© Springer-Verlag Berlin Heidelberg 1994

Mechanisms of gas and water transport in cuticles

Transport through the intact cuticle occurs by diffusion. Transport of an uncharged molecule across cuticles is proportional to its concentration gradient. An additional pressure gradient has never been found to increase transport rates, *i.e.*, there is no mass flow through pores. As mass flow of liquids or gases through pores requires a pore diameter greater than the respective mean free path length, pores — should they exist — would be smaller than ca. 0.8 nm in diameter (Scherer and Bolton, 1985). It follows that using the gradient of mole fraction as the driving force is inappropriate. Permeabilities of cuticles are, therefore, expressed as permeances P (m s^{-1}) rather than conductances. P is defined as flow (g) per unit area (m^{-2}) and time (s^{-1}), divided by the concentration gradient across the cuticle (g m^{-3}).

Waxes. The bulk of plant cuticles is made up of a strongly cross-linked polymer (cutin) network (Holloway, 1982). Apart from cutin, there may be a structurally different type of polymer present which has been called cutan (Holloway, this volume). Our understanding of transport processes in cuticles is, therefore, based on the concepts of diffusion in polymers. Thermal motion of chain segments leads to separations between polymer chains which may be wide enough to accomodate a molecule of the diffusing species, which moves from one random position to another due to its thermal energy. Diffusing gas molecules in polymers find themselves in an environment which can be treated for many practical purposes as an organic liquid. It follows that diffusing molecules in a polymer could as well be called solutes. Transport rates within a homogeneous polymer (above its glass transition temperature) are governed by only two parameters, the partition coeffient K and the diffusion coefficient D. The former equals the ratio of concentrations in the polymer and in the surrounding medium and describes a solute's solubility in the polymer, and the latter measures the mobility of the solute in the polymer network. Plant cuticles, however, are highly inhomogeneous structures, and breaking down permeabilities into apparent, overall partition and diffusion coefficients is of limited value for the understanding of transport processes.

It was shown that removal of waxes from cuticles results in an increase of gas and water permeabilities of up to three orders of magnitude (see Lendzian and Kerstiens, 1991). Our present understanding of how waxes accomplish their barrier function is based on the fact that waxes embedded in the cutin/cutan polymer are partly in a crystalline state. Schönherr and Riederer (1989) proposed that waxes form distinct crystallites, separated from each other due to crystal-lisation restraints in the cutin/cutan network or other defect-producing circumstances. Molecules in a crystal array show little thermal motion. This means that there is no opportunity for solutes to penetrate those regions of the cuticle occupied by wax crystallites. Solutes are forced to 'find their way' around the obstacles. Elongation of the mean diffusion path has the same effect as a reduction in solute mobility and decreases transport rates. The actual effect depends not only on the total fraction of cuticle volume thus excluded from diffusion paths, but also on the size and shape of the crystallites. This was shown for technical membranes, where the addition of impermeable flakes is used to lower permeabilities (Cussler *et al.*, 1988).

Recently Riederer has proposed a somewhat different model (see Riederer *et al.*, *this volume*), where crystalline waxes form excluded regions in a continuous, partly amorphous wax layer. Reynhardt and Riederer (1991) showed that cuticular waxes consist of a mixture of several phases with various degrees of molecular order and mobility. In this model, cuticular permeabilities are governed by the size, number and transport properties of non-crystalline regions within the wax layer. This layer (or layers) may be on the inside or on the outside of the cuticular membrane.

Our conception of how waxes determine the overall transport properties of cuticles has reached a high degree of complexity. However, it is not possible for example to predict how halving the wax load of a cuticle would influence its permeability. Wax load has been found to be correlated with cuticular water permeability in one study by Premachandra *et al.* (1992) carried out with entire detached leaves, but not in a study using isolated cuticles (Riederer and Schneider, 1990). Although there are some studies in which there appeared to be a correlation between wax load and cuticular water permeability, the common problem of these studies is that entire leaves were used (detached and wilting, or in darkness). The contribution of incomplete stomatal closure was assumed to be small, but could not be quantified. 'Cuticular' water permeabilities in these studies were usually much higher than found with stomata-free isolated cuticles (Lendzian and Kerstiens, 1991), and should better be called, for instance, 'minimum overall conductances', clearly including both cuticular and residual stomatal water loss. The paper by Premachandra *et al.* (1992) is an exception in as far as the values reported are within the range of water permeabilities found with isolated cuticles, indicating good stomatal closure.

Since differences in wax load in these studies were usually related to drought resistance of different cultivars, or to preceding drought treatments, effects on residual stomatal conductance (in darkness or after excision of leaves) may have influenced 'cuticular' transpiration rates. It appears that in near-darkness it is usual that at least a few stomata fail to close completely (Laisk *et al.*, 1980; Kappen *et al.*, 1987; Rawson and Clarke, 1988). I am not aware of any SEM studies examining stomatal closure of detached, wilting leaves. Aperture widths under 1 μm, which are difficult to assess by light microscopy, would still be large enough to allow relatively significant stomatal transpiration (Stålfelt, 1932; Kerstiens *et al.*, 1992). Small absolute changes in residual stomatal conductance may thus appear as large relative differences in apparent cuticular permeability.

Polysaccharides. A reticulum of fine polysaccharide fibrillae is present in most types of cuticles (Holloway, 1982). Gouret *et al.* (1993) recently found good correlations between cuticular wax load and permeability of a lipophilic herbicide, diuron, if the seven species examined were

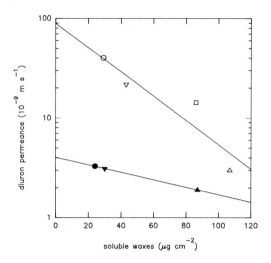

Figure 1   Diuron permeance of isolated cuticles versus soluble wax content. Open symbols: all-reticulate cuticles (□ *Capsicum annuum* fruit; ▽ *Galium aparine* leaf; ○ *Lyco-persicon esculentum* fruit; △ *Prunus laurocerasus* leaf). Closed symbols: outer layer of the cuticle lamellate or amorphous (▲ *Buxus sempervirens* leaf; ● *Hedera helix* leaf; ▼ *Vanilla planifolia* leaf). Data from Gouret, Rohr and Chamel (1993).

grouped according to their ultrastructure (Fig. 1). The grouping criterion was whether the cuticular polysaccharide reticulum reached the outer surface, or whether a lamellate or amorphous layer formed the outermost part of the cuticle. This result fits in well with speculations about the polysaccharide reticulum playing some special role in cuticular transport (see Lendzian and Kerstiens, 1991) which were based on earlier findings. Kerstiens and Lendzian (1989b) and recently Chamel *et al.* (1992) showed that around 75% of the water taken up by isolated tomato fruit (*Lycopersicon esculentum* Mill.) and white fir needle (*Abies alba* Mill.) cuticles were associated with cuticular polysaccharides. Mean water uptake was closely correlated with mean polysaccharide content of four species (Kerstiens and Lendzian, 1989b). The same was found to be true for the six species examined by Chamel *et al.* (1991) when the water uptake reported was compared with the polysaccharide content of the respective cuticles (estimates taken from Riederer and Schönherr, 1984; Kerstiens, 1988; Gouret *et al.*, 1993). Chamel *et al.* (1992), however, found no correlation between mean polysaccharide content of fir needles from different trees and their water uptake. Haas (1974) discovered that polysaccharide content of tomato fruit cuticles was correlated with their water permeability.

If the polysaccharide reticulum really does provide diffusion pathways with special properties, different from those encountered in the cutin/cutan polymer or the non-crystalline wax regions, then its importance will be determined to a large extent by its localisation in the cuticle. As the effective diffusion barrier is located in a rather narrow region along the outer surface (Schönherr and Riederer, 1989), polysaccharides would have to penetrate this region to provide effective pathways across the cuticle.

A survey of studies of water permeability where cuticles of known ultrastructure were used revealed that only cuticles possessing a non-reticulate outer layer were very impermeable (P $< 0.7 \cdot 10^{-5}$ m s^{-1}), whereas all the highest permeances (P $< 2.5 \cdot 10^{-5}$ m s^{-1}) were associated with all-reticulate cuticles (Table 1). There was a range of permeances (0.7-$2.1 \cdot 10^{-5}$ m s^{-1}) where the two ultrastructural groups overlapped. It has to be stressed, however, that the group of highly-permeable cuticles consisted almost entirely of fruit cuticles, which were absent from the lower and middle range of permeabilities, and that there may be other structural differences between fruit and leaf cuticles. Table 1 also contains results for conifer needles which were determined

Table 1   Water permeance P (m s^{-1} * 10^{5}) of cuticular membranes of known ultrastructure.

A. Outer lamellate or amorphous layer present	
Clivia miniata (leaf)[1,2]	0.1-0.5 [12]
Picea abies (needles)[4]	0.3 [7]
Pseudotsuga menziesii (needles)[1]	0.3 [10]
Ficus elastica (leaf)[1,5]	0.3-0.4 [12]
Hedera helix (leaf)[1,5]	0.3-0.6 [12]
Pyrus communis (leaf)[1,5]	1.2-2.1 [12]
Picea rubens (needles)[3]	1.2 [11]
Allium cepa (bulb scale)[2]	1.9 [12]
B. All regions reticulate	
Ilex aquifolium (leaf)[1]	0.8-1.1 [12]
Citrus aurantium (leaf)[2]	0.7-5 [12]
Pinus sylvestris (needles)[1]	1-3 [6,8,13]
Picea sitchensis (needles)[1]	1.4 [13]
Prunus laurocerasus (leaf)[1,5]	1.7 [12]
Abies balsamea (needles)[1]	≈3 [9]
Lycopersicum esculentum (fruit)[5]	5-14 [12]
Capsicum annuum (fruit)[5]	9-20 [12]

Ultrastructure references: [1] *Holloway, 1982 (and references therein);* [2] *Schönherr, 1982;* [3] *Percy et al., 1992;* [4] *Tenberge, 1992;* [5] *Gouret et al., 1993. Permeability references:* [6] *Pisek and Berger, 1938;* [7] *Baig and Tranquillini, 1980;* [8] *Cape and Fowler, 1981;* [9] *estimated from DeLucia and Berlyn, 1984;* [10] *Hadley and Smith, 1990;* [11] *Herrick and Friedland, 1991;* [12] *Lendzian and Kerstiens, 1991 (and references therein);* [13] *van Gardingen et al., 1991. Data come from investigations with isolated or non-isolated astomatous cuticles (leaves and fruits) or from transpiration-decline experiments (needles), and represent means.*

from weight-loss curves, where stomatal contributions could not safely be excluded, *viz.* minimum overall conductances. Only values within the range of permeances determined with isolated cuticles ($P < 10 \cdot 10^{-5}$ m s^{-1}) were included in Table 1, indicating that relatively good stomatal closure had taken place. Where different studies reported widely different values, only the lowest ones were used. The three conifer species with all-reticulate cuticles showed slightly or much higher minimum overall conductances than the three species with a non-reticulate outer layer. Non-reticulate layers have been found to appear after exposure to 250 ppb ozone (*Picea rubens* Sarg.; Percy *et al.*, 1992), or disappear following prolonged exposure to acidic rain (*Phaseolus vulgaris* L.; Percy and Baker, 1987). This may be more likely to cause significant effects on water permeability than changes in amount or composition of cuticular waxes.

The survey also showed that extrapolated hold-up times for water transport, a measure of how long it takes for water molecules to cross isolated cuticular membranes (Lendzian and Kerstiens, 1991), were above a certain threshold (600 s) only if cuticles possessed a non-reticulate outer layer (Fig. 2). No correlation with cuticular thickness or wax load was found. This may be taken as an indication that the polysaccharide reticulum offers relatively fast diffusion pathways, although it has to be kept in mind that speed alone does not necessarily imply a high contribution to overall flow, as long as the transport capacity of that network is unknown.

From micrographs (Holloway, 1982; Gouret *et al.*, 1993) the thickness of the polysaccharide strands can roughly be estimated. It amounts to only 5-10 nm, and it is, therefore, unlikely that the strands represent anything more complex than single cellulose microfibrils (*i.e.*, no fibres with inter-microfibrillar spaces). It has to be stressed that the chemical nature of the strands is still unclear, although cellulose certainly represents a major part of the material (Holloway, 1982). Cellulose microfibrils, however, are largely crystalline (Brett and Waldron, 1990), which poses the question of how water could diffuse in these elements. Diffusion may be restricted to amorphous regions, which are usually thought to make up only a small proportion of the cross-section. MacKay *et al.* (1988), however, hypothesised that 10-nm wide cellulose microfibrils in bean hypocotyl primary walls had a 'rigid' (but probably not crystalline), 2-nm thick outer sheath of hemicellulose II molecules. The sheath would, therefore, represent 64% of the cross-section of the fibril. An alternative diffusion pathway may exist along the surface of microfibrils. The latter phenomenon is not unknown from synthetic polymer membranes where embedded fibers are not 'well-wetted' by the polymer (*e.g.*, Aronhime *et al.*, 1987). I am unaware of any measurements of diffusion coefficients in or along microfibrils.

It has to be stressed that the involvement of polysaccharides in transport across cuticles is highly speculative, and that all the evidence is of a circumstantial nature. The study by Gouret *et al.* (1993) is the only systematic investigation into this field so far, and it relates to a lipophilic

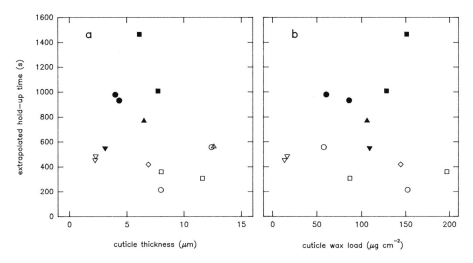

Figure 2a Extrapolated hold-up time of water diffusion across isolated cuticles versus thickness of the cuticular membranes. Open symbols: all-reticulate cuticles (□*Capsicum
annuum* fruit; ∇ *Citrus aurantium* leaf; Δ *Ilex aquifolium* leaf; ○*Lycopersicon
esculentum* fruit; ◊ *Prunus laurocerasus* leaf). Closed symbols: outer layer of the
cuticle lamellate or amorphous (▲ *Clivia miniata* leaf; ■ *Ficus elastica* leaf;
● *Hedera helix* leaf; ▼ *Pyrus communis* leaf). Data from Becker, Kerstiens and
Schönherr (1986), Kerstiens (1988), and unpublished data.

Figure 2b Extrapolated hold-up time of water diffusion across isoaled cuticles versus cuticular
wax load. Symbols and references as above. Wax load estimates from Riederer and
Schönherr (1984), Kerstiens (1988), and unpublished data.

substance where the interactions with the cuticle may differ from those of pollutant gases and
water.

Concentration dependence. The aspects of transport across cuticles discussed so far had much
to do with the mobility of solutes: impermeable barriers rendering diffusion paths very tortuous,
and a reticulum of potential pathways with diffusion properties different from the bulk polymer.
This section deals with a phenomenon which concerns the other governing parameter of transport
in polymers, solute solubility.

Kerstiens *et al.* (1992) described the concentration dependence of SO_2 sorption in isolated
cuticles. In white fir cuticles, the partition coefficient K rose by a factor of more than 200 when
SO_2 concentration was decreased from 10^6 ppm (pure SO_2 at 10^5 Pa) to 100 ppm. This was
interpreted as an indication that both SO_2 dissolution in the polymer (Henry sorption) and
adsorption at a limited number of appropriate sites in or on the cuticle occurred at the same time.
The data could be modelled as representing the sum of a linear Henry dissolution term and a

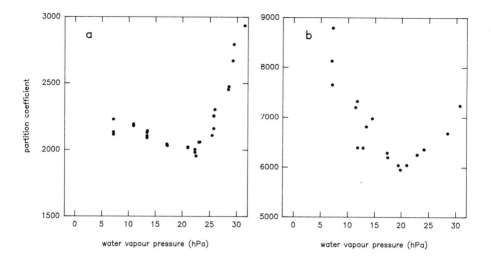

Figure 3   Partition coefficient of water for isolated *Citrus aurantium* (a) and *Picea abies* (b) leaf cuticles versus water vapour pressure at 25°C (100% r.h. = 32 hPa).

Langmuir adsorption term. The latter has a saturation characteristic. The mathematical model predicts that K would not rise much higher if the SO_2 concentration was lowered to ambient values. A similar observation was made for water sorption in isolated *Citrus aurantium* L. (bitter orange) and *Picea abies* (L.) Karst. (Norway spruce) leaf cuticles, where K was found to decrease steadily between 20 and 70% relative humidity. At higher humidity K rose again, probably due to the formation of water clusters (Fig. 3a, b).

The combination of a Henry and a Langmuir term is the standard way to analyse gas uptake of polymers below their glass transition temperature. The physical interpretation of 'dual-mode sorption' in glassy polymers is that there are permanent microvoids present in the polymer. Polymer chains cannot carry out certain types of thermal motion below a characteristic temperature. This leads to excess free space being 'frozen' in the polymer. It is believed that adsorption takes place on the walls of these microvoids.

The question whether plant cuticles are in a glassy state at typical temperatures cannot be answered conclusively (Lendzian and Kerstiens, 1991). It might depend on the water content of the cuticle, as water may act as a plasticizer by lowering the glass transition temperature. Since dry cuticles have often been used for the determination of gas permeabilities, and very high gas concentrations had to be used to detect fluxes, the applicability of these results to *in vivo* conditions has to be treated with a degree of caution.

The physical nature of adsorption sites that cause non-linear sorption behaviour of SO_2 and other gases (Lendzian and Kerstiens, 1991) may well turn out to be quite different from that in glassy polymers. The presence of polar groups in cutin, and of interfaces between polysaccharides and cutin/cutan are other possible explanations. Independently of the correct physical explanation, the existence of adsorption sites produces a range of new problems for modelling and prediction of gas permeabilites.

Paul and Koros (1976) modelled transport across polymer membranes in the glassy state as a function of the concentration and the mobility of the adsorbed population of a solute (expressed as a fraction of the mobility of the dissolved population). This model was applied to SO_2 and fir cuticles (Kerstiens et al., 1992). It predicts that, if the relative mobility of adsorbed molecules ranges from 0 (immobile) to 1 (adsorbed and dissolved molecules equally mobile), the permeability at SO_2 concentrations below 10 ppm would be between 1 and about 100 times as high as the permeability above 10^5 ppm. The function levels off at both low (< 1 Pa) and high (> 10^4 Pa) partial pressures of SO_2. The diffusion coefficient of SO_2 uptake into isolated cuticles increased strongly if solute concentration was increased (Kerstiens and Federholzner, unpublished data). As the proportion of adsorbed molecules is higher at low concentrations, it appears that the mobility of the adsorbed population of solute molecules was indeed lower than that of the dissolved population.

Both for SO_2 and for CO_2, data exist that show that permeances tended to be higher at 10^6 ppm than at 300 ppm (see Lendzian and Kerstiens, 1991). These findings contradict the predictions of the dual-mode sorption model. Water might have been responsible for this difference, as cuticles in the experiments with 300 ppm were dry, whereas in the high concentration experiments they were in contact with water. Water concentration in the cuticle increases steeply when relative humidity exceeds ca. 70% (Fig. 3). Water might have changed the state the cuticles were in (plasticization), or it may have produced pathways across the cuticles, e.g., by swelling polysaccharide strands or by producing very narrow channels consisting of a continuum of hydration water at polar groups and water clusters (Schönherr, 1982; Hauser et al., 1993). Plasticization of glassy polymers by the penetrating gas resulting in an inverse concentration/permeability relationship has also been observed with technical membranes (e.g., Sada et al., 1993). Water content of the cuticle was shown to affect water permeability of intact cuticles (Schönherr, 1982) and wax-free preparations of cuticular membranes (Becker et al., 1986).

In the real world, we have to deal with gas mixtures. Whereas dissolution in the cuticle is a process that is virtually independent for each species of the mixture, there will be competition for the limited number of adsorption sites. In general it is fair to say that the more easily condensable a gas is, the stronger it will compete for adsorption sites. Again, if adsorbed molecules are immobile, this would not change the transport characteristics. It is, however, not

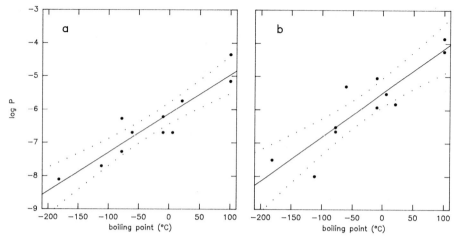

Figure 4 Logarithm of gas permeances P (m s^{-1}) versus boiling point of the gases for *Citrus aurantium* leaf (a) and *Lycopersicon esculentum* fruit (b) cuticles. Data points represent permeances for O_2, O_3, CO_2, H_2S, SO_2, CH_3SH, NO_2 and H_2O (from left to right). For references, see text.

very likely that this will be the case. It follows that, theoretically at least, the presence of water may increase gas permeability by plasticizing the cuticle or forming additional pathways, or decrease gas permeability by successfully competing against other, less condensable gases for adsorption sites.

Concentration-dependence of permeabilities also arises from a completely different set of causes: the specific chemical interactions between dissolved air pollutants and constituents of plant cuticles. Ozone was shown to be destroyed while passing through the cuticle, apparently without chemically changing the cuticle (Kerstiens and Lendzian, 1989a). Only at very high concentrations (2.5%) was the proportion of undestroyed ozone molecules high enough (1-5%) that transport across isolated cuticles could be detected. Such high concentrations also led to effects on water permeability (Kerstiens and Lendzian, 1989b). Nitrogen dioxide has also been shown to react with cuticles. It is bound irreversibly and can increase water permeability if present in high concentrations in the cuticle (see Lendzian and Kerstiens, 1991). As with O_3, an effect at ambient concentrations appears to be very unlikely (Kerstiens *et al.*, 1992).

Prediction of gas permeances. In spite of all the difficulties in understanding permeabilities in quantitative terms, it appears to be possible to estimate the permeance of a given membrane for a certain gas within about one order of magnitude if permeances for other gases are known. Logarithmic regressions of gas permeance (O_2, O_3, CO_2, H_2S, SO_2, CH_3SH, NO_2 and H_2O; data from Lendzian, 1982, 1984; Becker *et al.*, 1986; Lendzian *et al.*, 1986; Lendzian and Kerstiens, 1988, 1991; Kerstiens and Lendzian, 1989a, b; Geyer and Schönherr, 1990; Kerstiens *et al.*, 1992) versus the boiling point of gases were calculated for isolated *Citrus aurantium* leaf and tomato fruit cuticles (Fig. 4a, b). Permeability of both types of cuticles increased by one order of magnitude every time the boiling point of the gas rose by 80° (Kerstiens *et al.*, 1992). Both cuticles represent the all-reticulate ultrastructural type.

Air pollutant effects on cuticular water permeability

Treatment of isolated *Ilex aquifolium* L. (holly) cuticles with 1-1.5 ppm ozone and/or an acidic solution (pH 2) for 1 week did not significantly affect water permeability (Garrec and Kerfourn, 1989). Similarly, exposure of isolated cuticles of *Citrus aurantium, Ficus elastica* Roxb. (rubber tree) and *Hedera helix* L. (ivy) to a combination of frequent ozone (up to 130 ppb) and acid mist (pH 3) episodes for 10 months did not result in a change of water permeability (Kerstiens and Lendzian, 1989b).

Table 2   Effects of air pollutants and UV-B radiation on adaxial cuticular water permeance P $(m \ s^{-1} * 10^5)^a$

	P (treated)	P (control)
Fagus sylvatica		
30-120 ppb O_3	$2.54 \ (0.56)^b$	2.30 (0.56)
20-50 ppb SO_2	2.92 (0.67)	2.86 (0.73)
600 ppm CO_2 (1st yr of exposure)	2.87 (0.74)	2.85 (0.53)
600 ppm CO_2 (2nd yr of exposure)	2.15 (0.34)	2.15 (0.51)
300-400 ppb NO	1.59 (0.57)	1.61 (0.49)
30-130 ppb O_3 + mist at pH 3.0^c	3.87 (0.29)	3.74 (0.29)
Acer pseudoplatanus		
600 ppm CO_2	2.22 (0.60)	2.37 (0.53)
300-400 ppb NO	1.56 (0.30)	1.67 (0.41)
Betula pubescens		
50-60 ppb NO_2 + SO_2 (cabinets)	2.69 (0.98)	1.03 (0.61) *
20-70 ppb NO_2 + SO_2 (greenhouse)	1.65 (0.69)	1.38 (0.48)
Corylus avellana		
300-400 ppb NO	2.07 (0.79)	1.74 (0.37)
Prunus avium		
30-120 ppb O_3	0.61 (0.21)	0.56 (0.29)
300-400 ppb NO	1.05 (0.37)	0.92 (0.37)
Hedera helix		
30-130 ppb O_3 + mist at pH 3.0^c	0.28 (0.03)	0.31 (0.04)
6.3 kJ m^{-2} d^{-1} UV-B (plant-weighted)	0.44 (0.13)	0.25 (0.08) *

[a] *n = 6-12;* [b] *S.D.; * = significant difference (p 0.05);* [c] *Kerstiens and Lendzian (1989b).*

Exposure of deciduous trees or shrubs from before bud-break for several months to a variety of air pollutants had no effect on adaxial cuticular water permeability in most treatments (Table 2; Kerstiens, in prep.). Plants were grown and exposed in greenhouses (O_3, SO_2, CO_2, NO, NO_2 + SO_2) or in artificially illuminated growth cabinets or phytotrons (O_3 + acid mist, NO_2 + SO_2, UV-B). Control treatments received low levels of the respective pollutant gases and ambient levels of CO_2. The control group in the UV-B experiment received no UV-B. Water permeability of astomatous leaf surfaces was measured on the intact leaf with a highly sensitive moisture monitor (Kerstiens and Lendzian, 1989b).

In some cases conditions in both control and exposure cabinets reduced plant growth and caused visible changes in appearance compared with plants kept in a greenhouse. In these cases (the NO_2 + SO_2 treatment carried out in cabinets, and the UV-B treatment, Table 2), the respective treatments led to an increase of water permeability. Water permeability of greenhouse-grown control plants was between those of control and treated plants grown in cabinets. In the second NO_2 + SO_2 fumigation, which was carried out in a greenhouse, some leaves showed visible damage. This was not related to leaf age. These leaves also showed significantly higher water permeability than the control group, whereas there was no effect if the entire population of leaves grown under fumigation was examined.

These findings indicate that effects of gaseous air pollutants on cuticular water permeability, should they occur, are mediated by the plant's metabolism rather than being the result of direct chemical or physical interactions between pollutant and cuticle. Plants experience a variety of environmental stresses and when exposed to these stresses may be more at risk than plants grown under the well-watered, well-nourished, more or less herbivore-free growing conditions typically experienced by most experimental plants. These conditions are the exception rather than the rule when compared to the ambient environment. The possibility, therefore, exists that air pollution effects on cuticular water permeability may be less rare in nature than the results reported above would suggest.

Acknowledgements

I am grateful to Dr P. W. Lucas for his comments on an earlier draft of this manuscript.

References

Aronhime MT, Neumann S, Marom G (1987) The anisotropic diffusion of water in Kevlar-epoxy composites. J Mat Sci 22: 2435-2446

Baig MN, Tranquillini W (1980) The effects of wind and temperature on cuticular transpiration of *Picea abies* and *Pinus cembra* and their significance in dessication damage at the alpine timberline. Oecologia 47: 252-256

Becker M, Kerstiens G, Schönherr J (1986) Water permeability of plant cuticles: permeance, diffusion and partition coefficients. Trees 1: 54-60

Brett C, Waldron K (1990) Physiology and biochemistry of plant cell walls. Unwin Hyman - London etc.

Cape JN, Fowler D (1981) Changes in epicuticular wax of *Pinus sylvestris* exposed to polluted air. Silva Fenn 15: 457-458

Chamel A, Pineri M, Escoubes M (1991) Quantitative determination of water sorption by plant cuticles. Plant Cell Environ 14: 87-95

Chamel A, Escoubes M, Baudrand G, Girard, G (1992) Determination of water sorption by cuticles isolated from fir tree needles. Trees 6: 109-114

Cussler EL, Hughes SE, Ward WJ, Aris R (1988) Barrier membranes. J Membr Sci 38: 161-174

DeLucia EH, Berlyn GP (1984) The effect of increasing elevation on leaf cuticle thickness and cuticular transpiration in balsam fir. Can J Bot 62: 2423-2431

Garrec JP, Kerfourn C (1989) Effets de pluies acides et de l'ozone sur la perméabilité à l'eau et aux ions de cuticules isolées. Environ Exp Bot 29: 215-228

Geyer U, Schönherr J (1990) The effect of the environment on the permeability and composition of *Citrus* leaf cuticles. I. Water permeability of isolated cuticular membranes. Planta 180: 147-153

Gouret E, Rohr R, Chamel A (1993) Ultrastructure and chemical composition of some isolated plant cuticles in relation to their permeability to the herbicide diuron. New Phytol 124: 423-431

Haas K (1974) Untersuchungen zum chemischen Aufbau der Cuticula während der Organogenese von Blättern und Früchten sowie zur Cuticulartranspiration. Doctoral diss., Universität Hohenheim

Hadley JL, Smith WK (1990) Influence of leaf surface wax and leaf area to water content ratio on cuticular transpiration in western conifers, U.S.A. Can J For Res 20: 1306-1311

Hauser HD, Walters KD, Berg VS (1993) Patterns of effective permeability of leaf cuticles to acids. Plant Physiol 101: 251-257

Herrick GT, Friedland AJ (1991) Winter desiccation and injury of subalpine red spruce. Tree Physiol 8: 23-36

Holloway PJ (1982) Structure and histochemistry of plant cuticular membranes: an overview. *In* Cutler DF, Alvin KL, Price CE (*eds*) The plant cuticle. Academic Press, London, *pp* 1-32

Kappen L, Andresen G, Lösch R (1987) *In situ* observations of stomatal movements. J Exp Bot 186: 126-141

Kerstiens (1988) Funktionelle Veränderungen der pflanzlichen Kutikula durch Ozon. Doctoral diss., Technische Universität München

Kerstiens G, Lendzian KJ (1989a) Interactions between ozone and plant cuticles. I. Ozone deposition and permeability. New Phytol 112: 13-19

Kerstiens G, Lendzian KJ (1989b) Interactions between ozone and plant cuticles. II. Water permeability. New Phytol 112: 21-27

Kerstiens G, Federholzner R, Lendzian KJ (1992) Dry deposition and cuticular uptake of pollutant gases. Agric Ecosystems Environ 42: 239-253

Laisk A, Oja V, Kull K (1980) Statistical distribution of stomatal apertures of *Vicia faba* and *Hordeum vulgare* and the *Spannungsphase* of stomatal opening. J Exp Bot 31: 49-58

Lendzian KJ (1982) Gas permeability of plant cuticles: oxygen permeability. Planta 155: 310-315

Lendzian KJ (1984) Permeability of plant cuticles to gaseous air pollutants. *In* Koziol MJ, Whatley FR (*eds*) Gaseous air pollutants and plant metabolism. Butterworths, London, *pp* 77-81

Lendzian KJ, Kerstiens G (1988) Interactions between plant cuticles and gaseous air pollutants. *In* The Association of Applied Biologists (*ed*) Aspects of applied biology 17, part 2 Environmental aspects of applied biology, Wellesbourne, UK, *pp* 97-104

Lendzian KJ, Kerstiens G (1991) Sorption and transport of gases and vapors in plant cuticles. Rev Environ Contam Toxicol 121: 65-128

Lendzian KJ, Nakajima A, Ziegler H (1986) Isolation of cuticular membranes from various conifer needles. Trees 1: 47-53

MacKay AL, Wallace JC, Sasaki K, Taylor IEP (1988) Investigation of the physical structure of the primary plant cell wall by proton magnetic resonance. Biochem 27: 1467-1473

Paul DR, Koros WJ (1976) Effect of partially immobilizing sorption on permeability and the diffusion time lag. J Polym Sci B 14: 675-685.

Percy KE, Baker EA (1987) Effects of simulated acid rain on production, morphology and composition of epicuticular wax and on cuticular membrane development. New Phytol 107: 577-589

Percy KE, Jensen KF, McQuattie CJ (1992) Effects of ozone and acidic fog on red spruce needle epicuticular wax production, chemical composition, cuticular membrane ultrastructure, and needle wettability. New Phytol 122: 71-80

Pisek A, Berger E (1938) Kutikuläre Transpiration und Trockenresistenz isolierter Blätter und Sprosse. Planta 28: 124-155

Premachandra GS, Saneoka H, Fujita K, Ogata S (1992) Leaf water relations, osmotic adjustment, cell membrane stability, epicuticular wax load and growth as affected by increasing water deficits in sorghum. J Exp Bot 43: 1569-1576

Rawson HM, Clarke JM (1988) Nocturnal transpiration in wheat. Aust J Plant Physiol 15: 397-406

Reynhardt EC, Riederer M (1991) Structure and molecular dynamics of the cuticular wax from leaves of *Citrus aurantium* L. J Phys D: Appl Phys 24: 478-486

Riederer M, Jetter R, Markstädter C, Schreiber L (1994) Air pollutants and the cuticle: implications for plant physiology. *In* Percy KE, Cape JN, Jagels R, Simpson CM (*eds*) Air pollutants and the leaf cuticle. Springer-Verlag (*this volume, pp*)

Riederer M, Schneider G (1990) The effect of the environment on the permeability and composition of Citrus leaf cuticles. II. Composition of soluble cuticular lipids and correlation with transport properties. Planta 180: 154-165

Riederer M, Schönherr J (1984) Accumulation and transport of (2,4-dichlorophenoxy)acetic acid in plant cuticles: I. Sorption in the cuticular membrane and its components. Ecotoxicol Environ Safety 8: 236-247

Sada E, Kumazama H, Wang JS (1993) Concentration dependence of diffusivities of penetrants in glassy polymer membranes. J Appl Polym Sci 48: 939-943

Scherer JR, Bolton BA (1985) Water in polymer membranes. 5. On the existence of pores and voids. J Phys Chem 89: 3535-3540

Schönherr J (1982) Resistance of plant surfaces to water loss: transport properties of cutin, suberin and associated lipids. *In* Lange OL, Nobel PS, Osmond CB (*eds*) Physiological plant ecology, vol 2, Encyclopedia of plant physiology, vol 12B, Springer Verlag, Berlin, Heidelberg, New York, *pp* 153-179

Schönherr J, Riederer M (1989) Foliar penetration and accumulation of organic chemicals in plant cuticles. Rev Environ Contam Toxicol 108: 1-70

Stålfelt MG (1932) Der stomatäre Regulator in der pflanzlichen Transpiration. Planta 17: 22-85

Tenberge, K.B. 1992. Ultrastructure and development of the outer epidermal wall of spruce (*Picea abies*) needles. Can. J. Bot. 70: 1467-1487.

van Gardingen PR, Grace J, Jeffree CE (1991) Abrasive damage by wind to the needle surfaces of *Picea sitchensis* (Bong.) Carr. and *Pinus sylvestris* L. Plant Cell Environ 14: 185-193

Ion Transport Across Leaf Cuticles: Concepts and Mechanisms

Melvin T. Tyree
U.S.D.A. Forest Service, Aiken Forest Science Laboratory
P.O. Box 968, Burlington, Vermont 05403
USA

Introduction

The chemistry of leaf cuticles (*e.g.*, Holloway, 1994) and the permeation of cuticles by nonelectrolytes (*e.g.*, Kerstiens, 1994; Riederer *et al.*, 1994) are much better understood than is the permeation of ionic species, *e.g.*, salts and acids. Ions differ from nonelectrolytes in that they carry a net electric charge. Ions and nonelectrolytes both diffuse in response to concentration gradients in solution, but ions are unique in being moved by electric gradients in addition to concentration gradients. If the force associated with an electric gradient is larger in magnitude and opposite in direction to the concentration gradient, then ionic species can move from regions of low to high concentration. In general, when salts and acids diffuse, an electric gradient, called a diffusion potential is generated; this electric gradient will retard the rate of diffusion of some ions and speed up the rate of others. Failure to recognize the influence of electric gradients can lead to errors or vagueness in interpretation of results (see below).

A leaf cuticle can be viewed as an example of a membrane. When a substance passes through a membrane it must first dissolve into the chemical constituents of the membrane and then migrate through the membrane under the influence of thermodynamic forces. The processes involved are similar to those in water; a biological membrane can be viewed as a solvent (a membrane-solution) that is not soluble in water. As many polar and ionic substances are soluble in water, whereas nonpolar substances are not soluble in water, biological membranes tend to be composed of insoluble macromolecules: polymerized substances whose monomers may or may not be soluble in water or aggregates of nonpolar substance or of large nonpolar molecules with relatively smaller polar or ionic groups attached. The purpose of this paper is to review the physical chemistry of ion movement in water and membrane-solutions and to consider what happens at the interface between water and membrane-solution. Studies of ion migration through cuticles can be used to provide valuable insights into the structure of cuticles.

Some physicochemical principles

Space permits only a brief review of relevant concepts; readers interested in more in-depth treatments may wish to consult Chapter 3 of Nobel (1991), Robinson and Stokes (1970), and Crank and Park (1968).

NATO ASI Series, Vol. G 36
Air Pollutants and the Leaf Cuticle
Edited by K. E. Percy et al.
© Springer-Verlag Berlin Heidelberg 1994

Soluble solids dissolve in solvents because the intermolecular forces binding the solute to the solvent molecules are about as strong as or stronger than between the solute molecules in the solid form. Three conditions must be met simultaneously for a molecule to diffuse in a solvent: (1) the intermolecular forces between the solvent and solute must be broken momentarily to permit movement, (2) a hole must open up in the solvent in an adjacent solvation site (*i.e.*, intermolecular forces between solute molecules must be broken momentarily to form a space large enough for the solute to occupy), and (3) the molecule must be moving towards the hole (*i.e.*, the velocity vector for motion of the solute must be pointing between its present location and the hole and the velocity must be large enough to move the solute to the hole before the hole disappears). The rate at which solutes move in solution can be described by a fundamental property called its mobility (u). The u depends both on the properties of the solvent and the solute, and u can be explained qualitatively in terms of the kinetic energy of motion of solutes and solvents in relation to the energy of intermolecular forces restricting motion in solution.

The u of a molecule depends on the magnitude of the intermolecular weak bonds between the molecules (solvent-to-solvent and solute-to-solvent binding energies) as this determines the probability of holes developing in the solvent and of the solute breaking free of the solvent. The higher the binding energies, the lower the u. Mobility also depends on the mass of the solute and solvent molecules, because mass determines the velocity of molecules at any given kinetic energy. Velocity is inversely proportional to the square root of mass ($m^{-1/2}$). So the u of solutes in water decreases approximately with $m^{-1/2}$, *i.e.*, a solute with molecular weight m = 100 will be twice a mobile as a solute with m = 400. Deviations from this trend result from differences in binding energy between different solutes and water. Similarly any given solute is more mobile in a low molecular weight solvent than in a high molecular weight solvent, but intermolecular binding energies can dominate in solvents.

Solute movement can be described in terms of u, diffusion coefficient (D), permeability (P), and electrical conductivity (λ, for ions). But the last three quantities are all related to u. The relationship between μ and D can be established through analogy with Fick's first law of diffusion as follows.

The fundamental equation for solute motion is v = u F where v is the velocity of movement in solution ($m\ s^{-1}$) and F is the force acting on a mole of molecules. This equation is identical in form to one of Newton's laws of motion in a frictional world, if we replace u with 1/f, where f is the coefficient of friction. In the Newton's-law analogy, a large mass moves at a constant velocity when propelled by a constant force; the velocity is inversely proportional to the coefficient of friction. The force driving motion of solutes in solutions equals minus the gradient of the chemical potential (μ) and for nonelectrolytes is given by:

$$\mu = \mu^* + RT \ln(C/C^*) \qquad\qquad [1a]$$

where R is the gas constant, T is the Kelvin temperature, C is the concentration of the solute and superscript * refers to standard state. If flow is in the direction of the x-axis then:

$$F = -d\mu/dx = -(RT/C) \, dC/dx \qquad [1b]$$

Since v of solutes is hard to measure, movement is usually given in terms of flux density, J (mol s^{-1} m^{-2}), and J = vC. Thus the fundamental equation becomes J = vC = uCF and after substituting Eq. [1b] we have:

$$J = - uRT \, dC/dx. \qquad [2a]$$

Fick's first law is:

$$J = - D \, dC/dx \qquad [2b]$$

thus if follows that D = uRT.

Membrane systems are generally very thin so C can not be measured directly within the membrane. So J across membranes is usually described in terms of permeability (P) and the concentration difference between the solutions adjacent to the inside and outside surfaces of the membrane (Fig. 1A). Within the membrane, the solute concentrations can be higher or lower than in the water outside the membrane depending on binding energy between the solute and respective solvents. If the intermolecular binding energy between the solute and water is weaker than between the solute and membrane-solution then the concentration inside the membrane (C^m) is more than in the adjacent water layer (C). Similarly, if the binding energy between solute and water is stronger than that between solute and membrane-solution then C^m <C. This difference in concentration is given by the partition coefficient ($\alpha = C^m/C$) and is a measure of the relative solubility of the solute in the membrane relative to water. When the concentration of solute in the water on the two sides of the membrane is unequal, a concentration gradient as shown in Fig. 1A is established. Fick's first law applies within the membrane-solution and the gradient of C^m (dC^m/dx) is equal to $-(C^m_o-C^m_i)/\delta$, where δ is the thickness of the membrane. Fick's first law within the membrane would be given by:

$$J = - D(C^m_o-C^m_i)/\delta = -uRT(C^m_o-C^m_i)/\delta \qquad [3a]$$

or if we replace C^m with C we get:

$$J = -(\alpha D/\delta)(C_i-C_o) = -(\alpha uRT/\delta)(C_i-C_o). \qquad [3b]$$

in terms of P, Eq. 3b is usually written as $J = -P(C_i-C_o)$ from which it follows that:

$$P = (\alpha D/\delta) = (\alpha uRT/\delta) \qquad [3c]$$

Transport of ionic species differs from that of nonelectrolytes in that an extra term for electrical potential must be added to Eq. 1a. The electro-chemical potential of an ion, μ_i, is given by

$$\mu_i = \mu^*{}_i + RT \ln(C_i/C^*{}_i) + z_i F\psi \qquad [4a]$$

where z_i is the ionic valence with sign, F is the Faraday constant, and ψ is the electrical potential in volts. To illustrate, let us consider a simple acid such as HCl or HNO_3 diffusing through water with no other ions present. The driving force for the H+ and Cl⁻ (or NO3-) would be unequal because the z_i values would be +1 and -1, respectively.

$$d\mu_+/dx = (RT/C_+)dC_+/dx + Fd\psi/dx \text{ for } H^+ \text{ and} \qquad [4b]$$

$$d\mu_-/dx = (RT/C_-)dC_-/dx - Fd\psi/dx \text{ for } Cl^- \text{ or NO3-} \qquad [4c]$$

But the flux densities of the anion and cation, J_+ and J_-, must be equal to preserve change neutrality. The flux densities are given by

$$J_+ = -u_+C_+ \, d\mu_+/dx = -u_+RT \, dC_+/dx - Fd\psi/dx \qquad [5a]$$

$$J_- = -u_-C_- \, d\mu_-/dx = -u_-RT \, dC_-/dx + Fd\psi/dx \qquad [5b]$$

Figure 1b illustrates what happens. If there is no ψ gradient when diffusion starts, the force on each ion ($d\mu/dx$) is equal and the more mobile ion initially moves faster causing a slight charge separation which generates a ψ gradient. If $u_+ u_-$ then a diffusion potential is generated making ψ increase in the direction of decreasing C. The diffusion potential gradient reduces the force on the cation and increases the force on the anion so that they move at identical velocities. After some algebra in which we set Eq. 5a equal to 5b and solve for $d\psi/dx$ in terms of dC/dx and substituting the result back into Eq. 5a we get

$$J_+ = J_- = [2u_+u_-/(u_+-u_-)] \, RT \, dC/dx \qquad [6]$$

The same derivation can be done in the context of a membrane, and if we assume that the partition coefficient of the anion equals that of the cation then we can express the permeability of a simple acid (or salt pair) in terms of ratios of ionic permeabilities, $P_i = \alpha u_i RT/\delta$, where i = + or -. So when HCl or HNO_3 diffuses across a cuticle membrane, it will diffuse with an effective permeability, EP, given by

$$EP = 2P_+P_-/(P_+-P_-) \qquad [7]$$

Hauser, Walters and Berg (1993) have measured the EP of HCl and HNO_3 across cuticles and found EP differs for the two acids. They concluded that the anion must be influencing the permeability of the acid, but they never defined exactly what EP is in terms of ionic P's. In terms of Eq. 7a the EP measured can be viewed as a ratio and product of Ps in which the P of the Cl or NO_3 differ. In the limiting case when P of H is much more than P of the anion, then $EP = 2P_-$ for the above acids. Smalley, Hauser and Berg (1993) have also measured EP of H_2SO_4. A similar derivation for this case yields $EP = 3P_+P_-/(P_++2P_-)$ with a limiting value of $EP = 1.5P_-$ for H_2SO_4 when $P_- \ll P_+$. It must be stressed that EP will be defined by a different equation than (7) if other

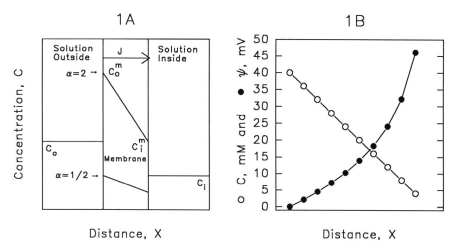

Figure 1A Diagram of a cuticle membrane separating two solutions. Co and C_i = solute concentrations in the outside and inside solutions, respectively; C^m_o and C^m_i = corresponding concentrations in the membrane altered by the partition coeficient (α). Direction of flux (J) is from left to right as indicted by the arrow.
B: Linear concentration profile (open circles) of a mono-monovalent salt during diffusion in water or a membrane-solution and the predicted diffusion potential gradient (ψ). The equation that predicts ψ during salt diffusion depends only on concentration ratios and not distances, so distance on the x-axis is not specified. The equations that applies is $\psi = k\ln(C_o/C)$ where $k = 2u_+u_-RT/(F(u_++u_-))$ and C_o is the concentration at x = 0 and ψ at x = 0 is taken as 0. Note that C declines linearly with distance but ψ increases exponentially.

ions are present while diffusion of acids occurs across a cuticle, because other diffusing species will contribute to the overall diffusion potential and thus will affect the rate of diffusion of the acid.

The equations that govern the diffusion of mixtures of two or more salts are more complex. For example, MacFarlane and Berry (1974) studied the diffusion of MCl salts where M = Li, Na, K, Cs or Rb. MacFarlane and Berry attempted to devise an experimental procedure that would eliminate the influence of diffusion potentials and to obtain values of cation permeability, but their experiments were conceptually flawed. Figure 2 illustrates one of these experiments in which 0.5 M KCl was placed on one side of a cuticle and 0.5 M LiCl was placed on the other side. In their experiments the flux of K from left to right was about twice the flux of Li from right to left. Since the Cl concentration was the same on both sides they assumed Cl must not be moving and that the P of each ion could be calculated from J/C for each ion (*i.e.*, ignoring the

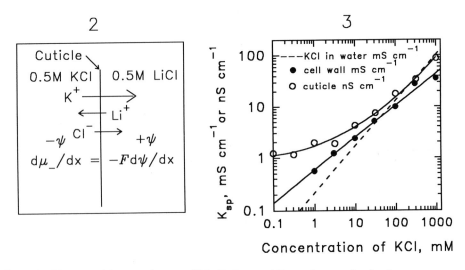

Figure 2 Diagram of the experiments of MacFarlane and Berry. See text for details.

Figure 3 The x-axis is KCl concentration and y-axis is specific condutance, K_{sp}, of KCl in water (dashed line), of cell wall (open circles) equilibrated with various concentrations of KCl in bathing medium, and of citrus cuticles (closed circles) equilibrated with various concentrations of KCl in bathing medium.

term containing ψ). The error was to assume that unequal fluxes of K and Li would cause no ψ gradient. If there was no ψ gradient initially, then the higher flux of the more mobile species (K) would cause a charge separation causing ψ to be positive on the right and negative on the left. This voltage difference would provide a driving force on Cl ions equal to $-Fd\psi/dx$ which would: (a) drive Cl ions from left to right, (b) speed up the flux of Li from right to left, and (c) slow down the flux of K from left to right. So the P values they calculated were not correct, but would reflect a ratio of permeabilities of all diffusing ions. For example, if we assume that is the same for all ions, then it can be shown that P'_K actually measured by MacFarlane and Berry was given by $P'_K = P_K (2P_{Li} + P_{Cl})/(P_K + P_{Li} + P_{Cl})$. But it is unlikely that α is the same for K, Li, and Cl ions; when this is taken into account, a much more complex ratio results where each P term is multiplied by ratios of α's for all ions.

From the above consideration, it can be seen that it is difficult to measure ionic P's in a straight-forward manner. In some cases EP values suffice and we do not need to know individual ionic P's. But in order to understand how acidic precipitation on leaves influences the rate of ion leaching across cuticles we must have values for individual ionic P's and the diffusion potentials must be measured.

Ion transport across cuticles and implications regarding structure

One way to compute ionic P's in cuticles is to measure diffusion potentials, $E^{io} = \Delta\psi$, and electrical conductance, λ, because the former gives information about the ratio of P's and the latter gives the sum of P's (Tyree *et al.*, 1991). For monovalent salts (MCl) it can be shown that

$$P_+ + P_- = \lambda RT/(az^2 F^2 C) \qquad [8]$$

where λ (S) is the conductance in a cuticle disk of surface area = a (m^2) and z is the valence of the salt. In Equation (8) it is presumed that λ is measured in a cuticle in equilibrium with MCl at concentration C (mol m^3). Also it can be shown that

$$P_+/P_- = (e^x - C_R)/(1 - e^x C_R) \qquad [9]$$

where $C_R = C_i/C_o$ is the concentration ratio across the cuticle causing an E^{io} and $x = FE^{io}/RT$. Measurements done this way on citrus cuticles have revealed P's in the range of 2 to 20 X10^{-9} m s^{-1} for Cl and the monovalent alkali metals (H through Cs in the periodic table). In dilute solutions (2 mM) the alkali metals were two to eight times more permeable than Cl. In concentrated solutions (500 mM) all P's were up to five times lower but the P of Cl was higher than that of Li, K, and Na (Tyree *et al.*, 1991).

Studies of how λ and E^{io} change with concentration in cuticles as compared to similar studies on ion exchange resins can provide valuable insights into the structure of cuticles and mechanisms of transport. For example, cuticles have a substantial Cation Exchange Capacity (CEC) equal to 150 mM when expressed in concentration units. This is comparable to the CEC of plant cell walls (300 mM, Tyree, 1968). Exchangeable cations in cell walls contribute to λ and thus to P_+. Exchangeable cations in cell walls are dissolved in the water (which makes up half the volume of cell walls) and are relatively mobile. Cuticles contain much less water (by volume) so exchangeable cations may be less mobile and may contribute much less to cation permeation rates.

Figure 3 shows the specific conductance ($K_{sp} = \lambda$ measured across two parallel faces of a 1-cm cube) of KCl in water versus C. Compare these values to the K_{sp} of cell walls equilibrated in KCl over the same concentration range. It can be seen that cell wall K_{sp} exceeds that of KCl in water over most of the range, and K_{sp} of walls approaches that of KCl in water at 1000 mM. This indicates that exchangeable cations in cell walls are in aqueous solution and mobile, *i.e.*, contributing to conductance. A detailed analysis of the shape of the K_{sp} curve for cell walls suggested that exchangeable cations were not as mobile as an equivalent concentration of ions in water. The limiting conductance at low KCl concentration can be attributed to a mobile concentration of 40 mM whereas the CEC value in concentration units was 300 mM (Tyree, 1968). In marked contrast, the K_{sp} of citrus cuticles was 10^6 to 10^7 times smaller and declined approximately linearly with decreasing KCl in the equilibration solution. Since no limiting value is reached at low KCl concentration, the exchangeable cations in citrus cuticles did not contribute much to conductance and, therefore, contributed little to K mobility or permeation. This is consistent with a bilayer model of a cuticle in which the CEC is confined to the polymerized cutin layer on the inner surface of cuticles and where the mobility of ions is limited by the outer waxy layer were there is little or no CEC (Tyree et al., 1991).

A bilayer model of cuticle structure was also supported by an observed asymmetry in diffusion potentials, E^{io}. The asymmetry was duplicated in a model experimental system consisting of two paper layers with different P values for anions and cations. The Goldmann equation predicts a nonzero E^{io} across a membrane when unequal concentrations are present on the two sides and when the P's of the anion and cation are unequal. The Goldmann equation is a variation of Eq. [9] in which E^{io} is solved in terms of P_R and C_R, i.e., $E^{io}=(F/RT)\ln[(1+P_RC_R)/(C_R+P_R)]$. Tyree et al. (1990) have shown that diffusion potentials across paper follow the Goldmann equation when experiments were designed to maintain a constant average ionic strength across the paper-membrane. Different papers have different P_R and thus generate different E^{io} values at any given C_R, but the relationship was symmetrical, i.e., $E^{io} = y$ mV when $C_R = x$ and $E^{io} = -y$ when $C_R = 1/x$ (Fig. 4). When a bilayer paper membrane was made of two sheets of paper with different P_R, the symmetry predicted by the Goldmann equation was no longer observed. E^{io} of cuticles were also asymmetrical in the same way; thus cuticles could be viewed as a bilayer of cutin and wax with different P_R values.

Measured values of D also provide valuable information about the ease with which ions move through cuticles compared to membranes with higher water content. Ions are about as mobile in cell walls and ion exchange resins as in water. This follows because D in ion exchange resins is not much less than in water (D's are a half or third that in water, Crank and Park, 1968). This means that the molecular interactions are predominately those between the ions and water rather than between water and resin polymer. There is much less water in cuticles, so D might be much smaller because of interactions between the ions and the waxes or between ions and the cutin polymer. D could be measured in cuticles by measuring the time it would take for solute to pass through cuticles and comparing that to solutions of Fick's second law which give time for penetration in terms of functions of D and cuticle thickness. One special solution of Fick's second law relates the average distance, x, a molecule can diffuse to the time, t: $x^2=2Dt$. Leaf cuticles are of the order of 10^{-6} m thick. The D of many solutes in water is of the order of 10^{-9} m^2 s^{-1}. So if D of solutes in cuticles were the same as in water, the a solute would pass through a cuticle in

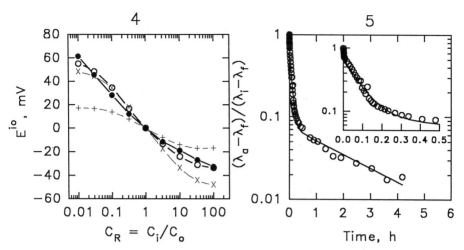

Figure 4   Diffusion potential in two different papers (+ and x), in a paper bilayer (open circles), and in maple leaf cuticles (closed circles).

Figure 5   Washout kinetics of cuticle conductance, λ, versus time (x-axis) after transfering a citrus cuticle from an initial KCl concentration of C to a final concentration of 0.1C. The y-axis is normalized by the maximum change of conductance from the intial and final solutions, λ_i and λ_f respectively. λ_a is the cuticle conductance at the time plotted on the x-axis.

$t = x^2/2D = (10^{-6})^2/2 \times 10^{-9} = 0.0005$ s. But the time required for solute to pass through cuticles ranged from 10^2 to 10^4 s, from which we can conclude that D must be very low.

The time of penetration is usually deduced from solutions of Fick's second law that relate more measurable quantities such as: (1) how long it takes J to approach steady (constant flux) from the time a concentration difference is applied across the membrane, or (2) how long it takes solute C to fall from one equilibrium value to another after a cuticle is transferred from one concentration of solution to another. It is not possible to measure concentrations in cuticles directly, but for ions an indirect measure of concentration comes from measurements of λ which is proportional to ionic C in cuticles. For nonelectrolytes, the only option is to measure J and how long it takes J to approach steady values. Figure 5 is a typical "washout" curve showing how long it takes to fall from one equilibrium value to another after reducing the C of KCl in the bathing solution by a factor of 10. As the C of KCl in the cuticle falls so does λ. The time it took λ to fall to within 10% of its final value gave the time it took approximately 90% of the ions to diffuse out of the cuticle (about 500 s). Values of D can be computed by using solutions of Fick's second law to analyze the shape of this curve. Values for D in cuticles of small nonelectrolytes (including water) and of KCl are in the range of 10^{-15} to 10^{-18} m^2 s^{-1} (Tyree *et al.*, 1991; Becker *et al.*, 1986; Reiderer, 1994). Schönherr (1976) has suggested that small polar solutes pass through the cuticle via small polar pores whose diameter is not much more than that of the solute. Diffusion through such confined spaces would cause stearic hindrance of motion that could result in low D values. Alternatively, small molecules may move slowly through a solution consisting of large molecules and polymers. In this model of diffusion D would be low because of the excessive energy required to create solvation holes in the solute as the small solute passes through.

More studies of ion permeation through cuticles are needed. Measurement of transport parameters such as E^{io}, P, D, and λ provide information on the rate at which ions move across cuticles and may also provide information on the mechanism of ion permeation. Future work on ion permeation through artificial wax sheets (artificial cuticles) could also provide information on how wax chemistry influences ion permeation rate. Substantial ion fluxes might occur across cuticles during acid rain events, *i.e.*, heavy metals contained in acid rain might migrate across cuticles and enter leaf cells or important nutrient ions (Ca, Mg, K etc) might be leached out at harmful rates. In order to predict rates of ion movement in and out we must know individual ionic P's and E^{io} values during acid rain events. In one experiment, artificial acid precipitation was placed on the outer surface of a cuticle and an artificial apoplastic solution was placed on the inner surface (Tyree *et al.*, 1990). Depending on pH and solution concentrations, the E^{io} generated by these mixed salt solutions ranged from 52 to 140 mV (inside negative). The observed E^{io} was sufficient to alter the driving force and thus the ionic J's by up to a factor of 20 and in some cases reversed the direction of J of some divalent cations so that they were accumulated against a concentration gradient. Work in the future must take into account the influence of $E^{io} = \Delta\psi$ on the rate of ion movement across cuticles.

References

Becker M, Kerstiens G, Schönherr J (1986) Water permeability of plant cuticles: permeance, diffusion and partition coefficients Trees 1: 54-60

Crank J, Park GS (1968) *Diffusion in Polymers* Academic Press. London New York.

Holloway PJ (1994) The plant cuticle: Biosynthesis and physicochemical characteristics. *(This volume, pp 1-13)*

Hauser HD, Walters KD, Berg VS (1993) Patterns of effective permeability of leaf cuticles to acids. Plant Physiol 101: 251-257

Kerstiens G (1994) Air pollutants and plant cuticles: mechanisms of gas and water transport and effects on water permeability. *(This volume, pp 79-92)*

McFarlane JC, Berry WL (1974) Cation penetration through isolated leaf cuticles. Plant Physiol 53: 723-727

Nobel PS (1991) *Physicochemical and Environmental Plant Physiology* Academic Press. London Sydney Tokyo Toronto

Riederer M, Jetter R, Markstädter C, Schreiber L (1994) Air pollutants and the cuticle: Implications for plant physiology. (*This volume, pp*)

Robinson RA, Stokes RH (1970) *Electrolyte Solutions* Butterworths London

Schönherr J (1976) Water permeability of isolated cuticular membranes: the effect of cuticular waxes on diffusion of water. Planta 131: 159-164.

Smalley SJ, Hauser HD, Berg VS (1993) Effects of cations on effective permeability of leaf cuticles to sulfuric acid. Plant Physiol 103: 251-256

Tyree MT (1968) Determination of transport constants of isolated *Nitella* cell walls. Can J Bot 46: 317-327

Tyree MT, Tabor CA, Wescott CR (1990) Movement of cations through cuticles of *Citrus aurantium* and *Acer saccharum*: Diffusion potentials in mixed salt solutions. Plant Physiol 94: 120-126

Tyree MT, Scherbatskoy TD, Tabor CA (1990) Leaf cuticles behave as asymmetric membranes: Evidence from the measurement of diffusion potentials. Plant Physiol 92: 103-109

Tyree MT, Wescott CR, Tabor CA (1991) Diffusion and electric mobility of ions within isolated cuticles of *Citrus aurantium*. Plant Physiol 97: 273-279

Tyree MT, Wescott CR, Tabor CA, Morse AD (1992) Diffusion and electric mobility of KCl within isolated cuticles of *Citrus aurantium*. Plant Physiol 99: 1057-1061

Effects of Air Pollutants on Epicuticular Wax Chemical Composition

K.E. Percy, C.J. McQuattie[1] and J.A. Rebbeck[1]
Canadian Forest Service - Maritimes Region
Natural Resources Canada
P.O. Box 4000
Fredericton, N.B.
Canada E3B 5P7

Abstract

There are numerous reports in the literature of modifications to epicuticular wax structure as a consequence of exposure to air pollutants. Most authors have used scanning electron microscopy (SEM) to describe changes in wax crystallite morphology or distribution. "Erosion" or "weathering" of crystalline structure into an amorphous state is the most common observation, particularly in the case of conifer needles having the characteristic tube crystallites comprised of nonacosan-10-ol. Wax structure is largely determined by its chemical composition. Therefore, many of the reported changes in wax structure due to air pollutants probably arise from direct interactions between pollutants such as ozone and wax biosynthesis. The literature describing changes in wax composition due to pollutants is briefly reviewed. New evidence is introduced in support of the hypothesis for a direct interaction between air pollutants and epicuticular wax biosynthesis.

Introduction

The outermost layer of the plant cuticle comprises long-chain, usually saturated aliphatic molecules called epicuticular waxes. The epicuticular wax layer ranges from only a few nanometers to a few microns in thickness. Due to its position at the leaf surface it forms the barrier between a plant and its atmospheric environment and is, therefore, the first point of contact between air pollutants and plants.

Epicuticular wax physicochemical characteristics exhibit a high degree of interspecific variation (Baker, 1982). The most common even-carbon number constituents include fatty acids (C_{12}-C_{32}), aldehydes (C_{22}-C_{32}), primary alcohols (C_{22}-C_{32}) and alkyl esters (C_{32}-C_{72}). The most often resolved odd-carbon number constituents include hydrocarbons (C_{17}-C_{35}), secondary alcohols (C_{21}-C_{33}), and ketones (C_{23}-C_{33}). Cyclic constituents include triterpenoid acids and triterpenols.

The odd-carbon number diols (C_{25}-C_{31}) have been added to the list first published by Baker (1982). They are major constituents of some coniferous epicuticular needle waxes (Frannich *et*

---

[1]USDA Forest Service, Northeastern Forest Experiment Station, 359 Main Road, Delaware, Ohio, U.S.A. 43015

NATO ASI Series, Vol. G 36
Air Pollutants and the Leaf Cuticle
Edited by K. E. Percy et al.
© Springer-Verlag Berlin Heidelberg 1994

al., 1978; Gunthardt-Goerg, 1986; Percy and Baker, 1990; Percy *et al.*, 1992). Therefore, they are important to the following discussion.

The single homologue most indirectly studied with respect to air pollutant effects is the C_{29} secondary alcohol, nonacosan-10-ol (m/z M^+ 496; M^{-15}, 481). This homologue, which normally occurs in its metastable state (M. Reiderer, personal communication), forms characteristic tubes on conifer needles.

In addition to constituents produced by acyl-elongase enzyme systems, β-diketones (C_{29}-C_{33}) and hydroxy, β-diketones (C_{29}-C_{33}) are produced by a specialized beta-keto-acyl elongase system (Wettstein-Knowles, 1987). These are found in a limited number of species including *Eucalyptus*.

There are relatively few reports in the literature of pollutant-induced effects on the even-carbon constituents produced via the elongase-reductase biochemical pathway. There are, however, numerous reports of effects on odd-carbon constituents produced via the competing elongase-decarboxylase pathway.

It is well known that a variety of factors can affect epicuticular wax chemical composition (see reviews by Martin and Juniper, 1970; Baker, 1982). Prominent among these are genotype, environment, ontogeny and, of course, air pollutants. While interspecific differences in wax composition among nine *Picea* species were large (Table 1), differences between clones/provenances of some of these same species varied to a much lesser extent (Percy and Fowler, unpublished data).

Table 1. Epicuticular wax chemical composition of seedlings of nine *Picea* species grown in a uniform environment.

Species	Primary alcohols	Secondary alcohols	Alkanes	Diols	Fatty acids	Hydroxy acids	Alkyl esters
Norway Spruce	0.0	25.6	30.9	18.2	7.9	2.7	12.5
Sitka Spruce	1.8	34.8	15.4	27.2	4.3	0.6	11.7
Engelmann Spruce	0.8	35.8	10.5	26.3	2.7	0.0	20.4
Serbian Spruce	0.7	39.6	11.3	25.8	2.3	0.6	16.2
Black Spruce	0.9	40.8	10.0	31.0	1.9	0.0	11.5
Red Spruce	0.0	45.1	19.8	20.1	2.1	0.6	10.7
White Spruce	0.5	46.0	10.7	24.6	3.4	0.0	11.4
Mexican Spruce	0.0	49.8	12.4	23.6	0.9	0.0	10.9
Blue Spruce	0.0	54.0	5.9	26.9	0.0	0.0	10.8

(species arranged in order of increasing secondary alcohols)

The introduction of a point mutation, however, has been demonstrated to alter wax composition (Holloway *et al.*, 1977a & b).

The ontogenetic influence on wax composition is also strong. Wax constituents are deposited onto the leaf surface in an ordered sequence (Frannich *et al.*, 1978; Buckovac *et al.*, 1979; Baker and Hunt, 1981; Percy *et al.*, 1992) with a tendency for more polar wax classes to emerge later in leaf expansion. In some conifers a significant proportion of the dominant constituent non-acosan-10-ol is already deposited prior to bud break (Riding and Percy, 1985; Percy and Baker, 1990).

The environment in which a plant grows can affect epicuticular wax composition (Baker, 1982). However, only at extreme high temperatures, low relative humidities, high irradiances or excessive soil moisture deficit are wax biosynthesis and final composition modified to any degree. New research with four *Picea* species has, nevertheless, shown that light quality can exert a profound influence upon needle wax composition, selectively favoring one of the two major biosynthetic pathways (Cape and Percy, 1993). Composition can certainly be altered indirectly through the physical action of rain (Baker and Hunt, 1986) or abrasion (Wilson, 1984) which selectively remove certain classes of wax crystallites.

Timing of plant exposure to pollutants is, therefore, crucial. As the wax layer is deposited only during the period of leaf or needle expansion (Gunthardt, 1985; Percy and Baker, 1990), direct effects on wax composition due to air pollutants must occur during the initial growing season for species with long-lived needles. Changes in epicuticular wax characteristics during succeeding years are more likely to be caused by secondary factors other than air pollutants, such as physical abrasion from snow or rain (Percy *et al.*, 1993).

The literature is replete with references to structural changes in epicuticular waxes following exposure to air pollutants (see Turunen and Huttunen, 1990). The most frequently reported observation is the "fusion" of wax tubes between stomata and within epistomatal chambers of conifer needles. Acidic deposition and pollutant gases such as ozone and sulphur dioxide were said to act similarly in the "weathering" or "premature ageing" of leaf surface structures. Yet, in the case of at least one species, ozone and acidic fog elicited different responses such as increased occlusion of stomata due to ozone and the appearance of new plate crystallites following needle exposure to acidic fog at pH 3.0 (Percy *et al.*, 1990).

It is well established that wax structure is closely related to wax chemical composition. The experiments of Jeffree *et al.* (1975) provided confirmation of this relationship, which is summarized in Table 2.

Table 2.   Relationship of epicuticular wax structure to its chemical composition

Constituent class	Crystalline structure
hydrocarbons	plate
primary alcohols	plate
secondary alcohols	tube
aldehydes	rod
ketones	tube
alkyl esters	amorphous
β-diketones	tube
diols	ribbons
triterpenoids	amorphous
estolides	amorphous

Modified from Baker (1982).

As can be seen, hydrocarbons and primary alcohols crystallize as plates, while secondary alcohols and ketones form tubes. Some important constituents of conifer needle waxes appear as amorphous layers underlying the tube crystallites.

Therefore, it would seem logical that pollutant-induced modifications to wax structure so often visualized under the SEM should also be reflected in changes in chemical composition. Yet, the literature contains scores of references to wax "erosion" or what could be termed the *indirect mechanism* for interaction. This mechanism implies an undefined interaction between pollutants and the inert wax deposit *in situ*. Few authors have postulated a *direct mechanism* by which it can be hypothesized that exposure to ozone, sulphur dioxide or acidic deposition stimulates or inhibits the microsomal-based, epidermal elongase-decarboxylation or elongase-reductase enzyme systems for wax biosynthesis.

Air pollutant-induced changes in wax chemical composition

Gas chromatography/mass spectrometry (GC/MS) confirmed changes in wax chemical composition have been described for only a few species. Cape (1986) reported significant decreases in amounts of long-chain alcohols and ketones on Scots pine (*Pinus sylvestris* L.) needles growing in polluted air. The pollutant, although not identified, was probably sulphur dioxide. Shelvey and Koziol (1986) exposed two rye grass (*Lolium perenne* L.) clones to sulphur dioxide during both winter and summer experiments. Effects were dependant upon clone and season. In winter, a decrease in tetracosane coupled with an increase in tritriacontane was observed. In summer, pentacosane increased in both genotypes as a result of fumigation.

Percy and Baker (1987) examined the effect of simulated acid rain on epicuticular wax of a number of crop and deciduous species. Significant effects on wax composition were observed at pH's 4.6 or lower. Two of four crop species were affected. Constituents produced by both major biosynthetic pathways were decreased due to leaf treatment with simulated acid rain during the period of wax deposition.

Using cellulose acetate to remove crystalline tubes (nonacosan-15-ol) from expanding canola (*Brassica napus* L. cv Rafal) leaves Percy and Baker (1987) also determined that the rate of wax regeneration was slowed and the amounts of nonacosane and nonacosanone were reduced to a greater degree if the acid rain treatments coincided with the short period (days) during which tubes appear at the surface. Subsequent thin layer radio-chromatography experiments confirmed that the inhibition resulting from leaf pretreatment with simulated acid rain at pH ≤ 4.2 was due to effects on *de novo* wax synthesis and biosynthesis of major constituents.

The same authors treated two contrasting Sitka spruce (*Picea sitchensis* (Bong.) Carr.) clones with simulated acid rain (Percy and Baker, 1991). Proportions of nonacosan-10-ol increased with increasing acidity in both clones. Proportions of nonacosane diols and hydroxy-acids increased with rain acidity in one clone, while proportions of estolides increased in one clone and decreased in the other.

Lütz *et al.* (1990) exposed three Norway spruce (*Picea abies* (L.) Karst.) clones to combined ozone and acidic mist treatments. Despite differences across clones and needle age, production of nonacosan-10-ol was increased in all clones following treatment.

Percy *et al.* (1992) exposed red spruce (*Picea rubens* Sarg.) needles to ozone and/or acidic fog and recovered epicuticular wax at three intervals during the grand phase of needle elongation. Needles exposed to ozone at > 70 ppb had significantly less secondary alcohols, diols, esters and fatty acids. Needles exposed only to acidic fog at pH 3.0 manifested changes only in secondary alcohols.

Kerfourn and Garrec (1992) examined declining Norway spruce trees and Norway spruce and ivy (*Hedera helix* L.) seedlings exposed to ozone and acidic fog. They observed that alkane chain lengths increased naturally with leaf age, whereas treatment with pollutants caused a shortening of alkane chain lengths. They hypothesized that, for such changes to occur, the pollutants must interact directly with wax biosynthesis. This most recent evidence for changes in homologue composition complements that previously offered at the wax class level.

New evidence for a direct mechanism of interaction

Despite the limited, yet accumulating evidence for a direct mechanism, there still exists some controversy. In order to address the controversy we have been conducting a number of experiments to determine whether wax composition is modified passively at the leaf surface, or, in our opinion, by a direct pollutant interaction with wax biosynthesis.

This first set of experiments used recrystallized wax and two pollutants, ozone and simulated acidic deposition. The hypothesis tested was that ozone and acidity do not alter wax chemical composition once the epicuticular wax layer is crystallized *in situ*, as on the leaf surface.

Whole wax extracted from current-year, field-grown red spruce needles and greenhouse-reared sugar maple seedlings was recrystallized onto borosilicate glass. Single homologue references, representing all major predominant odd- and even-chain wax classes (*i.e.*, hexacosanol, 1,9-non-anediol, hexacosanoic acid, oleanloic acid, *etc.*) were also similarly recrystallized. To ensure quality control, recrystallized wax structure was examined using SEM prior to exposure, to confirm that it was representative of that observed on intact leaves, or expected based upon the homologue used.

Recrystallized deposits were exposed in CSTR's (Percy *et al.*, 1992) to charcoal-filtered air or one of two concentrations of ozone (70, 150 ppb). Fumigations lasted 8 h per day over 7 days. A replicate set of deposits was immersed in sulphuric/nitric acid at pH 3.0 or pH 1.0 to simulate acidic deposition onto the leaf surface. Immersion was complete and lasted for periods between 30 minutes and several hours. Sulphate exposure at pH 1.0 over 2 h was calculated to be in the same range (0.1-0.3 M h) commonly measured near the cloudbase in higher elevation forests (J.N. Cape, personal communication).

Chemical composition before and after treatment was then compared using GC-MS techniques described elsewhere (Percy *et al.*, 1993).

Exposure to 70 or 150 ppb ozone over 7 days did not alter chemical composition of recrystallized red spruce needle wax (Fig. 1). Proportions of the major constituents secondary alcohols, nonacosane-diols, alkyl esters and fatty acids in deposits exposed at up to 150 ppb remained unchanged relative to those measured for charcoal-filtered air. Sugar maple wax chemical composition was likewise unaffected following exposure to ozone.

Immersion of recrystallized red spruce wax at acidities of pH 3.0, representative of single ambient coastal fog events, did not result in any change in constituent proportions (Fig. 2). Immersion in pH 1 acid, however, did alter composition of recrystallized red spruce wax. While proportions of secondary alcohols and nonacosane diols remained unchanged, treatment with acid at pH 1

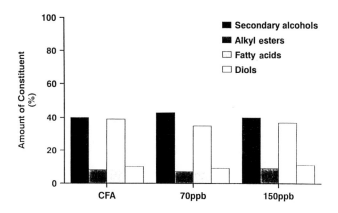

Figure 1   Chemical composition of recrystallized current-year red spruce needle wax exposed to ozone. CFA = charcoal-filtered air.

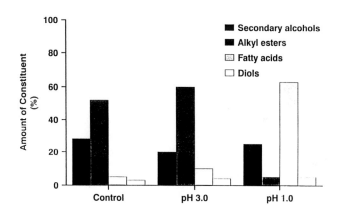

Figure 2   Chemical composition of recrystallized current-year red spruce needle wax treated with acid at pH 3.0 or 1.0.

resulted in a decrease in proportion of alkyl esters (Fig. 2). Fatty acids liberated from the red spruce esters by hydrolysis were increased.

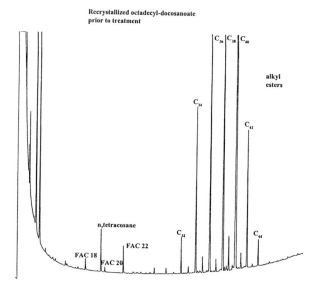

Figure 3   GC chromatogram of alkyl ester reference mixture prior to immersion in acid at pH 3.0 or 1.0. n,tetracosane is co-injected internal standard.

As alkyl esters (carbon chain C_{36}-C_{50} in red spruce) were the only class of constituents tested that were altered chemically following exposure to acidity, they were further investigated. Alkyl ester (mixture) was recrystallized and immersed under acid. The typical homologous series of carbon numbers C_{34} to C_{50} was determined by GC analysis (Fig. 3). Following immersion at pH 3.0, a series of fatty acids (C_{16} to C_{24}) were resolved by GC (Fig. 4). The original ester series was still resolved at this point. Following immersion at pH 1.0, however, the original ester series was almost completely hydrolyzed and the fatty acid series was exclusively resolved along with some smaller amounts of primary alcohols (Fig. 5).

It is important to note here the change in alkyl ester profile from control to pH 3.0. As ambient coastal fog or high elevation cloud events seldom have single event acidities lower than pH 3, it may be that only at extreme acidities are alkyl esters on foliage subject to hydrolysis. It is interesting to note, however, that in terms of total acid loading, the pH 1.0 treatment was in the range of sulphate loadings experienced by trees growing in or near the base of polluted clouds in certain areas. Similarly, accumulated acidity from successive coastal fog events, without wash-off, could produce such extreme acidities.

A wide range of single reference homologues representing the most common and several uncommon wax constituents were also recrystallized individually and exposed to ozone. Fumigations with up to 150 ppb ozone over 7 days did not alter the composition of any constituents examined, including the diol tested, 1,9-nonanediol (compare Figs. 6 and 7). Treatment of these reference compounds with acidity is pending.

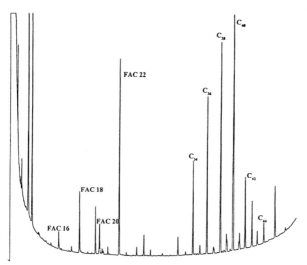

Figure 4   GC chromatogram of recrystallized alkyl ester following immersion at pH 3.0.
n,tetracosane is co-injected internal standard.

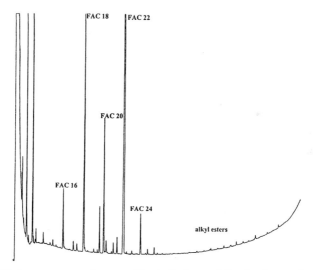

Figure 5   GC chromatogram of recrystallized alkyl ester following immersion at pH 1.0.
n,tetracosane is co-injected internal standard.

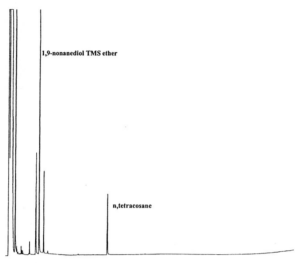

Figure 6   GC chromatogram of recrystallized diol exposed to charcoal-filtered air (0 ppb O$_3$).n,tetracosane is co-injected internal standard.

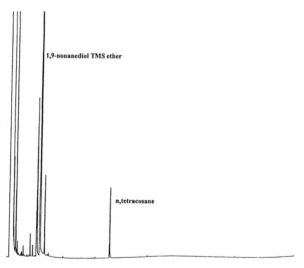

Figure 7   GC chromatogram of recrystallized diol exposed to 150 ppb ozone. n,tetracosane is co-injected internal standard.

Conclusions

In conclusion, the literature on effects of air pollutants on epicuticular wax chemical composition is limited. However, several workers have recently ascribed ozone- or acid mist-induced changes in wax composition to a direct interaction of the pollutant with wax biosynthesis, the so-called *direct* mechanism.

Certainly, it is well known that key wax enzyme synthesis systems are pH sensitive below the threshold range of 5 to 5.5, a range ten times less acidic than rain, and up to 500 times less acidic than coastal fog in eastern North America. Given the manifest role of genetics in wax biosynthesis and the determinate relationship between wax chemical composition and its resultant structure, it would seem logical to propose that modifications from crystalline wax to amorphous wax morphologies reported in the literature have resulted primarily from the *direct* not *indirect* mechanisms.

The evidence from recrystallized wax deposits as surrogates for waxes *in situ* provides strong evidence supporting the *direct* mechanism. The only exception may be the hydrolysis of alkyl esters under conditions of extreme acidity, normally encountered only under specialized conditions such as near the base of polluted cloud in high elevation forests of Europe and eastern North America, or coastal sites during successive fogs but little rain.

Radiolabelling studies on the effects of ozone and acidic fog will be undertaken to investigate further the pollutant effects on *de novo* wax synthesis and biochemical pathways.

Acknowledgements

The GC analysis of wax chemical composition was ably performed by Mr. C.K. McLaughlin, Canadian Forest Service - Maritimes Region. The seedling material used in the comparative GC analysis of wax composition in nine *Picea* species was kindly provided by Dr. D.P. Fowler, Scientist Emeritus, Canadian Forest Service - Maritimes Region, Fredericton.

References

Baker EA (1982) Chemistry and morphology of plant epicuticular waxes. *In* The Plant Cuticle. Cutler DJ, Alvin KL, Price C.E. (*eds*) Academic Press, London *pp* 139-165

Baker EA, Hunt GM (1981) Developmental changes in leaf epicuticular waxes in relation to foliar penetration. New Phytol 88: 731-767

Baker EA, Hunt GM (1986) Erosion of waxes from leaf waxes from leaf surfaces by simulated rain. New Phytol 102: 161-173

Baker EA, Buckovac MJ, Flore JA (1979) Ontogenetic variation in the composition of peach leaf wax. Phytochem 18: 781-784

Cape JN (1986) Effects of air pollutants on the chemistry of surface waxes of Scots pine. Water Air Soil Pollut 31: 393-399

Cape JN, Percy KE (1993) Environmental influences on the development of spruce needle cuticles. New Phytol 125: 787-799

Frannich RA, Wells LG, Holland PT (1978) Epicuticular wax of *Pinus radiata* needles. Phytochem 17: 1617-1623

Gunthardt MS (1985) Stomata and epicuticular wax formation on needles of *Pinus cembra* and *Picea abies*. Botanica Helvetica 95: 5-12

Gunthardt-Goerg MS (1986) Epicuticular wax of needles of *Pinus cembra, Pinus sylvestris* and *Picea abies*. Eur J For Path 16: 400-408

Holloway PJ, Brown GA, Baker EA, Macey MJK (1977) Chemical composition and ultrastructure of the epicuticular wax in four mutants of *Brassica napus* L. Chem & Physics Lipids 19: 114-127

Holloway PJ, Hunt GM, Baker EA, Macey MJK (1977) Chemical composition and ultrastructure of the epicuticular wax in four mutants of *Pisum sativum* L. Chem & Physics Lipids 20: 141-155

Jeffree CE, Baker EA, Holloway PJ (1975) Ultrastructure and recrystallization of plant epicuticular waxes. New Phytol 75: 539-549

Kerfourn C, Garrec JP (1992) Modifications in the alkane composition of cuticular waxes from spruce needles (*Picea abies*) and ivy leaves (*Hedera helix*) exposed to ozone fumigation and acid fog: comparison with needles from declining spruce trees. Can J Bot 70: 861-869

Lütz C, Heinzmann U, Gulz P-G (1990) Surface structures and epicuticular wax composition of spruce needles after long-term treatment with ozone and acid mist. Environ Pollut 64: 313-322

Martin JT, Juniper BE (1970) The Cuticles of Plants. Arnold, London.

Percy KE, Baker EA (1987) Effects of simulated acid rain on production, morphology and composition of epicuticular wax and on cuticular membrane development. New Phytol 107: 577-589

Percy KE, Baker EA (1990) Effects of simulated acid rain on epicuticular wax production, morphology, chemical composition and on cuticular membrane thickness in two clones of Sitka spruce (*Picea sitchensis* (Bong.) Carr.). New Phytol 116: 79-87

Percy KE, Krause CR, Jensen KF (1990) Effects of ozone and acid fog on red spruce needle epicuticular wax ultrastructure. Can J For Res 20: 117-120

Percy KE, Jensen KF, McQuattie CJ (1992) Effects of ozone and acid fog on red spruce needle epicuticular wax production, chemical composition, cuticular membrane ultrastructure and needle wettability. New Phytol 122: 71-80

Percy KE, Jagels R, Marden S, McLaughlin CK, Carlisle J (1993) Quantity, chemistry and wettability of epicuticular waxes on needles of red spruce along a fog-acidity gradient. Can J For Res 23: 1472-1479

Riding RT, Percy KE (1985) Effects of SO_2 and other air pollutants on the morphology of epicuticular waxes of needles of *Pinus strobus* and *Pinus banksiana*. New Phytol 99: 555-563

Shelvey JD, Koziol MJ (1986) Seasonal and SO_2 induced changes in epicuticular wax of ryegrass. Phytochem 25: 415-420

Turunen M, Huttunen S (1990) A review of the response of epicuticular wax of conifer needles to air pollution. J Environ Qual 19: 35-45 von Wettstein-Knowles P (1987) Genes, elongases and associated enzyme systems in epicuticular wax synthesis. *In* Stumpf PK, Mudd JB, Nes WD (*eds*) The Metabolism, Structure and Function of Plant Lipids. Plenum Press New York *pp* 489-498

Wilson J (1984) Microscopic features of wind damage to leaves of *Acer pseudoplatanus* L. Ann Bot 53: 73-82

Effects of Air Pollutants on Epicuticular Wax Structure

Satu Huttunen
Department of Botany
University of Oulu
P.O. Box 400
SF-90571 Oulu
Finland

Abstract

In xerophytes, like conifers, the epicuticular wax is well developed. Especially in and around stomatal entrances, a thick wax coating is present. Epicuticular waxes are modified by changes in plant growth conditions such as temperature, relative humidity, irradiance, and wind, or acid rain. The fine structure of epicuticular waxes, their chemistry, and ecophysiological function are modified, especially in evergreen, long-lived conifer needles with characteristic crystalline wax structures. During needle flushing and development, wax structure is easily modified. Acid rain-treated Scots pine needles had 50% less epicuticular waxes in early August. Pollution-induced delayed development, destruction, and disturbances have been identified in many plant species. The structural changes in wax crystals are known. Acid rain or polluted air can destroy the crystalloid epicuticular waxes in a few weeks. In *Pinus sylvestris*, the first sign of pollution effect is the fusion of wax tubes. In *Picea abies* and *P. sitchensis*, modifications of crystalloid wax structure are known. In Californian pine trees phenomena of recrystallization of wax tubes on second-year needles were observed after delayed epicuticular wax development in *Pinus ponderosa* and *P. coulteri*. Thus, the effects of air pollutants are modified by climate.

Accelerated senescence of leaves and needles have been associated with natural and anthropogenic stresses. The accelerated erosion rate of epicuticular waxes has been measured under air pollution conditions. Many short-term air pollution experiments have failed to show any structural changes in epicuticular wax structures. The quantity and quality of needle waxes grown in open-top chambers, glass houses, or polluted air before treatment, differ from field conditions and make it difficult to detect effects of any treatment.

Introduction

In xerophytes, as in conifers, the epicuticular wax is well developed. There is a thick wax coating, especially in and around the stomatal entrances. The wax crystal morphology can vary from rods, plates, filaments and tubes to granules and ribbons. Tube-type waxes are present in many of the higher plant groups. They are the dominant wax crystal type in the *Gymnospermae* and the *Graminae*, and have been recorded in a wide range of *Angiosperm* families, mostly dicotyledons (Bukovac *et al.*, 1981; Jeffree, 1986; Kerfourn, 1992). The epicuticular waxes and the plant cuticle are a combined product of genetics and the environment (Kerfourn, 1992). The wax ultrastructure and its chemistry are highly dependent on each other (Baker, 1982; Jeffree, 1986). Secondary alcohols, *e.g.*, nonacosane-10-ol, and homologies crystallize as squat-type tubes.

NATO ASI Series, Vol. G 36
Air Pollutants and the Leaf Cuticle
Edited by K. E. Percy et al.
© Springer-Verlag Berlin Heidelberg 1994

Many species (*Pinus sylvestris, Picea pungens*) have a protective tubular wax architecture, especially in and on the stomatal cavities. Some species have tubular waxes only in the stomatal cavities (*e.g., Pinus muricata, Pinus contorta* (Bukovac *et al.*, 1981)), while some others have them all over the surface (*e.g., Picea abies, Picea mariana*), and yet others only in the stomatal rows (*Pinus sylvestris*). The epicuticular waxes have many protective functions on plant surfaces, *e.g.*, they prevent water loss. In conifers this function is of crucial importance due to their longevity and evergreen life form. The protection against water loss, however, seems to be most effective in current-year needles. The epicuticular wax morphology changes along with needle age and is disturbed by polluted air (sulphur dioxide, nitrogen oxides), or acidic fog (Huttunen and Laine, 1983; Mengel *et al.*, 1989; Turunen and Huttunen, 1990). The effects of air pollutants on epicuticular waxes may be mediated by metabolic interference in the wax biosynthetic pathways (Kerfourn, 1992), by preceding chemical alterations (Kerfourn, 1992), or by physico-chemical contact reactions (Riederer, 1989).

The clogging of the stomata of *Pinus nigra* needles as a consequence of smoke injury was one of the early observations related to air pollution and epicuticular waxes (Rhine, 1924). Some recent reviews (Riederer, 1989; Turunen and Huttunen, 1990) give an overview of the effects of air pollutants on the epicuticular waxes of conifer needles. There is, however, less information available on the effects of air pollution on the epicuticular waxes of other species. Changes in the epicuticular waxes and surface structures caused by polluted air have been observed in *Quercus pubescens, Fagus sylvatica* (Bottaci *et al.*, 1988), *Acer rubrum* (Krause, 1981), *Ulmus glabra, Quercus robur,* and *Acer platanoides* (Huttunen and Ruonala, 1986). The variability of leaf age and the shorter life span of broadleaved trees make them less indicative of the effects of pollutants on their epicuticular waxes or cuticles. Particle deposition seems to be one deleterious factor affecting broadleaved surfaces. Dwarf shrub epicuticular waxes indicate pollution changes in *Vaccinium vitis-idaea* L. and *Empetrum nigrum* L. (Mikkonen and Huttunen, 1981). Among crop plants, acid rain effects on cabbage epicuticular waxes have been observed (Adams *et al.*, 1990).

The structural response of the epicuticular waxes to air-borne pollutants, especially in conifers, will be discussed here.

Some aspects of the methods and materials

The structural sensitivity of epicuticular waxes is remarkable. Changes in epicuticular wax structures occur during sample preparation and the sources of error are numerous (Reed, 1982; Crang and Klomparens, 1988).

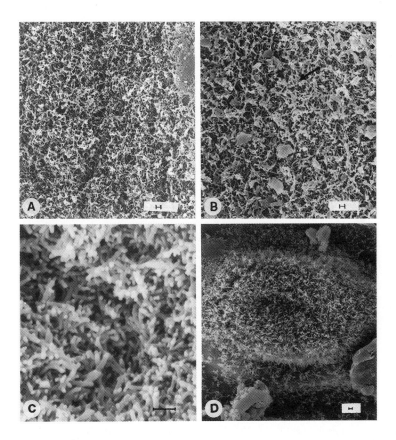

Figure 1   Epicuticular waxes of *Pinus sylvestris* needles preserved by air drying (A) and
            freeze drying (B) in liquid nitrogen. An arrow indicates more fusion of wax tubes
            in B. The epicuticular waxes of *Picea abies* in young needles. Tubular waxes on
            stomata (C) and the whole stoma (D).

It is not always possible to use fresh leaf samples. Freeze drying samples for storage (*e.g.*, liquid
nitrogen) and critical point drying of samples may destroy the architecture and ultrastructure of
epicuticular waxes (Figure 1a, 1b). This may cause difficulties in interpreting the morphology
of freeze-dried material. Many researchers use air drying at mild room temperatures for
preserving and dehydrating samples for wax morphology studies (Bermadinger *et al.*, 1987;
Turunen and Huttunen, 1991; Kerfourn, 1992; Tuomisto and Neuvonen, 1993). Some researchers fix fresh wax material in 2% (W/v) osmium vapor before coating it with gold-palladium
(Krause and Houston, 1983; Percy *et al.*, 1990).

An increase in surface temperatures (+40° ±50°C) during the experiment (open top chambers)
or sample transportation may cause melting damage to the epicuticular waxes (Bytnerowicz *et
al.*, 1989). The artificial wind and light conditions in growth chambers may also have an effect
on the development of epicuticular wax structures. Current methods favour the use of mild room

temperatures for drying the samples. After gentle drying, needle samples retain their epicuticular wax structure well. Several ambient and low temperature scanning electron microscopy methods have recently been reviewed (Jeffree and Read, 1991). Many species need to be tested in order to establish the best method for preserving epicuticular wax or surface structure.

When the morphology of epicuticular wax is studied, it is difficult to assess the role of cuticle-embedded waxes. A combination of scanning electron microscopy and transmission electron microscopy gives optimal results in this respect.

Air pollution and *Picea* species

Young needles of Norway spruce, *Picea abies*, have thick, crystal, epicuticular wax tube formations concentrated on the stomata, but the needle surface between the stomata is also covered with sparse, wax, tubular crystals (Figure 1c, 1d). The densely arranged tubes are short (0.5 -1.1 μm) and cylindrical (0.1 - 0.2 μm diameter) (Baker, 1982). A significant proportion of these tubes lie partly embedded within the amorphous wax film, but the majority project away from the epidermis.

Gunthardt-Goerg (1987) demonstrated at the Alpine timberline that the epicuticular wax layer of *Picea abies* is formed by successive layers and not by one layer of lipid mixture exuded all at once. The ultrastructure and the development of the outer epidermal wall of current needles reach maturity in European spruce forests in October (Tenberge, 1992).

The normal aging of needles causes visible changes in the epicuticular wax in and around the stomata (Figure 2a-2l). The tubular wax crystals are converted into flattened and fused crystalloid formations. The needle age of Norway spruce may be from 11 to 14 years in northern conditions. In polluted air, the mean age of the needles is shortened and the erosion rate of the tubular epicuticular wax accelerated. The crystalloid epicuticular waxes of Norway spruce stomatal antechambers show some typical signs of aging erosion. From current to 4 years, crystalloid wax tubes can be observed in and outside the stomatal rows on the needle surfaces. After that the surface is smoothened and the stomatal antechambers show abundant cracks and eroded crystalloid wax forms. From the fifth needle year onwards, further decay of the stomatal antechambers is observable and empty cavities in the stomatal chambers can be seen (Karhu and Huttunen, 1986).

Microscopic observations of epicuticular wax structures have, for a long time, suggested links between pollution and aging effects. A chemical study of alkanes has permitted a distinction between aging response and pollution symptoms. Pollution induced shorter carbon chains in the alkane composition of Norway spruce needle and ivy leaf waxes, while aging was characterized by longer chain alkanes (Kerfourn, 1992).

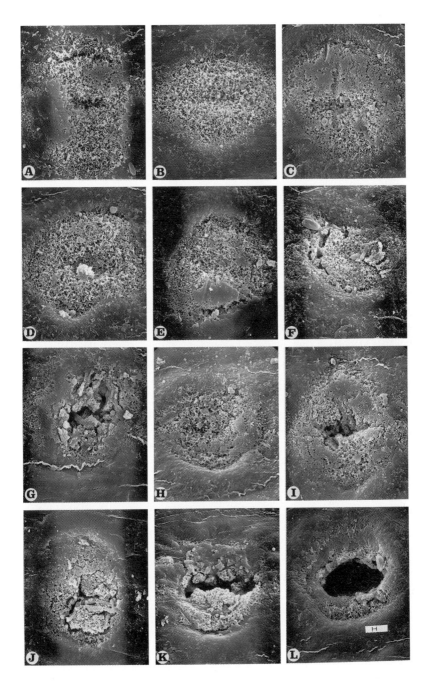

Figure 2   The aging erosion of *Picea abies* needles in northern Finland. Samples obtained
from Kiiminki in March. The current-year needles already exhibit erosion phenomena in their tubular waxes in late winter (A). Erosion of a stomatal wax plug over
12 years. Decrease of tubular waxes after the fourth year of life (B-L).

Comparing *Picea abies* needles from areas with visible SO_2 vegetation damage with needles from areas without damage, Grill (1973) demonstrated a premature agglomeration of crystalloid wax in the epistomatal chambers under polluted conditions. Östensen and Gullvåg (1985) and Gullvåg and Östensen (1986) made similar observations. Sauter and Voss (1986) noted a greatly accelerated production of scale-like formations on the stomata in declining *Picea abies*. Sauter *et al.* (1987) showed that the degradation of the epistomatal wax deposits of *Picea abies* needles was also accelerated both by a 20-week exposure at the edge of a motorway and by a brief fumigation with exhaust gas. Magnesite plant dust also caused degradation in Norway spruce waxes (Bermadinger *et al.*, 1987). An interesting observation was made by Kim (1985), who reported that the degree of epicuticular wax tubule fusion decreased from the top to the bottom of a tree and was higher in sun-exposed than in shaded needles.

Gunthardt-Goerg and Keller (1987) studied the effects of 5 months of ozone fumigation on Norway spruce epicuticular wax and stomata. Flattened wax structures and fused wax fibrils also occurred in the controls and the authors, therefore, concluded that these phenomena cannot serve as measures of the ozone effects. The wax quantity was considerably reduced by fumigation with 300 μg^{m-3} ozone. Ojanperä and Huttunen (1989) studied a different *Picea abies* clone in the above-mentioned experiment and observed slightly increased erosion in the wax structure of the epistomatal chambers at concentrations higher that 200 μg^{m-3}. The methods of observation in these two papers differed somewhat. Ojanperä and Huttunen (1989) used air-dried samples, while Gunthardt-Goerg and Keller (1987) used liquid nitrogen freeze-dried ones. In the former experiment, moreover, the needles fumigated with ambient air and 100 μg^{m-3} ozone were infected by fungi, and their effects on the epicuticular waxes disturbed structural observations (Ojanperä and Huttunen, 1989).

Contrary to the above findings, Barnes *et al.* (1988) found ozone accelerated the structural degradation of epicuticular wax on Norway spruce needles. In four clones, O_3 fumigation resulted in 70-80% of the stomata on the previous year's needles being occluded in contrast to the 7-28% occlusion in charcoal-filtered air. Five of the clones showed a greater effect of ozone on the wax of the previous year's needles than on the current needles. Barnes *et al.* (1988) concluded that stomatal occlusion was a direct chemical effect of ozone.

Tuomisto and Neuvonen (1993) quantified the occurrence of different wax types on *Picea abies* needles and concluded that air pollution has a great effect on the morphology of epicuticular wax. Tubular wax types are more common in clean air than in polluted air, while the eroded forms (with the exception of amorphous wax) more commonly occur in polluted air.

Mengel *et al.* (1989) studied the effect of acidic fog on the needle surfaces and water relations of *Picea abies*. Under water stress conditions, the trees that had been exposed to acidic fog showed significantly higher transpiration rates than the control trees. Rinallo *et al.* (1986) studied the epicuticular waxes of the needles of *Picea abies* seedlings. Spraying with an acidified mist (pH 3.5) altered the epicuticular waxes. Tubes disappeared and the wax was fused and fissured in the stomatal antechambers. Our own observations on the acid rain effects on Norway spruce needle surfaces revealed that the margins of the stomatal area showed the first changed forms of crystalloid waxes. The second-year needles had lost the crystalloid wax tubes almost entirely. The acid rain effects may have interactions with needle fungi (Turunen and Huttunen, 1988; Turunen and Huttunen, 1991; Turunen *et al.*, 1993). Kerfourn (1992) studied the ozone and ozone/acids effects on Norway spruce epicuticular waxes. The structural changes were preceded by chemical changes. The effects of air pollution from smelters (Czechoslovakia) on Norway spruce epicuticular waxes are characterized by heavy metal deposition on surfaces and a deformed wax structure (Mankovska *et al.*, 1989).

Jagels (1991) studied the biophysical aspects of fog deposition on the needles of *Abies balsamea*, *Picea rubens* and *Pinus strobus*. In young, physiologically active needles of *Picea rubens* most of the fog was deposited on the epicuticular waxes which occlude the epistomatal chambers. This non-random depositional pattern was discussed with reference to the sensitivity of *Picea rubens* to acidic fog. The fog deposition pattern may also explain the observed field correlation between decline symptoms in *Picea rubens* and fog acidity (Jagels *et al.*, 1989) as well as the experimental symptoms that can be produced by exposing *Picea rubens* to acidic fog and ozone (Jacobson *et al.*, 1989; Leith *et al.*, 1989; Percy *et al.*, 1990; Krause and Cannon, 1991). Percy *et al.* (1990) observed new structures consisting of upright, irregular wax plates in needles exposed to acidic fog (pH 3.0). Krause and Cannon (1991) indicated morphological changes were moderate at pH 4.2 and 0.15 ppm ozone, and severe at pH 3.0 and 0.15 ppm ozone.

Ozone treatments increased mesophyll cell disruption in red spruce after frosts in early winter, but there was no correlation between histological injury and visible symptoms in spring. No changes in cuticle structure were observed after ozone exposure (Fincher and Alscher, 1992).

Air pollution and *Pinus* species

The micromorphology of young Scots pine (*Pinus sylvestris*) needle surfaces is characterized by tubular waxes on and between stomata. The interlacing wax tubes are about 0.06 - 1 μm long (Figure 3a, 3b). In young needles, the stomata are covered and occluded by crystalline wax (Huttunen and Laine, 1983). The mean needle age of Scots pine varies from 6 years on northern to 3-4 years on more southern sites. The weathering of Scots pine epicuticular wax in polluted and clean air has been described (Huttunen and Laine, 1983; Crossley and Fowler, 1986). The wax tubes are shortened, thickened, and fused into an amorphous surface "crust" with time. The first sign of change is the fusion of wax tubes. Fiedler *et al.* (1990) studied green and chlorotic

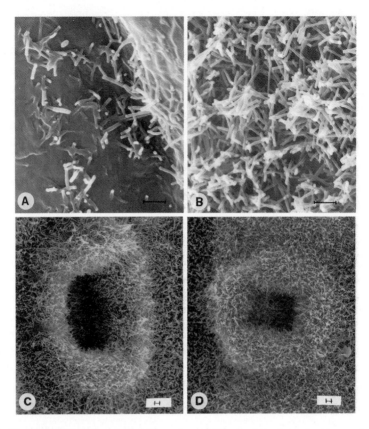

Figure 3   Young developing waxes of Scots pine needles flushing from the sheaths (A and B).
Young stoma of a *Pinus sylvestris* needle from Finnish Lapland (C) and one from
the Gothenburg region in southern Sweden (D) in June a few days after flushing.

Scots pine needles in the Dueben Heath and found accelerated aggregation of the epicuticular
wax. Wind (van Gardingen *et al.*, 1991) and other natural ecological factors tend to damage the
epicuticular wax surfaces. Grace (1990) concluded that, in Scotland, the pine needle cuticular
wax had stomatal dysfunctions caused by mechanical damage to the leaf rather than thinner or
less developed cuticle. The cuticular mass of pine needles collected from five altitude was
between 4 and 6 μg^{mm-2}. The quantity of waxes varies in pine needles from 0.5% to over 2% dry
weight. Yound developing needles have smaller percentages of wax (Huttunen *et al.*, 1990;
Turunen and Huttunen, 1991; Turunen *et al.*, 1993).

Comparisons of climatic and air pollution effects on needle epicuticular wax characteristics in
Scots pine (Turunen *et al.*, 1992) yielded the finding that, in Poland, only 10% of the studied
pine needles had well-developed and well-preserved epicuticular wax; the corresponding figure
in Finland being 50%. Further studies on epicuticular wax of Scots pine needles in Silesia
revealed that 72.3% of all needle samples had lost their crystalloid waxes (Huttunen and

Krodzinska, 1993). This difference is mainly related to the different levels of air pollution. The epicuticular wax structure of young, well-developed Scots pine needles is very similar on different sites and at different latitudes (Figure 3c, 3d). The erosion rate and mean age vary, however, as mentioned above. Increased transpiration rates of eroded needles, as already mentioned for *Picea abies*, have also been measured for Scots pine (Huttunen *et al.*, 1981; Huttunen and Laine, 1983; Mäkelä and Huttunen, 1987; Turunen and Huttunen, 1991).

In an acid rain experiment, Turunen *et al.* (1993) observed that the quantity of epicuticular waxes in 2-month-old pine needles was only 2/3 of that in 1-year-old needles, indicating incomplete wax synthesis. Wax production was slowest in pH 3 and pH 4 treated 2-month-old needles, which had 50% less waxes than in the water controls. This may lead to an increasing permeability of the cuticles (Huttunen *et al.*, 1989).

Fiedler *et al.* (1990) studied green and chlorotic pine needles in a polluted pine stand and observed an accumulation of gypsum crystals on latently damaged needles. The phenomenon was abundant in a simulated acid rain experiment with Scots pine and Norway spruce seedlings (Huttunen *et al.*, 1991).

The wax structure of developing needles of *Pinus sylvestris* progenies infected by *Lophodermella sulcigena* showed differences in the wax biosynthesis rate (Jalkanen *et al.*, 1981). Fungal cutinase activities (Kolattukudy *et al.*, 1987) have effects on Scots pine needle epicuticular waxes.

In *Pinus pinaster* needles, the epicuticular waxes consisting of crystalline structures with wax tubes 1.5-1.8 µm long are principally distributed inside the epistomatal chambers and, to a lesser extent, around and between adjacent chambers (Manes *et al.*, 1988). These structures appear morphologically quite similar in the abaxial and adaxial surfaces. The crystalline wax is naturally variable. The plants treated at pH 2.4 showed an increase in the percentage of stomata with large fissures in the wax structures from about the 5th week onwards.

In *Pinus pinea* needles, the epicuticular waxes are distributed on the epicuticular layer between the stomata and inside the epistomatal chamber, with some structural differences in the stomatal apparatus as compared with that observed in *P. pinaster* (Manes *et al.*, 1988).

The effects of photochemical smog were studied in an open-top chamber, but the short-term experiment did not show any significant changes in the epicuticular waxes of 1-year-old seedlings of *Pinus coulteri, P. ponderosa, P. jeffreyi,* and *P. sylvestris*. The difference between outside plots and open-top chamber needles was most pronounced (Bytnerowicz *et al.*, 1989). Yläsaari *et al.* (1987) studied the epicuticular wax surface structure of Californian pine species *Pinus attenuata, P. coulteri, P. muricata, P. albicauli, P. ponderosa,* and *P. jefferi*. All the needle samples obtained from San Bernardino mountains revealed somewhat damaged epicuticular waxes and stomatal plugs compared with cleaner sites and known species mottling symptoms.

Ozone-sensitive *Pinus strobus* has shown accelerated degradation of the wax morphology under polluted conditions (Percy and Riding, 1978; Krause and Dochinger, 1984).

Exposure of elongating needles of *Pinus strobus* to sulphur dioxide and other air pollutants delayed wax deposition in the epistomatal chambers. No alteration of wax form was evident on needles of *Pinus banksiana* (Riding and Percy, 1985). The structure and ontogeny of the stomatal complex in *Pinus strobus* and *P. banksiana* have been described by Johnson and Riding (1981).

Krause and Houston (1983) noticed that ambient air had no effect on the epistomatal plugs of ten sulphur dioxide-tolerant clones of *Pinus strobus*, whereas fissures occurred in 12 sensitive clones.

Conifer needles (*e.g.*, *Pinus densiflora*, *Pinus koraiensis*) exposed to ambient air pollutants revealed breakdown and the aggregation of wax structures on stomatal chambers (Kim and Lee, 1990).

Organic air pollutants

Inhibition of epicuticular wax biosynthesis is known to be caused by trichloracetate (Frannich and Wells, 1980). The structural changes of epicuticular waxes caused by organic micropollutants have not been described in detail. However, plant surfaces accumulate lipophilic compounds to a considerable extent (Reischl *et al.*, 1989), and they may have effects on epicuticular waxes.

UV-B radiation and waxes

The plant cuticle is the first and most important barrier to the penetration of near UV-radiation. Many waxes reflect strongly in the ultraviolet range. The glaucous bloom seems to make it possible for conifers to tolerate high light intensities without damage, particularly with respect to shorter wavelengths (Clark and Lister, 1975). Day *et al.* (1992) studied UV-B penetration in the foliage of different species. UV-B was completely attenuated by the epidermis of *Picea engelmannii*. The needle epidermis of *Abies lasiocarpa*, *Picea engelmannii* and *Pinus flexilis* was thinner in high elevation individuals and in older needles. However, no significant difference in the depth of UV-B penetration within these species across elevation or age treatments was observed. Essentially all UV-B was attenuated before it reached the mesophyll. Crystalline epicuticular waxes were not observed to be critical in UV-B screening, as their removal had no effect on the depth of UV-B penetration. Bornmann and Vogelmann (1988) found little changes in UV-A penetration following removal of epicuticular waxes from *Picea engelmannii* and *Abies lasiocarpa* needles. For most species, UV-B reflectance from the leaf is less than 5%, and most of the attenuation is the result of absorption and scattering within the epidermal tissue. There are few species which exhibit leaf surface reflectance of the order of 20-70% in the UV waveband. This has been shown to be true for glaucous surfaces, such as *Picea pungens* (Clark and Lister, 1975), or certain species with dense pubescence (Robberecht *et al.*, 1980). UV radiation has been observed to increase epicuticular wax production in plants (Steinmuller and Tevini, 1985). Ultraviolet B treatment increased the amount of tubular waxes on the needles of Scots pine seedlings (Huttunen, unpublished results).

Sullivan and Teramura (1988) tested seedlings of different conifer species. *Pinus contorta, P. resinosa*, and *P. taeda* exhibited damage symptoms after UV-radiation. *Abies fraseri, Picea glauca, Pinus strobus, Pinus edulis* and *Pinus nigra* were not sensitive. Sullivan and Teramura (1989, 1992) and Naidu *et al.* (1993) have further studied *Pinus taeda*. Dube and Bornmann (1992) studied UV-effects on *Picea abies*. In these, epicuticular waxes or cuticular aspects have not been discussed.

DeLucia and Berlyn (1984) studied the effect of increasing elevation on *Abies balsamea* leaf cuticle thickness and cuticular transpiration. The mean cuticle thickness on the adaxial needle surface decreased with increasing elevation from 3.01 to 2.21 µg. Epicuticular wax expressed as g wax/g dry weight slightly increased. The dense mesh of wax rodlets found between the stomata in the low elevation needles is replaced by predominantly laminar wax at the tree line.

Conclusions

The ultrastructure of epicuticular waxes and the distribution of tubular waxes are species-specific. The genotype and phenotype affect the ultrastructure of waxes. Air pollutants (sulphur dioxide, nitrogen oxides, acid rain) cause changes in the wax ultrastructure, including delayed crystallization of wax structures in developing needles, fusion or erosion of wax tubes in young mature needles, or other morphological changes observable in scanning electron microscopy. Mature needles are not considered to be able to, *de novo*, synthesize any waxes after their growth has ended. Recrystallization of deposited waxes may be observed on needle surfaces. pH or pollutant treatment has a tendency to reduce the concentration of waxes.

Epicuticular wax morphology shows typical changes as needles age and this is duplicated, at a more rapid rate, in the the presence of air pollutants and acidic precipitation. The morphological changes caused by ozone are questionable, when the saturated character of the wax chemistry is considered, but many possibilities for physico-chemical changes exist, when interactions with sunlight, UV-radiation, and wet surfaces are additionally considered. Riederer (1989) postulated the morphological changes are not a direct impact of air pollution. However, the preceding chemical changes and disturbances in biosynthesis, the effects of aerosols, organic compounds, and particles, and the accelerated erosion rate suggest both direct and indirect effects.

Acknowledgements

This work was financed by the Academy of Finland. The language of the manuscript was checked by Ms. Sirkka-Liisa Leinonen.

References

Adams CM, Caporn SJM, Hutchinson TC (1990) Crystal occurrence and wax disruption on leaf surfaces of cabbage treated with simulated acid rain. New Phytol 114: 147-158

Bäck J, Huttunen S (1992) Structural responses of needles of conifer seedlings to acid rain. New Phytol 120: 77-88

Baker EA (1982) Chemistry and morphology of plant epicuticular waxes. *In* Cutler DF, Alvin KL, Price CE (*eds*) The plant cuticle. Academic Press, London *pp* 139-166

Barnes JD, Davison AW, Booth TA (1988) Ozone accelerates structural degradation of epicuticular wax on Norway spruce needles. New Phytol 110: 309-318

Bermadinger E, Grill D, Golob P (1987) The different influence of magnesite emissions on the surface waxes of Norway spruce and silver fir. Can J Bot 66: 125-129

Bornmann J, Vogelmann T (1988) Penetration of blue and UV radiation measured by fiber optics in spruce and fir needles. Physiol Plant 72: 699-705

Bottacci A, Brogi L, Bussotti F, Cenni E, Clauser F, Ferretti M, Gellini R, Grossini P, Schiff S (1988) Inquinamento ambientale e deperimento del bosco in Toscana. Regione Toscana. Società botanica italiana 134 *pp*

Bukovac MJ, Rasmussen HP, Shull VE (1981) The cuticle: surface structure and function. Scanning Electron Microscopy III: 213-223

Bytnerowicz A, Olszyk DM, Huttunuen S, Takemoto B (1989) Effects of photochemical smog on growth, injury, and gas exchange of pine seedlings. Can J Bot 67: 2175-2181

Clark J, Lister G (1975) Photosynthetic action spectra of trees II. The relationship of cuticle structure to visible and ultraviolet spectral properties of needles from four coniferous species. Plant Physiol 55: 407-413

Crang FE, Klomparens KL (1988) Artifacts in biological electron microscopy. Plenum Press New York and London 233 *pp*

Crossley A, Fowler D (1986) The weathering of Scots pine epicuticular wax in polluted and clean air. New Phytol 103: 207-218

Day TA, Vogelmann TC, DeLucia EH (1992) Are some plant life forms more effective than others in screening out ultraviolet-B radiation? Oecologia 92: 513-519

Dube S, Bornmann J (1992) Response of spruce seedlings to simultaneous exposure to ultraviolet-B radiation and cadmium. Plant Physiol Biochem 30(6): 761-767

DeLucia EH, Berlyn, GP (1984) The effect of increasing elevation on leaf cuticle thickness and cuticular transpiration in balsam fir. Can J Bot 62: 2423-2431

Fiedler HJ, Baronius G, Ehrig F (1990) Rastereletronenmikroskopische und chemische Untersuchungen gruner und chlorotischer Nadeln eines immissionsgeschädigten Kiefernbestandes. Flora 184: 91-101

Fincher J, Alscher RG (1992) The effect of long-term ozone exposure on injury in the seedlings of red spruce (*Picea rubens* Sarg). New Phytol 120: 49-59

Franich RA, Wells LG (1980) Inhibition of *Pinus radiata* primary needles epicuticular wax biosynthesis by trichloroacetate. J Exp Bot 31: 829-838

Grace J (1990) Cuticular water loss unlikely to explain tree-line in Scotland. Oecologia 84: 64-68

Grill D (1973) Rasterelektronenmikrosckopische Untersuchungen an SO_2 belasteten Fichtennadeln. Phytopath Z 78: 75-80

Gullvåg BM, Östensen H (1986) Wax layer erosion in spruce needles — an indicator of air-borne pollution. J Ultrastruct Res 94: 280

Gunthardt-Goerg MS (1987) Epicuticular wax formation on needles of *Picea abies* and *Pinus cembra*. *In* Stumpf PK, Gunthardt-Goerg MS, Keller T 1987 Some effects of long-term ozone fumigation on Norway spruce. Trees 1: 145-150

Gunthardt MS, Wanner H (1982) Veränderungen der Spaltöffnungen und der Wachsstructur mit zumehmendem Nadelalter bei *P. cembra* und *P. abies* L. Karsten an der Waldgrenze. Bot Helv 92: 47-60

Huttunen S (1992) Responses of northern confires to changes in pollution and climate. *In* Teller A, Mathy P, Jeffers, JNR (*eds*) Response of forest ecosystems to environmental changes. Elsevier Applied Science. Commission of the European Communities 1009 *pp* 515-519

Huttunen S, Havas P, Laine K (1981) Effects of air pollutants on the wintertime water economy of the Scots pine *Pinus sylvestris*. Holarctic Ecology 4(2): 94-101

Huttunen S, Laine K (1983) Effects of air-borne pollutants on the surface wax structure of *Pinus sylvestris* needles. Ann Bot Fennici 20: 79-86

Huttunen S, Ruonala K (1986) Comparisons of leaf surface structures of elm, oak, and maple in urban and rural trees. J Ultrastruct & Molec. Struct Res 94: 280

Huttunen S, Turunen M, Reinikainen J (1989) Studies on Scots pine (*Pinus sylvestris* L) and Norway spruce (*Picea abies* L. Karst) needle cuticles. Ann Sci For 46 suppl: 553-556s

Huttunen S, Reinikainen J, Turunen M (1990) Wintering response of conifers to acid rain treatment under northern conditions. *In* Kauppi P, Kenttämies K, Anttila P (*eds*) Acidification in Finland. Springer-Verlag Berlin *pp* 607-633

Huttunen S, Turunen M, Reinikainen J (1991) Scattered $CaSO_4$-crystallites on needle surfaces after simulated acid rain as an indicator of nutrient leaching. Water Air Soil Pollut 54: 169-173

Huttunen S, Krodzinska K (1993) Epicuticular waxes of Scots pine needles in Katowice region. Unpublished data

Jacobson JS, Lassoie JP, Osmeloski J, Yamada K (1989) Changes in foliar elements in red spruce seedlings after exposure to sulphuric acid and nitric acid mist. Water Air Soil Pollut 48: 141-160

Jagels R (1991) Biophysical aspects of fog deposition on the needles of three conifers. J Exp Bot 42: 757-763

Jagels R, Carlisle J, Cunningham R, Serreze S, Tsai P (1989) Impact of acid fog and ozone on coastal red spruce. Water Air Soil Pollut 48: 193-208

Jalkanen R, Huttunen S, Väisänen S (1981) The wax structure of the developing needles of *Pinus sylvestris* progenies infected by *Lophodermella sulcigena*. Silva Fennica 15: 377-381

Jeffree CE 1986 The cuticle, epicuticular waxes and trichomes of plants, with reference to their structure, functions and evolution. *In* Juniper B, Southwood R (*eds*) Insects and the Plant Surface. Edward Arnold *pp* 23-64

Jeffree CE, Read ND (1991) Ambient- and low temperature scanning electron microscopy. *In* Hall JL, Hawes C (*eds*) Electron microscopy of plant cells. Academic Press London *pp* 313-413

Johnson RW, Riding RT (1981) Structure and ontogeny of the stomatal complex in *Pinus strobus* L and *Pinus banksiana* Lamb. Am J Bot 68: 260-268

Karhu M, Huttunen S (1986) Effects of aging and air pollution on Norway spruce needles. J Ultrastruct & Molec Struct Res 94: 281

Kerfourn C (1992) Impacts des polluants atmosphériques acides (H_2SO_4, HNO_3) et photo-oxydants (O_3) sur l'intégrité des cuticules d'Epicea (*Picea abies*) et de lierre (*Hedera helix*). Leur rôles possibles dans le dépérissement des forêts. Université de Nancy I Thèse 142 *pp*

Kim Y.S. (1985) REM Beobachtungen immissionsgeschädigter Fichtennadeln. Cbl ges Forstw 102: 96-105

Kim YS, Lee JK (1990) Chemical and structural characteristics of conifer needles exposed to ambient air pollution. Eur J For Path 20: 193-200

Kolattukudy PE, Ettinger WF, Sebastian J (1987) Cuticular lipids in plant-microbe interactions. *In* Stumpf PK, Mudd JB, Nes W (*eds*) The metabolism, structure, and function of plant lipids. Plenum Press New York and London *pp* 473-480

Krause CR (1981) Diagnosis of ambient air pollution injury to red maple leaves. Scanning Electron Microscopy III: 203-206

Krause CR and Dochinger LS (1984) Surface changes to pine needles induced by ambient particles. Phytopath 74: 870

Krause CR, Houston DB (1983) Morphological variation in epicuticular wax of SO_2-sensitive and -tolerant eastern white pine clones. Phytopath 73: 1266-1269

Krause CR, Cannon WN (1991) Epistomatal wax injury to red spruce needles (*Picea rubens* Sarg) growth in elevated levels of ozone and acidified rain. Scanning Microscopy 5(4): 1173-1180

Leith ID, Murray MB, Sheppard LJ, Cape JN, Deans JD, Smith RI, Fowler D (1989) Visible foliar injury of red spruce seedlings subjected to simulated acid mist. New Phytol 113: 313-320

Manes F, Altieri A, Angelini R, Bruno F, Cortiello M, Del Caldo L (1988) Micromorphological and biochemical changes in *Pinus pinea* L., *Pinus pinaster* Aiton, *Nicotiana tabacum* L in relation to atmospheric pollutants. *In* Cape JN, Mathy P (*eds*) Scientific basis of forest decline symptomatology. Commission of the European Communities. Directorate General for Science, Research and Development, Environmental Research Programme. Proceedings of a workshop jointly organized by the Commission of the European Communities, and the Institute of Terrestrial Ecology, Bush Estate Research Station, Edinburgh, Scotland, 21-24 March 1988 *pp* 342-353

Mankovska B, Huttunen S, Peura R (1989) The effect of air pollution from the Krompachy and Rudnany smelteries on *Picea abies* L. Karst. Ekologia (CSSR) 8(1): 49-58

Mengel K, Hogrebe AMR, Esch A (1989) Effect of acidic fog on needle surface and water relations of *Picea abies* Physiol Plant 75: 201-207

Mikkonen H, Huttunen S (1981) Dwarf shrubs as bioindicators. Silva Fennica 15: 475-480

Mäkelä A, Huttunen S 1987 Cuticular needle erosion and winter drought in polluted environments. A model analysis. Working paper 87.48 International Institute for Applied Systems Analysis. Luxemburg 25 *pp*

Naidu S, Sullivan T, Teramura A, DeLucia E (1993) The effects of ultraviolet-B radiation on photosynthesis of different aged needles in field-grown loblolly pine. Tree Physiol 12: 151-162

Ojanperä K, Huttunen S (1989) Interactions of ozone and pathogens on the surface structure of Norway spruce needles. Ann Sci For 46 suppl: 543-546s

Östensen H, Gullvåg, BM (1985) The wax layer of *Picea abies* needles studied from different German and Norwegian localities subjected to airborne pollution. J Ultrastruct Res 91: 268

Percy, KE, Riding RT (1978) The epicuticular waxes of *Pinus strobus* subjected to air pollution. Can J For Res 8: 474-477

Percy KE, Baker EA (1990) Effects of simulated acid rain on epicuticular wax production, morphology, chemical composition and on cuticular membrane thickness in two clones of Sitka spruce (*Picea sitchensis* (Bong.) Carr.). New Phytol 116: 79-87

Percy KE, Krause CR, Jensen KF (1990) Effects of ozone and acidic rain on red spruce needle epicuticular wax ultrastructure. Can J For Res 20: 117-120

Reed DW (1982) Wax alteration and extraction during electron microscopy preparation of leaf cuticles. *In* Cutler DF, Alvin KL, Price CE (*eds*) The Plant Cuticle. The Linnean Society of London. Academic Press *pp* 181-195

Reischl A, Reissinger M, Hutzinger O (1989) Organic micropollutants and plants. *In* Schulze ED, Lange OL, Oren R (*eds*) Ecological Studies Vol 77 Springer-Verlag Berlin Heidelberg *pp* 193-209

Rhine JB (1924) Clogging of stomata of conifers in relation to smoke injury and distribution. Bot Gasezette 78: 226-232

Riederer M (1989) The cuticles of conifers: structure, composition, and transport properties. *In* Schulze ED, Lange OL, Oren R (*eds*) Ecological Studies Vol 77 Springer-Verlag Berlin Heidelberg *pp* 157-192

Riding RT, Percy KE 1985 Effects of SO_2 and other air pollutants on the morphology of epicuticular waxes of needles of *Pinus strobus* and *Pinus banksiana*. New Phytol 99: 555-563

Rinallo C, Raddi P, Gellini R, DiLonardo V (1986) Effects of simulated acid deposition on the surface structure of Norway spruce and silver fir needles. Eur J For Path 16: 440-446

Robberecht R, Caldwell MM (1980) Leaf ultraviolet optical properties along a latitudinal gradient in the arctic-alpine life zone. Ecology 61(3): 612-619

Sauter JJ, Voss JU (1986) SEM-observations on the structural degradation of epistomatal waxes in *Picea abies* (L) Karst and its possible role in the "Fichtensterben". Eur J For Path 16: 408-423

Steinmuller D, Tevini M (1985) Action of ultraviolet radiation (UV-B) upon cuticular waxes in crop plants. Planta 164: 557-564

Sullivan J, Teramura A (1988) Effect of ultraviolet-B irradiation on seedling growth in Pinaceae. Am J Bot 75(2): 225-230

Sullivan J, Teramura A (1989) The effects of ultraviolet-B radiation on the loblolly pine. Growth, photosynthesis and pigment production in greenhouse grown seedlings. Physiol Plantar 77: 202-207

Sullivan J, Teramura A (1991) The effect of ultraviolet-B radional on loblolly pine. II. Growth of field grown seedlings. Trees 6: 115-120

Tenberge KB (1992) Ultrastructure and development of the outer epidermal wall of spruce (*Picea abies*) needles. Can J Bot 70: 1467-1487

Tuomisto H, Neuvonen S (1993) How to quantify differences in epicuticular wax morphology of *Picea abies* L. Karst. needles. New Phytol 123: 787-799

Turunen M, Huttunen S (1988) Preliminary results on the effects of acid rain on pine and spruce needle surfaces. Poster presented at the workshop "Scientific basis of forest decline symptomatology" in Edinburgh, Scotland, 21-24 March 1988

Turunen M, Huttunen S (1990) A review of the response of epicuticular wax of conifer needles to air pollution. J Environ Qual 19: 35-45

Turunen M, Huttunen S (1991) Effects of simulated acid rain on the epicuticular wax of Scots pine needles under northerly conditions. Can J Bot 69: 412-419

Turunen M, Huttunen S, Staszewski T, Poborski P (1992) Influence of the climate and air pollution on needle surface characteristics in the Scots pine (*Pinus sylvestris* L). *In* Teller A, Mathy P, Jeffers JNR (*eds*) Response of forest ecosystems to environmental changes. Elsevier Applied Science. Commission of the European Communities. *pp* 643-644

Turunen M, Huttunen S, Bäck J, Lamppu J (1993) Effect of acid rain treatment on cuticular characteristics in needles of Scots pine and Norway spruce seedlings. Manuscript submitted to Can J For Res

van Gardingen PR, Grace J, Jeffree CE (1992) Abrasive damage by wind to the needle surfaces of *Picea sitchensis* (Bong.) Carr. and *Pinus sylvestris* L. Plant Cell and Environ 14: 185-193

Yläsaari K, Huttunen S, Bytnerowicz A (1987) Ilmansaasteiden aiheuttamat pintarakenteen muutokset amerikkalaisilla Pinus-suvun neulasilla (An estimation of the damage to the surface structure of the epicuticular waxes of American pine needles) Aquilo Ser Bot 25: 193-197

Leaf Wettability as a Measure of Air Pollution Effects[1]

Richard Jagels
Department of Forest Biology
University of Maine
5755 Nutting Hall
Orono, ME 04469-5755
U.S.A.

Abstract

Droplet contact angle (DCA) is a technique that can be used to measure wettability and, in turn, provide an assessment of the physical and chemical characteristics of a surface. As adapted to plant biology, DCA measurements have been useful in characterizing changes in the type or condition of leaf epicuticular waxes. Environmental as well as temporal factors can modify the biophysical features of epicuticular wax surfaces and thereby affect DCA measurements. An understanding of the role of these non-pollutant factors is necessary before pollution damage can be accurately assessed. Controlled chamber experiments and field pollutant gradient studies have shown that DCA is generally reduced when plants are exposed to air pollutants such as ozone, So_2, and acidic fog. In some cases, environmental influences, such as temperature, have been separated from the pollutant effect. However, mixtures of anthropogenic pollutants or anthropogenic and natural compounds (sea salts, dust particles) which are often present in field studies can confound the interpretation of DCA measurements. A few studies that attempt to separate these factors have been conducted, but more are needed before the potential for using DCA measurements in long-term bioindicator studies can be fully realized. Some studies have demonstrated that pollutants do not necessarily affect leaf surfaces in a uniform patter, but rather are specific for certain structures such as stomates or trichomes; deposition levels can also be different on ad- and abaxial surfaces. The degree to which these inhomogeneities of action can affect DCA measurements needs further study.

Introduction

Waxes that are produced on plant surfaces, particularly leaf cuticles, serve multiple functions. The most often cited role for epicuticular leaf waxes is the control of water and solute loss or uptake (Mecklenburg *et al.*, 1966; Bain and McBean, 1967; Baker, 1974; Sherbatskoy and Klein, 1983; Schönherr *et al.*, 1984; Waldman and Hoffman, 1988; Schuepp and Hendershot, 1989). Restriction of gas exchange, a barrier to insects and diseases, and reflection of selected wavelengths of light have also been suggested or demonstrated as roles of epicuticular waxes (Martin and Juniper, 1970; Hanover and Reicosky, 1971; Jeffree *et al.*, 1971; Clark and Lister, 1975; Walla and Peterson, 1976; Baker *et al.*, 1983; Berg, 1987). Indirectly, the status of epicuticular waxes may influence physiological processes such as chilling injury or winter

---

[1] Report No. 1821 of the Maine Agricultural and Forestry Research Station.

NATO ASI Series, Vol. G 36
Air Pollutants and the Leaf Cuticle
Edited by K. E. Percy et al.
© Springer-Verlag Berlin Heidelberg 1994

hardiness (Franssen, 1991; McDonald *et al.*, 1993; Jagels, unpublished data). Abrasion of surface waxes may lead to direct injury as in the case of wind erosion of surface waxes (Wilson, 1984; van Gardingen *et al.*, 1991; Hoad *et al.*, 1992).

Wettability and surface characteristics

In theory, many of the morphological features, quantitative aspects and chemical properties of epicuticular wax surfaces, should affect leaf wettability, as measured by the droplet contact angle method (Fogg, 1947; Leyton and Juniper, 1963; Troughton and Hall, 1967) — a technique borrowed from surface science physicists. Measurements of leaf wettability should provide insight into changes in epicuticular waxes that may affect leachability of solutes, residence time for aqueous-borne pollutants, propensity for water loss from leaves, selected wavelength reflectance properties, and substrate suitability for insects or pathogens.

Holloway (1970) reviewed the physico-chemical properties that can affect leaf wettability, and defined two major factors — surface chemistry and roughness. He showed that isolated classes of leaf surface waxes had different droplet contact angles. Alkanes were the most hydrophobic (106-109°); esters, ketones and secondary alcohols were intermediate; and diols were the least hydrophobic (70-71°). Other investigators have confirmed the importance of wax chemistry on leaf wettability (Netting and von Wettstein-Knowles, 1973; Percy and Baker, 1990). Holloway concluded, however, that the wide range of wettabilities found for intact, native plant cuticles cannot be accounted for based solely on wax composition. Chloroform removal of surface waxes generally reduced the contact angle measurement by varying percentages, depending upon the species. However, in a few cases, an unaccountable increase in contact angle occurred after wax stripping. For the species investigated, contact angles after wax removal ranged from 10-154°, indicating that surface roughness also plays a critical role.

Leaf roughness, as defined by Holloway (1970), included venation pattern, shape and size of epidermal cells, cuticular ornamentation and trichomes. He characterized trichome distributions as being either "open," in which case wettability is enhanced, or "closed," in which case the surface becomes more water repellent. The morphology of the waxes could also influence wettability — those with a distinct bloom generally being less wettable (Holloway, 1970). Glaucousness in wheat has also been correlated with measured contact angles (Netting and von Wettstein-Knowles, 1973).

Holloway's chemical effects can be more broadly defined as molecular effects, and these would include normal electrical or ionic fields across the cuticle, and thickness of cuticle, which can affect the energy of adhesion (Finch and Smith, 1979). The energy of adhesion may not be uniform over leaf surfaces, at least for some species (Jagels, 1991). Surface contamination, whether natural or anthropogenic in origin, can also affect "molecular" wettability, and is the basis for using droplet contact angle measurements to monitor air pollution effects on leaf surfaces (Schwartz and Garoff, 1985; Cape et al., 1989).

Leaf geometry and deformability must be added to surface roughness as geometric factors that can significantly affect the angles measured. The cross-sectional geometries of conifer needles, ranging from nearly terete to triangular, present multiple arcuate surfaces which will cause contact angles to deviate from those measured on planar surfaces (Good, 1979; Yuk and Jhon, 1985). Leaf deformability is important as it may be influenced by leaf turgor pressure. Droplet contact angle measurements have been shown to vary depending on the time of day that leaves are measured, presumably as a consequence of osmotic changes within the leaf (Fogg, 1944). Surface roughness can also be affected over time as a consequence of colonization by microflora and fauna or by wind erosion of waxes (Turunen and Huttunen, 1990; van Gardingen et al., 1991; Hoad et al., 1992).

Since pure, flat surfaces have a specific surface free energy (SPSE) which is directly related to the molecular properties of the surface (Gray, 1967), real surfaces, with contamination and micropores, change entropy and adsorption, reduce SPSE from its pure value, and affect droplet contact angles. However, for very rough surfaces (some leaves) geometric forces may overwhelm molecular forces (Good, 1979). Leyton and Armitage (1968) relate this to the pressure of an air film between the droplet and surface. A consequence of these physical principles is that one may be able to effectively measure the effect of air pollution on leaf wettability in certain plant species, but not for others. The likelihood of finding a measurable pollution effect should increase as the geometric effects decrease. An exception to this may be the case of a leaf with a mostly "closed" trichome system, where pollution deposition may act to increase the capillary action between trichomes such that the closed system acts more like an "open" system (as defined by Holloway, 1970). For each leaf system the relative roles of molecular and geometric effects should be assessed in relation to presumed presence or absence of pollution effects.

Thus far the leaf surface has been discussed in its static mode, but one also should consider the leaf from a dynamic perspective to fully evaluate pollution effects. Schönherr et al. (1984) report that lipophilic non-electrolytes are absorbed through the leaf cuticle at rates based on solubility constants, while anions are not sorbed in any significant amount and lipophilic cations will be pH dependent in their sorption. Organic acids may play a significant role for wetted surfaces. Berg (1987) notes that while protons move into a leaf, mineral ions move out, through the cuticle, at slow rates. Measurements of wettability could, thus, be influenced by a combination of dynamic events which may show diurnal variability as well as variability on a longer time scale. Spatial variability is also possible based on the heterogeneity over a leaf surface. Jagels (1991) has shown that pollutants may be deposited on conifer leaf surfaces in non-random patterns.

Finally, heterogeneity between trees at a site needs to be considered in relation to genetic and edaphic variability (Banks and Whitecross, 1971; von Wettstein-Knowles, 1974; Avato *et al.*, 1984).

Measuring wettability

The accuracy and repeatability of droplet contact angle measurements depend upon factors such as purity of water droplets, temperatures of the solid, liquid and gas phases, and droplet size (Good, 1979; Ponter and Yekta-Ford, 1985). The rapidity with which droplet angles must be measured depends on factors such as relative humidity of the surrounding air and hysterisis of advancing and receding droplet angles (Joanny and de Gennes, 1984).

In order to accurately assess the wettability of leaf surfaces, field measurements are generally needed within 1-2 h of leaf collection. Thus, many of the factors that are carefully controlled by physicists are not realistically possible for botanists. However, the quality of the water should be controlled with the use of freshly distilled solutions which have had purity checks (Ponter and Yekta-Ford, 1985), and droplet size should be carefully measured and standardized. Contact angles have been reported to either decrease or increase with decreasing droplet size, depending on the gaseous environment and surface being measured (Ponter and Yekta-Ford, 1985). Thus, droplets need to be of a uniform size and contact angles need to be measured before droplet size changes.

Diurnal fluctuations in droplet contact angle measurements on leaves (Fogg, 1944) as well as controlled measurements on deformable solids (Yuk and Jhon, 1985) suggest that contact angle measurements for an experiment should be standardized to a particular time of day, and position on leaf. Hysterisis, defined in this special case, as the difference between the advancing and receding contact angles, has been extensively discussed in the physics literature (Good, 1973; Finch and Smith, 1979; Joanny and de Gennes, 1984; Schwartz and Garoff, 1985). One solution is to measure the advancing contact angle on a slightly tilted stage, but probably the most practical solution is to measure contact angle within 10-15 seconds after droplet is applied (Dettre and Johnson, 1967). Multiple measurements will confirm whether the range of variability is acceptable.

Pollutant effects

Turunen and Huttunen (1990) reviewed the literature for air pollution effects on conifer needle epicuticular waxes, and elaborated on a number of morphological changes, which will not be restated here. Among ecophysiological consequences they noted that leaf wettability can be a measure of wax structural changes.

Cape (1993) further assessed the literature for leaf-wettability properties of plants exposed to acid rain or polluted cloud. Reductions in contact angle measurements were cited for five broadleaved trees and four conifers exposed to natural or simulated fogs or rain with pH values of 3.0 to 4.2 (Cape, 1993). Trees growing in artificial versus natural environments, trees of varying ages, or leaves in different developmental stages, showed different leaf wettability responses.

Berlyn et al. (1993) found a chamber effect on wettability for red spruce but no treatment (acid mist) effects. Horntvedt (1988) had previously shown a lack of correlation between acid rain treatment and epicuticular wax quantity for Norway spruce and lodgepole pine. Boyce et al. (1991) found that species, age and canopy position as well as elevational changes, affected droplet contact angle measurements for red spruce and balsam fir. Some of the field differences, particularly elevational ones, may be a consequence of varying wind erosion of epicuticular waxes (Wilson, 1984; van Gardingen et al., 1991; Hoad et al., 1992).

Reductions in contact angles for leaves exposed to ozone in chambers have been reported (Barnes et al., 1990; Percy et al., 1992). Percy et al. (1992) found that leaf wettability responded more quickly to ozone than to acid mist treatments of 1-year-old potted red spruce. However, a field study of red spruce along a well-documented pollutant (ozone and acid fog) gradient revealed that a reduction in wettability for red spruce needles was correlated with the greatest exposures to acid fog (pH 3.2) but not with high levels of ozone (Percy et al., 1993). Wax quantity was not correlated with either ozone or fog acidity, but was correlated with total fog exposure.

Other natural or anthropogenic deposits on leaves may affect leaf wettability (Turunen and Huttunen, 1990). Cape et al. (1989) found that leaf wettability increased with increasing amounts of dust ("a mixture of soil-derived particles, soot, biological debris and inorganic salts") on leaf surfaces. Gellini et al. (1985) reported epicuticular wax damage as a consequence of a synergism between surfactants and salts, scavenged by winds and deposited on coastal forests in Italy. Jagels et al. (1989) similarly showed salt deposits for coastal red spruce in the eastern U.S.

The potential synergisms between uncontrolled factors such as those just cited, and the air pollutants being studied create two dilemmas: (1) the pollutant effect on leaf wettability may be partially masked, and (2) the contact angles measured may not be readily compared to other sites or canopy age classes. An example of point (2) can be seen in the wettability measurements for greenhouse-grown, 2-year-old, red spruce seedlings, with contact angles ranging from 82° to 65°, depending on treatment, as compared to 70-year-old trees on the coast of Maine, with lower

102

contact angles ranging from $75°$ to $55°$, depending on exposure to acid fog and ozone (Percy *et al.*, 1992; Percy *et al.*, 1993).

Future possibilities

Cape *et al.* (1989) attempted to assess on a regional basis the effects of multiple air pollutants on leaf wettability of Norway spruce and Scots pine. Leaves were more wettable from low-altitude sites in Britain and the Netherlands than for high altitude sites in Germany (where decline symptoms were most notable). Wax quantity decreased with increasing wettability.

Whether these results are simply a reflection of different habitats, as suggested by the altitudinal differences reported by Boyce *et al.* (1991) or some combination of site and pollution stress is not resolved by this study. But it raises the question: can droplet contact angle measurements be used as a tool for biomonitoring? The studies of Cape *et al.* (1989) and Percy *et al.* (1992, 1993) would suggest that on a region-wide basis, or across age classes, the observed differences will be difficult to interpret. The greatest promise may be for assessing long-term change within a site. This kind of study would also need to be carefully controlled so that measurements would be standardized for: time of year, time of day, position in plant canopy, developmental stage of leaf, proximity in time to pollutant or rain events or other meteorological anomalies (Giese, 1975; Haas, 1977; Golz, 1984). Multiple measurements over leaf surfaces would be needed to ascertain inhomogeneities due to morphological features such as stomates (Jagels, 1991), or previously discussed mechanical abrasion, or epiphyte colonization. Using a set of stringently controlled protocols, changes in leaf wettability over time could provide an early warning for potential forest health risks and as such would be a useful adjunct to air pollution monitoring in rural areas.

References

Avato P, Bianchi G, Salamini F (1984) Genetic control of epicuticular lipids in maize (*Zea mays* L.). *In* Structure, function and Metabolism of Plant Lipids. Siegenthaler PS, Eichenberger W, (*eds*). Elsevier. *pp* 503-506
Bain JM, McBean DG (1967) The structure of the cuticular wax of prune plums and its influence as a water barrier. Aust J Biol Sci 20: 895-900
Baker EA (1974) The influence of environment on leaf wax development in *Brassica oleracea* var. *gemmifera*. New Phytol 73: 955-966
Baker EA, Hunt GM, Stevens PJG 1983 Studies of plant cuticle and spray droplet interactions: A fresh approach. Pesticide Sci 14: 645-658
Banks JCG, Whitecross MI (1971) Ecotypic variation in *Eucalyptus viminalis* Labill. I. Leaf surface waxes, a temperature x origin interaction. Aust J Bot 19: 327-334
Barnes JD, Eamus D, Davison AW, Ro-Poulsen H, Mortensen L (1990) Persistent effects of ozone on needle water loss and wettability in Norway spruce. Environ Pollut 63: 345-363

Berg VS (1987) Plant cuticle as a barrier to acid rain penetration. *In* Effects of Atmospheric Pollutants on Forests, Wetlands and Agricultural Ecosystems Hutchinson TC, Meema KM (*eds*) NATO ASI series, vol. G16 Springer-Verlag *pp* 145-154

Berlin GP, Anoruo AO, Johnson AH, Vann DR, Strimbeck GR, Boyce RL, Silver WL (1993) Effects of filtered air and misting treatments on cuticles of red spruce needles on Whiteface Mountain, NY. J Sustainable Forestry 1(1): 25-47

Boyce RL, McCune DC, Berlyn GP (1991) A comparison of foliar wettability of red spruce and balsam fir growing at high elevation. New Phytol 117: 543-555

Cape JN 1993 Direct damage to vegetation caused by acid rain and polluted cloud: definition of critical levels for forest trees. Environ Pollut 82: 167-180

Cape JN, Paterson IS, Wolfenden J (1989) Regional variation in surface properties of Norway spruce and Scots pine needles in relation to forest decline. Environ Pollut 58: 325-342

Clark JB, Lister GR (1985) Photosynthetic action spectra of trees. I. The relationship of cuticle structure to the visible and ultraviolet spectral properties of needles from four coniferous species. Plant Physiol 55: 407-413

Dettre RH, Johnson RE (1967) Contact angle hysteresis — porous surfaces. *In* Wetting, SCI monograph 25, London. pp. 144-155

Finch JA, Smith GW (1979) Contact angle and wetting. Minerals Sci Engineering 11(1): 36-63

Fogg GE (1944) Diurnal fluctuation in a physical property of leaf cuticle. Nature 3912: 515

Fogg GE (1947) Quantitative studies on the wetting of leaves by water. Proc Royal Soc B 134: 503-552

Franssen I (1991) Changes in frost hardiness and epicuticular wax in Norway spruce seedlings in response to frequency of acid mist application. Joint Report of Dept. of Air Pollution, Wageningen, The Netherlands, and Institute of Terrestrial Ecology, Edinburgh, Scotland. 67 pp

Gellini R, Pantani F, Grossoni P, Bussotti F, Barbolani E, Rinnalo C (1985) Further investigation on the causes of disorder of the coastal vegetation in the park of San Rossore (central Italy). Eur J For Path 15: 145-157

Giese BN (1975) Effects of light and temperature on the composition of epicuticular wax of barley leaves. Phytochem 14: 921-929

Golz P (1984) Composition and surface structures of epicuticular waxes from different organs of jojoba. *In* Structure, Function and Metabolism of Plant Lipids Siegenthaler PA, Eichenberger W, (*eds*) Elsevier. *pp* 507-511

Good RJ (1979) Contact angles and the surface free energy of solids. Surface Colloid Sci 11: 1-29

Good WR (1973) A comparison of contact angle interpretations. J Colloid Interface Sci 44(1): 63-71

Gray VR (1967) Contact angles, their significance and measurement. *In* Wetting. SCI monograph 25, London. *pp* 99-111

Haas K (1977) Einfluss von Tempatur und Blattalter auf das Cuticularwachs von *Hedera helix*. Biochem Physiol Pflanzen 171(5): 25-31

Hanover JW, Reicosky DA (1971) Surface wax deposits on foliage of *Picea pungens* and other conifers. Amer J Bot 58: 681-687

Hoad SP, Jeffree CE, Grace J (1992) Effects of wind and abrasion on cuticular integrity in *Fagus sylvatica* L. and consequences for transfer of pollutants through leaf surfaces. Agri, Ecosystems and Environ 42: 275-289

Holloway PJ (1970) Surface factors affecting the wetting of leaves. Pesticide Sci 1: 156-163

Horntvedt R (1988) The effect of acid precipitation on epicuticular wax in Norway spruce and lodgepole pine. Medd Norsk Inst Skogforskning 40(13): 1-13

Jagels R (1991) Biophysical aspects of fog deposition on the needles of three conifers. J Exp Bot 42(239): 757-763

Jagels R, Carlisle J, Cunningham R, Serreze S, Tsai P (1989) Impact of acid fog and ozone on coastal red spruce. Water Air Soil Pollut 48: 193-208

Jeffree CE, Johnson PC, Jarvis PG (1971) Epicuticular wax in the stomatal antechamber of Sitka spruce and its effects on the diffusion of water vapour and carbon dioxide. Planta 98: 1-10

Joanny JF, de Gennes PG (1984) A model for contact angle hysteresis. J Chem Phys 81(1): 552-562

Leyton L, Armitage IP (1968) Cuticle structure and water relations of pine needles of *Pinus radiata* (D. Don). New Phytol 67: 31-38

Leyton L, Juniper BE (1963) Cuticle structure and water relations of pine needles. Nature 198: 770-771

Martin JT, Juniper BE (1970) The Cuticles of Plants. Edward Arnold Ltd. London.

McDonald RE, Nordby HE, McCollum TG (1993) Epicuticular wax morphology and composition are related to grapefruit chilling injury. HortScience 28(4): 311-312

Mecklenburg RA, Tukey HP Jr, Morgan JV (1966) A mechanism for the leaching of calcium from foliage. Plant Physiol 41: 610-613

Netting AG, von Wettstein-Knowles P (1973) The physico-chemical basis of leaf wettability in wheat. Planta 114: 289-309

Percy KE, Baker EA (1990) Effects of simulated acid rain on epicuticular wax production, morphology, chemical composition and on cuticular membrane thickness in two clones of Sitka spruce (Picea sitchensis (Bong.) Carr.). New Phytol 116: 79-87

Percy KE, Jensen KF, McQuattie CJ (1992) Effects of ozone and acidic fog on red spruce needle epicuticular wax production, chemical composition, cuticular membrane ultrastructure and needle wettability. New Phytol 122: 71-80

Percy KE, Jagels R, Marden S, McLaughlin CK, Carlisle J (1993) Quantity, chemistry and wettability of epicuticular waxes on needles of red spruce along a fog-acidity gradient. Can J For Res 23(7): 1472-1479

Ponter AB, Yekta-Ford M (1985) The influence of environment on the drop size -contact angle relationship. Colloid and Polymer Sci 263: 673-681

Schönherr J, Kerler F, Riederer M (1984) Cuticular lipids as interface between plant and environment. *In* Structure, Function and Metabolism of Plant Lipids Siegenthaler PA, Eichenberger W (*eds*) Elsevier *pp* 491-498

Schuepp PH, Hendershot WH (1989) Nutrient leaching from dormant trees at an elevated site. Water Air Soil Pollut 45: 253-264

Schwartz LW, Garoff S (1985) Contact angle hysteresis on heterogeneous surfaces. Langmuir 1(2): 219-232

Sherbatskoy T, Klein RM (1983) Response of spruce and birch foliage to leaching by acid mists. J Environ Qual 12: 189-195

Troughton JH, Hall DM (1967) Extracuticular wax and contact angle measurement on wheat (*Triticum vulgare* L). Aust J Biol Sci 20: 509-525

Turunen M, Huttenen S (1990) A review of the response of epicuticular wax on conifer needles to air pollution. J Environ Qual 19: 35-45

van Gardingen PR, Grace J, Jeffree CE (1991) Abrasive damage by wind to the needle surfaces of *Picea sitchensis* (Bong) Carr and *Pinus sylvestris* L. Plant, Cell Environ 14: 185-193 von Wettstein-Knowles P (1974) Gene mutation in barley inhibiting the production and use of C_{26} chains in epicuticular wax formation. FEBS Letters 42: 187-191

Waldman JM, Hoffman MR (1988) Nutrient leaching from pine needles impacted by acidic cloudwater. Water Air Soil Pollut 37: 193-101

Wilson J (1984) Microscopic features of wind damage to leaves of *Acer psendoplatanus* L. Annals of Botany 53: 73-82

Yuk SH, Jhon MS (1985) Contact angles on deformable solids. J Colloid Interface Sci. 110(1): 252-257

Air Pollutants and the Cuticle: Implications for Plant Physiology

Markus Riederer, Reinhard Jetter, Claus Markstädter and Lukas Schreiber
Physiologische Ökologie
Universität Kaiserslautern
Postfach 30 49
D-67653 Kaiserslautern
Federal Republic of Germany

Abstract

The physiologically most important function of the plant cuticle is to control the loss of water and of inorganic and organic constituents of plants via the surfaces of leaves and fruits. In a polluted environment, the cuticle may also affect the rates of uptake of extraneous chemicals. It will be shown how the essential transport properties of plant cuticles can be determined experimentally using intact leaves, isolated cuticles, and reconstituted cuticular waxes. The transport properties will be related to the physico-chemical properties of the permeants in order to achieve a general description of pollutant transport across the leaf/atmosphere interface and to assess the relative contributions of the cuticular and the stomatal pathways to the total flow rate. The correlation of the transport properties of cuticles with their chemical composition will be discussed and a model of the molecular structure of the transport-limiting barrier of the cuticle and of epicuticular waxes be presented. The effects of chemicals of anthropogenic and biogenic origin on cuticular permeability will be described quantitatively.

Introduction

In a physiological sense, the most important function of the plant cuticle is to control the rate of exchange of matter between the interior of leaves, fruits or primary stems of higher plants and the environment. This applies primarily to the exchange of water (transpiration), endogenous organic and inorganic compounds (leaching), and the penetration of inorganic and organic pollutants. Air pollutants may interact with the cuticle in two different ways: (*i*) they may be transported across the cuticle, and (*ii*) they may affect the transport properties of the leaf/atmosphere interface. The transport of pollutants across this interface can be studied at three levels of complexity by using (*i*) whole leaves, (*ii*) isolated cuticular membranes, and (*iii*) reconstituted cuticular waxes.

Investigations into the uptake of organic solutes from an aqueous solution into intact needles from different species of conifers showed that needles are very efficient scavengers for lipophilic organic pollutants from precipitation. A rapid adsorption process to the microscopically rough surface of the needle cuticle was followed by a slow penetration across the transport barrier of the cuticle into the interior of the needles (Schreiber and Schönherr, 1992). The degree of scavenging and the rates of uptake increased with increasing effective surface areas. The effective

NATO ASI Series, Vol. G 36
Air Pollutants and the Leaf Cuticle
Edited by K. E. Percy et al.
© Springer-Verlag Berlin Heidelberg 1994

surface area reflects the roughness arising from epicuticular wax structures and can be obtained from adsorption isotherms (Schreiber and Schönherr, 1993a).

Isolated cuticular membranes can be used to examine how cuticular permeance of pollutants depends on various factors. The permeance is the proportionality coefficient relating a given driving force to the resulting flow rate. It is a composite entity consisting of the mobility of the permeant (expressed by the diffusion coefficient), its relative solubility (expressed by the partition coefficient), and the thickness of the transport barrier. The permeances of 2,4-dichlorophenoxyacetic acid (2,4-D) across isolated cuticular membranes from 10 plant species varied over more than two orders of magnitude. Fruit cuticles generally had higher permeances than leaf cuticles (Riederer and Schönherr, 1985). The permeance of the cuticular membrane of a given plant species depends primarily on the lipophilicity of the solute (expressed either by the cuticle/water or the octanol/water partition coefficient). Quantitative relationships are available for predicting cuticular transport properties from basic physico-chemical properties (Kerler and Schönherr, 1988a, 1988b; Schönherr and Riederer, 1989) and non-empirical descriptors of molecular structure (Sabljic et al., 1990).

Volatile pollutants can potentially take two parallel pathways across the leaf/atmosphere interface: the stomatal and the cuticular path. Which one of the two is preferred depends on the transport properties of the cuticle and the properties of the pollutant (Riederer, 1990; Riederer, 1994). For a given leaf cuticle, the ratio of cuticular to total flow across the interface is high for compounds with low volatility (expressed by Henry's law constants or air/water partition coefficients) and/or high lipophilicity (expressed by the octanol/water partition coefficient). The cuticular component of total flow will be negligible for compounds with high volatility and/or low lipophilicity. Thus, lipophilic organic pollutants will be primarily taken up via the cuticle while stomatal transport will account for most of the uptake of inorganic pollutants. When the stomata are closed or absent (e.g., in fruit) the cuticle is the only port of entry available for all types of pollutants.

Pollutants and other environmental factors may also affect the properties of the cuticular transport barrier. Various naturally occurring and anthropogenic organic compounds (including alcohols, organic pollutants and surfactants) have been shown to increase the permeance of plant cuticles (Riederer and Schönherr, 1990; Geyer and Schönherr, 1989; Schönherr et al., 1991; Schönherr, 1993a, 1993b).

The prerequisite for analysing and understanding these effects is a deeper knowledge of the molecular structure of the cuticular transport barrier. Based on solid state nuclear magnetic resonance, x-ray diffraction, and differential scanning calorimetry studies as well as on the quantitative analysis of selected cuticular waxes by capillary gas chromatography-mass spectrometry a tentative model for the structure of cuticular waxes has been proposed (Basson and

Reynhardt, 1988; Riederer and Schneider, 1990; Reynhardt and Riederer, 1991, 1993; Riederer and Schreiber, 1993). According to this model, cuticular wax consists of three zones differing in molecular arrangement and composition: (*i*) the crystalline zone A (regular arrangement of the long aliphatic chains of the wax constituents in an orthorhombic crystal subcell), (*ii*) the solid amorphous zone B (chain ends of long-chain aliphatics together with some short-chain aliphatics and cyclic compounds), and (*iii*) the amorphous zone D (short-chain aliphatics and cyclic compounds) having a solid amorphous and a liquid amorphous fraction.

Diffusion of solutes across cuticular wax can occur only in the amorphous zone while the crystalline zone A represents an excluded volume. Consequently, in terms of diffusive transport, cuticular wax is comparable to a technical barrier membrane consisting of a permeable matrix and impermeable flakes embedded within this matrix. The impermeable flakes (in waxes: crystalline domains) reduce the cross-sectional area available for diffusion and, due to tortuousity, increase the actual length of the diffusion path. Any factor reducing the volume fraction of the crystalline zone A and/or the lateral extension of the crystalline flakes will increase the diffusion coefficient of a permeating solute (Riederer and Schreiber, 1993). Potential factors having this effect can be chemical or physical factors and an altered composition of cuticular waxes.

A model system has been devised for investigating the effects of external factors on the mobility of permeants in cuticular waxes (Schreiber and Schönherr, 1993b). ^{14}C-labelled solute is mixed with cuticular wax and this mixture is deposited as a thin film on the surface of an inert substrate. The kinetics of desorption of this solute into an aqueous receiver medium are measured and the diffusion coefficient is obtained by applying an appropriate form of the Second Fickian law. First results show that this system is a very potent tool for investigating pollutant effects on the cuticular transport barrier.

In addition to the impact of chemical and physical factors on the physical structure of cuticular waxes, changes in composition may also affect their transport properties. Such alterations may result from effects on wax biosynthesis and/or on the cuticular wax already deposited in and on the surface of the cuticle. First experimental evidence for the latter possibility has been obtained from studies on the composition of the cuticular waxes of *Fagus sylvatica* leaves during the course of a vegetation period (Markstädter, 1993). The coverages of hexacosanal and octacosanal rapidly declined after they had reached a maximum just when leaf expansion had come to a halt. Simultaneously, the coverages of hexacosanoic and octacosanoic acids increased. In vitro experiments showed that UV-B radiation may induce this reaction by transforming long-chain alkanals in the solid state partly to the corresponding alkanoic acids and partly to a insoluble residue of as yet unknown composition and structure.

Numerous reports show that external factors may also influence the fine structure of epicuticular wax structures. Evidence has been produced showing that the tubular crystals found on the cuticular surfaces of conifers and many additional plant species consist of the S enantiomer of nonacosan-10-ol. In vitro experiments demonstrated that the formation of tubular aggregates from this compound proceeded spontaneously under kinetic control (rapid crystallisation from solution). The crystal habit formed was independent of the substrate on which the crystallisation had been performed and was also independent of the solvent used. Under thermodynamic control (slow crystallisation from solution or from the melt), nonacosan-10-ol crystallised in platelets. This finding demonstrates that both tubules and platelets are two habits of the crystals of one and the same compound. The large surface energy associated with the tubular habit leads to the thermodynamic instability of this form and consequently can be regarded as the driving force for the transition from the tube-like to the plate-like habit (Jetter 1993). This transition from one crystal habit to another may be accelerated by the action of pollutants and various environmental and physiological factors.

References

Basson I, Reynhardt EC (1988) An investigation of the structures and molecular dynamics of natural waxes: II. Carnauba wax. J Phys D: Appl Phys 21: 1429-1433

Geyer U; Schönherr J (1989) In vitro test for effect of surfactants and formulation on permeability of plant cuticles. *In* Cross B, Scher HB (*eds*) Pesticide formulations: innovations and developments. ACS Symposium Series 371, American Chemical Society, Washington, *pp* 22-33

Jetter R (1993) Chemische Zusammensetzung, Struktur und Bildung röhrenförmiger Wachskristalle auf Pflanzenoberflächen. Doct. Diss., Universität Kaiserslautern

Kerler F, Schönherr J (1988a) Accumulation of lipophilic chemicals in plant cuticles: prediction from octanol/water partition coefficients. Arch Environ Contam Toxicol 17: 1-6

Kerler F, Schönherr J (1988b) Permeation of lipophilic chemicals across plant cutiles: prediction from partition coefficients and molecular volumes. Arch Environ Contam Toxicol 17: 7-12

Markstädter C (1993) Die Wirkung von Umweltfaktoren auf die Zusammensetzung der kutikulären Wachse von Blättern von *Fagus sylvatica* L. Doct. Diss., Universität Kaiserslautern

Reynhardt EC, Riederer M (1991) Structure and molecular dynamics of the cuticular wax from leaves of *Citrus aurantium* L. J Phys D: Appl Phys 24: 478-486

Reynhardt EC, Riederer M, Schneider G (1993) Structures and molecular dynamics of plant waxes. II. Cuticular waxes from leaves of *Fagus sylvatica* L. and *Hordeum vulgare* L. Eur Biophys J (*in press*)

Riederer M, Schönherr J (1985) Accumulation and transport of (2,4-dichlorophenoxy)acetic acid in plant cuticles: II. Permeability of the cuticular membrane. Ecotoxicol Environ Safety 9: 196-208

Riederer M, Schönherr J (1990) Effects of surfactants on water permeability of isolated plant cuticles and on the composition of their cuticular waxes. Pestic Sci 29: 85-94

Riederer M, Schreiber L (1993) Waxes — the transport barriers of plant cuticles. *In* Hamilton RJ (*ed*) Waxes. The Oily Press, West Ferry (*in press*)

Riederer M (1990) Estimating partitioning and transport of organic chemicals in the foliage/atmosphere system: discussion of a fugacity-based model. Environ Sci Technol 24: 829-839

Riederer M (1994) Partitioning and transport of organic chemicals between the atmospheric environment and leaves. *In* Trapp S, McFarlane C (*eds*) Plant contamination: Modeling and simulation of organic chemicals processes. Lewis Publishers, Chelsea, MI (*in press*)

Riederer M; Schneider G (1990) The effect of the environment on the permeability and composition of *Citrus* leaf cuticles. II. Composition of soluble cuticular lipids and correlation with transport properties. Planta 180: 154-165

Sabljic A, Güsten H, Schönherr J, Riederer M (1990) Modeling plant uptake of airborne organic chemicals. 1. Plant cuticle/water partitioning and molecular connectivity. Environ Sci Technol 24: 1321-1326

Schönherr J, Riederer M (1989) Foliar penetration and accumulation of organic chemicals in plant cuticles. Rev Environ Contam Toxicol 108: 1-70

Schönherr J, Riederer M, Schreiber L, Bauer H (1991) Foliar uptake of pesticides and its activation by adjuvants: Theories and methods of optimization. *In* Frehse H (*ed*) Pesticide chemistry, VCH Verlagsgesellschaft, Weinheim, *pp* 237-253

Schönherr J (1993a) Effects of monodisperse alcoholethoxylates on mobility of 2,4-D in isolated plant cuticles. Pestic Sci 38: 155-164

Schönherr J (1993b) Effects of alcohols, glycols and monodisperse ethoxylates alcohols on mobility of 2,4-D in isolated plant cuticles. Pestic Sci (*in press*)

Schreiber L, Schönherr J (1992) Uptake of organic chemicals in conifer needles: Surface adsorption and permeability of cuticles. Environ Sci Technol 26: 153-159

Schreiber L, Schönherr J (1993a) Contact areas between waxy leaf surfaces and aqueous solutions: Quantitative determination of specific leaf surface contact areas. J Exp Bot 44 (*in press*)

Schreiber L, Schönherr J (1993b) Mobilities of organic compounds in reconstituted cuticular wax of barley leaves: Determination of diffusion coefficients. Pestic Sci 38: 353-361

Cuticular Characteristics in the Detection of Plant Stress Due to Air Pollution — New Problems in the Use of these Cuticular Characteristics

Jean-Pierre Garrec
INRA - Centre de Recherches forestières de Nancy
Laboratoire Pollution atmosphérique
54280 Champenoux
France

Abstract

The foliar surface, and particularly the cuticle, is the first zone of impact of air pollutants on leaves. At the level of the cuticle, it is mainly studies on the modifications of the physico-chemical properties of the waxes that allow us to detect and estimate plant stress. However, during recent years, with modifications in the nature and level of air pollution (decrease of primary pollutants: SO_2, HF; increase of secondary pollutants: O_3, acid deposits; increase of nitrogen deposits; increase of organic micropollutants; appearence of global environmental problems: CO_2, climatic change), the physiological impact on plants and in particular on the cuticle is different.

For this reason, new problems have appeared and use of cuticular characteristics in the detection of plant stress due to air pollutants has recently evolved. Some examples are given, but much remains to be done to understand the effects on the cuticle of these new modifications of the atmospheric environment of plants.

Introduction

The cuticular characteristics most widely used for detection of air pollution impact on leaves are:

Epicuticular wax morphology

These characteristics describe destruction and disturbance (erosion, fusion, flattening, melting) of epicuticular waxes. Information is gathered from observations by scanning electron microscopy (SEM), but some authors have tried to quantify their observations, *e.g.*, partitioning into different classes (Turunen and Huttunen, 1991; Tuomisto and Neuvonen, 1993), or physical data from the SEM (Schreiber and Rentschler, 1990). Generally, morphological and chemical features of cuticular waxes are closely related.

Droplet contact angle

This technique characterizes and measures changes in the type of condition of epicuticular waxes and, at the same time, is a measure of leaf wettability (cf. this workshop).

NATO ASI Series, Vol. G 36
Air Pollutants and the Leaf Cuticle
Edited by K. E. Percy et al.
© Springer-Verlag Berlin Heidelberg 1994

Quantity of waxes

These characteristics provide a measure not only of observable changes at the epicuticular wax level, but also of hidden modifications at the level of intracuticular waxes.

The quantity of cuticular waxes may be determined gravimetrically or colorimetrically (Ebercon *et al.*, 1977).

Remarks

On conifer needles, observation of changes in epicuticular waxes caused by air pollutants has often been conducted at the level of the stomata. But experiments with trichloroacetate (T.C.A.) have demonstrated that epistomatal waxes have a different biosynthesis than epicuticular waxes *sensu stricto* (Frannich and Wells, 1980). An understanding of the specific reactions of these two surface waxes is needed.

It should also be noted that to use cuticular characteristics and to understand the relation between air pollutants and their effects on the leaf surface, we must first consider three problems:

i)	the evolution of the nature and level of air pollutants up to now;
ii)	the new atmospheric environment of the leaf; and
iii)	the interactions in the gas mixture at the leaf surface.

The evolution of the nature and level of air pollutants up to now

Since the begining of the industrial era, the air pollution history has continuously evolved (Garrec, 1993) and in western Europe we can identify two different periods up to the present day:

- 1900-1980
- 1980-1990

Briefly, the first period is characterized by high air concentration of primary pollutants (SO_2, HF). These pollutants came from easily identifiable sources and initiated local pollution.

At the level of the effect of these primary air pollutants on trees, they were characterized by a high physiological impact with specific foliar necrosis and by tree mortality in localized areas of polluted forests.

However, the air pollutants present during the second period are generally secondary air pollutants (*e.g.*, O_3, wet and dry acid deposits) at a lower air concentration. They originate from reactions of different emissions from remote sources difficult to identify, and are involved in large-scale, trans-boundary pollution.

The interaction of these secondary pollutants with trees is characterized by a loosely defined physiological impact: yellowing of the leaves and a decrease in the vitality of the trees. These pollutants initiate, generally in combination with climatic stress, forest decline with very irregular localization over a regional scale.

We have to keep in mind this evolution of the nature and level of air pollutants before using cuticular characteristics to detect plant stress due to air pollution.

As an illustration of this, we have established an inexhaustive compilation of the scientific literature in relation to the effect of air pollutants on cuticular characteristics over these two periods (Table 1).

Table 1   Effect of air pollutants on cuticular characteristics from the scientific literature

Air Pollutant	Cuticular characteristic				
	Wax erosion (morphological modification)	No wax erosion	Increasing wax amount	Decreasing wax amount	No effect on wax amount
SO$_2$	*******	****	**	**	**
O$_3$	*****	*****		**	**
Acid rain	******	***	*	*	**
Acid mist	**	**			**
NH$_3$	**	**			

The data presented in Table 1 show the variability of the response of the plant surface and/or the inhomogeneity of the action of these pollutants.

However from these data, it seems likely that primary air pollutants, such as SO$_2$, have a deleterious effect on cuticular wax characteristics.

Unlike the concentrated primary pollutants, secondary air pollutants, such as O$_3$ or acid deposits, seem to have a less evident impact on the waxes. Indeed most of the results indicate that the effect of these less concentrated secondary pollutants resembles the aging process and is not at all pollutant specific (Gunthardt-Goerg and Keller, 1987; Lutz *et al.*, 1990).

The new atmospheric environment of the leaf

In future, in relation to the continuous evolution of air pollution such as the increasing levels of trace gases in the atmosphere, new environmental problems are likely to occur at the leaf surface.

Some of these new problems have already been defined:

- increasing CO_2 levels;
- higher flux of UV-B radiation due to increasing concentration of CFC and N_2O;
- increasing level of organic micropollutants; and
- increasing nitrogen deposits from industrial (NOx) or agricultural (NH_3) activities.

Although we have little information on the repercussions of these new problems on cuticular characteristics, their potential effects could be important and have to be considered, in conjunction with the effect of the secondary air pollutants already present.

The first results suggest a significant effect of increasing levels of CO_2 and UV-B on wax quantity (Thomas and Harvey, 1983; Steinmüller and Tevini, 1985) but actually conflicting results have been obtained (cf. this workshop).

It has been demonstrated that a large accumulation of organic micropollutants occurs in the cuticular waxes (Schönherr and Riederer, 1989; Granier and Chevreuil, 1992). From this observation, a new method could be developed using this cuticular characteristic to evaluate the level of organic pollutants in the air and potential effects on the leaf. But, at the same time, little is known about the impact of these organic micropollutants on the physico-chemical properties of cuticular waxes. As a lot of organic pollutants are present in the atmosphere, much remains to be done to understand their specific interactions with cuticular waxes.

Increasing levels of nitrogen deposition have recently been observed at the plant surface (Favilli and Messini, 1990; Thijsse and Baas, 1990). These high inputs may increase the leaf surface microflora and modify the relation between air pollutants and the cuticular waxes, with consequently a different impact of the pollutants at the leaf surface (Schreiber and Schönherr, 1992).

We have also to consider that, at the level of the whole tree, CO_2 and NOx act as fertilizers, and different experiments have shown that fertilization of trees increases their cuticular wax quantity (Chiu et al., 1992).

The interactions in the gas mixture at the leaf surface

At present due to the simultaneous presence, in particular at low concentrations of oxidants and organic compounds in the air, the possibility of reactions between these anthropogenic gases, the biogenic gases, and the leaf surface has to be taken into account.

The boundary layer, a zone close to the leaf surface where there is a transition from turbulent to molecular diffusion of gases (laminar flow) is mainly concerned with these reactions.

Indeed this zone is defined by high aerodynamic (or diffusive) resistance compared to free atmosphere, which depends particularly on wind velocity and leaf micromorphology (surface roughness).

Consequently, air pollutants and other gases are temporarily "confined" in this layer before reaching the cuticular waxes and foliar tissues through the stomata.

It may be considered that three phases exist simultaneously at the boundary layer:

- a liquid phase which corresponds to the currently observed film of water on the leaf surface, and water linked with the polar groups of the cuticle;
- a lipid phase determined by the epicuticular waxes, but also by the cutin; and
- a gas phase at the level of the boundary layer *sensu stricto*.

Two sources of gases supply the boundary layer:

gases from the free atmosphere

- air pollutants (SO_2, O_3, NOx, VOC)
- naturally occurring gases (CO_2, H_2O)

gases from the interior of the leaf originating from leaf metabolism

- natural emissions: H_2O, CO_2, terpenes (α pinene), isoprene (Rasmussen, 1972)
- stress emissions: C_2H_4 from the effect of air pollutants
- biological reduction of pollutants: H_2S from SO_2 and NH_3 from NOx. A schematic representation of what happens at the boundary layer is shown in Figure 1.

The lipid phase

This phase acts first as a large sink of organic micropollutants in relation to their large accumulation in the epicuticular waxes (Schönherr and Riederer, 1989).

But reactions of secondary air pollutants on waxes may occur:

- reactions of H_2SO_4 with hydroxyl groups of long chain primary and secondary alcohols (Holloway *et al.*, 1976) give sulphated and sulphonated compounds such as polar products with surfactant properties (for example sodium lauryl sulphonate).
- reactions of O_3 on waxes:
  * reaction of O_3 on lipids (lipid peroxidation), but other oxidants like PAN, OH radicals may give the same products.
  * reaction of O_3 on unsaturated hydrocarbons which gives aldehydes (reaction catalyzed by H_2O).

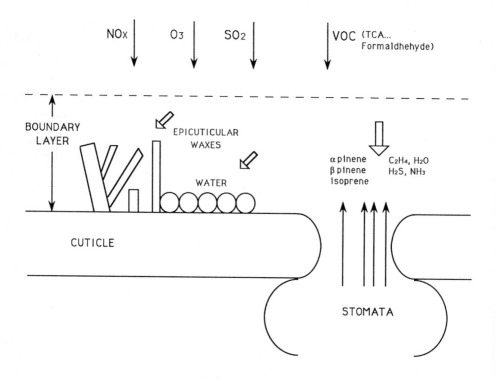

Figure 1   Principal components acting in the boundary layer reactions.

      *   reaction of O_3 on saturated hydrocarbons (alkanes) which gives alcohols (reaction catalyzed by H_2O).

This phase is also a sink for primary pollutants:

- a large accumulation of SO_2 in the waxes is observable;
- an accumulation of NOx in the cuticle exists with phenolics nitrated by gaseous NO_2.(Van Hove *et al.*, 1989; Kisser-Priesack *et al.*, 1990).

The liquid phase (water)

This phase may be a sink for many soluble pollutants: NH_3, SO_2, O_3, TCA, formaldehyde.

But formation of new products may occur in this phase:

- $NH_3 + SO_2 \rightarrow (NH_4)_2 SO_4$: formation of ammonium sulfate
- $O_3 + H_2O \rightarrow H_2O_2$: formation of hydrogen peroxide
- $O_3 + H_2O \rightarrow OH^-$: formation of hydroxyl radicals
- formation of acids: $SO_2 + H_2O \rightarrow H_2SO_4$
                          $NOx + H_2O \rightarrow HNO_3$

These reactions are catalyzed by O_3 or NH_3 or hydrocarbons (terpenes).

N.B. In the liquid phase, numerous ions are also present, from the leaching of foliar mineral elements.

The gas phase

In this phase we can observe:

- sources of oxidants
  $NO_2 + O_2 \rightarrow NO + O_3$
  $NO_2 + O_2 \rightarrow PAN$ (peroxyacetyl nitrate)

These reactions are catalyzed by UV radiation and unsaturated hydrocarbons (anthropogenic hydrocarbons or isoprene, α pinene) (Elstner *et al.*, 1985).

- sources of acids
  $SO_2 + O_3 \rightarrow SO_4^{--}$
  $NOx + O_3 \text{ Æ } NO_3^-$

These reactions are catalyzed by terpenes (Stangl *et al.*, 1988)

- Interactions of O_3 with unsaturated hydrocarbons
  $O_3 + C_2H_4 + H_2O_2 \rightarrow 2 HCHO + H_2O_2$ (formaldehyde + hydrogen peroxide (Elstner *et al.*, 1985).
  $O_3 + C_2H_4$ (ethylene) $\rightarrow HOCH_2O_2H$
  $O_3 + C_5H_8$ (isoprene) $\rightarrow HOCH_2O_2H$ or $HCHO$ (formaldehyde)

This formation of hydroxymethyl hydroperoxide ($HOCH_2O_2H$) is catalyzed by H_2O (Gäb *et al.*, 1985)

$O_3 + \alpha$ pinene $\rightarrow$ pinonaldehyde (Yokouchi and Ambe, 1985).

- Interactions of O_3 with vapor phase water
  $O_3 + H_2O \rightarrow OH^- + 2O_2$ $OH^- + C_5H_8$ (isoprene) $\rightarrow HCHO$ (formaldehyde)

(Cox *et al.*, 1980)
$$O_3 + H_2O \rightarrow H_2O_2$$

- Other reactions exist:
$$SO_2 + NH_3 \rightarrow (NH_4)_2SO_4$$
$$SO_2 + formaldehyde \rightarrow hydroxymethanesulfonate$$

Generally speaking, it appears that on the leaf surface at the boundary layer the lipid phase is mainly a sink of organic pollutants, the liquid phase a source of acids and OH radicals, and the gas phase a large source of new organic products.

Remember that the different reactions noted in the different phases are expected to happen, and that the probabilities of such reactions depend upon many factors: presence of the reactive gases, presence of water, velocity of the reactions, minimal concentration of the gases.

We think that these reactions and accumulation at the boundary layer have to be increasingly taken into account, as they can have a significant additive effect upon the physiological impact of the presently low concentration of pollutants. But their specific impact on waxes is still unknown and has to be studied.

In conclusion, from all these reactions and accumulations at the boundary layer, we can hypothesize that the gases reaching the epicuticular waxes and the plant tissues will be:

- the air pollutants present in the free atmosphere but at a different concentrations;
- new reactive products (acids, organic compounds) which could be more phytotoxic than the products they originated from.

In relation to these remarks, it is easy to understand that difficulties will arrive when we try to establish the real relationship between the concentration of the pollutants in the free atmosphere and their observed physiological effects on the cuticular waxes.

Conclusion

It is observed that at the leaf surface, cuticular characteristics are modified by air pollutants. However, with the evolution of different air pollutants and the possible presence of new reactive products at the boundary layer, it seems increasingly difficult to use "classical" cuticular characteristics to specifically detect plant stress due to air pollutants.

The use of more sophisticated cuticular characteristics, such as the modification of chemical composition of cuticular waxes could, in future, be a more appropriate and more sensitive method of detecting new plant stress and understanding at what level these recent air pollutants act: have they a direct (chemical) effect on the waxes, or an indirect effect on the wax biosynthesis or a more general impact on the plant metabolism (aging)?

References

Chiu ST, Anton LH, Ewers FW, Hammerschmidt R, Pregitzer KS (1992) Effects of fertilization on epicuticular wax morphology of needle leaves of Douglas fir, *Pseudotsuga menziesii* (Pinaceae). Amer J Bot 79: 149-154

Cox RA, Derwent RG, Williams MR (1980) Atmospheric photooxidation reactions, rates, reactivity and mechanisms for reaction of organic compounds with hydroxyl radicals. Environ Sci Technol 14: 57

Ebercon A, Blum A, Jordan WR (1977) A rapid colorimetric method of epicuticular wax content of sorghum leaves. Crop Sci 17: 179-180

Elstner EF, Osswald W, Youngman RJ (1985) Basic mechanisms of pigment bleaching and loss of structural resistance in spruce (*Picea abies*) needles: advances in phytomedical diagnostics. Experientia 41: 591-597

Favilli F, Messini A (1990) Nitrogen fixation at phyllospheric level in coniferous plants in Italy. Plant Soil 128: 91-95

Franich RA, Wells LG (1980) Inhibition of *Pinus radiata* primary needle epicuticular wax biosynthesis by trichloroacetate. J Exp Bot 31: 829-838

Gäb S, Hellpointner E, Turner WV, Korte F (1985) Hydroxymethyl hydroperoxide and bis (hydroxymethyl) peroxide from gas-phase ozonolysis of naturally occurring alkenes. Nature 316: 535-536

Garrec JP (1993) Évolution de la pollution atmosphérique en France. De la pollution locale à la pollution globale. Ann. Géographie (*in press*)

Granier L, Chevreuil M (1992) On the use of tree leaves as bioindicators of the contamination of air by organochlorines in France. Water Air Soil Poll 64: 575-584

Günthardt-Goerg MS, Keller T (1987) Some effects of long-term ozone fumigation on Norway spruce. II Epicuticular wax and stomata. Trees 1: 145-150

Holloway PJ, Jeffree CE, Baker EA (1976) Structural determination of secondary alcohols from plant epicuticular waxes. Phytochemistry 15: 1768-1770

Kisser-Priesack GM, Bieniek D, Ziegler H (1990) NO_2 binding to defined phenolics in the plant cuticle. Naturwissenschaften 77: 492-493

Lütz C, Heinzmann V, Gülz PG (1990) Surface structures and epicuticular wax composition of spruce needles after long term treatment with ozone and acid mist. Environ Poll 64: 313-322

Rasmussen RA (1972) What do the hydrocarbons from trees contribute to air pollution? J Air Pollut Ass 22: 537-543

Schönherr J, Riederer M (1989) Foliar penetration and accumulation of organic chemicals in plant cuticles. Rev Environ Contam Toxicol 108: 1-70

Schreiber H, Rentschler I (1990) Eine quantitative methode zur charakterisierung von oberflächenstrukturen auf blättern und nadeln. Angew Bot 64: 37-50

Schreiber L, Schönherr J (1992) Leaf surface microflora may significantly affect studies of foliar uptake of chemicals. Bot Acta 105: 345-347

Stangl H, Kotzias D, Geiss F (1988) How forest trees actively promote acid deposition. Naturwissenschaften 75: 42-43

Steinmüller D, Tevini M (1985) Action of ultraviolet radiation (UV-B) upon cuticular waxes in some crop plants. Planta 164: 557-564

Thijsse G, Baas P (1990) "Natural" and NH_3-induced variation in epicuticular needle wax morphology of *Pseudotsuga menziesii* (Mirb.) Franco. Trees 4: 111-119

Thomas JF, Harvey CN (1983) Leaf anatomy of four species grown under continuous CO_2 enrichment Bot Gaz 144: 303-309

Tuomisto H, Neuvonen S (1993) How to quantify differences in epicuticular wax morphology of *Picea abies* (L.) Karst. needles. New Phytol 123: 787-799

Turunen M, Huttunen S (1991) Effect of similated acid rain on the epicuticular wax of Scots pine needles under northerly conditions. Can J Bot 69: 412-419

Van Hove LWA, Adema EH, Vredenberg WJ, Pieters GA (1989) A study of the adsorption of NH_3 and SO_2 on leaf surfaces. Atmos Environ 23: 1479-1486

Yokouchi Y Ambe Y (1985) Aerosols formed from the chemical reaction of monoterpenes and ozone. Atmos Environ 19: 1271-1276

Evaluation of Pollutant Critical Levels from Leaf Surface Characteristics

J Neil Cape
Institute of Terrestrial Ecology
Bush Estate
Penicuik
Midlothian EH26 0QB
United Kingdom

Abstract

The Critical Level for a given pollutant must be determined from controlled experiments, although it will be applied under field conditions. Experiments that have studied leaf surface properties in response to air pollutants are reviewed in terms of their relevance to the establishment of Critical Levels, with particular reference to conifers. Although all pollutants may have an indirect effect on leaf surfaces by affecting the biosynthesis of cuticle and surface waxes, organic vapours and acidity in cloud and rain may also have direct effects on waxes *in situ*. Leaf surface characteristics include quantity and quality of epicuticular waxes, and leaf wettability. Previously unpublished data on leaf wettability of spruce species exposed in the field and in controlled environments to a range of pollutants are used to illustrate some of the problems of interpretation that may arise.

Introduction

The concept of Critical Levels has been developed as a tool to aid in the formation of policy for air pollution control. The concept relies on the identification of limits of exposure to pollutants that will protect vegetation from any measurable adverse effects. Mapping of pollutant concentrations then identifies regions of 'exceedence' where vegetation may be regarded as 'at risk' for damage. Critical Levels may, in principle, be defined for specific vegetation types or ecosystems, but in practice they are defined at the simplest level in terms of the most sensitive ecosystem or vegetation type in a given region. As information becomes available, higher level maps may be produced to take into account the different sensitivities of plant species, or the interaction of pollutant effects with climatic and edaphic factors.

Two aspects of air pollution research must be used to define the Critical Level maps. One is the accurate establishment of pollutant concentrations in air or in precipitation across a region, both in terms of long-term averages and short-term peak concentrations; the other is the development of reliable dose-response relationships that can be used to set the Critical Level for a given pollutant, *i.e.*, the largest concentration (or more precisely, the greatest exposure) at which no adverse effect can be measured. The Critical Level for a given pollutant, as defined above, depends on the type of measurement used to assess plant response. For agricultural crops, dose-response experiments have used crop yield as the appropriate measure, but there is no

NATO ASI Series, Vol. G 36
Air Pollutants and the Leaf Cuticle
Edited by K. E. Percy et al.
© Springer-Verlag Berlin Heidelberg 1994

obvious measure generally applicable to natural vegetation. Responses may be measured, for example, in terms of reduced growth, change in species composition, visible injury, reduced photosynthetic activity or in changes to leaf surface properties.

The leaf surface is the barrier between a plant and the atmosphere, and controls the uptake of both gaseous and aqueous pollutants from the atmosphere. As such, it is the part of the leaf most exposed to attack by air pollutants, and any changes in its structure induced by air pollutants may have far reaching consequences for the whole plant. The physical and chemical structure of the leaf surface, and the ways in which the exchange of gases and ions are regulated by the leaf surface, have been widely studied in relation to air pollution, often as diagnostic markers of air pollution stress in industrialised areas (*e.g.*, Huttunen and Laine, 1983; Cape, 1986; Crossley and Fowler, 1986; McIlveen, 1992) or in relation to perceived 'decline' of forest trees (*e.g.*, Grill *et al.*, 1987; Simmleit and Schulten, 1987; Cape *et al.*, 1989).

The effects of air pollutants on leaf surfaces, both in the field and in controlled experiments, have been reviewed recently (Cape, 1988; Turunen and Huttunen, 1990; Huttunen, *this volume*; Percy *et al.*, *this volume*). This paper examines the extent to which the effects of air pollutants on leaf surfaces, as opposed to whole leaves or whole plants, may be used to define 'Critical Levels' for individual pollutants and thereby identify geographical regions 'at risk' from air pollution damage.

Potential interactions of pollutants with leaf surfaces

Before considering the available data on pollutant effects, it will be helpful to identify the potential mode of action of the major air pollutants on leaf surfaces. Any gaseous pollutant that enters the leaf through stomata has the potential to cause some disturbance to the normal metabolic processes of the leaf, and may, therefore, indirectly affect the leaf surface by modifying the biosynthesis of cuticle or surface waxes. Changes to metabolic processes may also be caused by ions in aqueous solution on the leaf surface, if they penetrate the leaf. These will be referred to as **indirect** effects of pollutants on leaf surfaces. The chemical action of air pollutants on leaf surface structures will be referred to as **direct** effects.

Ozone is a powerful oxidant which is known to affect plant metabolic processes after foliar absorption. It reacts with unsaturated molecules, leading to fragmentation of long-chain molecules, but such compounds are rarely present in leaf surface waxes. Large atmospheric concentrations of ozone are associated with high levels of photochemical activity involving the rapid production and consumption of a wide range of highly reactive free-radicals. These may be able to react directly with the saturated hydrocarbons of leaf surface waxes, but no experimental data exist to demonstrate the importance of this type of chemical reaction. Ozone itself, therefore, may have little direct effect on leaf surfaces, but its presence may indicate the possibility of changes caused by free-radicals.

Sulphur dioxide also affects plant metabolic processes and may, therefore, influence the biosynthesis of leaf surface components. In terms of direct chemical effects it may react with aldehydes, if present in leaf surface waxes, but is more likely to have an effect through its dissolution in water to form an acid, with the resultant acid hydrolysis of long-chain esters in leaf surface waxes (see below).

Nitrogen oxides (NO and NO$_2$) are lipid soluble, and may react directly with the cuticle, but only after very long exposure to very large concentrations (Lendzian and Kerstiens, 1988). This reaction is unlikely to be important in most situations. Both gases may also cause disruption to metabolic processes following foliar absorption, but much less is known about potential effects than for ozone or sulphur dioxide.

Ammonia may also affect plant metabolism and, therefore, leaf surface development, but the potential for direct effects is likely to be negligible.

Organic compounds such as solvents and biogenic molecules (terpenes, isoprene, *etc.*) are very soluble in lipids, and may accumulate from the atmosphere, leading to changes in the physical properties and structure of the semi-crystalline surface waxes (Riederer, *this volume*). Indirect effects on plant metabolism following absorption are not known. Plants themselves may be major sources of such molecules, usually released through stomata, so that the leaf surface around the stomata may show the greatest effects. As emission of small organic molecules (ethene, ethane, ethanol) can be stimulated by stress to the plant, including pollutant-induced stress, this may be a potential route for the indirect effect of pollutants which do not themselves react directly with surface waxes.

Acidity and other ions in solution in rain and cloud may also have indirect effects, but direct reaction with leaf wax molecules is unlikely, with the possible exception of ester hydrolysis after long or frequent exposure to large concentrations. Percy *et al.* (*this volume*) has shown that significant hydrolysis of isolated wax esters can occur after exposure to acid at pH 1 for 1-3 h, *i.e.*, a dose of 0.1 - 0.3 mol l^{-1}.h. At high elevations, cloud with an average pH of 3.5 may occur for over 1000 h per year (Cape, 1993), giving an equivalent dose of more than 0.3 mol l^{-1}.h even neglecting periods when surfaces are wet after immersion in cloud. As esters usually comprise only a small proportion of surface waxes, the overall role of ester hydrolysis on wax structure and leaf surface chemistry is not known.

Particles of soot or dust, whether suspended in air or in water droplets, are unlikely to cause adverse indirect effects unless they accumulate to the extent where stomata are clogged or light is excluded from the leaf surface. They may, however, have a direct physical effect on leaf surface structures by abrasion, or by lowering the surface free energy of wax crystallites, permitting more rapid transition to amorphous structures (Riederer, *this volume*).

In addition to pollutant effects, leaf surfaces are subject to physical abrasion by other leaves, by wind-borne dust, by impacting rain and cloud droplets, and by snow. Although most gaseous and aqueous pollutants have the potential to disrupt the development of leaf surfaces, only organic molecules and acid solutions, and possibly nitrogen oxides, are likely candidates for causing direct effects on established leaf surfaces.

Methods for studying pollutant effects on leaf surfaces

Three techniques have been widely used to investigate the effects of air pollutants on leaf surfaces: electron microscopy, to study morphological changes; measurement of leaf wettability (contact angle) as an integrating assessment of physical and chemical change which may have a lasting influence on leaf vitality; and chemical composition of leaf surface waxes, as an indicator of direct chemical effects and/or changes in biosynthesis.

Effects of pollutants observed by scanning electron microscopy (SEM) are often described as the erosion or melting of the surface waxes which have a semi-crystalline structure during and immediately after leaf expansion (Huttunen, *this volume*). The effects may be seen as the acceleration of a natural process of 'erosion' with age, but is more properly described as a transition to a more stable amorphous form of the principal component responsible for the tubular structures on leaf surfaces, 10-nonacosanol (Riederer, *this volume*). Changes in structure are usually accompanied by changes in wettability (Jagels, *this volume*). Chemical changes in surface waxes have shown a preference for shorter chain lengths possibly leading to softer, more erodible waxes. The proportions of wax compounds with different functional groups (alcohols, alkanes, esters, *etc.*) and the timing of wax production may also be affected (Percy *et al.*, *this volume*).

Critical Levels and leaf surface properties

The latest Critical Levels for the major air pollutants are shown in Table 1, as amended by a Workshop on Critical Levels held at Egham (UK) in 1992 (UNECE, 1993). The value for ozone was defined in terms of the concentration above a threshold concentration (40 ppbV[1]) during daylight hours, when plant stomata are expected to be open, and able to absorb the gas. This definition is a measure of the cumulative dose above the threshold which is absorbed by the plant leaf. The current level is tentative, and will be reviewed in November 1993, but is greatly

---

[1] 1 ppbV = 10^{-9} atm = 1 nl l[-1]

Table 1. Critical Levels (UNECE, 1993)

Ozone

Expressed as cumulative (daylight hours x concentration above 40 ppbV) during the growing season. Critical Level = 300 ppbV.h

Sulphur dioxide
annual and winter means (μg m^{-3})

agricultural crops	30
natural vegetation and forests	20
cyanobacterial lichens	10

Nitrogen oxides (NO + NO$_2$)
all vegetation (μg m^{-3})

annual mean	30
4-h mean	95

Ammonia
all vegetation (μg m^{-3})

1 hour	3300
1 day	270
1 month	23
1 year	8

Ions in cloud/rain
forests in cloud 10% time: 0.3 mM (H$^+$) with 0.15 mM non-sea SO$_4$=.

---

exceeded over most of Western Europe. It has also been greatly exceeded in controlled experiments that have studied effects of ozone on leaf surfaces. No obvious effects on surface waxes were observed by SEM of Norway spruce needles exposed to 50 or 150 ppbV ozone, even though underlying cuticular structures were altered (Günthardt-Goerg and Keller, 1987). Other SEM studies have observed 'melting' or 'erosion' of surface waxes at similar concentrations at or above 50 ppbV ozone (see Turunen and Huttunen, 1990). There is no evidence of direct effects caused by short-term exposure to much higher concentrations (Trimble et al., 1982; Kerfourn and Garrec, 1992; Percy et al., this volume).

Changes in chemical composition have been noted after exposure to concentrations of 70 ppbV and above over 42 days (Percy et al., 1992).

Increases in wettability (decreases in contact angles) have been observed after exposure of Norway spruce needles to 78 ppbV (Barnes et al., 1990a) or 100 ppbV (Barnes et al., 1990b), but measurements were made on air-dried needles, whose surfaces may have been altered by different rates of drying (Barnes et al., 1990a). Contact angle measurements are very sensitive

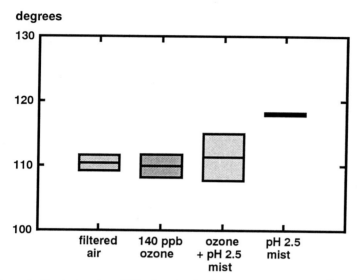

Figure 1   Contact angles of 0.2-μL water droplets on current-year needles of Norway spruce
seedlings exposed to episodes of ozone at 140 ppb, or to filtered air, in combination
with twice weekly applications of acidic mist (H_2SO_4 + NH_4NO_3) at pH 2.5 (Cape
et al., 1990). Boxes show the range of mean vaues from two replicate chambers per
treatment.

to leaf turgor (Fogg, 1944). Contact angle measurements (Cape *et al.*, 1990) on fresh Norway
spruce needles exposed to episodes of 140 ppbV ozone throughout the growing season showed
no change in wettability (Figure 1), even with the addition of acid mist.

From these results it would appear that leaf surface properties may not be sensitive indicators of
ozone exposure, even for concentrations well above the Critical Level.

For sulphur dioxide, much of the morphological information from SEM studies has come from
field sampling along gradients of sulphur dioxide concentration, where SO_2 has been assumed
to be the pollutant responsible for enhanced 'erosion' of leaf surface structures. Effects are
observed in the range 10-50 μg m^{-3} (see Turunen and Huttunen, 1990). However, controlled
experiments with seedlings have not shown such a clear picture, with long-term exposure to
concentrations up to 150 μg m^{-3} having no apparent effect on Norway spruce (Günthardt-Goerg
and Keller, 1987). 'Erosion' of pine waxes has, however, been seen at similar concentrations
(Riding and Percy, 1985; Krause and Houston, 1983). Measurements of wettability (contact
angle) from a range of controlled environment experiments with SO_2 have shown systematic
increases in contact angle in response to SO_2 concentrations close to the Critical Level (Table
1).

degrees

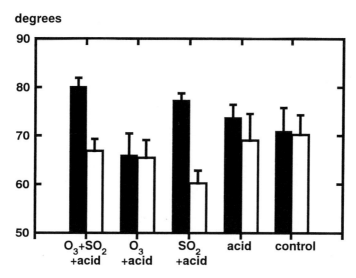

Figure 2   Contact angles of 0.2-µL water droplets on Norway spruce needles. Saplings were exposed over 30 months in open-top chambers at Hohenheim, Germany, to SO_2 (average 50 µg m^{-3}), O_3 (summer average 70 µg m^{-3}) and/or acid rain (pH 4) with
'control' treatment of filtered air and rain at pH 5 (Seufert *et al.*, 1990); samples
were taken in October 1987, and contact angles were measured according to Cape
et al.(1989). Error bars are standard deviation of five trees per chamber. Solid bars:
current-year needles, open bars: 1-year-old needles.

Long-term exposure of saplings in chambers (Figure 2), or of large trees to filtered and unfiltered
air in field exclusion chambers (Figure 3) show similar enhancements in contact angle to those
measured on needles from saplings from a field fumigation experiment (Figure 4). In the latter
case, there was a clear positive correlation between contact angle and sulphur content of the
needles (Cape *et al.*, 1994). Similar results were observed on seedlings exposed to episodes of
SO_2 in closed chambers (Figure 5). Concentrations of SO_2 close to the Critical Level clearly
show measurable responses in leaf surface properties, so that changes in these properties may be
useful in refining the Critical Levels for conifers, and possibly for other natural vegetation.

There have been no relevant studies involving exposure of plants to NO or NO_2 alone, although
these gases have been components of exposures by road sides (see below). In these experiments,
however, it is more likely that hydrocarbon vapours caused the observed effects.

There have been a few studies with ammonia, some at concentrations approaching the Critical
Levels listed in Table 1. Thijsse and Baas (1990) exposed Douglas fir over 14 months to a range
of concentrations between 25 and 100 µg m^{-3}, as well as to ambient and filtered air. Increased

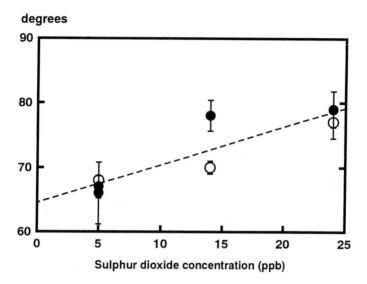

Figure 3   Contact angles on fresh needles from mature Norway spruce trees growing in an open-top chamber filtration experiment at Edelmannshof, Germany (Arndt, 1987). Samples were taken from four trees in each treatment (filtered or unfiltered chambers, or open air) in August 1988 and measured using the method of Cape et al. (1989). Boxes show 95% Confidence Intervals.

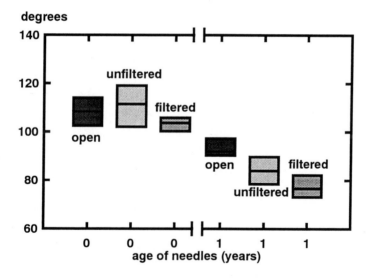

Figure 4   Contact angles of 0.2-μL water droplets on current-year Norway spruce needles. Variation of contact angle with SO_2 concentration in an open-air fumigation experiment at Liphook, southeast England (Cape et al., 1994). Error bars are standard deviation of six trees per plot. Solid symbols: ambient O_3, open symbols: 1.3 x ambient O_3.

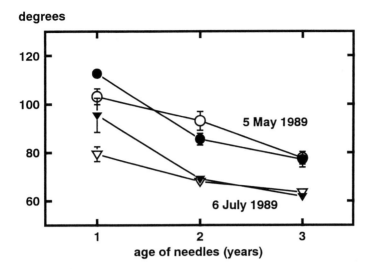

Figure 5 Contact angles of 0.2-μL water droplets on Norway spruce needles after exposure in hemispherical glasshouses at Lancaster University (Lucas *et al.*, 1987) to summer ozone fumigation (70 ppb, 7 h d⁻¹, 5 d wk⁻¹) followed by short episodes of up to 200 ppb SO_2 at 3-week intervals between March and May 1989. Contact angles were measured according to Cape *et al.* (1989). Error bars show range of means from two replicate chambers. Open symbols : filtered air, solid symbols: SO_2 treated.

fusion of wax tubules was observed at all concentrations above ambient. Another fumigation at higher concentrations (180 μg m⁻³ over 13 weeks) also showed fusion of surface waxes on Douglas fir (van der Eerden *et al.*, 1992). By contrast, winter fumigation (August - May) of Scots pine with 60 or 100 μg m⁻³ showed no effect (Bacic *et al.*, 1992). In this case it is significant that fumigation was not applied during needle expansion and development of the leaf surface.

The role of organic pollutants has been tested in both laboratory and field experiments. Raddi *et al.* (1992) treated three conifer species with solutions containing an ionic surfactant at concentrations similar to those observed during rain storms, and showed significant fusion of surface waxes after 10 weeks of treatment, similar to those observed in the field (see also Paoletti, *this volume*). Wax degradation was observed, using SEM, after exposing young Norway spruce and silver fir trees in summer beside a motorway (Sauter *et al.*, 1987; Sauter and Pambor, 1989). Significant wax degradation was seen, particularly in Norway spruce, after only 1 week. In view of these findings, it may be appropriate to attempt to set Critical Levels for volatile organic compounds (VOCs) in addition to inorganic pollutants.

The largest body of literature on air pollutant effects on leaf surfaces is related to exposure to acidic rain or mist. Studies up to 1989 were reviewed by Turunen and Huttunen (1990), who highlighted the sensitivity of leaf surface wettability to acidic solutions with pH as high as 4.6 (Percy and Baker, 1987). For conifers, the acidity at which effects have been observed is at pH 3.5 and below, and this was the basis for setting the Critical Levels for ions in cloud (Table 1; see also Cape, 1993). The explicit inclusion of sulphate concentrations reflects results from experiments that showed a different pattern of response to nitric acid and sulphuric acid at the same pH (Rinallo et al., 1986). Further evidence for an effect of sulphate ions comes from experiments with Douglas fir, where treatment with ammonium sulphate solutions at a concentration of 2.5 mM led to collapse of wax surface structures (van der Eerden et al., 1992). Different effects of solutions containing nitrate and sulphate ions on the wettability of Norway spruce have also been observed in chamber experiments (Figure 6).

The dose-response of contact angle for simulated mist containing all four major ions (H^+, NH_4+, $SO_4=$, NO_3-) was also investigated; a clear treatment effect in autumn (Figure 7) was less pronounced in winter, 8 weeks after the experiment ceased and plants were exposed to rain and snow (Figure 8). Absolute values for the contact angles in these two sets of measurements are

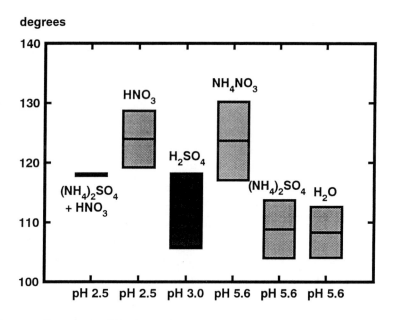

Figure 6   Contact angles of 0.2-μL water droplets on current-year Norway spruce needles exposed to simulated mist in open-top chambers at ITE Edinburgh. Boxes show the range of mean values for two replicate chambers for each treatment. Measurements were made according to Cape et al. (1989). For experimental details see Cape et al.(1988).

degrees

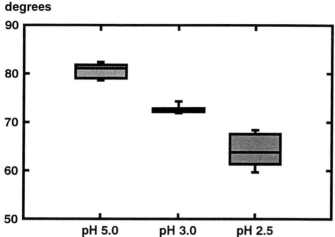

Figure 7   Contact angles of 0.2-μL water droplets on current-year red spruce needles exposed to simulated
             mist in open-top chambers at ITE Edinburgh. Measurements were made in autumn during the period
             of treatment using the method of Cape *et al.*(1989). For experimental details see Fowler *et al.*(1989).
             Boxes show the 95% limits to mean values of five trees per treatment.

degrees

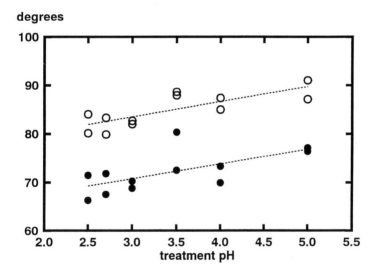

Figure 8   Contact angles of 0.2-μL water droplets on current-year red spruce needles exposed to simulated mist
             in open-top chambers at ITE Edinburgh. Measurements were made in February after exposure during
             the previous growing season, using the method of Cape *et al.* (1989). For experimental details see
             Fowler *et al.* (1989). Individual points are the means of five trees per chamber, with two replicate
             chambers per treatment. open symbols: current-year needles (formed during treatment) solid symbols:
             1-year-old needles (formed before treatment)

not directly comparable, as slightly different methods were used. The similar response of 1-year-old needles (Figure 8), formed before the treatments started, suggests that the effect of the acidic mist was a direct effect on the leaf surface, and not simply an effect on wax biosynthesis.

This response of contact angle to acid mist treatment is not limited to red spruce; experiments in the same chambers with clonal grafts of Sitka spruce also showed a significant increase in wettability (decrease in contact angle) in both clones measured (Figure 9). Similar effects for Norway spruce seedlings were seen in glasshouse experiments using the same treatments (Figure 10).

Although these experiments have been conducted with concentrations well above the Critical Level of concentration, they show a uniformity of response in three spruce species. Other recent experimental studies of the response of leaf surface wettability to simulated acid mist, and recent field experiments, have been summarised by Cape and Percy (1993). Measurable effects in terms of changes in surface wax chemistry and leaf wettability are observed at concentrations and exposures observed in the field. The Critical Level for ions in cloud (Table 1) was partly derived from measurements on leaf surfaces (Cape, 1993), and such measurements may be useful in extending and refining the Critical Level for other tree species and for natural vegetation.

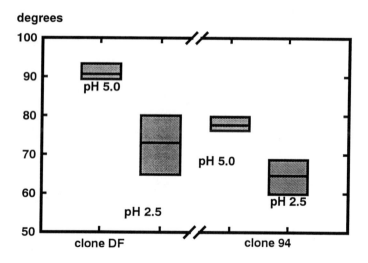

Figure 9   Contact angles of 0.2-μL water droplets on current-year Sitka spruce needles, measured using the method of Cape *et al.* (1989). Clonal grafts were treated with simulated acid mist in open-top chambers; for experimental details, see Leith *et al.* (1992). Boxes show the range of mean values for two replicate chambers per treatment.

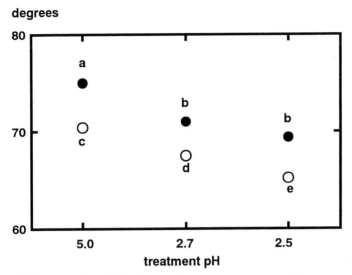

degrees

Figure 10 Contact angles of 0.2-μL water droplets on current-year Norway spruce needles. Two-year-old seedlings were raised in a glasshouse and misted using a hand sprayer during needle elongation (Franssen, 1991). Open symbols: after 8 weeks treatment, solid symbols: after 11 weeks treatment. Values with the same letter are not significantly different (p > 0.05).

Conclusions

In controlled experiments, leaf surface properties are sensitive indicators of exposure to some pollutants, notably sulphur dioxide and acidity in simulated cloud and rain. It is not yet clear whether observed changes have been caused indirectly, through effects on the development of leaf cuticles, or are the result of a direct effect on wax components on the leaf surface. There is very little information on effects of ammonia or of nitrogen oxides on leaf surface properties. By contrast, leaf surfaces appear to be rather insensitive to ozone in experiments, but may show a greater response to the wide range of airborne compounds and free radicals that make up the photochemical air pollution for which ozone is a useful surrogate. In particular, the potential for direct effects of organic vapours on leaf surfaces should be addressed experimentally, with a view to defining Critical Levels for volatile organic compounds (VOCs).

The sensitivity of leaf surface structures to concentrations of pollutants close to the Critical Level suggests that the use of such measurements may be helpful in refining the Critical Level for individual plant species. Care must be taken, however, in controlled experiments, to be sure that the observed changes are caused by exposure to the pollutant of interest, and not by the growing conditions used. Whether plants are grown in controlled environment chambers or in a glasshouse can cause large changes in leaf surface properties (Cape and Percy, 1993).

Acknowledgments

Fergus MacLean, Bruce Riddoch and Alison Shaw contributed to the measurements of contact angles presented above. Grateful thanks go also to researchers throughout Europe, for access to plant material from the experiments cited above. The research projects that provided material at ITE Bush were supported by the United States Department of Agriculture (Spruce/Fir Co-operative), the Commission of the European Communities, the UK Department of the Environment and the Natural Environment Research Council.

References

Arndt U (1987) Open-top chamber projects in Hohenheim and Edelmannshof. *In* Microclimate and Plant Growth in Open-Top Chambers. Air Pollution Report 5 (EUR 11257), Commission of European Communities, Brussels. *pp* 299-317

Baic T, Baas P, van der Eerden, LJM (1992) Needle wax surface structure of *Pinus sylvestris* as affected by ammonia. Acta Bot Neerlandica 41: 167-181

Barnes JD, Brown KA (1990a) The influence of ozone and acid mist on the amount and wettability of the surface waxes in Norway spruce [*Picea abies* (L.) Karst.]. New Phytol 114: 531-535

Barnes JD, Eamus D, Davison AW, Ro-Poulsen H, Mortensen L (1990b) Persistent effects of ozone on needle water loss and wettability in Norway spruce. Environ Poll 63: 345-363

Cape JN (1986) Effects of air pollution on the chemistry of surface waxes of Scots pine. Water Air Soil Poll 31: 393-399

Cape JN (1988) Air pollutant effects on conifer leaf surfaces. *In* Scientific Basis of Forest Decline Symptomatology Cape JN Mathy P (*eds*) Air Pollution Report 15, CEC, Brussels, Belgium. *pp* 149-159

Cape JN (1993) Direct damage to vegetation caused by acid rain and polluted cloud: definition of critical levels for forest trees. Environ Poll 82: 167-180

Cape JN, Paterson IS, Wolfenden J (1989) Regional variation in surface properties of Norway spruce and Scots pine needles in relation to forest decline. Environ Poll 58: 325-342

Cape JN, Fowler D, Eamus D, Murray MB, Sheppard LJ, Leith ID (1990) Effects of acid mist and ozone on frost hardiness of Norway spruce seedlings. *In* Environmental Research with Plants in Closed Chambers Payer HD, Pfirrman T, Mathy P (*eds*) Air Pollution Report 26, CEC, Brussels, Belgium. *pp* 331-335

Cape JN, Percy KE (1993) Environmental influences on the development of spruce needle cuticles. New Phytol 125: 787-799

Cape JN, Sheppard LJ, Binnie J (1994) Leaf surface properties of Norway spruce needles exposed to sulphur dioxide and ozone in an open-air fumigation system at Liphook. Plant Cell Environ (*in press*)

Fogg GE (1944) Diurnal fluctuation in a physical property of leaf cuticle. Nature 154: 515

Fowler D, Cape JN, Deans JD, Leith ID, Murray MB, Smith RI, Sheppard LJ, Unsworth MH (1989) Effects of acid mist on the frost hardiness of red spruce seedlings. New Phytol 113: 321-335

Franssen I (1991) Changes in frost hardiness and epicuticular wax in Norway spruce seedlings in response to frequency of acid mist application. Internal report: Institute of Terrestrial Ecology, Edinburgh, UK

Grill D, Pfeifhofer H, Halbwachs G, Waltinger H (1987) Investigations on epicuticular waxes of differently damaged spruce needles. Eur J For Path 17: 246-255

Günthardt-Goerg MS, Keller T (1987) Some effects of long term ozone fumigation on Norway spruce. II. Epicuticular wax and stomata. Trees 1: 145-150

Huttunen S, Laine K (1983) Effect of air-borne pollutants on the surface wax structure of *Pinus sylvestris* needles. Ann Bot Fenn 20: 79-86

Kerfourn C, Garrec JP (1992) Modifications in the alkane composition of cuticular waxes from spruce needles (*Picea abies*) and ivy leaves (*Hedera helix*) exposed to ozone fumigation and acid fog: comparison with needles from declining spruce trees. Can J Bot 70: 861-869

Krause CR, Houston DG (1983) Morphological variation in epicuticular wax of SO_2 sensitive and tolerant eastern white pine clones. Phytopathology 73: 1266-1269

Leith ID, Sheppard LJ, Cape JN, Crossley A (1992) Effects of acid mist on visible foliar injury and needle characteristics of mature clonal grafts of Sitka spruce. *In* Air Pollution and Interactions between Organisms in Forest Ecosystems Tesche M, Feiler S (*eds*) IUFRO Working Party P 2.05, Technische Universität Dresden. *pp* 110-114

Lendzian KJ, Kerstiens G (1988) Interactions between plant cuticles and gaseous air pollutants. Aspects of Applied Biology 17, Part 2: 97-104. Association of Applied Biologists , Wellesbourne, Warwick, UK

Lucas PW, Cottam DA, Mansfield TA (1987) A large scale fumigation system for investigating interactions between air pollution and cold stress in plants. Environ Poll 43: 15-28

McIlveen WD (1992) The application of early diagnostic tests for tree dieback to the Ontario situation. For Ecol Manage 51: 61-67

Percy KE, Baker EA (1987) Effects of simulated acid rain on production, morphology and composition of epicuticular wax and on cuticular membrane development. New Phytol 107: 577-589

Percy KE, Jensen KF, McQuattie CJ (1992) Effects of ozone and acid fog on red spruce needle epicuticular wax production, chemical composition, cuticular membrane ultrastructure and needle wettability. New Phytol 122: 71-80

Percy KE, McQuattie CJ, Rebbeck JA (1994) Effects of air pollutants on epicuticular wax chemical composition. *In* Percy KE, Cape JN, Jagels R, Simpson CM (*eds*) Springer, New York (*this volume, pp* 67-79)

Raddi P, Moricca S, Gellini R, di Lonardo V (1992) Effects of natural and induced pollution on the leaf wax structure of three cypress species. Eur J For Path 22: 107-114

Riding RT, Percy KE (1985) Effects of SO_2 and other air pollutants on the morphology of epicuticular waxes on needles of *Pinus strobus* and *Pinus banksiana*. New Phytol 99: 555-563

Rinallo C, Raddi P, Gellini R, di Lonardo V (1986) Effects of simulated acid deposition on the surface structure of Norway spruce and silver fir needles. Eur J For Path 16: 440-446

Sauter JJ, Kammerbauer H, Pambor L, Hock B (1987) Evidence for the accelerated micromorphological degradation of epistomatal waxes in Norway spruce by motor vehicle emissions. Eur J For Path 17: 444-448

Sauter JJ, Pambor L (1989) The dramatic corrosive effect of road side exposure and of aromatic hydrocarbons on the epistomatal wax crystalloids in spruce and fir- and its significance for the 'Waldsterben'. Eur J For Path 19: 370-378

Seufert G, Hoyer V, Wöllmer H, Arndt U (1990) General methods and materials. Environ Poll 68: 205-229

Simmleit N, Schulten, HR (1987) On the impact of acidic precipitation on the epicuticular wax of spruce needles. *In* Acid Rain: Scientific and Technical Advances. Perry R, Harrison RM, Bell JNB, Lester JN (*eds*) Selper Ltd., London. *pp* 546-553

Thijsse G, Baas P (1990) "Natural" and NH3-induced variation in epicuticular needle wax morphology of *Pseudotsuga menziesii* (Mirb.) Franco. Trees 4: 111-119

Trimble JL, Kelly JM, Tolin SA, Orcutt DM (1982) Chemical and structural characterization of the needle epicuticular wax of two clones of *Pinus strobus* differing in sensitivity to ozone. Phytopathology 12: 652-656

Turunen M, Huttunen S (1990) A review of the response of epicuticular wax of conifer needles to air pollution. J Environ Qual 19: 35-45

UNECE (1993) Mapping Critical Levels and Loads. Manual 25/93. Umweltbundesamt, Berlin

van der Eerden LJ, Lekkerkerk LJA, Smeulders SM (1992) Effects of atmospheric ammonia and ammonium sulphate on Douglas fir (*Pseudotsuga menziesii*). Environ Poll 76: 1-9

New Analytical Techniques for Cuticle Chemical Analysis

Hans-Rolf Schulten
Fachhochschule Fresenius
Department of Trace Analysis
Dambachtal 20
65193 Wiesbaden
Germany

Abstract

1) The analytical methodology of pyrolysis-gas chromatography/mass spectrometry (Py-GC/MS) and direct pyrolysis-mass spectrometry (Py-MS) using soft ionization techniques by high electric fields (FI) are briefly described. Recent advances of Py-GC/MS and Py-FIMS for the analyses of complex organic matter such as plant materials, humic substances, dissolved organic matter in water (DOM) and soil organic matter (SOM) in agricultural and forest soils are given to illustrate the potential and limitations of the applied methods.

2) Novel applications of Py-GC/MS and Py-MS in combination with conventional analytical data in an integrated, chemometric approach to investigate the dynamics of plant lipids are reported. This includes multivariate statistical investigations on maturation, senescence, humus genesis, and environmental damages in spruce ecosystems.

3) The focal point is the author's integrated investigations on emission-induced changes of selected conifer plant constituents. Pattern recognition of Py-MS data of desiccated spruce needles provides a method for distinguishing needles damaged in different ways and determining the cause. Spruce needles were collected from both controls and trees treated with sulphur dioxide (acid rain), nitrogen dioxide, and ozone under controlled conditions. Py-MS and chemometric data evaluation are employed to characterize and classify leaves and their epicuticular waxes. Preliminary mass spectrometric evaluations of isolated cuticles of different plants such as spruce, ivy, holly, and philodendron, as well as ivy cuticles treated *in vivo* with air pollutants such as surfactants and pesticides are given.

Introduction

Most of the organic carbon on the Earth's surface is bound in fossil fuels, humic substances, and biological macromolecules and is heteropolymeric, polydisperse, and, to a large extent, insoluble in organic solvents. Therefore, from the standpoint of analytical chemistry, the direct application of wet-chemical, chromatographic and mass spectrometric methods is limited. Whereas the analysis of constituents of natural waxes and epicuticular plant waxes by soft ionization mass spectrometry (Schulten *et al.*, 1986a, 1987) could be performed after extraction, plant materials such as isolated cuticles, leaves, twigs, bark, wood and roots had to be tackled by analytical pyrolysis (Simmleit and Schulten, 1989c). Thus, temperature-controlled thermal degradation of the complex materials was combined with in-source field ionization mass spectrometry of leaves

NATO ASI Series, Vol. G 36
Air Pollutants and the Leaf Cuticle
Edited by K. E. Percy et al.
© Springer-Verlag Berlin Heidelberg 1994

of coniferous and deciduous trees. The main aim was to identify chemical changes due to air pollution on a molecular-chemical basis. Hence, to determine the causes of the widespread forest damages in Germany, spruce (*Picea abies*) (Schulten *et al.*, 1986b) and beech (*Fagus sylvatica*) (Schulten and Simmleit, 1986) were investigated by Py-FIMS in comprehensive, collaborative studies.

The results clearly indicated that the observed forest damage was a multifactor problem. The surfaces of the conifer needles were irreversibly polluted and one interesting point was that manganese dioxide had been impacted into the epicuticular wax layer and was proposed as a possible catalyst in the initial phytotoxic process (Simmleit *et al.*, 1989). Mass spectrometric analyses of the epicuticular wax of spruce showed estolides up to 1800 Dalton and confirmed increasing polymerization of the wax constituents with increasing needle age and, drastically, for needles of the same age, but with increasing damage by pollutants. Moreover, the combination of data from silviculture, botany, meteorology, biochemistry, soil science, *etc.* showed that essentially acid rain causes the observed tree damage (Simmleit *et al.*, 1990).

Multivariate statistical analysis allowed the differentiation and classification of spruce needles by integrated Py-FI mass spectra (Simmleit and Schulten, 1989a,b). Pattern recognition of the thermal degradation products of spruce needles enabled prediction of the specific kind of pollutant damage with about 7% accuracy (Simmleit *et al.*, 1990). It is noteworthy that, due to the complex variation of environmental effects and genetically-derived fluctuations, the epicuticular wax layer could <u>not</u> be used as a bioindicator for leaf damage.

Materials and methods

Cuticle preparations

The investigated isolated cuticles of four plant species, namely spruce, ivy, holly, and philodendron, were a gift from Dr. J.P. Garrec, Centre de Recherche forestière, Laboratoire d'étude de la Pollution atmosphérique, Seichamps, France. In addition, the upper surface of ivy (*Hedera helix*) leaves were treated *in situ* with surfactants and pesticides (Dr. Garrec). The different treatments were with: a) water (T_1); b) tween 80 (0.5%) + DMSO (1%) (T_2), both as standards; c) 9-thiodocanoate (2 mM) + T_2; d) diclofop-methyl (1 mM) + T_2; and e) clofibrate (7 mM) + T_2.

Curie-point pyrolysis-gas chromatography mass spectrometry (Py-GC/MS)

The experimental set-up for Curie-point pyrolyzer coupled to a gas chromatograph on-line with a double-focusing Finnigan MAT 212 mass spectrometer is shown in Figure 1 (Schulten and Schnitzer, 1992).

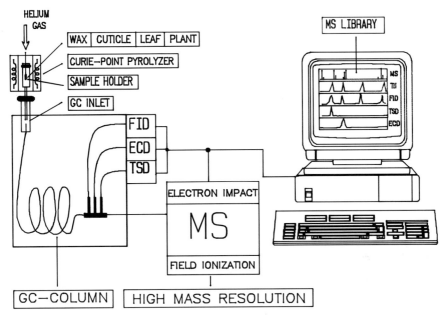

Figure 1   Schematic display of the instrumental set-up of Curie-point Py-GC/MS which monitors the total ion
            intensity (TII) of the mass spectrometer in combination with flame ionization (FID), electron capture
            (ECD) and thermo-sensitive (TSD) detectors. These four independent detector systems for the pyrol-
            ysis products of plant materials give *on-line* information on all ions recorded by electron impact or
            field ionization (FI) for the identification and quantification of organic-, halogene- and nitrogen/
            phosphorous-containing compounds (Schulten *et al.*, 1989).

Direct pyrolysis-field ionization mass spectrometry (Py-FIMS)

For temperature-resolved Py-FIMS, 100-200 µg of a homgeneous, representative sample (wax, cuticle, leaf, root or whole plant) are thermally degraded in the ion-source of a mass spectrometer for a global characterization of the complex biological materials (Schulten *et al.*, 1989). Figure 2 shows schematically the direct introduction system with the quartz crucible for the dried and ground sample which is transferred into the ion source by a heatable/coolable probe, adjusted to the +8 kV potential of the ion source and FI emitter (Schulten *et al.*, 1987). All samples are routinely heated *in vacuo* from 50 to 700°C at a heating rate of 0.5 K^{-1}. About 60 magnetic scans are recorded for the mass range 16-1000 Dalton. These single mass spectra are integrated by the data system, resulting in summed spectra. In general, three to six replicate measurements are performed and the summed spectra averaged to give survey spectra of good reproducibility which is an essential prerequisite for chemometric evaluation of pyrolysis data. For the integration of ion intensities characteristic for classes of compounds, the molecular ions of marker molecules are selected as previously described (Schnitzer and Schulten, 1992). Recently, the potential and

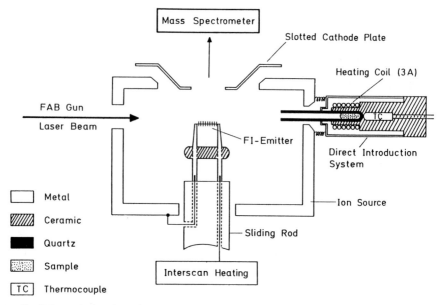

Figure 2   Schematic drawing of the modified experimental set-up for direct pyrolysis-field
ionization mass spectrometry (Schulten *et al.*, 1987).

limitations of analytical pyrolysis for direct, integrated studies of complex organic matter in
geochemistry, agriculture and ecology have been reviewed (Schulten, 1993).

Results and discussion

As illustrated in Figures 3 and 4, the Py-FI mass spectra of isolated cuticles of different plant
species such as spruce, ivy, holly, and philodendron upon visual inspection are clearly different.
Because with soft ionization mainly molecular ions of the pyrolysis products are generated and
mass spectrometric fragmentation is strongly reduced, the base peaks in the spectra at m/z 286,
m/z 584, and m/z 394 allow already qualitative and quantitative distinctions due to specific cuticle
constituents. However, the spectra show high information density with more than 800 nominal
masses and an exhaustive interpretation would be tedious taking into account that many of these
masses are occupied by molecular ions of different chemical composition and isomeric structures.
Thus, as in investigations of the complex organic matter in soils (Schnitzer, 1991; Schnitzer and
Schulten, 1992), it appeared promising to select characteristic classes of compounds as
biomarkers that represent 10-50% of the recorded total ion intensity (TII). As shown in Figure

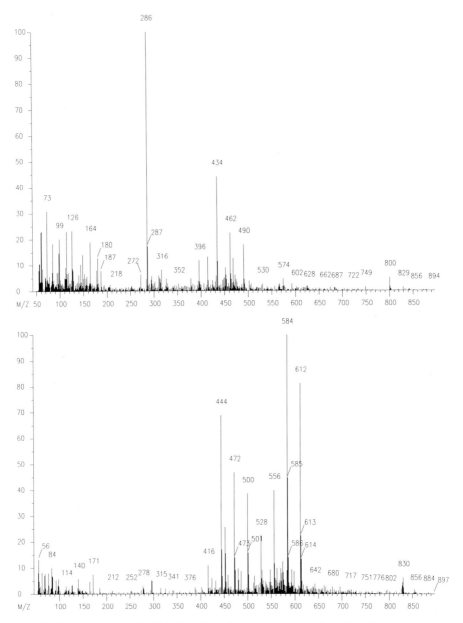

Figure 3 Py-FI mass spectra of isolated cuticles of spruce (upper part) and ivy (lower part).

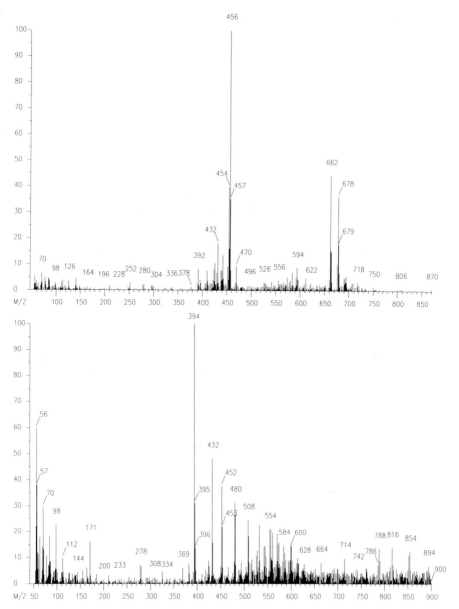

Figure 4   Py-FI mass spectra of isolated cuticles of holly (upper part) and philodendron (lower part).

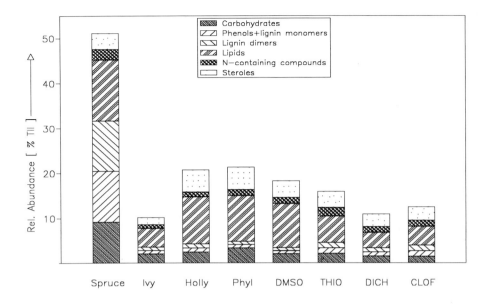

Figure 5   Histogram of selected classes of compounds such as carbohydrates, phenols, and lignin monomers, lignin dimers, lipids, N-containing compounds and steroles tentatively assigned to pyrolysis products of isolated cuticles of spruce, ivy, holly and philodendron (cf. FI mass spectra in Figs 3 and 4). For comparison, similarly obtained data for the *in situ* treatments of the upper surface of ivy (*Hedera helix*) leaves: b) tween 80 (0.5% + <u>DMSO</u> (1%) (T_2); c) 9-<u>thio</u>docanoate (2 mM) + T_2; d) <u>diclo</u>fop (1 mM) + T_2; e) <u>clo</u>fibrate (7 mM) + T_2, are shown to give weak but distinct differences (abbreviations underlined).

5, the differentiation of the four genuine plant cuticles is easily achieved on this wider molecular-chemical basis. The different phytotoxic treatments DMSO, THIO, DICH, and CLOF, however, resulted only in small chemical differences and the effect of air pollution on the ivy cuticle is better analyzed by multivariate statistical methods using pattern recognition, principal component-, factor- and canonical variation-analyses. This chemometric, integrated evaluation of Py-FI mass spectra of whole leaf samples together with environmental, biometric, physiological, chemical, microscopic, and spectroscopic parameters gave reliable and highly reproducible results on the impact of air pollution on spruce needles (Simmleit and Schulten, 1989a,b; Simmleit *et al.*, 1991).

Conclusions

The characterization of forest ecosystems and chemodynamics of plant constituents during maturation and senescence (Hemplfling *et al.*, 1991) indicated that Py-FIMS in combination with

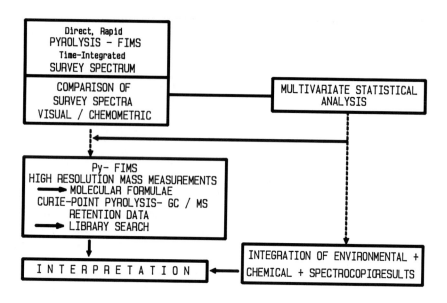

Figure 6   General strategy for the analytical, molecular-chemical investigations of complex mixtures of macro-molecular components by the combination of Curie-point Py-GC/MS and direct Py-FIMS. In an integrated approach, quality control and chemometric evaluation are performed.

pattern recognition is capable of detecting and distinguishing subtle differences in the molecu-lar-chemical composition of complex organic matter. For future work on isolated cuticles and cuticular waxes in connection with the impact of environmental pollutants, it appears that 1) intra- and interlaboratory reproducibility, and 2) objective evaluation (no descriptive approach, no personal effects!) of the data in an integrated multivariate, statistical calculation could be an attractive, complementary tool to the existing methods of cuticle analysis (cf Figure 6).

References

Hemplfling R, Simmleit N, and Schulten H-R (1991) Characterization and chemodynamics of plant constituents during maturation, senescence and humus genesis in spruce ecosystems. Biogeochemistry 13: 27-60

Schnitzer M (1991) Soil organic matter — the next 75 years. Soil Sci 151: 41-58

Schnitzer M and Schulten H-R (1992) The analysis of soil organic matter by pyrolysis-field ionization mass spectrometry. Soil Sci Soc Am J 56: 1811-1817

Schulten H-R (1993) Analytical pyrolysis of humic substances and soils: geochemical, agricul-tural and ecological consequences. J Anal Appl Pyrolysis 25: 97-122

Schulten H-R, Murray KE, and Simmleit N (1987) Natural waxes investigated by soft ionization mass spectrometry. Z Naturforsch 42c: 178-190

Schulten H-R, Schnitzer M (1992) Structural studies on soil humic acids by Curie-point pyrolysis-gas chromatography / mass spectrometry. Soil Sci 153: 205-224

Schulten H-R, Simmleit N (1986) Impact of ozone on high-molecular constituents of beech leaves. Naturwissenschaften 73: 618-620

Schulten H-R, Simmleit N, and Müller R (1987) High-temperature, high-sensitivity pyrolysis-field ionization mass spectrometry. Anal Chem 59: 2903-2908

Schulten H-R, Simmleit N, and Müller R (1989) Characterization of plant materials by pyrolysis-field ionization mass spectrometry: high resolution mass spectrometry, time-resolved high resolution mass spectrometry, and pyrolysis-gas chromatography/mass spectrometry of spruce needles. Anal Chem 61: 221-227

Schulten H-R, Simmleit N, and Rump HH (1986a) Soft ionization mass spectrometry of epicuticular waxes isolated from coniferous needles. Chem Phys Lipids 41: 209-224

Schulten H-R, Simmleit N, and Rump HH (1987b) Forest damage: characterization of spruce needles by pyrolysis-field ionization mass spectrometry. Intern J Environ Anal Chem 27: 241-264

Simmleit N, Herrmann R, Wild A, Forschner W, Gärtner E, Eichhorn J, and Schulten H-R (1990) Multivariate statistical evaluation of biometric, physiological, and chemical parameters describing the vitality of Norway spruce trees. Sci Total Environ 106: 195-219

Simmleit N, Schulten H-R (1989a) Differentiation of spruce needles by integrated field ionization mass spectra and principal component analysis. Biomed Environ Mass Spectrom 18: 1023-1029

Simmleit N, Schulten H-R (1989b) Pattern recognition of spruce trees: an integrated, analytical approach to forest damage. Environ Sci Technol 23: 1000-1006

Simmleit N, Schulten H-R (1989c) Analytical pyrolysis and environmental research. J Anal Appl Pyrolysis 15: 3-28

Simmleit N, Toth A, Szekely T, and Schulten H-R (1989) Characterization of particles adsorbed on plant surfaces. J Environ Anal Chem 36: 7-11

Leaf Cuticles as Mediators of Environmental Influences: New Developments in the Use of Isolated Cuticles

Tim Scherbatskoy
School of Natural Resources
University of Vermont
Burlington, VT 05405 USA

Abstract

Isolated leaf cuticles have been used in our research to characterize trans-cuticular ion diffusion rates under various environmental treatments and to measure cuticular attenuation of solar radiation. These studies have been conducted to understand better the role of the leaf cuticle as a protective barrier against potential environmental stressors including acid rain, ozone and ultraviolet radiation. These studies provide examples of a variety of current research uses for isolated leaf cuticles.

Ion permeability coefficients and exchange rates in isolated cuticles of *Acer, Prunus* and *Citrus* species have been studied using several experimental approaches, including measurement of adsorption kinetics, electrical potential and conductance, and perfusion rates.

Measured electrical (diffusion) potentials under KCl gradients across isolated cuticles are positive, indicating greater cation permeability. Electrical potentials (and permeability coefficients) vary with ionic strength and pH, and affect the driving force for ion diffusion through cuticles. Ion permeability in cuticles of *Prunus serotina* foliage was affected by experimental exposure to ozone and ultraviolet treatments. These studies indicate that cuticle permeability properties can be significantly altered by environmental factors. These and related studies on the ion exchange kinetics of *Acer saccharum* leaf cuticles suggest that foliar "leaching" is dominated by cuticle surface exchange mechanisms, with the magnitude of cuticular ion permeation being relatively small.

In working with various hardwood species, we observed that the success rate for cuticle isolation varies with tree species and time of year. Scanning electron micrographs of inner cuticle surfaces indicate that the effects of enzymatic digestion could vary with exposure time, possibly affecting transport properties of isolated cuticles. Experimental work to test this in *Citrus*, however, showed no significant effect of isolation time on measured diffusion potentials.

Current research to characterize absorption spectra of isolated cuticles is providing information on the optical properties of these cuticles, particularly in the ultraviolet range, where there appear distinct absorption peaks occurring at 304 and 346 nm.

Introduction

The purpose of this paper is to describe several different approaches we have taken to understand the role of leaf cuticles in modulating effects of environmental change on plants. Plants today are subject to a potentially stressful environment that includes precipitation containing various pollutants, tropospheric ozone and other trace gases, increased UV-B radiation, and climate

NATO ASI Series, Vol. G 36
Air Pollutants and the Leaf Cuticle
Edited by K. E. Percy et al.
© Springer-Verlag Berlin Heidelberg 1994

change. For this reason it is important to understand the biological and chemical interactions between the environment and plant canopies, which are often the first parts of plants to encounter these stressors.

As the cuticle covers all portions of the foliage of plants, it serves a role of mediating many environmental signals. Some of these roles are fairly well understood, such as limiting the exchange of gases such as CO_2, O_2, and water vapor. The cuticle is also the structure that ions and molecules must pass through during foliar leaching and uptake, but its role in these processes is not well understood. Other important processes involving leaf cuticles, such as attenuation of solar radiation or control of insect and fungal invasion, have received almost no attention.

The research discussed here deals with our efforts to understand the function of the leaf cuticle in mediating interactions between leaves and acid rain, trace metals, ozone, and ultraviolet radiation. Much of this research has used isolated leaf cuticles to study effects, so this report provides recent examples of this approach. A major thrust of this work is aimed at elucidating the mechanisms of ion transport through the cuticle, which is necessary to quantify accurately and model ion exchange in foliar leaching, foliar uptake and throughfall. In addition, work is presented on aspects of cuticle isolation methods, effects of ozone and ultraviolet radiation on cuticle structure and function, and light absorbance characteristics of isolated cuticles.

Ion exchange properties of cuticle surfaces

There is ample literature describing the contribution of forest canopy leaching to throughfall chemistry (Eaton *et al.*, 1973; Lovett *et al.*, 1985) and the ecological significance of this process in ecosystem nutrient cycles (Parker, 1983). There has been little work, however, investigating the mechanisms of foliar exchange. Both laboratory and field research in this area still tends to treat foliage as a "black box", measuring incident and throughfall solution chemistry and extrapolating plant or ecosystem nutrient fluxes from these measurements. These methods are appropriate for modelling some ecosystem processes, but are not sufficiently exact to predict responses of leaves or whole plants to precipitation or other atmospheric events. Nor does this approach elucidate mechanisms controlling the magnitude, rate or direction of chemical flux. The critical problem here is the lack of information on ion behavior on and in the cuticle, which is the main barrier between the leaf interior and exterior.

We have conducted studies using cleaned surfaces of whole leaves to measure the kinetics of ion exchange between the cuticle and artificial precipitation under controlled conditions. The goals of these experiments were to (a) develop techniques for measuring fluxes of ions between leaf surfaces and individual drops of precipitation, (b) measure the kinetics of ion exchange at pH 5.4 and 3.8, and (c) infer the relative importance of surface ion exchange and trans-cuticle ion diffusion in foliar leaching processes. These studies have been described in detail by Scherbatskoy and Tyree (1990).

Briefly, mature leaves of field-grown sugar maple (*Acer saccharum* Marsh.) were rinsed in deionized water for 1.3 min, surface-dried and placed in a glove box at 90-100% relative humidity. Individual 50-μL drops of artificial precipitation at pH 3.8 and 5.4, representative of regional deposition were applied to the adaxial and abaxial surfaces of leaves, and then quantitatively removed after various time intervals for analysis by graphite furnace atomic absorption spectrometry. Preliminary experiments showed no significant difference in the chemistry of drops placed on or off veins; the literature on foliar exchange over specific parts of leaves, however, is equivocal on this subject (Dybing and Currier, 1961; Lord *et al.*, 1979). Analysis of variance of spatial variability indicated that within the area drops were applied to (no closer than 1 cm to the leaf margins and not on a vein) there were no significant effects of location on drop chemistry. Additional experiments (not discussed here) were also performed by immersing entire leaves in solutions of artificial precipitation, yielding comparable results. It is important to keep in mind that the leaves used in these studies were selected to be free of obvious surface damage.

These experiments showed that Cu^{2+} and Pb^{2+} were rapidly removed from the drops of artificial precipitation, while K^+, Ca^{2+}, and Mg^{2+} increased in drops, and Zn^{2+} concentrations were unaffected (Scherbatskoy and Tyree, 1990). The removal of Cu^{2+} and Pb^{2+} from the drops was very rapid and was affected by solution pH, with greater removal from solution at pH 5.4. For the macro-nutrient cations (K^+, Ca^{2+}, and Mg^{2+}), greater solution concentrations were observed at pH 3.8. These observations are consistent with the cuticle acting as a weak-acid type cation exchanger, in which ions rapidly exchange between solutions and the ionized sites in the outer-most portions of the cuticle. Decreased Cu^{2+} and Pb^{2+} adsorption at the lower pH suggests a reduction in available exchange sites for cation adsorption because these sites would be preferentially occupied by H^+. Increased H^+ concentration would also favor the release of K^+, Ca^{2+} and Mg^{2+} by H^+ exchange from sites on the cuticle surface.

The rate and amount of exchange was significantly reduced on the abaxial surfaces of these maple leaves, which is covered with considerable epicuticular wax. Visual observation suggested that contact angles of drops on the abaxial surfaces were much greater than on the adaxial surface (which is free of epicuticular wax), although we made no rigorous measurement of contact angles.

One of the objectives of this work was to evaluate the relative importance of surface ion exchange and trans-cuticular ion permeation during precipitation-foliage contact. Calculation of an apparent permeability coefficient (P) (Scherbatskoy and Tyree, 1990) from the kinetics of these experiments provided reasonable values of P ($5x10^{-10}$ to $2x10^{-11}$ ms^{-1}) for the flux of K^+, Ca^{2+} and Mg^{2+} from the leaf to the drops, consistent with published values of P for these cations

(McFarlane and Berry, 1974; Reed and Tukey, 1982). On the other hand, the kinetics of exchange for Cu^{2+} and Pb^{2+} yielded values of P of 10^{-6} to10^{-7} ms^{-1}, which are about four orders of magnitude greater than values of P reported in the literature for cuticular ion diffusion. This observation suggests that surface ion exchange, not cuticular permeability, is the likely mechanism for Cu^{2+} and Pb^{2+} exchange. On the other hand, the apparent permeability coefficients calculated for K^+, Ca^{2+} and Mg^{2+} support the hypothesis of trans-cuticular diffusion for these cations. Because leaves used in these experiments were well rinsed, removing much of the surface deposits of these ions, diffusion through the cuticle could explain the observed data for these K^+, Ca^{2+}, and Mg^{2+}.

These data demonstrate that diffusion of ions through intact cuticles is not likely to be biologically important during foliar leaching events. A half-time for ion depletion from a leaf under conditions of continuous precipitation was calculated (Scherbatskoy and Tyree, 1990), assuming trans-cuticular diffusion is the dominant process and a representative permeability coefficient of 10^{-10} ms^{-1}. Under these conditions, the time that would be required for half the K^+, for example, within a leaf to be lost to the precipitation is approximately 10 days. This suggests that (for healthy leaves with intact cuticles) foliar leaching *via* trans-cuticular ion diffusion is not a biologically significant process. This also implies that other mechanisms must be involved in foliar leaching in the field, since measured cation increases in throughfall (approximately 40 μeq l^{-1} for K^+) are many times greater than the increases observed in these drop exchange experiments (about 1 μeq l^{-1}). There are a number of factors that could explain cation efflux from foliage without invoking rapid cuticular permeation, including (a) ion exchange at necrotic regions, trichomes or hairs, margins, bark, or with leaf surface micro-flora, (b) wash-off of dry deposition or substances slowly accumulated near the cuticle surface, or (c) cation exchange with exchange sites that are part of the chemical structure of the cuticle itself. These possible mechanisms are still in need of further examination through experimental research.

Other researchers have also used leaf surfaces to examine aspects of the mechanisms controlling foliar leaching. The work of Adams and Hutchinson (1987) and Hutchinson and Adams (1987) measured the rate of neutralization of acid rain droplets on leaf surfaces as affected by surface properties, nutrition and aerosol content of the air. Their observations were consistent with the results described above, and support the concept of the cuticle as a weak-acid cation exchanger.

In extending these results to nutrient cycling in plant canopies, there is some disparity between exchange rates calculated from throughfall measurements and those predicted from cuticle studies. Current research by Scherbatskoy and Lovett (unpubl.) is examining the role of the cuticle surface in controlling the chemistry of foliar leachate or throughfall. The goal of this work is to sort out the varying contributions to throughfall chemistry due to cuticle surface ion exchange, branch and twig leaching, leaf surface micro-flora, damage to the cuticle, dry deposition accumulation on the leaf surface, trans-cuticular ion diffusion, and effects of varying acidity conditions. These, we believe, are some of the important research areas still needing attention in order to understand the role of the leaf cuticle and leaf surface in chemical interactions between the atmosphere and whole plants.

Ion diffusion through the cuticle

The discussions above and, indeed, most discussions about ion flux between leaf surfaces and precipitation assume that concentration gradients alone provide the driving force for ion diffusion and flux. But diffusion of ions should also be affected by electrical forces that may arise in the cuticle. Because of the negatively charged nature of the cuticle matrix (arising from polyuronic and other carboxylic acid constituents in it), electrical (diffusion) potentials will arise in cuticles due to the differential permeability of cations and anions diffusing through the cuticle. Thus, proper consideration of ion diffusion in a cuticle should incorporate three important parameters controlling ion flux across the cuticle: (a) concentration difference, (b) diffusion potential, and (c) the permeability coefficient (which incorporates membrane thickness, ion mobility and ion partition coefficient). If diffusion potentials of significant magnitude occur in cuticles, they may have an effect on ion flux by altering the electrochemical gradient (Scherbatskoy, 1989; Tyree *et al.*, 1990a). The cuticular diffusion potential has generally not been considered in evaluations of transcuticular ion flux and ion permeability coefficients; the fundamental importance of this is discussed in detail by Tyree (*this volume*).

Techniques for measuring diffusion potentials across isolated leaf cuticles are described in detail in Tyree *et al.* (1990a). Briefly, these involve mounting a 1-cm diameter piece of enzymatically isolated *Acer* or *Citrus* cuticle between two halves of a flow cell and pumping unbuffered KCl solutions across the two sides of the cuticle to create ion concentration gradients. Diffusion potentials across the cuticle were measured at various KCl concentration ratios between the outside and inside of the isolated cuticle. There are several important observations about cuticles arising from this work. First, diffusion potentials do develop across leaf cuticles, and most certainly do exist in intact leaf-cuticle systems. The magnitude of these potentials can be quite large (up to ~100 mV), and, as explained in Tyree *et al.* (1990b), affect the driving force for ion diffusion through the cuticle. Secondly, these potentials are asymmetrical, being 1.3 to 4 times greater depending on the orientation of the concentration gradient with respect to the cuticle inner and outer surfaces. This measured asymmetry suggests there is a structural and/or chemical asymmetry in the cuticle matrix itself, due to greater amounts of ionizable molecules (*e.g.*, carboxylic acid substituents) in the morphological inner side of the cuticle (Scherbatskoy, 1989; Tyree *et al.*, 1990a).

Considerable research on the electrophysiology of leaf cuticles has continued in our laboratory. Recent work has focused on measuring the electrical conductance and diffusion potential in isolated cuticles in order to calculate cation and anion permeabilities (Tyree *et al.*, 1991). This work has provided new insights into the structure of the cuticle and the mechanisms of ion transport through it, particularly the observation that ion conductance appears to be rate limited mainly by the outer waxy portions of the cuticle.

Isolated cuticles have also been used in several other laboratories to investigate properties of permeation of various substances through the cuticle, including water vapor transport (Becker *et al.*, 1986), H+ transport (Hauser *et al.*, 1993), uptake and penetration of trace metals (Chamel *et al.*, 1984) and herbicides (Chamel, 1986), effects of acidity or ozone on cuticle permeability (Garrec and Kerfourn, 1989; Kerstiens and Lendzian, 1989; Scherbatskoy, unpubl.), and others. Some of the most extensive and rigorous evaluation of transport in isolated cuticles has been conducted in the laboratories of Schönherr (Schönherr, 1976, 1982; Schönherr and Riederer, 1989) and Riederer *et al.* (*this volume*).

Cuticle isolation

In the course of our research with isolated leaf cuticles, scanning electron micrographs (SEM) images were taken of adaxial and abaxial surfaces of intact leaves, particularly of sugar maple, and of outer and inner (epidermal) surfaces of isolated cuticles. In addition, leaves were sampled from a variety of deciduous tree species in order to determine which of the more common tree species in this region easily yield isolated cuticles. Table 1 summarizes the tree species that were tested and provides information about their locations, sampling dates, and the ease of cuticle isolation.

Procedures for cuticle isolation were modified from the basic enzymatic approach of Orgell (1955). Leaves were lightly abraded on their abaxial surfaces with 120 grit sandpaper to facilitate entry of enzyme solution. Leaf disks (10-14 mm diameter) were cut from each leaf, avoiding major veins, and were vacuum infiltrated in flasks containing filtered pectinase (E.C. 3.2.1.15) and cellulase (E.C. 3.2.1.4) (both from ICN Biochemicals, Cleveland OH, USA) in 0.1 M Na-Acetate buffer at pH 3.7 or 4.5. To prevent microbial contamination, 1 mM NaN3 was added to the solutions.

Concentrations of enzymes used varied with species being isolated. *Citrus* or other easily isolated species could be isolated in 1-3 days using a solution of 1% pectinase and 0.1% cellulase (w/v); this is the ratio given by Orgell (1955). *Acer* cuticles proved to be particularly difficult to isolate; they adhere tightly to the underlying cells, particularly over the vascular network, and are relatively thin. We tested a range of enzyme combinations at various concentrations and found

Table 1   Sources of foliage used in cuticle isolations. All leaves were sampled from southerly branches receiving some direct sunlight; all trees were field grown except *Citrus*, which was grown in a greenhouse. Percent success rate refers to the number of intact isolated cuticles removed from leaf disks as a percentage of the total number of leaf disks attempted; this provides and index of the difficulty of cuticle isolation.

Species and dates sampled	Location	% success
Acer platanoides L.		
08/25/87	Williston, VT	50
06/07/88	" "	80
06/23/88	" "	80
Acer rubrum L.		
07/07/88	Underhill, VT	10
Acer saccharum Marsh.		
08/06/87	Burlington, VT	30
09/12/87	" "	30
10/06/87	" "	30
05/24/88	" "	60
06/29/88	" "	50
07/07/88	Underhill, VT	40
Betula papyrifera Marsh.		
07/07/88	Underhill, VT	0
Betula alleghaniensis Britt.		
07/07/88	Underhill, VT	0
Citrus aurantium L.		
10/10/87	Burlington, VT	95
04/12/88	" "	95
Fagus grandifolia Ehrh.		
07/07/88	Underhill, VT	0
Fraxinus americana L.		
07/07/88	Underhill, VT	60
Ginkgo bilboa L.		
10/29/87	Burlington, VT	85
Liquidambar styraciflua L.		
06/28/88	Raleigh, NC	0
Populus tremuloides Michx.		
10/29/87	Burlington, VT	30
06/01/88	So. Burlington, VT	30
Prunus serotina Ehrh.		
07/07/88	Underhill, VT	90
Quercus velutina Lam.		
06/09/88	Williston, VT	75

10% pectinase and 2% cellulase (w/v) was most effective, allowing adaxial *Acer* cuticles to be removed in 1-2 weeks. Pectinase (10%) alone was ineffective for *Acer*; the addition of cellulase increased the ease of cuticle isolation, with no additional benefit above 2% cellulase. Addition of up to 5% hemicellulase did not improve maple cuticle isolation. After approximately mid-July *Acer* cuticle removal became more difficult; cuticles seemed to be more strongly attached to the underlying vascular network.

For SEM, most specimens were simply air dried at room temperature. Some specimens were dehydrated in a graded ethanol series (10-min immersions in 30, 50, 75, 85, 95, and 100% ethanol), followed by critical point drying with CO_2 using a SamDri model PVT-3B. Comparison of the air and critical-point dried specimens did not reveal differences in the appearance of surface features, and air drying has the advantages of convenience and not exposing cuticles to ethanol, which could have solvent actions on some cuticular waxes. All specimens were coated with palladium-gold using a Poloran model E-5100 sputter coater. Images were made with a JEOL 100CX scanning-transmission electron microscope operated at accelerating voltages of 20-40 kV.

Figure 1 (labeled as plate 4.04 A and B) shows the outer and inner surfaces of enzymatically isolated sugar maple adaxial cuticles. Notice in plate 4.04A that except for a somewhat flatter appearing image, typical surface features were preserved through the isolation procedure, including the cuticular ridges due to the epidermal cell wall ridges. Since this cuticle retained these features after removal from the underlying cell wall, an additional build-up of cuticular wax over these areas is suggested. Plate 4.04B shows distinct cuticular projections into the intercellular lamellae of the epidermis which are typical of inner surfaces of isolated cuticles (Holloway, 1982; Chamel, 1986). In Figure 2 (plates 4.05 A and B), higher magnifications reveal an apparent progression of enzymatic digestion of the inner cuticular surface. It appears that as the inner surface material (probably consisting largely of pectin and cellulose) is digested, these circular pits enlarge and leave behind the deeper regions outlined by the intercellular cuticular projections. The outer and inner surfaces of enzymatically isolated adaxial Norway maple (*Acer platanoides* L.) cuticles (not shown) are very similar in appearance to sugar maple. Figure 3 (labeled 4.06 A and B) shows the outer and inner surfaces of isolated adaxial *Citrus aurantium* cuticles. Although the surface wax structure appears quite different from maple, the inner surface bears some similarity. In particular, the inner surface seems to show signs of the progressive deterioration of the inner structural layers as seen for maple.

The physical and chemical structure of the inner (epidermal) side of cuticles may have effects on the transport properties of isolated cuticles. The degree of enzymatic degradation of the polysaccharides in the boundary between the cuticle and the epidermal cell wall could affect the transport properties of the cuticle by altering the concentration and distribution of negatively

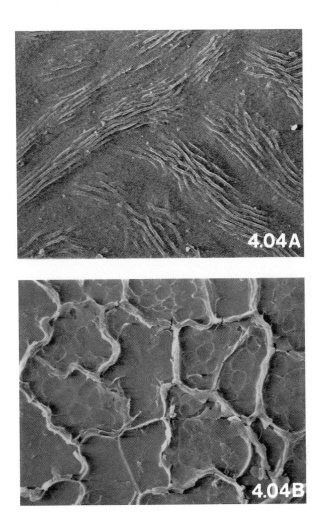

Figure 1   Morphological outer (4.04A) and inner (4.04B) surfaces of isolated *Acer saccharum* adaxial cuticles. Both at 800X.

charged sites in the cuticle matrix. Cuticles isolated for longer times might have thinner polysaccharide layers associated with their inner surfaces and concomitantly reduced concentrations of negative charge. Thus, isolated cuticles may have different transport and ion exchange properties than intact cuticles on whole leaves. This would be important in considering species such as maple which may require several weeks to isolate cuticles.

We examined this effect in *Citrus* cuticles by measuring diffusion potentials as a function of the time they were exposed to the enzymatic isolating solutions. *Citrus aurantium* cuticles were isolated in the minimum possible time and diffusion potentials measured according to procedures

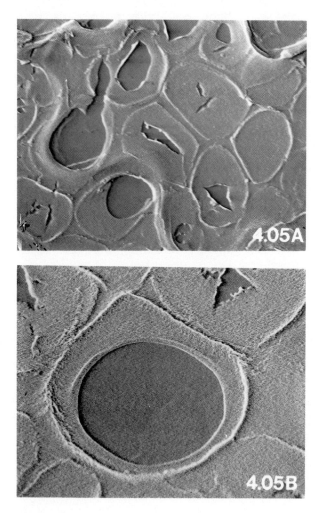

Figure 2   Morphological inner surface of isolated *Acer saccharum* adaxial cuticle at 3,000X
(4.05A) and 6,000X (4.05B).

described above and in Tyree *et al.* (1990b). The enzyme solution was then pumped across the
two faces of the cuticle overnight without removing it from the flow cell, and the diffusion
potential measurements were repeated. This cycle was repeated for up to 4 days. There was no
significant difference in diffusion potential due to the amount of exposure to the enzyme solutions
(Tyree *et al.*, 1990b). This suggests that, for easily isolated cuticles such as *Citrus*, diffusion
potentials and hence transport properties are probably stable with respect to isolation treatment
time. This assessment, however, needs to be confirmed for other species, such as maple.

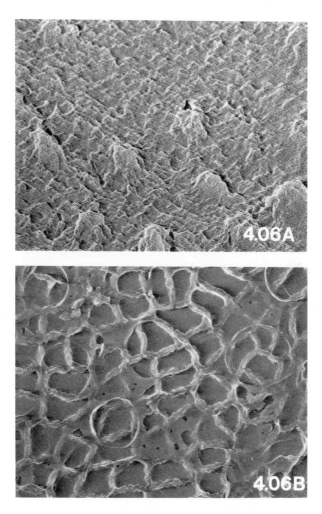

Figure 3   Morphological outer (4.06A, at 500X) and inner (4.06B, at 800X) surfaces of isolated *Citrus aurantium* adaxial cuticles.

Effects of ozone and UV-B

Other work in progress in our laboratory has examined the effects of ozone and ultraviolet
radiation (UV-B) singly and in combination on cuticle structure and function in seedlings of
sugar maple, black cherry (*Prunus serotina* L.) and clones of hybrid poplar (*Populus deltoides*
x *trichocarpa*). This involved exposing these seedlings (1-3 years age) in open-top chambers to
combinations of episodic ozone treatments (4-5 days at 0.012-0.015 ppmv once every 3 weeks)

and additional UV-B corresponding to a 30% decrease in stratospheric ozone. Treatment combinations were charcoal-filtered air (CF), charcoal-filtered air with additional ozone (O_3), charcoal-filtered air with additional ultraviolet radiation (UV-B), combined ozone and ultraviolet radiation (O_3+UV-B), and controls grown outside the chambers in ambient air. This multi-disciplinary study included examination of treatment effects on fungal infection processes, stomatal and cuticular CO_2 conductance, biomass accumulation, leaf surface structure using SEM and cuticular ion permeability.

During the June-September study period, leaf samples were collected monthly for evaluation of treatment effects on leaf surface structures and for isolation of leaf cuticles from maple and cherry for ion permeability studies (poplar was not included as it is amphistomatous). Leaf disks were air dried and examined by SEM as described earlier. Adaxial leaf cuticles were sampled from maple and cherry at these times and ion permeabilities measured according to the methods described in detail in Tyree *et al.* (1991). Briefly, this involved measuring both diffusion potential and electrical conductance in a specially equipped flow cell under a range of ion concentration ratios. From these measurements cation and anion permeabilities in the isolated cuticles were calculated.

Examination of leaf surfaces by SEM did not reveal any obvious differences in the structure of adaxial or abaxial cuticle features in any species due to treatments. No effort was made to quantify wax content or contact angles. Fungal hyphae were often observed on the surfaces of cherry (unrelated to the experimental treatments, and unrelated to the fungal infection component of this study, which was conducted with poplar).

Table 2   Ratios of ion permeability coefficients (P+/P-) for cuticles of black cherry (*Prunus serotina*) foliage exposed to four treatments. Means and standard deviation of three cuticles on each of four dates (n=12) . Treatments are explained in the text. * indicates statistically different from Control at p=0.05.

TREATMENT	MEAN (SD)	
Control (CF)	20.27 (14.45)	
O_3	6.36 (4.02)	*
UV-B	9.35 (6.82)	
O_3+UV-B	11.70 (10.25)	

Evaluation of cuticle permeability data are in progress, but preliminary data indicate a significant effect due to ozone treatments on the ratio of cation to anion permeability (P+/P-) in cherry (Table 2). This indicates that the relative permeabilities of cation and anion were altered by the ozone treatments, but does not indicate whether this effect was due more to the cation or anion. It does clearly suggest, however, that ozone treatment altered the physical and/or chemical structure of the cuticle in such a way as to affect ion permeability. The data also suggest a trend indicating UV-B also reduced the permeability ratio and that the combined O_3+UV-B treatment may have reduced this effect.

Light absorbance of cuticles

There is very limited research on the role of leaf surfaces in modifying light reaching the interior of leaves (Robbrecht and Caldwell, 1978; Bornmann and Vogelmann, 1991). These studies measured the characteristics of light passing though the cuticle and epidermis together. There is no work we are aware of, however, on radiation attenuation by the cuticle itself. Given the current concerns about increasing levels of UV-B exposure due to stratospheric ozone depletion, and the lack of information about the role of the cuticle itself in modifying the light environment of the leaf interior, this is an important area needing investigation. We are currently studying the light absorbance properties of isolated leaf cuticles from a number of broad-leaf tree species, including *Acer*, *Prunus* and *Citrus*. To do this, isolated cuticles are mounted in a scanning spectrophotometer and light absorbance is measured between wavelengths of 210 and 1100 nm. Cuticles used in this study were from the plants treated with ozone and UV-B, as described earlier.

Preliminary results from limited data indicate that isolated sugar maple leaf cuticles have characteristic absorption peaks at 304 and 345 nm. Percent transmittance in these cuticles is relatively constant across the scanned range except at these peaks, ranging from approximately 20% at 200 nm, 30% at 500 nm to 55% at 1100 nm. To date, we have only examined maple cuticles from the experiments described earlier. There does not appear to be a significant difference in the absorbance spectra of cuticles due to the treatments. Continuing research will examine effects for other species.

Conclusions

Several examples of recent work were summarized here in order to provide a sense of the types of investigations that are possible using isolated leaf cuticles. These studies generally focused on the transport of ions or transmittance of light through the cuticle because of our belief that the leaf cuticle is a very important boundary between the plant and its external environment. If environmental influences alter the structure or function of the cuticle, these processes could potentially be affected. In general, the cuticle appears to be resistant to the effects of the environmental stressors examined so far, although some effects were identified. More importantly, perhaps, studies with isolated cuticles can be helpful in shedding light on their physical and chemical properties. Although not discussed in detail here, isolated cuticles also have an important role in our understanding of the chemical properties and composition of the leaf cuticle (Baker *et al.*, 1982; Holloway, 1982), and of the transport properties of cuticles with respect to a large class of organic substances such as agro-chemicals. There is still much we do not know about the functional aspects of the leaf cuticle, but it is clear that continued research is important in order to better understand its fundamental properties and its role in mediating environmental changes.

Literature cited

Adams CM, Hutchinson TC (1984) A comparison of the ability of leaf surfaces of three species to neutralize acidic rain drops. New Phytol 97: 463-478

Baker EA, Bukovac MJ, Hunt GM (1982) Composition of tomato fruit cuticle as related to fruit growth and development. *In* The Plant Cuticle. Linnean Society of London International Symposium, London, 8-11 Sept. 1980. Cutler DF, Alvin KL, and Price CE (*eds*) London, Academic Press *pp* 33-44

Becker M, Kerstiens G, and Schönherr J (1986) Water permeability of plant cuticles: permeance, diffusion and partition coefficients. Trees 1: 54-60

Bornmann JF, Vogelmann TC (1991) Effect of UV-B radiation on leaf optical properties measured with fiber optics. J Exper Bot 42: 547-554

Chamel A, Gambonnet B, Genova C, and Jourdain A (1984) Cuticular behavior of cadmium studied using isolated plant cuticles. J Environ Qual 13: 483-487

Chamel A (1986) Foliar absorption of herbicides: study of the cuticular penetration using isolated cuticles. Physiol Veg 24: 491-508

Dybing CD, Currier HB (1961) Foliar penetration of chemicals. Plant Physiol 36: 169-174

Eaton JS, Likens GE, and Bormann FH (1973) Throughfall and stemflow chemistry in a northern hardwood forest. J Ecol 61: 495-508

Garrec JP, Kerfourn C (1989) Effets des pluies acides et de l'ozone sur la perméabilité à l'eau et aux ions de cuticules isolées. Implication dans le phénomène de dépérissement des forêts. Environ Exper Bot 29: 215-228

Hauser HD, Walters KD, and Berg VS (1993) Patterns of effective permeability of leaf cuticles to acids. Plant Physiol 101: 251-257

Holloway PJ (1982) The chemical constitution of plant cutins. *In* The Plant Cuticle. Linnean Society of London International Symposium, London, 8-11 Sept. 1980. Cutler DF, Alvin KL, and Price CE (*eds*) Academic Press, London. *pp* 45-85

Hutchinson TC, Adams CM (1987) Comparative abilities of leaf surfaces to neutralize acidic raindrops. I. The influence of calcium nutrition and filtered air on leaf response. New Phytol 106: 169-183

Kerstiens G, Lendzian KJ (1989) Interactions between ozone and plant cuticles. New Phytol 112: 13-19

Lovett GM, Lindberg SE, Richter DD, and Johnson DW (1985) The effects of acidic deposition on cation leaching from three deciduous forest canopies. Can J For Res 15: 1055-1060

Lord WG, Greene DW, and Emino ER (1979) Absorption of silver nitrate and lead nitrate into leaves of McIntosh apple. Can J Plant Sci. 59: 137-142

McFarlane JC, Berry WL (1974) Cation penetration through isolated leaf cuticles. Plant Physiol 53: 723-727

Orgell WH (1955) The isolation of plant cuticle with pectic enzymes. Plant Physiol 30: 78-80.

Parker GG (1983) Throughfall and stemflow in the forest nutrient cycle. Advan Ecol Res. 13: 57-133

Reed DW, Tukey HB (1982) Permeability of Brussels sprouts and carnation cuticles from leaves developed in different temperatures and light intensities. *In* The Plant Cuticle. Linnean Society of London International Symposium, London, 8-11 Sept. 1980. Cutler DF, Alvin KL, and Price CE (*eds*) Academic Press, London. *pp* 267-278

Riederer M, Jetter R, Markstädter C, Schreiber L (1994) Air pollutants and the cuticle: implications for plant physiology. *In* Percy KE, Cape JN, Jagels R, Simpson CM (*eds.*) Springer, New York. (*This volume, pp* 67-79)

Robbrecht R, Caldwell M (1978) Leaf epidermal transmittance of ultraviolet radiation and its implications for plant sensitivity to ultraviolet-radiation induced injury. Oecologia 32: 277-287

Schönherr J (1976) Water permeability of isolated cuticular membranes: the effect of cuticular waxes on diffusion of water. Planta (Berlin) 131: 159-164

Schönherr J (1982) Resistances of plant surfaces to water loss: transport properties of cutin, suberin, and associated lipids. *In* Encyclopedia of Plant Physiology, New Series, Physiological Plant Ecology. Lange OL, Nobel PS, Osmund CB, and Ziegler H (*eds*) Springer-Verlag, Berlin. *pp* 153-179

Schönherr J, Riederer M (1989) Foliar penetration and accumulation of organic chemicals in plant cuticles. Rev Environ Contam and Toxicol 108: 1-70

Scherbatskoy TD (1989) Ionic relations of leaf cuticles. PhD Diss, University of Vermont, Burlington. 185 *pp*

Scherbatskoy T, Tyree MT (1990) Kinetics of exchange of ions between artificial precipitation and maple leaf surfaces. New Phytol 114: 703-712

Tyree MT, Scherbatskoy TD, and Tabor CA (1990a) Leaf cuticles behave as asymmetric membranes: evidence from measurement of diffusion potentials. Plant Physiol 92: 103-109

Tyree MT, Tabor CA, and Wescott CR (1990b) Movement of cations through cuticles of *Citrus aurantium* and *Acer saccharum*. Plant Physiol 94: 120-126

Tyree MT, Wescott CR, and Tabor CA (1991) Diffusion and electric mobility of ions within isolated cuticles of *Citrus aurantium*. Plant Physiol 97: 273-279

SECTION II - NEW METHODS AND CONTRIBUTIONS

The Effect of the Environment on the Structure, Quantity and Composition of Spruce Needle Wax

M.S.Günthardt-Goerg
Eidgenössische Forschungsanstalt für Wald, Schnee und Landschaft
CH-8903 Birmensdorf

Abstract

The tubular structure (10-nonacosanol), as formed in spring on the was surface of new spruce needles (*Picea abies* (L.) Karst.), or as regenerated on previous-year needles, becomes gradually fused and flattened in relation to needle exposure, particularly wind and rain. Structural flattening does not necessarily imply changes in wax quantity, composition or lead to changes in needle transpiration or photosynthesis, and was approximately reproduced by bathing excised twigs in water (with pH having little effect). In 4-year-old plants of one clone planted out at a Swiss plateau and alpine sites, changes in wax structure were similar to those found in mature trees. No such changes were found in plants with O_3, SO_2, ambient air, charcoal-filtered air, or in plants grown outside the chambers but shielded from rain.

Area-related needle wax quantity in mature trees differed between the two sites, but did not differ in young plants under different treatments (fumigation or planted out at the sites). Minor differences in wax composition, however, were found to be related to the ozone dose of the fumigation or the ambient ozone dose at the sites. In each needle wax sample, 68 compounds grouped into 12 constituent classes were quantified. The quantity of the individual substituent classes varied among wax samples from genetically different mature trees at the two sites in a tree-specific way. Variation of these quantities was not larger than among young cloned plants after different treatments.

Introduction

The outermost coating of needles is a wax layer composed of up to 100 normal saturated hydrocarbons (C_{12} - C_{64}), grouped into at least 12 substituent classes having different functional groups (Günthardt-Goerg, 1986; Günthardt-Goerg *et al.*, 1994). During the last 20 years, structural changes on the wax surface (revealed by means of scanning electron microscopy) have been mostly interpreted in relation to environmental conditions (Turunen and Huttunen, 1990). Fumigation experiments were used in an attempt to reproduce changes in wax structure seen in the field (Günthardt-Goerg and Keller, 1987; Lütz and Heinzmann, 1990). Analytical approaches have been critically reviewed by Riederer (1989). In this paper, I summarize my own observations and experiments on the structure, amount, and composition of spruce needle wax.

NATO ASI Series, Vol. G 36
Air Pollutants and the Leaf Cuticle
Edited by K. E. Percy et al.
© Springer-Verlag Berlin Heidelberg 1994

Materials and methods

From a total of 55 4-year-old clonal Norway spruce plants (*Picea abies* (L.) Karst.), 35 were exposed to O_3 and SO_2 in the Birmensdorf field fumigation chambers (five plants per regime, one plant per chamber, various concentrations — Table 1). Precipitation was simulated by bathing the twigs of five plants for 5 h in ten different solutions having pH's 1 - 9.8. Five plants from each treatment were planted in a forest of the Swiss Plateau (665 m a.s.l.), on a subalpine site (1660 m a.s.l.), and on an open field site (550 m a.s.l., shielded from precipitation). Four needles per seedling (same age and exposure) were examined by scanning electron microscopy (210 samples in total). Wax quantity (extracted with chloroform) excluding leaf pigments and p-hydroxyacetophenone, was determined in 62 samples, and 68 components were quantified in each of 30 samples (without saponification, limitation of reliable detection of estolides by capillary gas chromatography = 64 C-atoms). Details of procedures can be found in Günthardt-Goerg *et al.* (1994).

Variation in needle wax structure due to needle age, position, and location on the needle within one mature tree was investigated. Gas exchange was measured in parallel (Häsler *et al.* 1991). Variation in structure, quantity and composition of needle wax from six mature trees each of the Swiss Plateau and the subalpine site was determined in 264 (structure), 36 (quantity), and 24 (composition) needle samples.

Table 1 Mean gaseous pollutant concentration ($\mu g/m^3$) during exposure period

	O_3	SO_2	NO_2	NO
Fumigations				
filtered air (fa)	<1	0	0	8
ambient air, 2 years (aa)	51-56	4-5	26	6
fa + O_3	28	0	0	8
fa + O_3	82	0	0	8
aa + SO_2	56	70	26	6
aa + SO_2	56	200	26	6
Swiss Plateau site				
May - October	76	5	24	3
November - April	39	13	24	3
Swiss subalpine site				
May - October	65	2	5	0.4
November - April	62	5	5	0.4

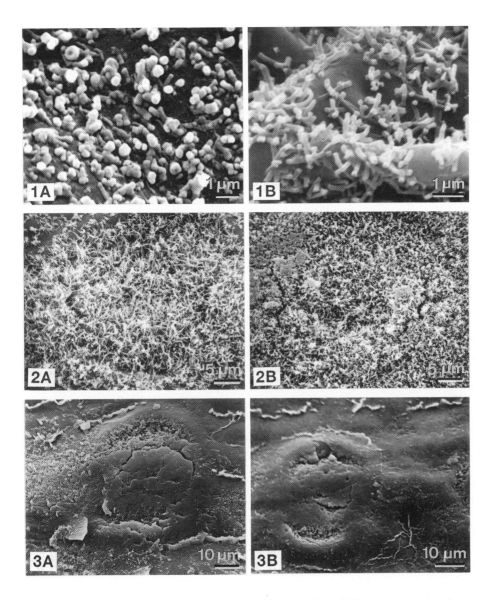

Figure 1   Wax structure on spruce needles at bud break. A: "Crumbly" wax structure on the needle tip; B: Wax tubes on a subsidiary cell.

Figure 2   Wax structure on stomatal openings of 0.5-year-old needles from clonal plants. A: After different exposure in fumigation chambers; B: After exposure in the field, but shielded from rain. Arrow: zone with fused wax tubes.

Figure 3   Needles bathed in Aq. dest; A: With acids added to pH 2.5; B: With detergents added to pH 9.6.

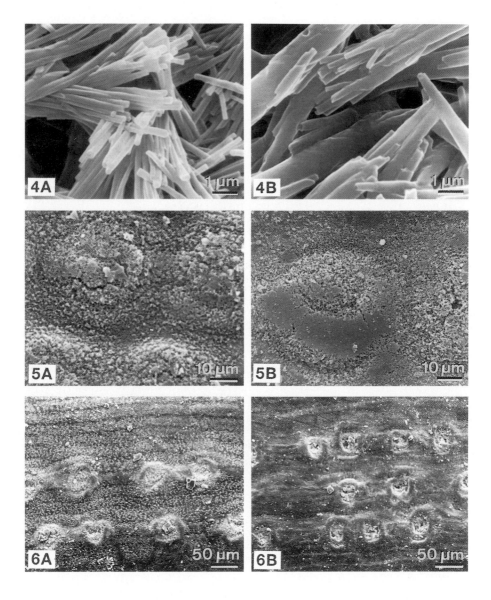

Figure 4   A: wax tubes of pure 10-nonacosanol; B: Fused tubes after bathing in acid solution
            pH 2.5.

Figure 5   0.5-year-old needles from clonal spruce plants; A: Exposed at the Swiss Plateau;
            B: At the subalpine site.

Figure 6   Mature tree at the Swiss Plateau site, shade crown in July, previous-year needle; A:
            Abaxial, B: Adaxial needle side.

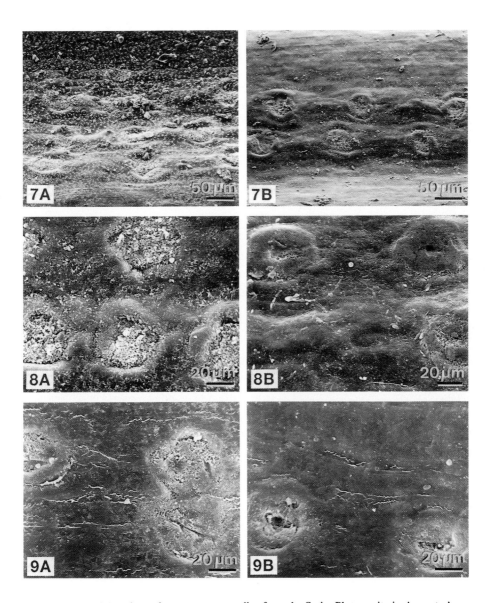

Figure 7   Adaxial surface of current-year needles from the Swiss Plateau site in August; A:
From the sun crown; B: From the shade crown of a mature spruce tree.

Figure 8   Mature trees without needle loss at the Swiss Plateau site, 3-year-old needles, same
exposure in a dominant tree (A), or a suppressed tree (B).

Figure 9   Dominant mature trees at the subalpine site, 3-year-old needles, same exposure in a
tree with 5 % (A), or 80 % (B) needle loss.

Results

Structure of needle wax in clonal plants

When buds flush in spring, "crumbly" wax structures appear on the needle surface, and tubular wax forms at the rim of the guard cell mother cells (Fig. 1A,B). After 5 months exposure, wax structures (Fig. 2A) were not altered by the different fumigation regimes shown in Table 1. Trees exposed in the field but shielded from precipitation had only small zones with fused wax tubes (Fig. 2B). Fusing, flattening, and formation of wavy lines in the wax structure were increased in needles bathed in different solutions but showed little relation to acidity (Fig. 3A,B).

Needle wax was a chemical mixture comprising single compounds having different structures. The main component, 10-nonacosanol, had a tubular form. However, the tubes were fused after bathing in acid solution (Fig. 4A,B). Estolides formed a perfectly smooth layer that did not respond to bathing. The plate-like rhomboid structure of the most prominent free fatty acid C_{24} showed distinct facets after bathing in low pH (not shown). In the clonal plants, needle wax structures were flattened after their exposure in the forest sites in a similar way to that found on mature trees (Fig. 5A,B).

Needle wax structure in mature trees

Wax tubular structure becomes aggregated and flattened with increasing needle age. This process was accelerated on the adaxial compared to the abaxial needle surface (Fig. 6A,B). On the abaxial surface of overwintered needles, wax tubes newly formed in spring remained intact until July (Fig. 6A). In the shade crown, the process of structural wax flattening preceded that in the sun crown by about 1 month (Fig. 7A,B). At the Swiss Plateau site, wax flattening was enhanced in needle samples (same age and exposure) from suppressed trees (Fig. 8A,B), and at the subalpine site this flattening was enhanced in trees having increased needle loss (Fig. 9A,B). Stomata unoccluded by wax were not found. CO_2 assimilation rate decreased with needle age in the sun crown, but was low and stable with increasing needle age in the shade crown (Fig. 10).

Wax quantity and composition

In clonal plants (exposed in the chambers or planted in the field) wax quantity per needle area and quantitative wax composition differed from those in mature trees (Fig. 11, Fig. 12A,B, last columns). The standard deviations of the mean total wax quantity and substituent classes were similar in mature trees and in the different seedling treatments. The same 68 compounds (grouped in 12 substituent classes with different polarity) were detected and quantified in all wax samples. When compared to filtered air (Fig. 12A) needle wax from clonal plants after fumigation with 82 $\mu g/m^3$ O_3 or exposure at the field sites (76 or 65 μg) was enriched in 10-nonacosanol and secondary diols at the expense of estolides and free ω-hydroxy fatty acids. Similarly, wax in

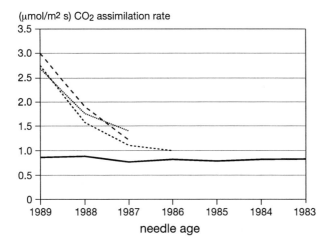

Figure 10 Swiss plateau site (same spruce tree as Fig 6 and 7). Assimilation rate in needles of different age in the sun crown (data shown from – – – 8.9.1989, ⋯⋯ 18.9.1989, - - - - - 20.9. 1989) and in the shade crown (——— 22.9.1989) after R. Häsler *et al.* 1991.

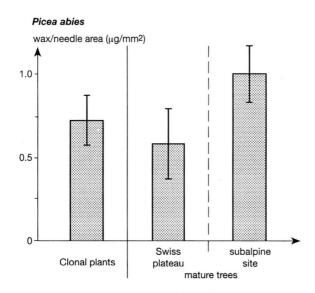

Figure 11 Mean wax amount in needle samples of clonal spruce plants (n = 36) and mature trees at the two sites (each n = 18).

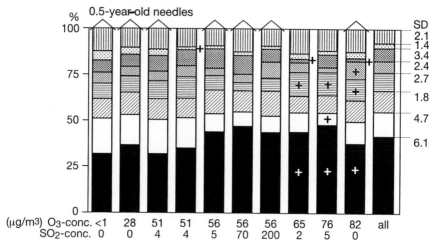

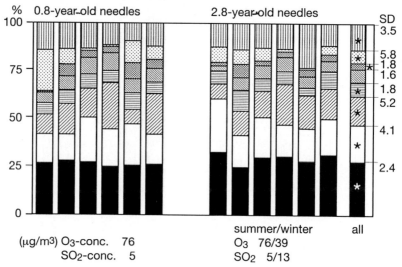

Figure 12 Weight sum (= 100 %) of 68 spruce needle wax compounds grouped in substituent
classes: ■ 10-nonacosanol, ☐ free 3-hydroxy fatty acids, ▨ free fatty acids,
▤ nonacosanediol, ▧ unknown diols, ▨ 12 estolides, ▦ hentriacontanol.
▥ Minor substituent classes without significant differences between trees or
treatments have been combined. The column 'all' represents mean values (+ SD)
of all preceeding columns.
A: Clonal plants, wax composition after different exposure to O_3 or SO_2. ∧ = exposure in chambers. + = mean value different from lowest ozone concentration (p<0.01).
B: Mature trees: * = different from clonal plants (p<0.01).

2.8-year-old needles of mature trees (Fig. 12B) contained more 10-nonacosanol than did 0.8-year-old needles. In the individual samples no correlation was found between wax substituent classes, extracted wax quantity or wax structure.

Conclusions

The fusing of wax tubes or flattening of wax structures occurs through the micromechanical action of precipitation, wind, and particles such as sand, dust or salt. Therefore, it depends on the exposure of the individual needle on the branch, crown, and tree to the meteorological conditions. Structural changes in the wax could not be related to the impact of the gaseous pollutants. Flattened structures at the surface of the wax layer do not necessarily imply decreased wax quantity or changed composition. Wax quantity rather reflects genetic differences, whereas minor quantitative changes in wax composition indicate changes during wax formation. Wax compounds are chemically very stable and are unlikely to react with air pollutants. Gas exchange (occurring through wax plugs in the stomatal antechamber) was closely related to the meteorological conditions at the two investigated sites (Häsler et al. 1991). Also, although wax structure is flattened as a result of meteorological conditions, structural changes do not necessarily lead to changes in gas exchange behaviour. Only drastic abrasion of the wax layer can increase epidermal conductance (Hoad et al., 1992).

Acknowledgements

The collaboration of Dr. C. Scheidegger (low temperature SEM, Fig. 6 and 7), Urs Jauch (Institute of Plant Biology, University of Zürich, Figs. 1-5, 8, and 9), Dr. R. Matyssek, and Dr. J. Innes is gratefully acknowledged.

References

Günthardt-Goerg MS (1986) Epicuticular wax of needles of *Pinus cembra, Pinus sylvestris* and *Picea abies*. Eur J For Path 16: 400-408

Günthardt-Goerg MS, Keller T (1987) Some effects of long-term ozone fumigation on Norway spruce. II Epicuticular wax and stomata. Trees 1: 145-150

Günthardt-Goerg MS, Keller T, Matyssek R, Scheidegger C (1994) Structural and chemical variation in the wax of Norway spruce needles from mature trees at two forest sites and from young plants experimentally exposed to O_3 or SO_2. Eur J For Path (*submitted*)

Häsler R, Savi C, Herzog K (1991) Photosynthese und stomatäre Leitfähigkeit der Fichte unter dem Einfluss von Witterung und Schadstoffen. *In* Lufthaushalt, Luftverschmutzung und Waldschäden in der Schweiz: Bd 5: Luftschadstoffe und Wald. Stark M (*ed*). Zürich: Verlag der Fachvereine, *pp* 143-168

Hoad SP, Jeffree CE, Grace J (1992) Effects of wind and abrasion on cuticular integrity in *Fagus sylvatica* L. and consequences for transfer of pollutats through leaf surfaces. Agriculture Ecosystems Environment 42: 3-4

Lütz C, Heizmann U (1990) Surface structures and epicuticular wax composition of spruce needles after long-term treatment with ozone and acid mist. Environmental Pollution 64: 313-322

Riederer M (1989) The cuticles of conifers: structure, composition and transport properties. *In* Ecological Studies 77: Forest decline and air pollution. Schulze ED, Lange OL, Oren R (*eds*) Springer Berlin Heidelberg New York, *pp* 158-192

Turunen M, Huttunen S (1990) A review of the responses of epicuticular wax of conifer needles to air pollution. J Environ Qual 19: 35-45

Effect of Ozone and Elevated Carbon Dioxide on Cuticular Membrane Ultra-structure of Yellow Poplar (*Liriodendron tulipifera*)

Carolyn J. McQuattie and Joanne Rebbeck
USDA Forest Service, Northeastern Forest Experiment Station
Forestry Sciences Laboratory
359 Main Road
Delaware, Ohio 43015
USA

Abstract

Ozone causes damage to leaves of many tree species and has been shown to increase cuticular membrane thickness in a conifer (red spruce). It has been suggested that elevated carbon dioxide can protect plants against air pollutants by reducing pollutant flux into the leaves, but it is not known whether ozone-induced changes in the leaf cuticle will be altered by elevated carbon dioxide. In 1991, white pine (*Pinus strobus*) and yellow poplar (*Liriodendron tulipifera*) seedlings were planted in a previously forested area. In May 1992, seedlings were enclosed in open-top chambers and the following treatments were initiated: 1) charcoal-filtered (CF) air, 2) ambient air (1X ozone), 3) two times ambient ozone (2X ozone), and 4) 2X ozone plus 350 ppm carbon dioxide (2X plus CO_2). First-year leaf samples were collected in August 1992. Midregions of white pine needles and yellow poplar leaves were prepared for electron microscopy by conventional methods and examined in a transmission electron microscope. The cuticular membrane of white pine grown in CF air was approximately 500 nm thick and consisted of an amorphous outer region and an inner reticulate region. Cuticular membrane thickness and wax tubule diameter were slightly greater in white pine needles grown in 2X plus CO_2. The cuticular membrane of yellow poplar leaves grown in CF air was approximately 200 nm thick and consisted of an outer polylamellate region and a reticulate inner region. Cuticular membranes of leaves grown in 2X plus CO_2 were also approximately 200 nm thick, but the outer membrane region had an amorphous structure. The cuticular membrane of yellow poplar leaves grown in 2X ozone were approximately 150 nm thick due to a thinner reticulate region. Second-year white pine and yellow poplar leaves will be collected in late August 1993, and cuticular membrane structure will be compared with the 1992 results.

Introduction

Ozone is an atmospheric pollutant that causes damage to leaves of many tree species. Morphological studies examining the effect of ozone on leaf surfaces have shown premature degradation of epicuticular wax structures (Barnes *et al.*, 1988; Percy *et al.*, 1990). The effect of ozone on the cuticular membrane, the cutin-containing region between the epicuticular wax layer and the epidermal cell wall (Holloway, 1982), has been less well characterized. Percy *et al.* (1992), measuring cuticular membrane thickness of red spruce (*Picea rubens*) exposed to ozone for one growing season, reported an increase in thickness due to the presence of a new amorphous layer.

NATO ASI Series, Vol. G 36
Air Pollutants and the Leaf Cuticle
Edited by K. E. Percy et al.
© Springer-Verlag Berlin Heidelberg 1994

Little work has been done, however, on the effects of ozone on the cuticular membrane of leaves from deciduous trees, particularly using longer-term ozone fumigations.

Forest trees, exposed to a steadily rising concentration of carbon dioxide in the atmosphere (Keeling, 1986), are likely to undergo alterations in growth responses (Graham et al., 1990). Bazzaz et al. (1990) have reported increased biomass in five tree species exposed to elevated carbon dioxide in growth chambers. It has been suggested that increased carbon dioxide may reduce the amount of ozone that is taken up by the leaf due to reduced stomatal conductance, thus protecting the plant (Allen, 1990). It is not known if the presence of elevated carbon dioxide will modify forest tree response to ozone. Furthermore, it is not known if ozone-induced changes in the leaf cuticular membrane will be altered by elevated carbon dioxide.

At the Delaware, Ohio, USDA Forest Service Laboratory, a long-term open-top chamber study has been designed to examine growth and physiological effects of ozone and the combination of ozone plus elevated carbon dioxide on yellow poplar (*Liriodendron tulipifera*) and white pine (*Pinus strobus*). This paper reports ultrastructural changes observed in the cuticular membrane of yellow poplar leaves after 2 years' exposure to ozone alone or in combination with elevated carbon dioxide.

Material and methods

In May of 1992, yellow poplar seedlings from a private nursery in Pennsylvania were planted in a previously forested area at the Delaware, Ohio, USDA Forest Service Lab and 12 seedlings per chamber were enclosed in standard open-top chambers (Rebbeck, 1993). The following fumigation treatments were initiated in late May: (1) charcoal-filtered air (CF-air); (2) two times ambient ozone concentration (2x ozone-air); (3) two times ambient ozone plus 300 ppm CO_2 above ambient (2x ozone + CO_2). There were three replicate chambers for each treatment. Ozone was generated using an OREC ozone generator from liquid oxygen, and carbon dioxide was added from a liquid CO_2 reservoir (see Rebbeck 1993 for details of design). Seedlings were exposed to treatments 24 h/day from May to mid-October throughout the 1992 and 1993 growing seasons.

In August of 1993, mature leaves from two seedlings (nodes 9, 10 or 11 from the apex) were taken from two replicate chambers of each treatment. To prepare leaf tissue for electron microscopy, interveinal leaf segments were cut into 1 mm^2 pieces and immersed in glutaraldehyde. Tissue was then post-fixed in osmium tetroxide, dehydrated in ethanol, and embedded in epoxy resin. Ultrathin (90 nm) cross sections of the leaves were cut on an ultramicrotome, collected on copper grids, and stained with uranyl acetate and lead citrate. All sections were examined and photographed in a Hitachi HU-11E transmission electron microscope. Cuticular membrane thickness was measured from the central periclinal wall of adaxial epidermal cells (10 micrographs per treatment), and differences in thickness due to treatment were analyzed using analysis of variance and the Scheffe Means Comparison Test (SAS Institute, Cary, North Carolina, USA).

Results

Yellow poplar leaves grown in CF-air were generally green, with little chlorosis. In contrast, leaves grown in 2x ozone-air were chlorotic, and some leaves had necrotic spots. Yellow poplar leaves grown in 2x ozone + CO_2 also showed chlorotic regions, but chlorosis was less severe than in the 2x ozone treatment.

Mean thickness of the cuticular membrane from leaves of yellow poplar grown in CF-air was significantly greater ($p < .001$) than cuticular membrane thickness from the other treatments (Table 1). The cuticular membrane consisted of a thin polylamellate outer region and a thicker reticulate inner region (Figure 1). This description corresponds to the cuticular membrane designation Type 1, as classified by Holloway (1982). At the junction between the reticulate region of the cuticular membrane and the cell wall, electron lucent deposits were observed (Figure 1). These extracellular deposits were similar in location to calcium oxalate crystals observed in conifer cell walls by Fink (1991).

Table 1   Cuticular membrane thickness of leaves from yellow poplar seedlings grown in charcoal-filtered air, two times ambient ozone, or two times ambient ozone plus elevated carbon dioxide for two growing seasons.

Treatment	Cuticle thickness (nm)
CF-air	618 ± 32 a
2x ozone-air	223 ± 28 b
2x ozone + CO_2	348 ± 16 c

Means + standard error of the mean followed by different letters are significantly different (p = 0.05) according to Scheffe's Means Comparison Test.

Cuticular membranes from yellow poplar leaves exposed to 2x ozone-air were 64% thinner than those of seedlings grown in CF-air. Ultrastructural characteristics of the cuticular membrane, a polylamellate outer region and a reticulate inner region (Figure 2), were the same in ozone-treated yellow poplar as in those grown in CF-air. The difference in thickness resulted from a thinner reticulate region in the 2x ozone-grown trees. Small electron translucent deposits (Figure 2) were

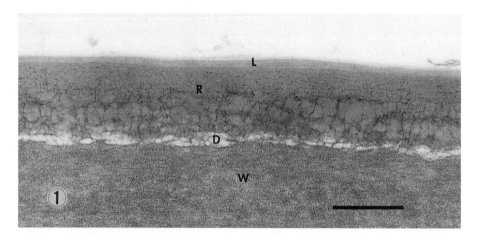

Figure 1   Cuticular membrane from a yellow poplar leaf grown in carbon-filtered air consisted of a thin lamellate outer region (L) and a thicker reticulate inner region (R). Lamellae were oriented parallel to the leaf surface. The inner region contained both fine and coarse reticulate subregions. Deposits (D) between the reticulate membrane region and the cell wall (W) may be composed of calcium. Bar = 500 nm.

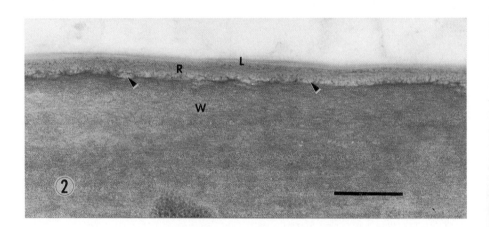

Figure 2   Cuticular membrane from a yellow poplar leaf exposed to 2x ozone-air. Outer poly-lamellate (L) and inner reticulate (R) regions were observed. The reticulate region is reduced in thickness compared to this region from leaves grown in CF-air. Very small electron lucent areas (arrows) were seen at the distinct boundary between the cuticular membrane and the epidermal cell wall (W). Bar = 500 nm.

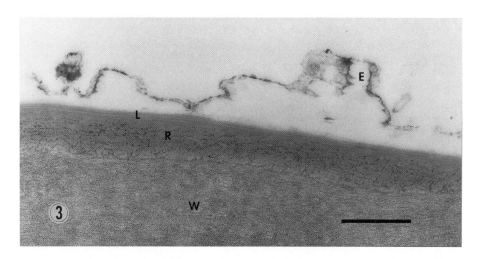

Figure 3   Structure of the cuticular membrane from a yellow poplar leaf grown in 2X ozone +
             CO$_2$. The outer polylamellate region (L) was similar in thickness and number of
             lamellae to the corresponding region from leaves of the other treatments. The inner
             reticulate region (R) was thicker than the reticulate region in leaves grown in 2X
             ozone air (compare to Figure 2) but thinner than leaves from the CF-air treatment
             (Figure 1). E, epicuticular wax. Bar = 500 nm.

observed at the junction of the reticulate region and the epidermal cell wall in some leaf sections
from this treatment.

Cuticular membrane thickness in yellow poplar leaves exposed to 2x ozone + CO$_2$ (Table 1) was
36% greater than cuticular membrane thickness from leaves treated with 2x ozone-air, but it was
significantly reduced when compared with membrane thickness from leaves grown in CF-air (a
44% reduction). The structure of the cuticular membrane (outer polylamellate and inner reticulate
regions, Figure 3) was the same as observed in the other treatments. In the three treatments
compared in this study, the outer polylamellate layer was consistently similar in thickness
(approximately 50 nm) regardless of treatment; however, the thickness of the inner reticulate
region appeared to vary with treatment. The boundary between the cuticular membrane and the
epidermal wall was less well-defined in many leaf sections from the 2x ozone + CO$_2$-grown
trees.

Alterations in epidermal cell walls were observed in the leaves grown in either 2x ozone-air or
2x ozone + CO$_2$ when compared with the CF-grown trees. Deterioration of epidermal walls (*i.e.*,

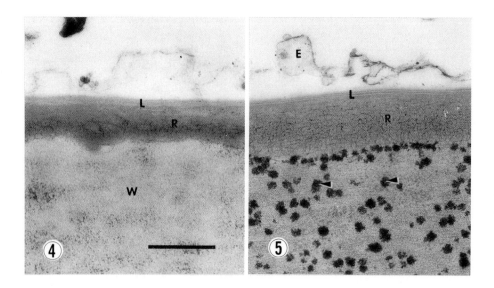

Figure 4   Deterioration of epidermal wall structure in a yellow poplar leaf grown in 2x ozone-air. Cell wall (W) lacks characteristic fibrillar structure. The cuticular membrane retained the polylamellate (L) and reticulate (R) regions.

Figure 5   Dense recipitate (arrows) formed in the epidermal wall of a leaf grown in 2x ozone + CO_2. However, cuticular membrane structure was similar to the structure of unaffected leaves. E, epicuticular wax. Bar = 500 nm.

loss of fibrillar structure) was often observed in yellow poplar leaves grown in 2x-ozone air (Figure 4). The formation of dense precipitates in the cell walls of two leaves grown in 2x ozone + CO_2 (Figure 5) was also observed. These aberrations in cell wall structure did not result in a change in the basic structure or the thickness of the cuticular membrane (Figures 4, 5).

Discussion

Cuticular membrane thickness in yellow poplar leaves decreased significantly after two seasons of seedling exposure to 2x ozone-air. This finding contrasts with the report by Percy *et al.* (1992), who found an increase in cuticular membrane thickness in red spruce after one season of ozone exposure. Differences in these results may be due to ozone exposure dynamics (*i.e.*, duration, diurnal fluctuation), inherent differences between conifer and deciduous trees (leaf life span), and differences in growing conditions (field chambers or environmentally-controlled chambers). Changes in plant metabolism and carbon allocation have been reported due to ozone exposure (Mooney and Winner, 1988). Yellow poplar, a fast-growing hardwood species, increased at least

2 m in height in all treatments during 1993 (J.Rebbeck, pers. comm.). It is possible that exposure to 2x ozone-air for two growing seasons altered the amount of photosynthate that was allocated to yellow poplar cuticle formation in the second year.

The significant reduction in cuticular membrane thickness found in leaves from trees grown in 2x ozone-air and 2x ozone + CO_2 compared with those grown in CF-air was due to a visible decrease in the thickness of the inner reticulate region. This region is mixture of cell wall compounds and cutin (Holloway, 1982). Further work is needed to determine whether the decrease in thickness of this reticulate region may be related to the production of cell wall material or cutin.

Elevated CO_2 added to 2x ozone increased cuticular membrane thickness compared to 2x ozone alone. Growth data from this study showed a significant growth increase in yellow poplar seedlings grown in 2x ozone + CO_2 compared to seedlings grown in 2x ozone alone (Rebbeck, manuscript in preparation). Whether this increase in growth and cuticular membrane thickness may be due directly to a CO_2 effect (increase in photosynthate) or indirectly due to a decrease in ozone uptake is yet to be determined.

The plant cuticle, comprised of the cuticular membrane plus epicuticular waxes, has been characterized as a non-living, non-cellular membrane that restricts water loss and protects the leaf from its environment (Bukovac et al., 1981). Although the resistance of the cuticle to ion movement is primarily due to the epicuticular wax layer (Schier and Jensen, 1992), it is possible that a reduction in the thickness of the cuticular membrane due to ozone exposure may increase permeability. Ozone has been shown to enchance ion leaching in Norway spruce (Skeffington and Roberts, 1985); whether an ozone-induced decrease in cuticular membrane thickness could further enchance ion loss has not been quantified. In this study, a significant increase in the thickness of the cuticular membrane was found with the combination of ozone and elevated CO_2. What role elevated CO_2 may play in ameliorating ozone-induced ion loss in leaves is unknown.

In summary, exposure of yellow poplar seedlings to 2x ozone-air over two growing seasons significantly reduced cuticular membrane thickness compared to seedlings grown in CF-air. This ozone effect was not completely ameliorated by addition of elevated CO_2 to 2x ozone-air, although cuticular membrane thickness was increased significantly compared with 2x ozone-air alone. The reduction in cuticular membrane thickness appears to correspond to a reduced inner reticulate region. Leaf samples will be collected yearly from this long-term study to further evaluate effects of ozone and ozone plus elevated CO_2 on the leaf cuticular membrane. These measurements will be correlated with epicuticular wax chemistry, leaf anatomy/morphology, growth, and biomass production for a more complete picture of forest tree response to changing environmental conditions.

References

Allen LH, Jr. (1990) Plant responses to rising carbon dioxide and potential interactions with air pollutants. J Environ Qual 19: 15-34

Barnes JD, Davison AW, Booth TA (1988) Ozone accelerates structural degradation of epicuticular wax on Norway spruce needles. New Phytol 110: 309-318

Bazzaz FA, Coleman JS, Morse SP (1990) Growth responses of seven co-occuring tree species of the northeastern United States to elevated CO_2. Can. J. For. Res. 20: 1479-1498

Bukovac MJ, Rasmussen HP, Shull VE (1981) The cuticle: surface structure and function. Scanning Electron Microscopy III: 213-223

Fink S (1991) Comparative microscopical studies on the patterns of calcium oxalate distribution in the needles of various conifer species. Bot Acta 104: 306-315

Graham RL, Turner MG, Dale VH (1990) How increasing CO_2 and climate change affect forests. BioScience 40: 575-587

Holloway PJ (1982) Structure and histochemistry of plant cuticular membranes: an overview. *In* The plant cuticle, Cutler DF, Alvin KL, Price CE (*eds*) Academic Press, London *pp* 1-32.

Keeling CD (1986) Atmospheric CO_2 concentrations. Mauna Loa Observatory, Hawaii 1958-1986. Oak Ridge Nat Lab Rep NDP-001/R1

Mooney HA, Winner WE (1988) Carbon gain, allocation, and growth as affected by atmospheric pollutants. *In* Air pollution and plant metabolism, Schulte-Hostede S, Darrall NM, Blank LW, Wellburn AR (*eds*) Elsevier Applied Science, London *pp* 272-287

Percy KE, Jensen KF, McQuattie CJ (1992) Effects of ozone and acidic fog on red spruce needle epicuticular wax production, chemical composition, cuticular membrane ultrastructure and needle wettability. New Phytol 122: 71-80

Percy KE, Krause CR, Jensen KF (1990) Effects of ozone and acidic fog on red spruce needle epicuticular wax ultrastructure. Can J For Res 20: 117-120

Rebbeck J (1993) Investigation of long-term effects of ozone and elevated carbon dioxide on eastern forest species: first-year response. Proceedings of the Air & Waste Management Association, 86th Annual Meeting, 1993 June 13-18, Denver, CO. Series 93-TA-43.02: 1-10

Schier, GA, Jensen KF (1992) Atmospheric deposition effects on foliar injury and foliar leaching in red spruce. *In* Ecology and decline of red spruce in the Eastern United States, Eager C, Adams MB (*eds*) Springer-Verlag, New York *pp* 271-294

Skeffington RA, Roberts M (1985) Effect of ozone and acid mist on Scots pine and Norway spruce - an experimental study. *In* Waldshaden, VAI Berichte 560, *pp* 747-760

Spatial Distribution of Sulphate Uptake by Wind-Damaged Beech Leaves

C.E. Jeffree, J. Grace, and S.P. Hoad
University of Edinburgh
Division of Biological Sciences
The King's Buildings
Mayfield Road
Edinburgh, EH9 3JH, U.K.

Abstract

Exposure of beech leaves to wind damage increased the amount and spatial variability of sulphate uptake from solutions in contact with the astomatous adaxial leaf surface. Drying of the droplets on the leaf surface enhanced uptake by up to three orders of magnitude compared with uptake from solution. Sulphate was not transported far from entry points provided by cuticular lesions. Cuticular integrity, assessed using dye tracers, was breached by wind damage caused by repeated abrasion and impacts between leaves and buds, and by ballistic impaction of wind-borne particles. Cuticular lesions provide acid rain and mist with access to mesophyll domains delimited by minor veins. Wind damage and weathering may, therefore, increase the magnitude and heterogeneity of solute uptake via leaf surfaces by damaging cuticular integrity.

Introduction

The permeability of plant cuticles to solutes is usually measured using cuticular membranes, enzymically-isolated from pristine leaves (*e.g.*, Kerler *et al.*, 1984; Schönherr and Riederer, 1989). In this way, the conductance of cuticles has been measured for water (Schönherr, 1982), and organic molecules (Schönherr and Riederer, 1989; Riederer, 1989), and ion transport and exchange properties of the cuticular membrane have been measured (Schönherr and Bukovac, 1973; Schönherr and Huber, 1977; Tyree *et al.*, 1990). An important advantage of the use of isolated cuticles for measuring permeance is that the driving forces for ion and molecular transport across the membrane are readily determined and can be dynamically controlled, and the same piece of cuticular membrane may be conditioned and manipulated successively to provide data for the conductance of the membrane to several ion species. However, there are also significant disadvantages in the use of isolated cuticles. In particular: [1] Satisfactory measurements depend crucially on complete cuticular integrity. Thus the conductance of plant surfaces in real-life situations, where the cuticle may be abraded, insect-bitten and otherwise injured, is certainly underestimated. [2] Measurements using cuticle discs have low spatial resolution, and are also limited to locations from which complete leaf discs can be obtained, thus excluding leaf tips and edges, which are particularly vulnerable to abrasive wind damage. [3] Measurements using isolated cuticles may be inappropriate for microphyllous needle-leaved species, such as conifers and heaths, from which it is impossible to isolate astomatous cuticular membranes of

NATO ASI Series, Vol. G 36
Air Pollutants and the Leaf Cuticle
Edited by K. E. Percy et al.
© Springer-Verlag Berlin Heidelberg 1994

useful size. **[4]** The chemical properties of the cuticular membrane may be altered in the process of isolation (see, *e.g.*, Schönherr and Riederer, 1986). **[5]** Permeability of isolated cuticular membranes may be sensitive to mechanical damage during preparation arising from some of the very processes (abrasion, torsion, tension, flexing, *etc.*) whose effect on cuticular permeability *in vivo* we are attempting to isolate.

The objective of this study was to assess the influence of wind damage on sulphate uptake from acidic solutions placed on the surface of beech leaves grown in exposed lowland and upland locations. The approach was designed to permit the analysis of the magnitude and variability of sulphate uptake at various levels of spatial resolution.

Materials and methods

Plant material: Seedlings of beech (*Fagus sylvatica* L.) raised under glass for two seasons in a potting mixture of sand, gravel and compost were acclimatised in a glass open-top shelter for a further season prior to transfer to an upland hill site at Dunslair Heights, Scotland, 42 km south of Edinburgh (55° 41' N, 3° 08' W, altitude 600 m) as described by Hoad *et al. this volume.* Leaves were also taken from a long-established 3-m high beech hedge at Edinburgh, one side of which was exposed to prevailing westerly winds, and the other side of which was sheltered by nearby trees and hedges. **Application of sulphate solutions to leaf surfaces:** Radioactively-labelled sulphate solutions were made as 2.5 mM or 3.3 mM solutions of $H_2[^{35}S]O_4$ with a specific activity of about 42 GBq mol^{-1}. The solutions were either used at native pH, or were adjusted to a specific pH with ammonium hydroxide. Uptake of sulphate was measured using intact leaves which had been exposed to solutions of ammonium $[^{35}S]$sulphate or $[^{35}S]$sulphuric acid, either as droplets, or uniformly over their surfaces. In some experiments, droplets were applied in wells made from silicone rubber rings bonded to the adaxial leaf surface with dental silicone rubber (Reflect Wash, Kerr U.K., Ltd., Peterborough)(Hoad *et al.*, 1992). Ten µL of sulphate solution was placed in each well and the leaves incubated for 5 h, either at 100% humidity to maintain droplet volume, or in open air, allowing the solution to evaporate. Alternatively, leaves were uniformly exposed to the solutions by floating them, adaxial surface downwards, on a pool of solution. **Scintillation counting:** Leaf discs (3.01 mm dia.: 7.41 mm^2) were digested in 100 µL of 1% aq. sodium docenyl sulphate at 95 °C for 16 h, decolourized by addition of 100 µL of 30% w/v H_2O_2 (95 °C, 4 h), and mixed with 1.8mL of Triton scintillant (0.33% PPO and 0.033% POPOP in 2:1 Toluene / Triton X100). Sulphate uptake (µmol m^{-2}) was calculated from duplicate scintillation-counts using a 2σ counting error of 0.5% or less, after subtraction of background. The spatial distribution of uptake was reconstructed by systematic leaf-disc sampling from recorded positions in leaves which had been exposed uniformly to sulphate solutions over their adaxial surfaces. For **Autoradiography** leaves were freeze-dried and autoradiographed by

Table 1   Uptake of sulphate (μmol m^{-2}) by the adaxial surfaces of beech leaves from sheltered and exposed sites at Dunslair Heights (600 m elevation) from 10-μL droplets of 2.5mM (NH$_4$)2[^{35}S]O$_4$ solution

	Sheltered site	Exposed site	Sheltered site	Exposed site
Site:				
Treatment:	Wet droplets	Wet droplets	Dried droplets	Dried droplets
Time:	5 h	5 h	5 h	5h
Mean uptake	1.1	34.2	813.0	1028.5
Standard error of the mean	0.2	6.2	163.6	232.4
Min.	0.0	0.4	51.4	8.7
Max.	3.7	78.1	2192.5	3156.8
N	26	16	22	23
Coefficient of Dispersion (Variance/Mean) random = 1	0.9	17.9	724.1	1207.8
Mean uptake % of sulphate in droplet	0.1	0.5	12.1	15.2
Minimum % uptake	0.0	0.1	0.8	0.1
Maximum % uptake	0.1	1.2	32.5	46.8

contact with DuPont Cronex 4 X-ray film for between 1 and 8 days. A **dye tracer** Coriphosphine O (Weis *et al.*, 1988) (1 mg/mL aq.) was used to reveal the locations of discrete cuticular lesions at which pectin was exposed at the surface. The distribution of the dye was detected by its fluorescence in long-wavelength UV radiation and photographed on Fuji Velvia colour film using an orange barrier filter.

Results

Leaves from sheltered and exposed sites at Dunslair Heights were exposed to 10-μL droplets of 2.5 mM ammonium [^{35}S]sulphate solution. Uptake of [^{35}S]sulphate via the astomatous adaxial surfaces of a sheltered beech leaf was very low, averaging 1.1 $\pm$ 0.2 μmol m^{-2} (N=26) (Table 1). Amounts of [^{35}S] sulphate taken up by individual discs ranged from undetectable to about 3.7 μmol m^{-2}. By contrast, mean uptake by an exposed leaf was 30 times greater than by the sheltered leaf. However, mean uptake remained very low, corresponding to about 0.5% of the sulphate available for uptake from the droplets. In the leaf from the exposed site the amounts taken up by individual discs showed a coefficient of dispersion (CD) of 17.87, indicating greater variability than would be expected of a randomly distributed sample with the same mean, while in the sheltered leaf a CD of 0.94 indicated variation closer to random.

When the droplets were evaporated to dryness on the leaf surface, sulphate uptake was greatly increased. Mean uptake from dried droplets was 813 $\pm$ 164 μmol m^{-2} by the sheltered leaf and 1028 $\pm$ 232 μmol m-^{2} by the exposed leaf, representing approximately 12% and 15% respectively of the sulphate available for uptake. The difference between sheltered and exposed leaves was not, in this instance, statistically significant. At the same time, the amounts taken up by the leaf discs from sheltered and exposed leaves were highly variable, showing a coefficient of dispersion of about 724 for the sheltered leaf, and of 1208 in the leaf from the exposed site (Table 1), significantly greater than would be expected for a random distribution.

Spatial distribution of sulphate uptake: When the values for sulphate uptake into leaf discs were compared with the locations of the samples, it was apparent that differences of two orders of magnitude or more occurred between samples with centres less than 5 mm apart. In further experiments the spatial distribution of sulphate uptake was mapped in leaves from sheltered and exposed leaves from a wind-exposed lowland site, by systematic sampling from recorded locations. Results for a leaf from the sheltered side of a lowland beech hedge (Fig. 1, A) showed a generally low level of uptake from 2.5 mM ammonium sulphate solution, with a mean of 5.6 $\pm$ 0.9 μmol m^{-2} (Table 2 A). However, individual samples close to the edge of the leaf, and some others in the distal half, showed uptake about an order of magnitude higher than the mean. By contrast, the leaf from the exposed side of the hedge showed mean uptake about 5-fold higher (33.4 $\pm$ 5.0 μmol m^{-2}) than in the sheltered leaf, again with maxima and minima an order of magnitude above and below the mean. The distribution map of sulphate uptake (Fig. 1, B) clearly demonstrates that the distal end of the leaf was most heavily labelled. In particular, samples at the leaf tip, one of the areas most vulnerable to abrasive wind damage, show the highest uptake with maximum values approaching 300 μmol m^{-2}, while the proximal end shows uptake closer to the range observed in the sheltered leaf. Especially in the exposed leaves, the statistical variability of the uptake data is again higher than would be expected of random data (Table 2

Table 2   Uptake (μmol m^{-2}) of sulphate by sheltered and exposed beech leaves from solutions applied uniformly to the whole of the adaxial surface into 3.01-mm diameter leaf disc samples.

	A] 2.5 mM (NH$_4$)$_2$[^{35}S]O$_4$		B] 2.5 mM H$_2$[^{35}S]O$_4$	
	Sheltered	Exposed	Sheltered	Exposed
Mean	5.6	33.4	11.8	28.8
Standard Error	0.9	5.0	1.7	2.8
Minimum	1.7	2.9	1.6	1.4
Maximum	51.9	277.5	107.2	194.8
N	79	89	105	120
Coefficient of Dispersion	11.7	67.6	26.2	33.3

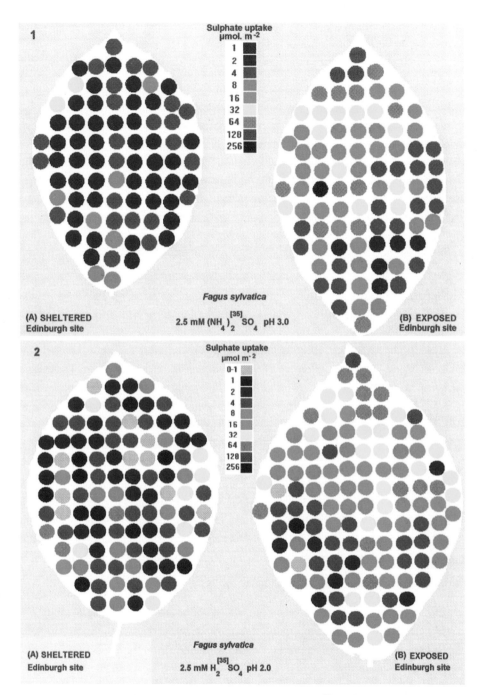

Figures 1 and 2. Distribution maps of sulphate uptake from uniformly-applied [^{35}S]sulphate solutions via the adaxial surface of beech leaves from sheltered and exposed sides of the same plant in a wind-exposed hedge at Edinburgh, U.K. Leaf-disc sample positions are colour coded to represent binary (2^n) intervals of sulphate uptake (see keys).

Figure 1   Uptake from a 2.5-mM pH 3.0 solution of (NH$_4$)$_2$[^{35}S]O$_4$ by (A) sheltered leaf (B) exposed leaf
Figure 2   Uptake from a 2.5-mM pH 2.0 solution of H$_2$[^{35}S]O$_4$ by (A) sheltered leaf (B) exposed leaf.

A), and the small-scale spatial variability is emphasised by the fact that adjacent samples often have values differing by more than an order of magnitude (Figs. 1 and 2).

In a parallel experiment, leaves from the sheltered and exposed sides of the same plant were exposed to 2.5mM sulphuric acid. Again the sheltered leaf shows generally low uptake (mean 11.8 ± 1.7 μmol m^{-2}: Table 2), with scattered peak values more than an order of magnitude above the general background (Fig. 2, A). The leaf from the exposed side of the hedge shows mean uptake of 28.8 ± 2.8 μmol m^{-2}, almost three times higher than in the sheltered leaf, and once again the distal end of the leaf showed highest uptake (Fig. 2B). In this experiment, the leaf from the sheltered side of the hedge showed little visible damage, and it was not always possible to associate the high-uptake leaf discs with visible imperfections. By contrast, the leaf from the exposed side of the hedge showed a pronounced gradient of visible damage features from the distal to the proximal end, including tattering of edges, areas of necrosis, minor scratches, and chlorotic mesophyll domains.

The predominantly distal distribution of sulphate uptake in this leaf (Fig 2, B) correlated broadly with the distribution of visible damage . However, the resolution of the leaf disc samples is too low to permit any direct connection to be made between uptake and individual damage events. To increase spatial resolution still further, distribution maps of radionuclide uptake were obtained by autoradiography of leaves, producing much higher resolution than is practical by disc-sampling, but with lower quantitative accuracy and dynamic range. Adaxial surfaces of leaves from the sheltered and exposed sides of the same plant at Edinburgh were uniformly exposed to a 3.3 mM $H_2[^{35}S]O_4$ solution, containing in addition the fluorochrome Coriphosphine O in order to stain the cell wall beneath damage microsites where the integrity of the cuticle had been compromised.

The sheltered leaf (Fig. 3) shows minor visible damage, in particular a healed perforation (Fig. 3, **p**) and a pair of minor necrotic lesions (not visible at the scale of this photograph). In the autoradiograph of the same leaf (Fig. 4) uptake of sulphate is low-level and diffuse, although there are small points of intense uptake. The edge of the perforation is strongly labelled with [^{35}S], but the label has penetrated only a few micrometres into adjacent tissues (Fig. 4, **p**). The positions of the two necrotic lesions are marked by strong labelling (Fig. 4, **n**). Again the label is closely confined to the injured area. Visible damage to the exposed leaf (Fig. 5) is much more conspicuous and affects larger areas. The leaf edges (Fig. 5, **m**) are browned, and tissue has been lost from a region of the leaf tip. Towards the distal end of the leaf is an arc of red-brown discoloration (**a**), resulting from repeated abrasive contacts with the tip of an adjacent leaf on the same branch. Although there is a diffuse increase in film density in the autoradiograph corresponding with this discoloured area (Fig. 6, **a**), the most strongly labelled sites within that area are small and labelled intensely (Figs. 6 and 8). These sites of intense uptake correlate exactly

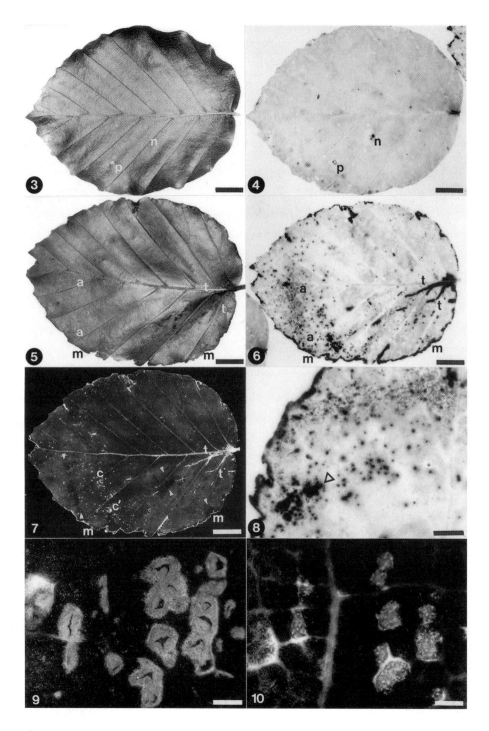

Captions to **Figures 3 to 10**: see page 193.

with the sites most strongly labelled with Coriphosphine O (Figs. 7; 9 and 10), and in general the pattern of dye uptake into the leaves closely corresponds with the distribution of the most intense [^{35}S]sulphate labelling. In particular, the visible lesions in the sheltered leaf, and the damaged leaf edges in the exposed leaf are strongly labelled by both the radionuclide (Figs. 4, 6, 8) and the dye (Fig. 7) as are the edges of torn areas near the leaf base (Figs. 6, 7) and the numerous damage microsites (Figs. 7 to 10). However, there is an inverse correlation between dye uptake and radionuclide uptake in the visibly-discoloured regions of the leaf. The dye has been taken up least in these areas (Fig. 7, **arrowheads**), while [^{35}S] uptake into the discoloured arc in the exposed leaf and from other strongly-discoloured regions is higher than in less-damaged adjacent areas (Figs. 6, 8).

A small irregular patch of intense [^{35}S] labelling is shown in Fig. 8. Seen at higher magnification in the fluorescence microscope (Fig. 9), this same feature consists of a cluster of fluorescently-labelled cuticular lesions, possibly caused by repeated impacts with adjacent leaves or buds. Neither the dye nor the [^{35}S] penetrate freely into the tissues from these entry points, but remain locally confined. When the same cluster is viewed from the abaxial leaf surface (Fig. 10) it becomes apparent that the dye has gained entry to internal tissue within single mesophyll blocks, or domains, but that the surrounding minor veins act as barriers to its further penetration.

Discussion

The amounts of sulphate taken up by undamaged beech leaves are small, consistent with our observations (Hoad *et al., this volume*) that acid mist at pH 3 and 5 has little measurable effect on the structure or function of undamaged leaves. Percy and Baker (1989) also recovered very little [^{35}S] from spruce needles exposed to sulphate solutions. However, even in apparently uninjured sheltered leaves, small breaches of cuticular integrity corresponding with the micro-scopic cuticular lesions (discussed by Hoad *et al., this volume*) permit high local uptake of sulphate. It follows that sulphate does not move rapidly from the point of entry, but may be immobilised, possibly by precipitation with Ca^{2+} as insoluble calcium sulphate. Entry via cuticular lesions leads to a spatially variable uptake that is apparent at both large and small scales, and is enhanced by the mechanical damage to leaf surfaces caused by exposure to wind. Consistent with earlier reports (Wilson, 1980, 1984) beech leaf tips and edges are vulnerable to wind damage, and sulphate uptake in these areas often shows the highest mean values and highest variance in wind-exposed leaves, emphasizing the importance of including the leaf margin, necessarily ignored in studies using isolated cuticles, in the analysis of uptake. Some other sites vulnerable to wind damage, such as the midrib and major veins (see Hoad *et al., this volume*) unexpectedly showed little uptake in wind-damaged leaves, and were often labelled to a lesser extent than was the lamina. At larger scale, a gradient of sulphate uptake from the leaf base (low) to the leaf tip (high) is common in wind-exposed beech leaves and has been observed in the samples shown here and many others. The data for sulphate uptake by wind-exposed leaves is also highly variable statistically, and this variance is significantly greater than would be expected to arise at random for samples with the same mean.

Both the mean uptake and the sample variance are substantially increased by droplet drying. Repeated cycles of acid mist deposition and drying-down (Milne *et al.*, 1990), or continuous deposition accompanied by evaporation (Unsworth and Crossley, 1987), could lead to the concentration of sulphate on the leaf surface and to decreasing pH, and chemically-induced cuticle damage may be greater under such circumstances. However, as noted by Unsworth and Crossley (1987), the significance of such processes on leaf surfaces remains to be demonstrated. Experimental analysis is necessary of the consequences of such cycles for cuticular integrity and chemistry, and of the consequences for cuticular uptake characteristics over the long term.

The exclusion of the dye tracer Coriphosphine by visibly-damaged areas of leaves, compared with the increased uptake of sulphate in the same areas, demonstrates that the enhancement of sulphate uptake in wind-damaged leaves is not exclusively by virtue of the provision of discrete breaches of cuticular integrity, which would not be expected to discriminate strongly between molecules. That cuticular permeability differs for molecules with different properties is widely known (see, *e.g.*, review by Lendzian and Kerstiens, 1991), but it would be relevant to know whether the properties of cuticle that are altered by abrasive damage and possible repair processes are primarily physical, for example influencing the molecular size-exclusion properties of the uptake pathway, or other properties such as their ion exchange capacity. Although dynamic changes in cuticle properties which could constitute one type of repair mechanism have been reported (Geyer and Schönherr, 1990), it is unclear whether a wind-damaged cuticle is in fact capable of repair, and thus whether it makes any difference whether the acid deposition event occurs concurrently with wind damage, or following a recovery period.

Sulphate can gain direct access to leaf mesophyll tissue via cuticular lesions which represent a cuticular bypass, and its containment within discrete mesophyll blocks or domains means that any immediate toxic effect is likely to cause spatially-patchy damage to metabolic processes. Such a bypass pathway circumvents any process of control by cuticular properties, and, therefore, in natural environments measurements of cuticular permeance provide an inadequate basis upon which to assess the interaction of leaves with pollutants. The fate of sulphate following uptake, and the consequences of its uptake, are still obscure. Although there is widespread concern about possible connections between acid deposition and forest decline, no confirmatory information has merged that the deposition of acid mist at realistic concentrations and pH's to intact cuticular membranes induces any physiologically-relevant response. The question of whether the presence of a droplet of 2.5mM sulphate resting on intact cuticle is actually perceived by the underlying cells is, as yet, unanswered. However, the conclusions of this work are that wind damages cuticular integrity, and influences both sulphate uptake from, and plant response to, acid mist. The influence of wind on cuticular integrity must, therefore, be controlled in experiments on the effects of acid mist and rain, and other atmospheric pollutants, on plant surface structure and function.

Acknowledgements

This study was funded by Natural Environment Research Council grant no. GR3/7175. Technical assistance provided by John Findlay is gratefully acknowledged. Grateful thanks is also extended to the Forestry Commission for help in siting and constructing the plant enclosures at Dunslair Heights.

References

Geyer U, Schönherr, J (1990) The effect of the environment on the permeability and composition of *Citrus* leaf cuticles. I. Water permeability of isolated cuticular membranes. Planta 180: 147-153

Hoad SP, Jeffree CE, Grace J (1992) Effects of wind and abrasion on cuticular integrity in *Fagus sylvatica* L. and consequences for transfer of pollutants through leaf surfaces. Agric Ecosystems Environ 42: 275-289

Kerler F, Riederer M, Schönherr J (1984) Non-electrolyte permeability of plant cuticles: a critical evaluation of experimental methods. Physiol plant 62: 599-606

Lendzian KL, Kerstiens G (1991) Sorption and transport of gases and vapors in plant cuticles. Rev Environ Contamin Toxicol 121: 65-128

Milne R, Crossley A, Henderson C (1990) Field measurements of the acidity of cloudwater deposited on polypropylene surfaces and Sitka spruce shoots. Trees 4: 205-210

Percy KE, Baker EA (1988) Effects of simulated acid rain on leaf wettability, rain retention and uptake of some inorganic ions. New Phytol 108: 75-82

Percy KE, Baker EA (1989) Effect of simulated acid rain on foliar uptake of Rb^+ and $SO_4$2- by two clones of Sitka spruce (*Picea sitchensis* (Bong.) Carr). *In* Air pollution and forest decline Bucher JB, Bucher-Wallin I (*eds*) Proc. 14th Int. Meeting for specialists in air pollution effects on forest ecosystems. IUFRO P2.05, 1988 *pp* 493-495

Percy KE, Baker EA (1990) Effects of simulated acid rain on epicuticular wax production, morphology, chemical composition and on cuticular membrane thickness in two clones of Sitka spruce [*Picea sitchensis* (Bong) Carr]. New Phytol 116: 79-87

Riederer M (1989) The cuticles of conifers: structure, composition and transport properties. *In* Schulze E-D, Lange OL, Oren R (*eds*) Ecological studies Vol 77. Springer-Verlag, Berlin *pp* 157-192

Schönherr J (1982) Resistance of plant surfaces to water loss: transport properties of cutin, suberin and associated lipids. *In* Lange OL, Nobel PS, Osmond CB, Ziegler CB (*eds*) Physiological plant ecology II. Water relations and carbon assimilation. Encyclopaedia of plant physiology. New Series, Volume 12B, Springer-Verlag, Berlin *pp* 153-179

Schönherr J, Bukovac MJ (1973) Ion exchange properties of isolated tomato fruit cuticular membranes: exchange capacity, nature of fixed charges and cation selectivity. Planta 109: 73-93

Schönherr J, Huber R (1977) Plant cuticles are polyelectrolytes with isoelectric points around three. Plant Physiol 59: 145-150

Schönherr J, Riederer M (1986) Plant cuticles sorb lipophilic compounds during enzymatic isolation. Plant Cell Environ 9: 459-466

Schönherr J, Riederer M (1989) Foliar penetration and accumulation of organic chemicals in plant cuticles. Rev Environ Contamin Toxicol 108: 1-70

Tyree MT, Scherbatskoy TD, Tabor CA (1990) Leaf cuticles behave as asymmetric membranes. Evidence from the measurement of diffusion potentials. Plant Physiol 92: 103-109

Unsworth MH, Crossley A (1987) Consequences of cloudwater deposition on vegetation at high elevation. *In* Hutchinson TC, Meema KM (*eds*) Effects of atmospheric pollutants on forests, wetlands and agricultural ecosystems. NATO ASI G16. Springer-Verlag, Berlin, Heidelberg *pp* 171-188

Weis KG, Polito VS, Labavitch JM (1988) Microfluorimetry of pectic materials in the dehiscence zone of almond (*Prunus dulcis* [Mill.] D.A Webb) fruits. J Histochem Cytochem 36: 1037-1041

Wilson J (1980) Macroscopic features of wind damage to leaves in *Acer pseudoplatanus* L. and its relationship with season, leaf age, and wind speed. Ann Bot 46: 303-311

Wilson J (1984) Microscopic features of wind damage to leaves of *Acer pseudoplatanus* L. Ann Bot 53: 73-82

Figures 3 to 10: Photographs (Figs. 3, 5), autoradiographs (Figs. 4, 6, 8) and fluorescence images (Figs. 7, 9, 10) of two leaves from sheltered (Figs. 3, 4) and exposed (Figs. 5 to 10) sides of the same beech plant in a wind-exposed lowland hedge. Leaf adaxial surfaces were uniformly exposed for 5 h to 3.3 mM $H_2[^{35}S]O_4$ containing 1 mg mL^{-1} of the fluorochrome Coriphosphine O.

Figure 3	Photograph of the sheltered leaf, showing only small numbers of visible defects. A perforation in the lamina is visible (**p**). In the original colour transparency two small necrotic lesions are visible at the point indicated (**n**). Bar = 10 mm.
Figure 4	Autoradiograph of the sheltered leaf, showing low-level labelling with [^{35}S]. The margin of the perforation indicated in Figure 5 is labelled with [^{35}S](**p**), and the two necrotic lesions are also strongly labelled (**n**). Bar = 10 mm.
Figure 5	Photograph of the exposed leaf showing a basal tear (**t**), damage to the leaf margin (**m**), and a discoloured arc caused by mutual leaf abrasion (**a**); unfortunately this region exhibits weak contrast when reproduced in black and white. Bar = 10 mm.
Figure 6	Autoradiograph of the exposed leaf, showing intense labelling of the leaf margins (**m**), the edges of a basal tear (**t**). Two arcs occur composed of scattered points of intense uptake. The most distal (**a - a**) has a background of diffuse uptake and corresponds with the discoloured arc shown in Fig. 5. Bar = 10 mm.
Figure 7	A fluorescence photograph of the exposed leaf showing Coriphosphine O uptake by the leaf margin (**m**), basal tear (**t**) and microscopic cuticular lesions (**c**). Note that uptake of the dye is reduced at three locations (**arrowheads**) where the lamina was visibly discoloured. Bar = 10 mm.
Figure 8	shows a detail from Figure 6. Arrowhead indicates a group of cuticular lesions which is also visible in the fluorescence image (Fig. 7), and at higher magnification in Figs. 9 and 10. Bar = 4 mm.
Figs. 9 and 10:	Fluorescence micrographs of Coriphosphine O labelling of tissue beneath the group of cuticular lesions shown in Figs. 7 (**c'**) and 8 (**arrowhead**). Fig. 9: View of the adaxial surface, clearly showing perforations in the cuticle. Fig. 10: View of the identical area from the abaxial surface, showing that the patches of fluorescence are confined to mesophyll blocks or domains bounded by minor veins. Bar = 250 μm.

Effects of UV-B Radiation on Wax Biosynthesis

Jeremy Barnes, Nigel Paul[1], Kevin Percy[2], Pam Broadbent[1], Chris McLaughlin[2],
Phil Mullineaux[3], Gary Creissen[3], and Alan Wellburn[1]
Department of Agricultural and Environmental Science
The Ridley Building
The University
Newcastle-Upon-Tyne
NE1 7RU. U.K.

Abstract

Two genotypes of tobacco (*Nicotiana tabacum* L.) were exposed in controlled environment chambers to three levels of biologically effective ultraviolet-B radiation (UV-B$_{BE}$; 280-320nm): 0, 4.54 (ambient) and 5.66 ($\approx 25\%$ enhancement) kJ m^{-2} d^{-1}. After 28 days, the quantity of wax deposited on leaf surfaces was determined gravimetrically; epicuticular wax chemical composition was determined by capillary gas chromatography with homologue assignments confirmed by gas chromatography-mass spectrometry. Leaf wettability was assessed by measuring the contact angle of water droplets placed on leaf surfaces. Tobacco wax consisted of three major hydrocarbon classes: straight-chain alkanes (C_{27}-C_{33}) which comprised $\approx 59\%$ of the hydrocarbon fraction, containing a predominance of odd-chain alkanes with C_{31} as the most abundant homologue; branched-chain alkanes (C_{25}-C_{32}) which comprised $\approx 38\%$ of the hydrocarbon fraction with anteiso 3-methyltriacontane (C_{30}) as the predominant homologue; and fatty acids (C_{14}-C_{18}) which comprised $\approx 3\%$ of the wax. Exposure to enhanced UV-B radiation reduced the quantity of wax on the adaxial surface of the transgenic mutant, and resulted in marked changes in the chemical composition of the wax on the exposed leaf surface. Enhanced UV-B decreased the quantity of straight-chain alkanes, increased the quantity of branched-chain alkanes and fatty acids, and resulted in shifts toward shorter straight-chain lengths. Furthermore, UV-B-induced changes in wax composition were associated with increased wettability of tobacco leaf surfaces. Overall, the data are consistent with the view that UV-B radiation has a direct and fundamental effect on wax biosynthesis. Relationships between the physico-chemical nature of the leaf surface and sensitivity to UV-B radiation are discussed.

Introduction

Depletion of stratospheric ozone by anthropogenically produced chlorine species (*e.g.*, chlorofluorocarbons) is leading to an increase in the amount of ultraviolet-B (UV-B) radiation

---

[1]Institute of Environmental and Biological Sciences, Lancaster University, Bailrigg, Lancaster LA1 4YQ. U.K.

[2]Canadian Forest Service, Natural Resources Canada, P.O. Box 4000, Fredericton, New Brunswick, Canada E3B 5P7.

[3]John Innes Institue, Colney Lane, Norwich, NR4 7UH United Kingdom

NATO ASI Series, Vol. G 36
Air Pollutants and the Leaf Cuticle
Edited by K. E. Percy et al.
© Springer-Verlag Berlin Heidelberg 1994

(280-320 nm) reaching the earth's surface (Stolarski *et al.*, 1991). This has prompted serious concern as numerous growth chamber, greenhouse and field studies have shown that UV-B radiation is potentially damaging to a wide range of plant species (Krupa and Kickert, 1989; Tevini and Teramura, 1989). However, considerable variation in response to enhanced UV-B radiation has been observed both within and between plant species (Barnes *et al.*, 1990; Ziska *et al.*, 1992). The basis of this variation is not well understood, but differences in the optical properties of outer tissue layers are widely considered to play an important role (Kulandaivelu and Maruthappan, 1986). To date, attention has remained firmly focused on the ability of the epidermis to achieve wavelength-specific absorption of UV-B through the accumulation of phenylpropanoid-type compounds (*e.g.*, flavonoids and flavones), and rather less emphasis has been placed on the way in which subtle physico-chemical differences in leaf surfaces may influence sensitivity to UV-B radiation.

The inert layer of epicuticular wax which generally covers the surface of leaves represents the first line of defence against a wide range of environmental factors, including UV radiation (Caldwell, 1981). Amongst its many functions (see Baker, 1982), this external layer influences both reception and penetration of incident radiation (Clark and Lister, 1975; Robinson *et al.*, 1993). Although exhibiting low absorption in the UV-B region (Wuhrmann-Meyer and Wuhrmann-Meyer, 1941), the waxes covering the surface of leaves are believed to play an important role in natural adaptation of plants to enhanced UV-B radiation (Clark and Lister, 1975; Roberecht *et al.*, 1980). This has led to proposals that UV radiation plays a regulatory role in wax biosynthesis (Tevini and Steinmüller, 1987). Enhanced levels of UV-B radiation are reported to alter wax composition in some crop plants (Steinmüller and Tevini, 1985), but the mechanisms underlying effects and the way in which these changes influence sensitivity to UV-B are poorly understood.

In this paper we report the results of collaborative experiments that have (a) examined changes in the amount and chemical composition of the waxes on the surfaces of tobacco (*Nicotiana tabacum* L.) leaves induced by enhanced UV-B radiation and (b) analysed how these changes influence leaf surface wettability. The possibility that differences in leaf surface characteristics may influence sensitivity to UV-B radiation is discussed.

Materials and methods

Plant material and growth conditions

Seeds of tobacco (*Nicotiana tabacum* L. cv Sansum) and a mutant GR 32-3 transgenic for chimeric glutathione reductase (GR: EC 1.6.4.3) genes based on a pea GR cDNA sequence, which in this case were targeted to the chloroplast, were grown individually from seed in a peat-based potting compost (Levington M3) in a thermostatically controlled glasshouse main-tained at 25°C with natural daylight supplemented by 100W metal halide lamps. After 28 d growth, plants were transferred to three controlled environment chambers, where they were grown in clean ambient air, under virtually identical environmental conditions; 16-h photoperiod, 55-65% RH, day/night temperature of $24\pm1.5°C/20\pm1.5°C$. Photosynthetically active radiation (PAR; 400-700 nm) was provided by a mixture of metal halide (MH; Osram HQI-T 400W) and high-pressure sodium lamps (HPS; Phillips 1000W SON-T), switched so that PAR was increased in two steps to a maximum of 985 μmol m^{-2} s^{-1} for 12 h each day. UV-A radiation (320-400 nm) was supplemented by Phillips TLD 36W/08 backlamps which together with the MH lamps produced a total UV-A flux of 0.98 ± 0.04 Wm^{-2} at plant height. UV-B radiation was provided by Phillips TL40/12 fluorescent tubes filtered with 0.1 mm thick cellulose diacetate (CA) to eliminate wavelengths below ≈ 292nm. CA filters were replaced every 2 days. Plants were kept well watered from below and were fertilized ("Miracle Gro" ICI Garden Products) at weekly intervals.

UV-B fluxes were measured and logged using a double monochromator scanning spectroradio-meter (Macam SR99, Macam Photometrics, Livingstone) linked to a microprocessor, calibrated for spectral irradiance against tungsten and deuterium sources (Macam SR903) traceable to National Physics Laboratory Standards and for wavelength accuracy against a mercury argon arc lamp (LOT Oriel, Surrey, England). UV-B radiation was provided for 7 h d^{-1} in the middle of the photoperiod, to provide daily biologically effective UV-B (UV-B$_{BE}$) fluences of 0, 4.54 and 5.66 kJ m^{-2} calculated using the generalized plant action spectrum normalized at 300 nm (Caldwell, 1971). The daily UV-B dose of 4.54 kJ m^{-2} is approximately equivalent to that presently received at Lancaster (England) under clear-sky conditions in mid-summer, modelled according to Bjorn and Murphy (1985). The "elevated" UV-B treatment represents a $\approx 25\%$ increase in this ambient flux.

Epicuticular wax production

After 28 d growth in controlled environment chambers, 4 x 10 cm^2 leaf discs were cut from each of leaves 2, 3 and 4 from five independent plants in each chamber. Epicuticular wax was removed from the adaxial and abaxial surfaces of leaves of individual plants by carefully dispensing HPLC grade chloroform across the leaf surface using a burette. Wax was collected separately from adaxial and abaxial leaf surfaces, then filtered [Whatman No. 1 paper followed by 0.2-μm Sartorious sieve], before removing the solvent under vacuum and drying to constant weight at room temperature as described elsewhere (Barnes et al., 1990; Barnes and Brown 1990). Wax samples were then transported to the Canadian Forest Service Laboratories in Fredericton (Canada) where wax samples were redissolved in chloroform, reduced in volume to 250 μL using a rotary evaporator and transferred to pre-weighed (± 10 µg) glass ampoules. The wax was then dried down under a constant stream of air at 30°C, and weighed (± 10 µg).

Epicuticular wax chemical composition

Quantitative analysis of epicuticular wax composition was completed using gas chromatography (GC). Wax samples were silylated with N,O-bis (trimethylsilyl) acetamide (TMS) at 50°C for 30 min and 1 µg wax injected onto a fused silica capillary column (10 m x 0.25 mm i.d.) with methyl-silicone liquid phase (0.1 µm film thickness) in a Varian 3410 gas chromatograph (GC) equipped with a flame ionization detector (FID) operated at 350°C. Column programming was: 80°C, hold 0.1 min; 81-120°C at 50°C min^{-1} and; 121-350°C at 6°C min^{-1}. Injector programming was: 120°C, hold for 0.1 min; 121-350°C at 300°C min^{-1}. Helium was used as carrier gas with a flow rate of 5 mL min^{-1} at 80°C. A Varian Star Workstation data system was used to integrate peak areas and calculate percentage homolgue composition. Relative retention times (RRT) were calculated by simultaneous co-injection of 0.5 µg n-tetracosane internal reference mixture. All GC homolgue assignments were confirmed by gas chromatography-mass spectrometry (GC-MS).

Leaf surface wettability

Wettability was assessed by measuring the static contact angle (θ) of water droplets on the surface of leaves. After 28 d growth in the chambers, 4 x 1cm^2 leaf discs were removed from the central region of non-shaded areas of the third leaf on six independent plants in each chamber and the contact angle of 0.2-µL glass-distilled water droplets placed on the adaxial and abaxial surfaces of leaves was determined as described by Barnes et al. (1990). The mean contact angle was measured for two droplets placed on the surface of each leaf disc, and this was used to calculate mean contact angles for each plant.

Results and discussion

The amount of epicuticular wax extracted from the surfaces of tobacco leaves was low (5-7 µg cm^2), with significantly (P < 0.01) greater deposition of wax on the adaxial surface of leaves. This pattern of wax deposition is characteristic of rapidly expanding leaves which are covered by a thin film of wax (Baker, 1982). Exposure to enhanced UV-B radiation markedly (c. 50%) decreased the amount of wax deposited on the adaxial surface of mutant 32-3, but there was no evidence of any effects of UV-B on the quantity of wax deposited on the abaxial surface of leaves (Figure 1). These data are consistent with the increased sensitivity of mutant 32-3 to UV-B radiation in terms of visible leaf injury (Barnes et al., 1994). It is, however, important to note that the increased sensitivity of mutant 32-3 is not a consequence of overexpressing GR (which in this line is 2.7-fold that of wild-type [31-31] Samsun levels), but is caused by either a

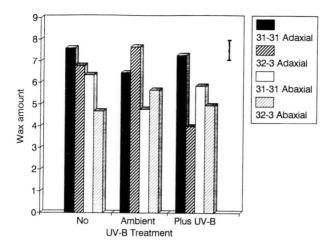

Figure 1. Effects of UV-B radiation on the quantity of wax ($\mu g\ cm^{2}$) deposited on the leaf surfaces of two genotypes of tobacco (*Nicotiana tabacum* L. cv. Samsun wild-type 31-31, transgenic for glutathione reductase; 32-3). LSD at P = 0.05 is presented.

somoclonal mutation arising from tissue culture, or because the T-DNA has inserted a UV-B responsive gene which causes altered expression or inactivation.

In agreement with previous reports (Carruthers and Johnstone, 1959; Kolattukudy, 1980), the epicuticular wax of tobacco was composed of three major classes: straight-chain alkanes (*n*-alkanes) in which odd carbon-numbered homologues predominated (C_{27}-C_{33}); branched-chain alkanes (*br*-alkanes) containing homologous series (C_{25}-C_{32}); and fatty acids in which even carbon-numbered homologues predominated (C_{14}-C_{18}). Approximate percentage compositions resolved by GC were *n*-alkanes ($\approx 59\%$), *br*-alkanes ($\approx 38\%$) and fatty acids ($\approx 3\%$), with C_{31} the predominant *n*-alkane homologue ($\approx 31\%$ of hydrocarbon fraction) and anteiso 3-methyltriacontane (C_{30}) the predominant *br*-alkane homologue ($\approx 15\%$ of hydrocarbon fraction). The chemical composition of the epicuticular wax was the same in the two genotypes, and was markedly influenced by UV-B radiation and the orientation of the leaf surface (Figure 2). Exposure to enhanced UV-B radiation resulted in a significant (P < 0.01) decrease in the content of *n*-alkanes and an increase (P < 0.05) in the content of *br*-alkanes and fatty acids in wax extracted from the adaxial leaf surface. However, there were no significant effects of UV-B on the chemical composition of the waxes on the abaxial leaf surface. Moreover, effects of UV-B

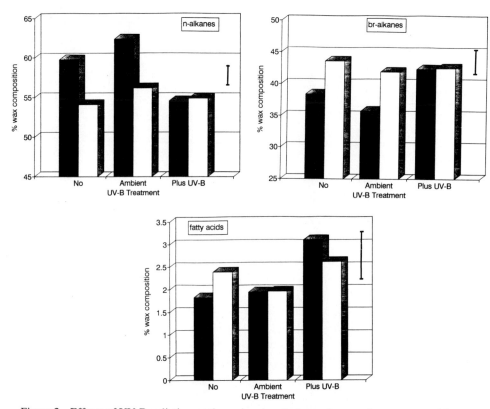

Figure 2. Effects of UV-B radiation on the major chemical constituents of wax extracted from the adaxial (■) and abaxial (□) surfaces of two lines of tobacco. As wax composition was the same for the two mutants, and there were no significant differences between the mutants in their response to UV-B radiation, data presented are meaned over the two genotypes. LSD at $P = 0.05$ is presented.

on adaxial leaf surface wax were associated with shifts in *n*-alkane homologue composition toward shorter chain lengths (Barnes *et al.*, 1994). These data support the view that UV-B radiation has a direct and fundamental effect on wax biosynthesis (Steinmüller and Tevini, 1985; Tevini and Steinmüller 1987), and are consistent with direct effects of UV-B on enzyme systems leading to a lessening of specificity and an increase in branching. The most likely explanation is that UV-B radiation affects microsomal membrane-based elongases responsible for the synthesis of the long-chain homologues characteristic of epicuticular waxes (see von Wettstein-Knowles, 1987). A similar conclusion was reached by Tevini and Steinmüller (1987) who studied the influence of UV-B radiation on wax biosynthesis of cucumber (*Cucumis sativus* L.) seedlings using specific inhibitors of the biosynthetic pathway.

UV-B-induced changes in wax chemical composition were associated with an increase in leaf surface wettability. Based on criteria for judging surface wettability (Crisp, 1963) the leaf surfaces of tobacco were wettable, exhibiting static contact angles (θ) for leaves grown at present day levels of UV-B of $105°$ and $110°$ for adaxial and abaxial surfaces, respectively. Exposure to enhanced UV-B radiation resulted in a significant (P < 0.001) reduction in θ for both leaf surfaces, showing that UV-B increased surface wettability (Figure 3), an effect that was most pronounced for the adaxial surface (surface* treatment interaction P < 0.01). The increase in leaf surface wettability is consistent with the presence of increased amounts of anteiso 3-methyltriacontane following exposure to enhanced UV-B radiation (Netting *et al.*, 1972) and would be expected to have far reaching physiological consequences for plants *in vivo* (Barnes and Brown, 1990; Brewer *et al.*, 1991).

It remains to be established whether changes in the amount and chemical composition of the surface waxes contribute to differences in the sensitivity of plants to UV-B radiation, or whether

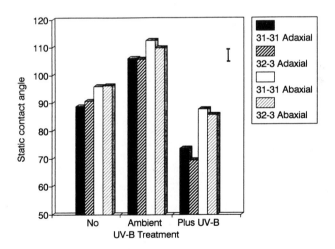

Figure 3. Influence of UV-B radiation on the static contact angle ($°$) of 0.2-µL glass-distilled water droplets placed on the adaxial and abaxial surfaces of leaves of two genotypes of tobacco. Wild-type cv. Samsun 31-31; transgenic for glutathione reductase 32-3. LSD at P = 0.05 is presented.

effects on wax biosynthesis simply reflect a direct manifestation of injury to epidermal cells. Some studies have concluded that epicuticular wax has little or no effect on the penetration of UV-B radiation into leaves (Day *et al.*, 1992; Bornman and Vogelmann, 1988). However, studies by Clark and Lister (1975) and preliminary studies conducted by Paul and Wellburn (unpublished) suggest that differences in the physico-chemical nature of the waxes may have an important role to play in determining sensitivity to UV-B radiation. Paul and Wellburn (unpublished) exposed twelve cultivars of pea (*Pisum sativum* L.), selected to represent a range of leaf glaucousness, to UV-B_{BE} fluxes between 2 and 8kJ m^{-2} d^{-1}. When the plants were assessed for their sensitivity to UV-B after 24 d of exposure there was a highly significant (P < 0.001) inverse correlation between sensitivity and glaucousness (Fig. 4). With the exception of a single cultivar ("Sugar Bon"), the most glaucous cultivars demonstrated the least sensitivity to UV-B radiation. Collaborative research is currently investigating two hypotheses; firstly, that water droplets on wettable leaf surfaces (less glaucous) act as plano-convex lenses magnifying the effects of UV-B radiation on the epidermis and upper mesophyll, and secondly, that differences in the amount and physico-chemical nature of the epicuticular wax influence reflectance of UV-B from the leaf surface.

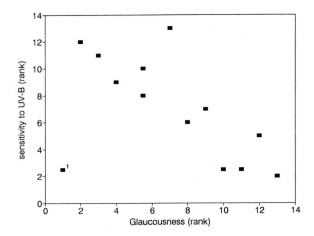

Figure 4. Rank correlationship between the sensitivity of cultivars of pea (*Pisum sativum* L.) to UV-B (measured as the mean time in days for visible symptoms to first appear) and glaucousness of leaves (expressed as the mean of visible rankings performed by six independent assessors). If the cultivar "Sugar Bon" (■[1]) is excluded, the Spearman Coefficient of Rank Correlation is -0.885, significant at P < 0.001.

Acknowledgements

The authors thank Mr. R. Taylor (Lancaster University) for technical assistance. This research was supported by The Royal Society, The U.K. Department of the Environment and the Canadian Forest Service.

References

Baker EA (1982) Chemistry and morphology of plant epicuticular waxes. *In* The Plant Cuticle. Cutler DJ, Alvin KL, Press CE (*eds*) Academic Press London *pp* 139-165

Barnes, JD, Brown KA (1990) The influence of ozone and acid mist on the amount and wettability of the surface waxes in Norway spruce (*Picea abies* [L.] Karst.). New Phytol 114: 531-535

Barnes JD, Eamus D, Davison AW, Ro-Poulsen H, Mortensen L (1990) Persistent effects of ozone on needle water loss and wettability in Norway spruce. Environ Poll 63: 345-363

Barnes PW, Flint SD, Caldwell MM (1990) Morphological responses of crop and weed species of different growth forms to ultraviolet-B radiation. Amer J Bot 77: 1354-1360

Björn LO, Murphy TM (1985) Computer calculation of solar ultraviolet radiation at ground level. Physiologie Végétale 23: 555-561

Bornman JF, Vogelmann TC (1988) Penetration of blue and UV radiation measured by fiber optics in spruce and fir needles. Physiol Planta 72: 699-705

Brewer CA, Smith WK, Vogelmann TC (1991) Functional interaction between leaf trichomes, leaf wettability and the optical properties of water droplets. Plant Cell Environ 14: 955-962

Caldwell MM (1971) Solar UV irradiation and the growth and development of higher plants. *In* Photophysiology. Giese AC (*ed*) Academic Press, New York *pp* 131-177

Caldwell MM (1981) Plant response to solar ultraviolet radiation. *In* Encyclopedia of Plant Physiology New Series Vol. 12A Physiological Plant Ecology. Lange OL, Nobel PS, Osmond CB, Ziegler H (*eds*) Springer-Verlag, New York, Heidelberg *pp* 169-197

Carruthers W, Johnstone RAW (1959) Composition of paraffin wax fraction from tobacco leaf and tobacco smoke. Nature 184: 1131-1132

Clark JB, Lister GR (1975) Photosynthetic action spectra of trees. II. The relationship of cuticle structure to the visible and ultraviolet spectral properties of needles from four coniferous species. Plant Physiol 55: 407-413

Crisp DJ (1963) Waterproofing mechanisms in plants and animals *In* Waterproofing and Water Repellency. Moilliet JL (*ed*) Elsevier, Amsterdam *pp* 416-481

Day TA, Vogelmann TC, DeLucia EH (1992) Are some plant life forms more effective than others in screening out ultraviolet-B radiation? Oecologia 92: 513-519

Kolattukudy PE (1980) Cutin, suberin, and waxes. *In* The Biochemistry of Plants, Vol. 4. Stumpf PK, Conn EE (*eds*) Academic Press, New York *pp* 571-645

Krupa S, Kickert RN (1989) The greenhouse effect: impacts of ultraviolet-B (UV-B) radiation, carbon dioxide (CO_2) and ozone (O_3) on vegetation. Environ Poll 61: 263-393

Kulandaivelu G, Maruthappan VM (1986) Characterization of epidermal transmittance and ultraviolet-B attenuation and the influence of light spectrum during growth. Plant Physiol Biochem 13: 82-89

Netting AG, Macey MJK, Barber HN (1972) Chemical genetics of a subglaucous mutant of *Brassica oleracea*. Phytochemistry 11: 579-585

Robberecht R, Caldwell MM, Billings WD (1980) Leaf ultraviolet optical properties along a latitudinal gradient in the arctic-alpine life zone. Ecology 61: 612-619

Robinson SA, Lovelock CE, Osmond CB (1993) Wax as a mechanism for protection against photoinhibition - A study of *Cotyledon orbiculata*. Bot Acta 106: 307-312

Steinmüller D, Tevini M (1985) UV-B-induced effects upon cuticular waxes of cucumber, bean and barley leaves. *In* Stratospheric Ozone Reduction, Solar Ultraviolet Radiation and Plant Life. Worrest RC, Caldwell MM (*eds*) Springer- Verlag, New York, Heidelberg *pp* 271-285.

Stolarski RS, Bloomfield P, McPeters RD (1991) Total ozone trends deduced from Nimbus 7 TOMS data. Geophys Res Lett 18: 1015-1018

Tevini M, Steinmüller D (1987) Influence of light, UV-B radiation, and herbicides on wax biosynthesis of cucumber seedlings. J Plant Physiol 131: 111-121

Tevini M, Teramura AH (1989) UV-B effects on terrestrial plants. Photochem & Photobiol 40: 479-487

von Wettstein-Knowles P (1987) Genes, elongases and associated enzyme systems in epicuticular wax synthesis. *In* The Metabolism, Structure and Function of Plant Lipids. Stumpf PK, Mudd JB, Mes WD (*eds*) Plenum Press, New York *pp* 489-498

Wuhrmann-Meyer K, Wuhrmann-Meyer M (1941) Untursuchungen über die absorption ultravioletter strahlen durch kutikular- und wachsschichten von blättern. I. Planta 32: 43-50

Ziska LH, Teramura AH, Sullivan JH (1992) Physiological sensitivity of plants along an elevational gradient to UV-B radiation. Amer J Bot 79: 863-871

Effects of Acid Rain and Surfactant Pollution on the Foliar Structure of Some Tree Species[*]

Paolo Raddi, Salvatore Moricca and Elena Paoletti
Centro di Studio per la Patologia delle Specie Legnose Montane
Consiglio Nazionale delle Ricerche
Piazzale delle Cascine 28
I-50144 Florence
Italy

Abstract

For 10 years we have been studying the effects of acid rain and ABS (a surfactant always found in sea aerosols) on several tree species. Alterations of the leaf structure were considered as damage index. We tried to quantify the damage to the wax structure by scoring in accordance with a damage scale given by SEM observations and by computing a damage index that allowed for a comparison among tree provenances and within individuals of the same provenance or clone. We tested the response of several species: Norway spruce, silver fir, cypress, London plane, chestnut, walnut, Italian alder, tree of heaven, common maple, European white elm, manna ash, holm oak, European beech. The different species exhibited different levels of damage in relation to the type of treatment: when ABS was present, the damage was always more severe. In the broadleaved trees, the most frequent disturbances noted were: erosion of the epicuticular wax, alterations in the stomata, lesions, abscission and/or alteration of hairs. Damage from ABS treatments was compared to damage observed in coastal vegetation after strong sea winds. By comparing natural and induced damage, we were able to demonstrate that ABS is one of the possible causes of coastal vegetation decline and that ABS may also impact significantly on vegetation growing far away from the sea.

Introduction

For about 10 years now, our research group has been using scanning electron microscopy (SEM) to highlight the effects of atmospheric pollutants on the morphology and structure of leaf waxes in a variety of different species of conifers and broadleaved trees. Our research work is part of the overall forest decline programme, and the basic hypothesis underlying our work is that the deposition of acidifying substances may be one of the primary causes of forest decline. The effects of acid deposition on the wax layer and on the occlusion of stomata have already been demonstrated, especially in conifers. For this reason, after an initial stage during which we studied the response of silver fir and Norway spruce cuticular wax to simulated treatments with acid pH solutions, our investigations were extended to include broadleaved trees as well.

Furthermore, as we have observed very widespread instances of forest decline along the Italian coastline, we also studied the possible interactions between acid depositions and simulated treatments with surfactants — pollutants of anthropogenic origin always present in sea aerosol.

[*] Research supported by National Research Council of Italy, Special Project RAISA, Sub-Project N. 2, Paper N. 1538

NATO ASI Series, Vol. G 36
Air Pollutants and the Leaf Cuticle
Edited by K. E. Percy et al.
© Springer-Verlag Berlin Heidelberg 1994

Surfactant pollution has been reported along the Tyrrhenian coast in Italy (Gellini *et al.*, 1983, 1985, 1987; Gisotti and De Rossi, 1980), in France (Devèze and Sigoillot, 1978; Garrec and Sigoillot, 1992), and in Australia (Pitman *et al.*, 1977; Truman and Lambert, 1978), but it is probably much more widespread. Synthetic surfactants, normally used as commercial detergents, are transported by surface waters; they then flow into the sea where they concentrate on the surface of the water (MacIntyre, 1974; Loglio *et al.*, 1989). Strong sea winds transport surfactants from the sea onto coastal vegetation, where they can cause severe damage. Surfactants may be responsible for direct damage by causing lipid degeneration of the chloroplasts in the chlorophyll parenchyma and especially in the stomatas' guard cells (Bussotti *et al.*, 1984). However, the main mechanism by which they damage the flora is that they increase the action of sea salt, enhancing its penetration and its accumulation in the leaves (Grieve and Pitman, 1978; Dowden *et al.*, 1978). Sea aerosols in any case can create highly stable suspensions, which can be transported over considerable distances. For example, in the area around Florence, more than 70 km from the coast, Grossoni *et al.* (1990) detected concentrations of MBAS (detergent content expressed as Methylene Blue Active Substances) between 2 and 4 mg/m^2, and Raddi *et al.* (1992), during occurrences of particularly strong winds, reported 5-10 mg/m^2 of MBAS in wet depositions at Vallombrosa, 120 km from the sea.

This paper reports the most significant results of our studies, as well as discussing the comparison between alterations in the cuticular structures observed in the field and those reproduced experimentally.

Materials and methods

Details on the individual treatments are described in the following subparagraphs. All samples were air-dried, sputtered with a gold palladium film using an S105A Edward sputter coater, and then observed with a Philips 505 SEM at 20 kV. Only needles from the experiment "Spraying with acid solution" were fixed in gluteraldehyde, first dehydrated in acetone to Critical Point, and lastly sputtered with gold.

In the case of broadleaved trees, as well as the morphology of epicuticular and epistomatal wax, we also examined characteristic alterations of the trichomes, of the glandular hairs (where present), and of the stomata. When we assessed the damage to the stomata (using a four-class damage scale), the minimum sample consisted in 100 stomata for each of the five trees, in other words 500 stomata: five trees x five samples per tree x 20 stomata per sample.

Induced Pollution

Seedlings were planted directly in the soil, in a special shelter with open sides and a roof that closed automatically when the relative humidity in the air exceeded 95%. This arrangement protected the trees from natural wet depositions, while ensuring natural conditions in almost all other respects.

The solutions were applied as a fog to the drip-point. As controls we used seedlings sprayed with demineralized water. The pH of the acid spraying was 3.5. The concentration of the surfactant (ABS: Sodium dodecylbenzene sulphonate) was 50 mg/L. Such a concentration is common in natural rainfall in coastal Tuscany during marine windstorms. All sprays were applied twice a week (once a week only for the experiment "Spraying with acid solution").

Spraying with acid solution

Five-year-old seedlings of silver fir (*Abies alba* Mill.) and Norway spruce (*Picea abies* (L.) Karst.) were sprayed for 20, 40, 50, and 60 weeks with solutions acidified either with H_2SO_4 or with HNO_3, or with both acids. After 20 acid sprays, subgroups were sprayed with demineralized water for 20, 30, and 40 weeks.

Spraying with acid solution and surfactant

Three-year-old seedlings of 10 species: common maple (*Acer campestre* L.), tree of heaven (*Ailanthus altissima* L.), Italian alder (*Alnus cordata* Loisel), chestnut (*Castanea sativa* Mill.), European beech (*Fagus sylvatica* L.), manna ash (*Fraxinus ornus* L.), walnut (*Juglans regia* L.), London plane (*Platanus acerifolia* Willd.), holm oak (*Quercus ilex* L.), and European white elm (*Ulmus laevis* Pall.) were treated with either demineralized water or acid solution (H_2SO_4:HNO_3 in a mass ratio of 5:2), or with demineralized water acidified as above with the addition of ABS. The solutions were applied for 6-7 weeks.

Spraying with surfactant

Five-year-old seedlings of pubescent oak (*Quercus pubescens* Willd.), Hungarian oak (*Q. frainetto* Ten.), holm oak (*Q. ilex* L.) and peduncolate oak (*Q. robur* L.), and 5-year-old seedlings of five Italian provenances of Norway spruce and 3-year-old seedlings of seven Italian provenances of European beech were sprayed for 10 weeks. For beech trees, a damage index was calculated for each tree: the number of stomata in each of the three damage stages (N_1, N_2, N_3) was multiplied by 1, 2 or 3, respectively. The products were added together and divided by the total number of stomata, which also included the undamaged ones (N_0)

$$DI = \frac{(N_1 \times 1) + (N_2 \times 2) + (N_3 \times 3)}{\Sigma (N_0 + N_1 + N_2 + N_3)}$$

Natural pollution

Near the coast

Trees of common cypress (*Cupressus sempervirens* L.), smooth cypress (*C. glabra* Sudw.), and Monterey cypress (*C. macrocarpa* Hartw.) were examined after a W-SW sea windstorm (Libeccio wind) and compared with 3-year-old seedlings of the same species artificially sprayed with ABS.

Far from the coast

We compared 1-, 6- and 12-year-old needles of two silver fir provenances, Vallombrosa (Tuscany, Central Italy) and Serra San Bruno (Calabria, Southern Italy). Of the two, the latter is described as more tolerant to forest decline. The samples were collected from adult trees in forest stands at Vallombrosa, 120 km from the coast, where severe forest decline has been observed. For the Serra San Bruno provenance, sample needles were gathered from trees growing both at Vallombrosa and in Calabria. Structural degradation was assessed in accordance with a four-stage classification scheme and the amount of wax was determined by extraction in chlorophorm (Raddi and Rinallo, 1989; Raddi *et al.*, 1990).

Results

Induced pollution

Spraying with acid solution

In needles of silver fir and Norway spruce a treatment with simulated acid deposition significantly altered both the epicuticular wax layer (flaking phenomenon) and the fibrillar wax structure in the epistomatal chambers, with fusion-grouping and fissuring. Of the three types of acidity examined, the most effective proved to be H_2SO_4, while HNO_3 produced the lowest levels of damage. Norway spruce appeared to be more sensitive than silver fir. Subsequent sprayings with demineralized water induced a slight reorganization of the wax structure, except in the case of HNO_3.

Spraying with acid solution and surfactant

All species were affected to some extent by simulated acid fog. When ABS was added, the damage was always more severe. The effects noted were (Figs. 9-12): 1. Erosion of the epicuticular wax structures and their migration, *e.g.*, into the stomata; 2. Alterations in the stomata, mainly consisting in a partial closure of the rimas due to the collapse of the guard cells or migration of the fused wax; 3. Lesions generally located near the stomata, the trichomes and the vascular tissues; 4. Abscission and/or morphological alterations of the trichomes and collapse

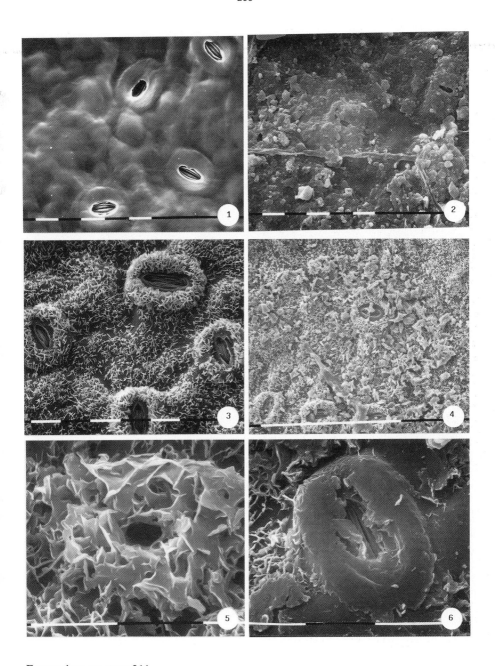

For captions see page 211

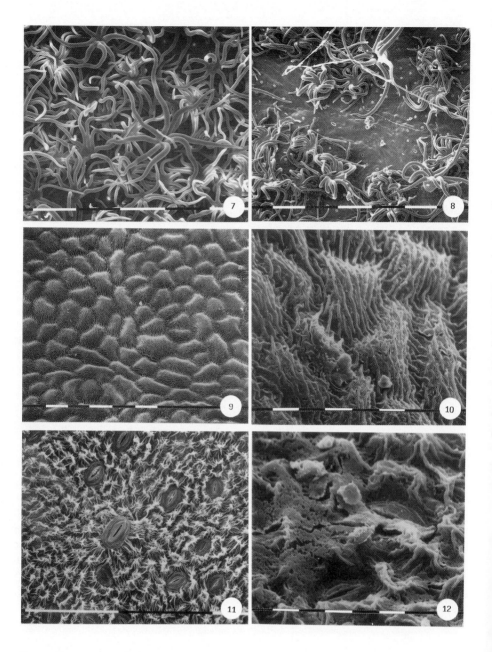

For captions see page 211

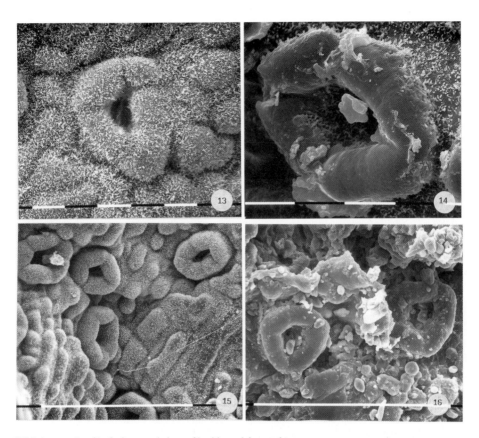

SEM photographs of leaf micromorphology of healthy and damaged trees.

Figure 1   European beech, abaxial surface: normal leaf wax structure with no sign of degradation (bar = 10 μm).

Figure 2   European beech, abaxial surface: severe structural degradation of leaf waxes, which project out of the originally smooth wax layer and cover most of the stomatal antechamber (bar = 10 μm).

Figure 3   Pedunculate oak, abaxial surface: normal distribution of waxes in vertical scales on the typically wrinkled epidermis; scales are more densely distributed around the stomata (bar = 10 μm).

Figure 4   Pedunculate oak, abaxial surface: structural degradation of waxy scales with formation of amorphous particles which partially occlude the stomatal openings (bar = 100 μm).

Figure 5   Pubescent oak, abaxial surface: detail of a stoma showing the beginning of degradation of the protective waxy scales (bar = 10 μm).

Figure 6   Pubescent oak: abaxial surface: severely damaged stoma with almost completely fused scales (bar = 10 μm).

Figure7   Holm oak, abaxial surface: epidermis entirely protected by a dense interlacing network of stellate trichomes; the stomata are not visible because of the dense tomentum (bar = 100 μm).

Figure 8   Holm oak, abaxial surface: abscission of trichomes, which now appear less densely distributed on the leaf surface (bar = 100 μm).

Figure 9   London plane, adaxial surface: typical finely striated epicuticular layer of an undamaged leaf (bar = 100 μm).

Figure 10   London plane, adaxial surface: marked alteration in the epicuticular wax structure (bar = 10 μm).

Figure 11   Tree of heaven, abaxial surface: stomata slightly sunken and crystalline epicuticular waxes (bar = 100 μm).

Figure 12   Tree of heaven, abaxial surface: the wax has fused and migrated over the stomata plugging them up almost completely (bar = 10 μm).

Figure 13   Common cypress: stoma with normal covering of wax microtubules (bar = 10 μm).

Figure 14   Common cypress: fusion of the microtubules and formation of amorphous plaques with partial damage to the stomatal rima (bar = 10 μm).

Figure 15   Monterey cypress: epidermis covered with a thick network of wax microtubules (bar = 100 μm).

Figure 16   Monterey cypress: severe erosion of the wax microtubules and partial closure of the stomatal antechambers by a mixture of fused wax and particulate matter (bar = 100 μm).

of the secretory head or disarticulation of the glandular hairs; 5. Hyperplasia and hypertrophy of the mesophyll, particularly in the walnut seedlings treated with the acid+ABS solution; 6. Development of fungal hyphae. The damage decreased in the following order: walnut, manna ash, common maple, European beech, chestnut, London plane, tree of heaven, European white elm, holm oak, Italian alder.

Spraying with surfactant

Even treatment with ABS alone can cause considerable damage in the treated plant, including (Figs. 1-8): 1. Disaggregation and fusion of the epicuticular and epistomatal wax; 2. Deactivation of the stomata, through occlusion or damage of the stomatal aperture, since it becomes plugged up by migrating fused wax or through impaired function of the guard cells; 3. Lesions and cracks in the cuticle; 4. Trichome abscission and destruction; 5. Collapse of the secreting heads of the glandular hairs. For oak species, damage decreased in the following order: pubescent oak, Hungarian oak, holm oak and pedunculate oak.

Different provenances of European beech and Norway spruce reacted differently to the treatment with ABS. For European beech, the damage to the stomatal waxes was quantified using a fairly large sample (500 stomata per treatment type per provenance), a four-point damage rating scale, and the transformation of the damage-stage frequency data into damage indices which made statistical analysis and comparisons possible. By measuring this damage index for control and treated plants before and after the treatments, it was possible to distinguish between the effects of natural aging and those of the treatments. A certain amount of wax degradation is always attributable to natural aging, a fact that must be taken into account when evaluating the results of experiments of this kind.

Even for Norway spruce provenances, the ABS treatment changed the distribution among the damage stages significantly and in a way that separated provenances, creating statistically significant differences between them (Raddi *et al.*, 1991). The effect of the treatment continued even after cessation of spraying, but degraded wax tubules were sometimes reconstituted or replaced by newly synthesised ones.

Natural pollution

Near the coast

In samples taken from cypress clones exposed to the action of sea aerosols containing surfactants, the microtubular wax network was fused into an amorphous plaque which had migrated so as to plug up and cover many of the stomata (Figs. 13-16). A very high amount of particulate matter was also observed; it consisted of sodium chloride crystals, pollen, fungal spores and dust. A hyperproduction of resin and some fungal hyphae were sometimes observed. Leaves taken from the leeward side of the same trees showed less complete but still severe structural degradation of the waxes. This confirmed that the sea aerosols transported by the wind caused an acute damage when they were deposited on the leaves. The ABS treatments caused damage similar to that observed in the directly exposed leaves, but no particulate matter was noted. By comparing natural and induced damage, it was possible to demonstrate that ABS is one of the possible causes of coastal vegetation decline.

Far from the coast

In silver firs (from both the Vallombrosa and the Serra San Bruno provenances) wax degradation consisting of both aggregation and fissuring in the epistomatal chamber and the creation of an amorphous wax type was a consequence of both natural needle aging and air pollution. There was a difference between the two provenances. In the Vallombrosa provenance, which is more sensitive to air pollution, more than half of the stomata on 6-year-old needles showed severe epistomatal wax damage, whereas in the Serra San Bruno provenance, which is quite tolerant, about 80% of these stomata were undamaged. For the Serra San Bruno provenance there was no difference in needle wax degradation between trees grown at Vallombrosa (a site with a high level of pollution) and those grown in Calabria (where the pollution is negligible). The amount of wax was always higher in the Serra San Bruno provenance.

Discussion and conclusions

The most important conclusions we can draw are the following: we have demonstrated experimentally that the surfactant ABS can cause severe damage to the epicuticular wax structures; this damage is structurally similar to naturally occurring damage and to damage caused by acid spraying; in combined treatments we find an overall worsening of damage, although it is not possible to distinguish damage caused by individual pollutants; aging also causes alterations in the epistomatal wax structures and in the stomata, alterations that are very similar to those caused by the pollutants we tested.

The two symptomatologies are very similar and this indicates that there is a direct causal relationship between the decline of coastal vegetation and the presence of surfactants in the sea aerosol. In areas very far away from the coast it becomes more difficult to define exactly the amount of damage caused by surfactants on the epicuticular wax structures, since these alterations may also be caused by other agents, such as acid atmospheric depositions, for example.

Since tests with chronic treatments last several years, it will be possible not only to evaluate the structural alterations of foliar wax structures over time, but also to examine the morphophysiological characteristics of these changes. We have already shown that short-term treatments with pollutants do not significantly affect the growth of trees, even though they can cause leaf yellowing and an abundant and early current-year leaf abscission in holm oak (Rinallo and Raddi, 1989a,b).

Since our research included a variety of coniferous and broadleaved species, we tried to highlight any relationship between morphological features of leaves and wax structures and the degree of sensitivity to pollutants. The wax structures of the species we studied behaved differently during the simulated treatments. But this varying degree of sensitivity does not appear to be directly connected to the microstructural characteristics of the wax, or to the presence of pubescences, although a thick trichome covering on the abaxial surface of the leaves may offer protection to the wax and stomata on the underside. And indeed, the underside of adult holm oak leaves is entirely covered with protective trichomes, and this species appears to be one of the most resistant to artificial treatments, although less tolerant than Italian alder or pedunculate oak, which have very few trichomes, if any. Furthermore, pedunculate oak, the oak species that is most tolerant to treatments, has waxes structured in vertical scales, a structure similar to that of pubescent oak - which is, on the other hand, very sensitive. It would seem, therefore, that the trend we were searching for does not correlate to wax damage severity. But it will be necessary to conduct more in-depth studies to justify the differences observed even in trees of the same species.

Although we tried to get some information on the chemical composition of the wax before simulated treatments and on the quality of the wax that is regenerated after interruption of those treatments, we did not succeed. A different chemical composition (either quantitative or qualitative) could perhaps justify the tolerance to atmospheric pollution displayed by different provenances of silver fir and Norway spruce, and especially in the Serra San Bruno provenance of silver fir. Studies on the wax composition in species tolerant to air pollution indicate that the low-molecular components of the paraffin and ester fractions decrease with increasing pollution (Schutt and Schuck, 1972). An indirect confirmation of this hypothesis could be provided by the fact that the degraded wax of Serra San Bruno silver firs does not attract saprophytic fungi, which are attracted by Vallombrosa silver firs. But it is unlikely that the chemical composition can provide the full explanation of this behaviour, for the tolerance to pollution may also be due to anatomical, morphological and genetic factors. Rinallo and Gellini (1987), in fact, reported that the Serra San Bruno provenance shows a relatively higher stomatal density, with stomata that are small and deeply embedded in the hypodermis, and epistomatal chambers that are very densely packed with fibrillar waxes, thicker mechanical tissues (epidermis and hypodermis) and a thicker layer of epicuticular wax.

Currently, the aim of our research is to clarify the relationship between the degradation of wax and other leaf structures and physiological factors, such as transpiration and stomatal conductance. For this research we are using self-rooted plants to evaluate exactly also the influence of aging and of environmental effects, and also to estimate how individual genetic variability interferes in the leaf structure responses to the pollutant being studied.

References

Bussotti F, Rinallo C, Grossoni P, Gellini R, Pantani F, Cenni E (1984) La moria della vegetazione costiera causata dall'inquinamento idrico. Monti e Boschi 35(6): 47-55

Devèze L, Sigoillot JC (1978) Les arbres malades de la mer. Aménagement de la région provençale 19: 13-24

Dowden HGM, Lambert MJ, Truman R (1978) Salinity damage to Norfolk Island pines caused by surfactants. II. Effect of sea water and surfactant mixtures on the health of whole plants. Aus J Plant Physiol 5: 386-396

Garrec J-P, Sigoillot J-C (1992) Les arbres malades de la mer. La Recherche 23: 940-941

Gellini R, Pantani F, Grossoni P, Bussotti F (1987) L'influence de la pollution marine sur la végétation côtière italienne. Bull Ecol t 18: 213-219

Gellini R, Pantani F, Grossoni P, Bussotti F, Barbolani E, Rinallo C (1983) Survey of the deterioration of the cosatal vegetation in the park of San Rossore in central Italy. Eur J For Path 13: 296-304

Gellini R, Pantani F, Grossoni P, Bussotti F, Barbolani E, Rinallo C (1985) Further investigation on the causes of disorder of the coastal vegetation in the park of San Rossore (central Italy). Eur J For Path 15: 145-157

Gisotti G, De Rossi C (1980) Il deperimento della vegetazione litoranea nell'ambito del degrado delle coste italiane. Ing Arch 5-6: 2-14

Grieve AM, Pitman MG (1978) Salinity damage to Norfolk Island pines caused by surfactants. III. Evidence for stomatal penetration as the pathway of salt entry to leaves. Aust J Plant Physiol 5: 397-413

Grossoni P, Bussotti F, Pantani F, Cini R, Gellini R (1992) Decline of *Pinus pinea* by polluted marine aerosols. Proc. Expertentagung Waldschadensforschung im ostichen Mitteleuropa und in Bayern, GFS-Bericht 24/91: 436-440

Loglio G, Degli Innocenti N, Gellini R, Pantani F, Cini R (1989) Detergents as a condition of pollution from coastal marine aerosol. Marine Poll Bull 20: 115-119

MacIntyre F (1974) The top millimeter of the ocean. Scient Amer 230: 62-77

Pitman MG, Dowden HGM, Humphrys FR, Lambert MJ, Grieve AM, Scheltema GH (1977) The outfall connection. Aust Nat Hist 19: 73-81

Raddi P, Moricca S, Di Lonardo V, Bruno E (1991) Alterations in the needle waxes of Norway spruce [*Picea abies* (L.) Karst.] caused by ABS: response of five provenances compared. *In* Giannini R (*ed*) Effects of Pollution on the Structure of Forest Tree Populations. CNR, Bertelli, Firenze *pp* 85-95.

Raddi P, Moricca S, Gellini R, Di Lonardo V (1992) Effects of natural and induced pollution on the leaf wax structure of three cypress species. Eur J For Path 22: 104-114

Raddi P, Rinallo C (1989) Variation in needle wax degradation in two silver fir provenances differentiated by tolerance to air pollution. *In* Scholz F, Gregorius H -R, Rudin D (*eds*) Genetic Effects of Air Pollutants in Forest Tree Populations. Springer-Verlag Berlin Heidelberg *pp* 67-76

Raddi P, Rinallo C, Moricca S (1990) Needle waxes from the silver-fir provenances of Vallombrosa and Serra San Bruno compared in relation to environmental pollution. Proc. International Workshop Mediterranean firs adaptation, selection and silviculture, INRA, Avignon, 11-15 June 1990: 349-357

Rinallo C, Gellini R (1988) Morphological and anatomical traits identifying the silver fir (*Abies alba* Mill.) from Serra San Bruno provenance. Giorn Bot Ital 122: 149-166

Rinallo C, Raddi P (1989a) Effects of simulated acid rain and ABS on leaf surfaces of some broadleaf seedlings. Eur J For Path 19: 151-160

Rinallo C, Raddi P (1989b) Effects of simulated acid fog on the leaves of some broadleaf seedlings. Phytopathol medit 28: 176-184

Schutt P, Schuck HJ (1972) Zusammenhzänge zwischen Rauchhärte und Cuticolawachsen bei Koniferen. Mitt Bundesversanst Wien 97: 399-417

Truman R, Lambert MJ (1978) Salinity damage to Norfolk Island pines caused by surfactants. I. The nature of the problem and effect of potassium, sodium and chloride concentration on uptake by roots. Aust J Plant Physiol 5: 377-385

Fourier Transform IR Studies on the Interaction of Selected Chemicals with Isolated Cuticles

Patricia Luque, F. Javier Ramírez[*], Antonio Heredia and Martin J. Bukovac[1]
Departamento de Bioquímica and [*]Departamento de Química Física
Facultad de Ciencias, Universidad de Málaga
29071 Málaga
Spain

Abstract

It is known that the plant cuticle represents the first barrier that must be overcome by any chemical reaching the plant surface from the atmosphere before entering the plant. Because of the imporance of the cuticle as a barrier to penetration of a wide variety of compounds, its morphology, chemistry, and permeability have been extensively studied. However, only limited information is available on the nature of functional chemical groups present and their interaction and role during the penetration process.

The usefulness of *in situ* Fourier transform infrared spectroscopy studies in identifying functional groups present in isolated cuticles is described and their relationships to the structure of the cuticular membrane are discussed. Applications of infrared spectroscopy on the presence and role of phenolics in the cuticle structure and during the cuticle development, nitrogen oxide binding to isolated cuticles, and the interactions between selected chemical probes during sorption by the cuticle are also described.

Introduction

The plant cuticle or cuticular membrane is the prime barrier to the sorption and subsequent uptake of xenobiotics deposited on plants from the atmosphere (Schönherr and Riederer, 1989). Nevertheless, identifying exogeneous chemical interactions with the cuticle currently requires a combination of destructive techniques. Thus, it is desirable to evaluate new experimental approaches that may yield useful information on specific interactions of penetrants with components of the cuticular membrane that are nondestructive and less time consuming.

We recently reported on the usefulness of Fourier transform infrared spectroscopy (FT-IR) for elucidating the presence of functional groups in isolated cuticles and for describing interactions between exogenously applied nitrogen dioxide, and the cuticular membrane (Ramírez et al., 1992; Luque et al., 1993). In this paper we present an overview of these findings and describe studies on the interaction of an organic molecular probe, dimethylsulfoxide, during sorption by isolated cuticles.

---

[1]Department of Horticulture, Michigan State University, East Lansing, MI 48824, USA

NATO ASI Series, Vol. G 36
Air Pollutants and the Leaf Cuticle
Edited by K. E. Percy et al.
© Springer-Verlag Berlin Heidelberg 1994

Material and methods

Cuticle isolation. Cuticular membranes (disks about 1 cm diameter) were isolated from mature tomato fruits (*Lycopersicon esculentum* Mill), grape berries (*Vitis vinifera* L.) and sour orange leaves (*Citrus aurantium* L.). Isolation was achieved with an aqueous mixture of pectinase (4% w/v), cellulase (0.4% w/v) and Na_3N (1 mM) in 50 mM sodium citrate buffer at pH 4.0 (Shafer and Bukovac, 1987) or with ammonium oxalate/oxalic acid (Roberts *et al.*, 1959). After isolation, cuticles were extensively washed in deionized water, air-dried and stored for further use.

Nitrogen oxide binding by isolated cuticles. Isolated cuticles held at about 20°C and 60% relative humidity were exposed to pure NO_2 in a small glass chamber. After 6 h the cuticles were removed, held for 1 h in air at room temperature to desorb gaseous NO_2 and washed three times (15 min each) with deionized water. The cuticles were then transferred to a desiccator and equilibrated in air over dry silica gel at room temperature.

Dimethylsulfoxide sorption by isolated cuticles. Segments (1 cm diameter) of dry isolated cuticles were exposed to vapors of dimethylsulfoxide (DMSO) for 1 h in a closed glass chamber at 35°C and 70% relative humidity. The cuticles were then washed extensively in deionized water and desorbed against air at room temperature.

FT-IR spectroscopy. IR spectra were obtained with a Perkin Elmer 1760X Fourier transform infrared spectrometer. The spectra were obtained on cuticular pieces mounted in a cell holder specially designed to perform IR studies on films. Membrane area exposed was 0.78 cm^2 and

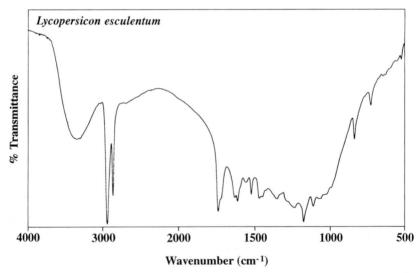

Figure 1   IR spectrum of mature tomato fruit cuticular membrane in the 4000-500 cm^{-1} region.

the sample chamber was purged with argon gas. The spectra were recorded with a resolution of 4 cm^{-1}. To enhance the signal-noise ratio 20 to 50 scans were accumulated for each sample. Spectra recorded from different samples of cuticular membranes gave essentially the same relative infrared absorption bands.

Results and discussion

FT-IR spectra of isolated cuticles. The IR spectrum between 4000 and 500 cm^{-1} for an isolated cuticular membrane from a mature tomato fruit is shown in Figure 1. The complex spectrum shows several strong absorption bands. The assignments for the absorption bands were facilitated by previous data on chemical composition of tomato fruit cuticle (Cutler *et al.*, 1982).

The broad band observed at about 3300 cm^{-1} was assigned to the stretching vibration of hydroxyl functional groups. The value of this frequency indicates that all hydroxyl groups are hydrogen bonded. The two strong absorption bands located near 2900 cm^{-1} were assigned to the asymmetric and symmetric stretching vibrations of the methylene groups, the most repeated structural unit in this biopolymer.

The strong band at 1730 cm^{-1}, with a shoulder at 1713 cm^{-1}, was assigned to the carbon-oxygen stretching vibration of the carbonyl group of the ester bond. The presence of the shoulder

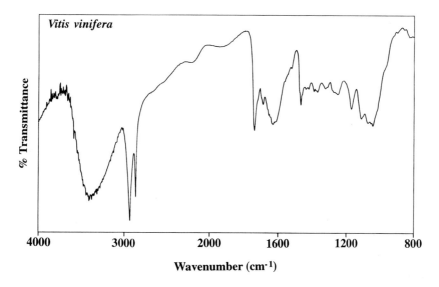

Figure 2   Infrared spectrum of grape berry cuticle in the 4000-800 cm^{-1}.

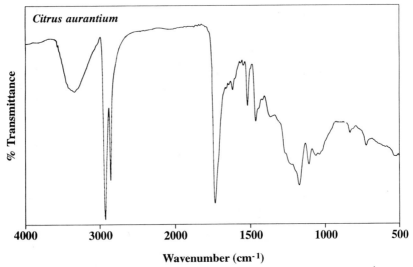

Figure 3   IR spectrum of *Citrus aurantium* leaf cuticle between 4000 and 500 cm^{-1}.

indicates that some of these functional groups are involved in hydrogen bonding. On the other hand, the two narrow bands at 1160 and 1100 cm^{-1} were assigned to the asymmetric and symmetric C-O-C stretching vibrations of ester bond, respectively.

The aromatic domain in the cuticle is characterized by a set of weak absorption bands located primarily between 1650-1500 cm^{-1} and 830 cm^{-1}. The relative intensities of these bands provide evidence for the existence of phenolics at the cuticular level (Ramírez *et al.*, 1992). The IR spectrum for isolated grape berry cuticles is shown in Figure 2. The strong absorption band observed at around 1600 cm^{-1} indicates the presence of phenolics of a different nature attached to the cuticular matrix. These results are in agreement with quantitative data previously obtained (Luque and Heredia, unpublished data). On the other hand, the infrared spectrum of isolated *Citrus* leaf cuticles (Figure 3) represents a good example of a very aliphatic cuticular membrane.

NO$_2$ *binding characterization by FT-IR spectroscopy.* It has been documented that nitrogen oxide, an air pollutant from diverse combustion processes, interacts with the plant cuticle and that the exposure of isolated plant cuticles to NO$_2$ shows irreversible sorption of the pollutant by the phenolic components of the cuticle (Kisser-Priesack *et al.*, 1987, 1990). This observation points to the ecotoxicological significance of the cuticle/nitroxide system.

Infrared spectra between 1800 and 600 cm^{-1} of untreated and NO$_2$-exposed cuticles are shown in Figure 4. The two spectra appear almost identical, but after careful study of the assignments one can elucidate the differences between the two isolated cuticles. The infrared spectrum of the

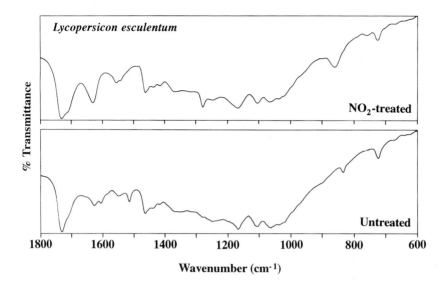

Figure 4   Infrared spectra of untreated and NO2-treated isolated tomato fruit cuticular membranes in the 1800-600 cm^{-1}.

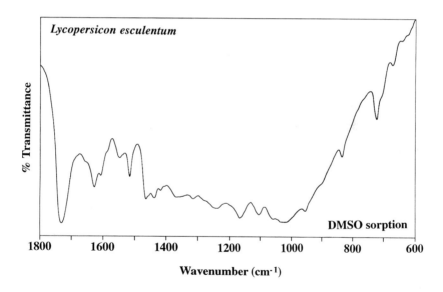

Figure 5   Infrared spectrum of tomato fruit cuticle after sorption of DMSO between 1800 and 600 cm^{-1}.

Table 1   Band frequencies (cm^{-1}) and assignments for DMSO and its complex with isolated
cuticular membranes (CM)

Assignment	CM	CM/DMSO	CM/DMSO (d)	Liquid DMSO
υ (C=O)	1731	1731	1731	-
υ (C=OH)	1715	-	1715	-
υ (S=O)	-	1018	-	1057
δ (SCH)	-	955 936	-	953 929
υ (C-S)	-	714	-	699

treated cuticle yields new bands in addition to some shifted frequencies in comparision to those
observed for the untreated cuticular membrane. New absorption bands appear at 1631, 1278 and
860 cm^{-1} and these were assigned to different nitrogen-oxygen vibrations (Luque et al., 1993).
The first two frequencies correspond to the asymmetrical and symmetrical stretching vibrations
of the NO_2 group, respectively. On the other hand, the absorption band at 860 cm^{-1} was assigned
to the NO_2 bending vibration. It is interesting to note that, when the NO_2 is sorbed, the absorption
bands assigned to the aromatic domain in the cuticle were shifted (Figure 4). This is spectroscopic
evidence that the nitration occurred in the phenolic components.

DMSO interaction with isolated cuticles. Isolated tomato fruit cuticular membranes sorb DMSO
to about 20% of their dry weight. The presence of the organic solvent in the cuticles was
confirmed by FT-IR spectroscopy. The infrared spectrum between 1800 and 600 cm^{-1} of the
tomato fruit cuticles after sorption of DMSO is shown in Figure 5.

Several significant changes were found in the infrared spectrum which reveal the interaction of
DMSO with the cuticular membrane. Thus, the weak IR absorptions at 1018, 950 and 714 cm^{-1}
can be assigned to different vibrations of the DMSO molecule (Table 1). Additionally, the weak
shoulder observed in the infrared spectrum of untreated tomato cuticles at 1713 cm^{-1} (Figure 1)
disappears when the DMSO is sorbed by the membrane (see Figure 5). It is important to point
out that after desorption of the DMSO from the treated cuticular membranes, the infrared
spectrum of the sample was essentially identical to the spectrum of the untreated cuticle,
including the reestablishment of the shoulder at 1713 cm^{-1} (Table 1). Further, the stretching
vibration of the SO bond, which is observed at 1057 cm^{-1} in the liquid DMSO, shifted to a lower
frequency when the organic solvent is sorbed by the cuticular membrane (Table 1). On the other
hand, the stretching vibration corresponding to the carbon-sulfur bond shifted to higher frequency
on sorption.

The analysis of these data indicates that a specific and reversible interaction occurs between
DMSO and selected chemical functional groups in the cuticle. The above spectral shifts are
indicative for hydrogen bonding between the oxygen of the SO functional group and a H-bond

acceptor group, putatively hydroxyl groups present in the cuticular membrane. A similar observation has been reported for other systems (Theng, 1974) and confirms the known role of DMSO as breaker of intermolecular H-bond interactions.

The existence of the interaction reported here may modify the physico-chemical properties of the polymer matrix of the cuticle. Thus, DMSO may plasticize the cuticle softening the intermolecular interactions that the highly cross-linked cutin imposes. Recent studies made on this hypothesis using calorimetric techniques confirm this point (Luque and Heredia, unpublished data).

Summarizing, our data demonstrate the usefulness of Fourier transform infrared spectroscopy as a complementary tool of *in situ* identification of interactions of chemicals at the cuticular level. Such interactions may be of great ecotoxicological importance in the case of irreversible uptake of pesticides or pollutants. In addition, FT-IR spectroscopy may yield structural information on the special arrangement of the different functional groups present in this biopolymer.

Acknowledgements

This research has been partially supported by a grant from NATO Scientific Affairs Division (CRG-901000) and from Dirección General de Investigación Científica y Técnica (Project PB91-0768), Spain.

Literature references

Cutler DF, Alvin KL, Price CE (*eds*) (1982) The Plant Cuticle. Academic Press, New York

Kisser-Priesack GM, Scheunert I, Gnatz G, Ziegler H (1987) Uptake of $^{15}NO_2$ and ^{15}NO by plant cuticles. Naturwissenschaften 74: 550-551

Kisser-Priesack GM, Bieniek D, Ziegler H (1990) NO_2 binding to defined phenolics in the plant cuticle. Naturwissenschaften 77: 492-493

Luque P, Heredia A, Ramírez FJ, Bukovac MJ (1993) Characterization of NO_2 bound to the plant cuticle by FT-IR spectroscopy. Z Naturforsch 48c: 666-669

Ramírez FJ, Luque P, Heredia A, Bukovac MJ (1992) Fourier transform IR study of enzymatically isolated tomato fruit cuticular membrane. Biopolymers 32: 1425-1429

Roberts MF, Batt RF, Martin JT (1959) Studies on plant cuticle. II. The cutin component of the cuticles of leaves. Ann Appl Biol 47: 573-582

Schönherr J, Riederer M (1989) Foliar penetration and accumulation of organic chemicals in plant cuticles. Rev Environ Contam Toxicol 108: 1-70

Shafer WE, Bukovac MJ (1987) Studies on octylphenoxy surfactants. III. Sorption of Triton X-100 by isolated tomato fruit cuticles. Plant Physiol 85: 965-970

Theng BK (1974) The chemistry of clay-organic reactions. Adam Hilger, Bristol

Effects of Wind and Simulated Acid Mist on Leaf Cuticles

S.P. Hoad , C.E. Jeffree, J. Grace
University of Edinburgh
Division of Biological Sciences
The King's Buildings
Mayfield Road
Edinburgh, EH9 3JH, U.K.

Abstract

The combined effect of wind and simulated acid mist on leaf cuticles was investigated in beech (*Fagus sylvatica* L.) and birch (*Betula pubescens* Ehr.). Macroscopic and microscopic features of wind damage are described. Visibly damaged leaf area and the numbers of microscopic cuticular lesions were measured. The cuticular conductance to water vapour (g_c) of the astomatous adaxial surfaces of the leaves was measured by a gravimetric method.

Field experimental sites were selected to provide either: 1] **Direct wind action** on widely-spaced plants caused by high wind speed and impaction of wind-blown particles, but with minimal mutual leaf abrasion 2] **Indirect wind action** via a high degree of mutual abrasion between closely-spaced plants. **Direct wind action** increased water loss via the leaf adaxial cuticle two-to three-fold in each species, by increasing the numbers of microscopic cuticular lesions. **Indirect wind action** caused more visible damage to leaves than direct wind action, increased g_c by about threefold compared with complete shelter, and induced the most cuticular lesions.

Acid mists at pH 3 or pH 5 were applied to the plants *in situ* at weekly intervals over a 100-day period. In sheltered plants, no effect of acid mist was detected on visibly damaged leaf area, the numbers of microscopic cuticular lesions, or on g_c. However, acid mists in combination with wind exposure caused significant effects on cuticular integrity that were dependent on the type of wind action. **Direct wind action** combined with pH 3 acid mist resulted in the largest numbers of microscopic cuticular lesions, and the highest g_c. By contrast, **indirect wind action** combined with pH 3 acid mist caused most visible damage to leaf tissue, but fewer microscopic lesions, and lower g_c, than in plants treated with water mist. In severely-abraded leaves exposed to indirect wind action and low-pH acid rain, g_c may be reduced by wound-isolation of blocks of non-functional leaf tissue.

Introduction

Vegetation in the British uplands experiences considerable stress from atmospheric pollutants in addition to climatic stresses imposed by low temperatures and high wind speeds (Grace and Unsworth, 1988). The effects of wind exposure on plants include loss of leaf area, structural damage to the cuticle and epicuticular waxes, damage to stomatal complexes and increases in leaf surface conductance to water vapour (Grace, 1974; Thompson, 1974; MacKerron, 1976; Grace and Russell, 1977; Wilson, 1978, 1980, 1984; Pitcairn *et al.*, 1986; van Gardingen, Grace and Jeffree, 1991; Hoad *et al.*, 1992). Although previous work provides some data on the

NATO ASI Series, Vol. G 36
Air Pollutants and the Leaf Cuticle
Edited by K. E. Percy et al.
© Springer-Verlag Berlin Heidelberg 1994

relationship between wind abrasion and cuticular conductance, there is little understanding of the relationship between wind damage and the susceptibility to pollution.

In undamaged and unstressed leaves, cuticular conductance in the gas phase (g_c) is approximately two orders of magnitude lower than stomatal conductance, g_s (van Gardingen and Grace, 1992). However, in leaves that have been stressed (*e.g.*, water-stressed, or damaged by wind or insect activity) resulting in stomatal closure, cuticular conductance and hence water loss may become a significant or the major component of total leaf surface conductance.

The impact of wind-blown particles (soil, plant debris, rain, ice crystals), and mutual impacts and abrasion between leaves, are components of a weathering process that modifies leaf surface characteristics. These changes may both degrade cuticle properties and breach cuticular integrity, leading to increases in exchange rate of solutes as well as gases. Consequently, wind-induced damage to the cuticle may influence leaf responses to atmospheric pollutants in cloud water, rain and the atmosphere. The objective of this study was to examine the effect on cuticular integrity of the application of simulated acid mist to undamaged and to wind-damaged leaf surfaces.

Materials and methods

Plant material: Birch (*Betula pubescens*) and beech (*Fagus sylvatica*) were used as experimental species for this study. Birch occurs naturally at high altitudes and experiences climatic stress from high winds and pollution stress from cloud water. Both species have an astomatous adaxial leaf cuticle, which enables measurement of g_c. Seedlings were raised for two seasons under glass in 4-L pots containing a potting mixture of sand, gravel and compost, and were acclimatised in a glass open-top shelter prior to transfer to field sites, where the pots were buried to half their depth in the soil.

Wind treatments: Different types of wind-damage were induced by locating the plants at contrasting locations. At an upland hill site at Dunslair Heights, Scotland (55°41'N, 3°08' W, altitude 600 m), plants were placed in wind-permeable wire-mesh animal exclosures at an open site exposed to prevailing wind, and at a sheltered site in a clearing within a conifer plantation. At Edinburgh, **direct wind action** was created by placing plants at 1-m spacing at an open field site. This site had a high level of wind-blown particles (Hoad *et al., submitted*) and plants oscillated freely with no mutual interaction between adjacent plants. **Indirect wind action** was created at a site protected from direct wind action, but mutual abrasion between adjacent plants was induced by close spacing (0.5 m). Sheltered plants were also grown, as a control, in a cold glasshouse.

Acid mist treatments: Simulated acid mists at pH 5 and pH 3 were formulated using equi-molar solutions of ammonium sulphate (($NH_4)_2SO_4$) and nitric acid (HNO_3) as described by Leith *et al.*

(1989). Deionised water mist was used as a control. Mists with a mean droplet diameter of 0.7 μm were applied with a hand-held aerosol unit (Humbrol sprayer, Border (UK) Ltd., Hull, UK) until leaves were thoroughly wet. A natural mist and cloud cover was simulated by covering each plant with a plastic enclosure immediately before and for 1 h following spraying. Mists were applied at weekly intervals, commencing on 15 June (day 0).

Damage assessments: Measurements of cuticular conductance (g_c) of the adaxial leaf surface, and assessments of leaf damage, were made on two occasions between 75 and 100 days after the start of mist application.

Visible leaf damage was measured *in situ* as described by Hoad *et al.* (*submitted*). Damage was assessed as a percentage of total leaf area, and included the sum total of dead (brown dry), blistered (tissue swollen yellow/green), chlorotic (yellowing) and necrotic (dark-coloured) tissue. Twelve randomly-selected leaves per treatment were measured on each occasion.

Microscopic cuticular lesions were identified by using ruthenium red as a dye tracer. Leaves were floated for 30 min on an aqueous solution of the dye (0.25 mg mL^{-1}) and mounted as described by Hoad *et al.* (1992). Counts were made of the numbers of microscopic cuticular lesions (diameter 0.01 - 0.1mm) per cm^2 of the adaxial leaf surface.

Cuticular conductance (g_c) of the astomatous adaxial surface to water vapour was determined gravimetrically using leaf-disc samples enclosed in a leaf-disc envelope designed to totally prevent water loss from the abaxial leaf surface and the cut edges of the disc (Fig. 1, Hoad *et al.*, *submitted*). Measurements of water loss from a defined area (3x3 mm) of the astomatous adaxial surface were made using a microbalance with a resolution of 0.01 mg (Cahn, Corritos, California, USA), inside a growth-room with environmental conditions as follows: day/night temperatures 18/12°C; day/night leaf-to-air Vapour Pressure Difference (D) 0.82/0.56 kPa (constant Relative Humidity of 60%); photoperiod 16 h; photon flux density at working height 300 %mol $m^{-2} s^{-1}$. Leaf-discs 8 mm in diameter were punched from an attached leaf and, within 60 s, enclosed in a leaf-disc envelope and weighed. Gravimetric measurements were made at 1- to 2-h intervals for 8 h. Leaf relative water content was maintained above 80% during the period of measurement, by replenishment of evaporated leaf water from the reservoir within the envelope (Fig. 1). Measurements were made on six disc samples taken from each of two leaf samples per mist treatment per site, and g_c was calculated from the rate of water loss (cuticular transpiration rate) and D using standard equations (Pearcy *et al.*, 1989).

For **low-temperature scanning electron microscopy (LTSEM)**, leaf samples were harvested and prepared at the field site to minimise damage during transportation. Briefly, samples up to 15 x 30 mm in size were excised from leaves, mounted on specimen stubs using Tissue-Tek OCT compound (Miles Laboratories, Naperville, Ill.) as a cryo-adhesive and frozen by plunging into

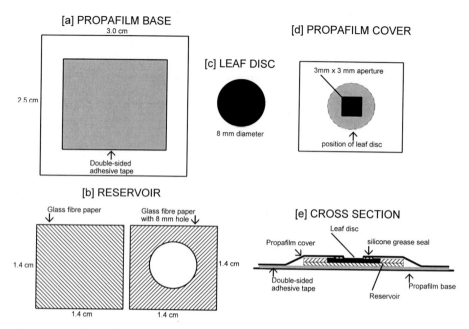

Figure 1   A diagram showing the construction of leaf-disc envelope used to measure cuticular conductance of a defined area of the astomatous adaxial leaf cuticular membrane. The individual components are shown in Fig. 1 a to d, and a cross-section of the completed assembly is shown in Fig. 1 e.

liquid nitrogen (-196°C) or subcooled liquid nitrogen (approx. -210°C). Field-mounted specimens were transferred to a cryo-specimen storage system (van Gardingen *et al.*, 1989; Jeffree and van Gardingen, 1993) for transport to the laboratory. In preparation for LTSEM, specimens were transferred to the cold stage of a Cambridge Instruments S250 SEM fitted with an Emscope SP2000 cryo system. As previously described (Jeffree and Read, 1991), surface-contaminating ice was sublimed by warming the specimen briefly to -80 °C before coating with gold in the specimen preparation chamber of the SP2000. Specimens were examined at below -160 °C at beam accelerating voltages of 5 or 10 kV.

Results

Macroscopic and microscopic features of wind damage to beech and birch leaves: In a pristine, incompletely expanded beech leaf, the adaxial surface is a pavement of convex cells with interlocked sinusoidal outlines. There is little visibly-crystalline epicuticular wax and the cell surfaces are smooth (Fig. 2). The veins stand proud of the surface, and are clothed with trichomes. Two types of trichome are visible in Figure 3, a glandular multicelled type and a single-celled clothing trichome. On the abaxial leaf surface the veins are more prominent, and more vulnerable to mechanical damage, and are also clothed in long, single-celled hairs. Shorter multicellular trichomes also occur on the abaxial lamina, and the stomata (shown in Figure 4 at various stages of differentiation) protrude above the general epidermal surface. The pristine leaf margin bears elongated fringing hairs and glandular trichomes (Fig. 5), which are vulnerable to mechanical damage.

In the early stages of leaf expansion, about 3-5 days after bud-break, the beech leaf is pleated, forming ridges of soft tissue between the main veins which are vulnerable to abrasive damage. Figure 6 shows two leaves from the relatively sheltered site at Dunslair Heights, that show different degrees of damage to the lamina in this intervein area, probably resulting from wind episodes shortly after bud-break. The leaf on the left shows large brown patches of dead tissue, while that on the right shows more limited damage, probably only affecting small groups of mesophyll blocks or domains.

The effects on the surface structure of young beech leaves of an episode of strong winds and rain of about 5 days duration shortly after bud-break are shown in Figures 7 to 11. Injury may occur to substantial areas of both adaxial and abaxial epidermises, causing cellular collapse, but without inducing conspicuous cuticular lesions. In Figure 7, groups of between 1 and about 20 epidermal cells have collapsed, without any visible loss of cuticular integrity. In a freeze-fracture through a similar region of lamina (Fig. 8) it is evident that the epidermal cell collapse does not necessarily involve the underlying palisade mesophyll, which, in this instance, is apparently healthy. Similarly, epidermal collapse occurs on the abaxial surface (Figs. 9 & 10), and may involve stomatal complexes as well as normal epidermal cells. In Figure 10 turgid stomatal complexes appear as islands in a sea of flaccid epidermis, indicating that they are more resistant to damage than the epidermis in general. At the periphery of the collapsed area of epidermis (Fig. 9) some stomata gape, suggesting that aperture control has been lost. The protruding major and minor veins are clearly vulnerable to mechanical damage, as shown in Fig. 11. On the other hand they also protect the underlying epidermis from abrasive damage by separating adjacent leaves from direct contact with the lamina. Note the trichome bases, remnants of hairs detached by abrasive damage (Fig. 11). The consequences of wind-induced abrasion on more mature leaves from samples taken at an exposed field site at Dunslair Heights, include smoothing and redistribution of the epicuticular wax (Fig. 12) and perforation of the cuticle (Fig. 13).

Visible damage: In water-misted beech controls, visibly-damaged leaf area was up to tenfold greater at wind-affected sites than under sheltered conditions (Figs. 14 a & b). Water-misted birch leaves showed approximately a fourfold increase in visibly-damaged leaf area compared with the sheltered controls, but in birch no significant difference was detected between the two

Figures 2 to 5: Surface structure of pristing beech leaves 3 days after bud-break

Figure 2   Adaxial leaf surface, showing turgid epidermal cells with sinusoidal outlines. LTSEM. Bar = 20 μm

Firgure 3   Glandular and covering trichomes on the major and minor veins, adaxial surface. LTSEM. Bar = 100 μm

Figure 4   Multicellular clothing trichomes on the abaxial surface. Stomatal complexes, in various stages of differentiation, protrud above the general epidermal surface. LTSEM. Bar = 20 μm

Figure 5   The leaf margin, seen fromthe abaxial surface, showing clothing and glandular hairs. LTSEM. Bar = 100 μm

Figure 6   Parts of two beech leaves from the more sheltered of the two sites at Dunslair Heights, showing wounding of the intervein lamina characteristic of wind damage to young leaves at the pleated stage soon after bud-break. In Fig. 6a, large brown patches of intervein tissue have been killed and have become desiccated following hydraulic isolation. In Fig. 6b, the injury is less severe, and similar to that seen in Fig. 7. Monochrome reproductions from colour slides. Bar = 5 μm

Figures 7 to 11: Consequences of wind abrasive damage to young leaves during an episode of strong winds and precipitation shortly after bud break.

Figure 7   A patch of collapsed adaxial epidermal cells alongside a minor vein, similar to the lesions seen in Fig. 6a. Note that there are no visible perforations in the cuticle. LTSEM. Bar = 20 μm

Figure 8   A freeze-fracture through a lesion similar to that shown in Fig. 7. The adaxial epidermal cells have collapsed, but the palisade mesophyll beneath appears to be undamaged. LTSEM. Bar = 10 μm

Figure 9   A large area of visible damage to the abaxial epidermis. In the band running diagonally from bottom left to top right, cellular collapse is probably confined to the epidermis. At top left, the sunken appearance indicates that the mesophyll is also injured, as in Fig. 6a. Isolated groups of turgid guard cells can be seen in the flaccid epidermis. LTSEM. Bar = 50 μm

Figure 10   The edge of a damaged area of abaxial epidermis, showing injury to epidermal cells and stomatal complexes, some of which may not yet have been fully developed. In several instances, one guard cell of a pair has lost turgor. LTSEM. Bar = 20 μm

Figure 11   Abrasive wind damage to the epidermis covering a major vein. Cells along the ridge are collapsed. Note the bases of uprooted trichomes (t). LTSEM. Bar = 50 μm

Figures 12 & 13: Consequences of wind abrasive damage to leaves at Dunslair Heights.

Figure 12   Smoothing and redistribution of epicuticular waxes on the adaxial cuticle. LTSEM. Bar = 10 μm

Figure 13   A perforation in the adaxial leaf surface, which has probably penetrated a group of epidermal cells beneath. Rhomboid crystals, possibly of solutes exuded from injured cells, occur in the vicinity of the wound. LTSEM. Bar = 40 μm

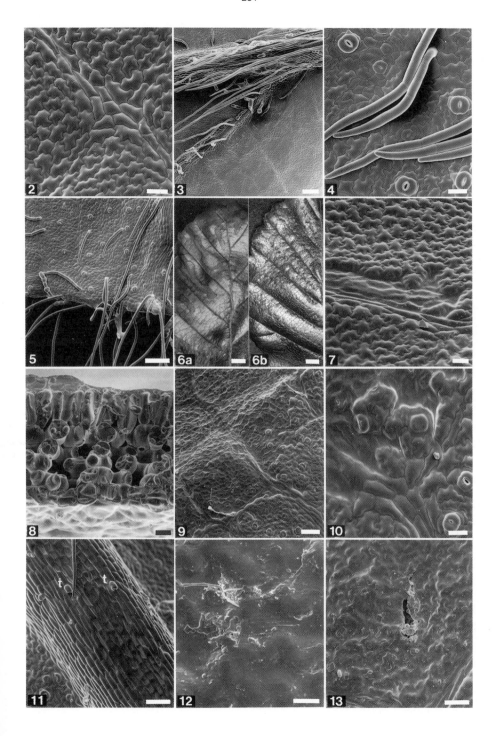

wind treatments. In beech (Fig. 14 b) the highest percentage of visibly-damaged leaf area was recorded in plants exposed to indirect wind damage.

Under complete shelter no significant effect of acid mist was observed on the percentage of visibly-damaged leaf area of either species. In beech, direct wind action combined with acid mist at both pH 3 and pH 5 caused more visible leaf damage than wind action alone, but both acid mist treatments induced similar effects. In birch, only pH 3 mist induced a significant increase in the visibly-damaged leaf area of plants exposed to direct wind action. Acid mist treatments combined with indirect wind action caused most visible damage in both species, above 30% of leaf area of beech, and about 20% of the leaf area in birch.

Microscopic damage to cuticular membrane: In water-misted plants, the numbers of microscopic cuticular lesions per cm^2 of leaf area, were at least an order of magnitude greater at wind-exposed sites than under complete shelter, and in both species were most numerous in plants exposed to indirect wind action (Figs. 14 c & d).

In neither species did acid mist induce significant changes in the numbers of microscopic lesions in sheltered plants. In both species, acid mist treatments produced significant increases in the numbers of microscopic cuticular lesions when combined with **direct wind action,** and pH 3 mist treatment combined with **direct wind action**, resulted in significantly more microscopic lesions than either pH 5 or control water mists. By contrast, in both species, a combination of **indirect wind action** and pH 3 mist resulted in significantly *fewer* microscopic lesions than did pH 5 or neutral mists, but in neither species was any effect detectable at pH 5.

Cuticular conductance: In water-misted plants of both species, g_c was two- to threefold greater following wind exposure compared to shelter, and was highest following indirect wind action with high mutual abrasion (Fig. 14 e & f). No significant effect of acid mist on g_c was observed in sheltered plants of either species. Cuticular conductance (g_c) was highest following a combination of pH 3 mist treatment and direct wind action. However, when combined with indirect wind action, pH 3 mist significantly *reduced* g_c. As noted for microscopic cuticular damage, pH 5 mist had no significant effect on g_c in plants exposed to indirect wind damage.

Discussion

In sheltered plants there was no evidence that acid mist causes visible macroscopic or microscopic damage to the leaf surface as suggested by Adams *et al.* (1990). Furthermore g_c was unaffected by acid mist in sheltered plants. This suggests that the physical structure of the cuticle in undamaged leaves is highly resistant to acid mist. Acid mist significantly influenced leaf structure and g_c only when the leaves had been (or were simultaneously being) damaged by wind action. Similarly, g_c of red spruce (*Picea rubens*) was unaffected by acid mist (Eamus *et al.*, 1989). By contrast, acid mist caused significant visible injury to red spruce needles and leaves of *Pisum sativum* and *Brassica napus* (Percy and Baker, 1987). Werkman (1993) found that fumigation of *Picea* with 140 ppb ozone had no effect unless the plants had been pre-treated by 120 h exposure to high wind speed in a controlled environment wind tunnel. Then, maximum assimilation rate was reduced by 20%.

Direct wind action may cause leaves to twist, bend and stretch to mechanical failure, as evidenced by the loss of leaf area in severe gusts. Presumably, just short of mechanical failure, such forces could result in cracking of the cuticle. Although smoothing of epicuticular waxes is reported to be a component of wind damage to strawberry leaves (MacKerron, 1976), our observations (Jeffree, unpublished) indicate that the fragile tubular wax crystals on Sitka spruce needles survive exposure to wind speeds well above natural magnitudes without detectable change. Leaf damage by direct wind action is probably by ballistic impaction of wind-blown soil, vegetation and ice particles, and wind-blown precipitation which may be composed of water, ice or mixtures of the two. These impactions may cause abrasion of the epicuticular waxes (Baker and Hunt, 1986; Mayeux and Jordan, 1987) and cuticle, and perforation of the cuticle or the underlying epidermal cell wall. Conceivably, a ballistic impact from large smooth object, such as a hailstone, may result in injury to and death of cells without the loss of cuticular integrity.

Indirect wind action, via mutual leaf impacts and abrasion, may remove and smooth epicuticular waxes, and perforate, score and crack the cuticle. The collapse of groups of epidermal or mesophyll cells may result from impacts between leaves, or between leaves and other plant organs (stems, buds). However, as noted above, these events may not always result in loss of cuticular integrity.

Since acid mist does not directly perforate undamaged cuticular membranes, the observation that low-pH acid mist increased the number of microscopic cuticular lesions in leaves exposed to direct wind action implies that the permeability of *pre-existing* microscopic damage sites is enhanced by acid damage. It is not clear how this might occur. Chemical degradation of the cuticle or cuticular waxes by acid mist is improbable, but acid hydrolysis of embedded polysaccharide constituents exposed at the surface of an abraded area might increase local permeability, and acid damage to cells might inhibit repair.

Although microscopic cuticular damage was highest at low mist pH when combined with direct wind action, visible damage to leaves was greatest as a result of indirect wind action and low pH, indicating that the latter environment was probably most damaging to overall leaf function. However, in both instances g_c was positively related to the number of microscopic cuticular lesions. The parallel reductions in the numbers of microscopic cuticular lesions and g_c in leaves subjected to indirect wind damage and low-pH acid mist (conditions which induced greatest visible damage) thus appear counterintuitive. Two possible contributory factors are advanced

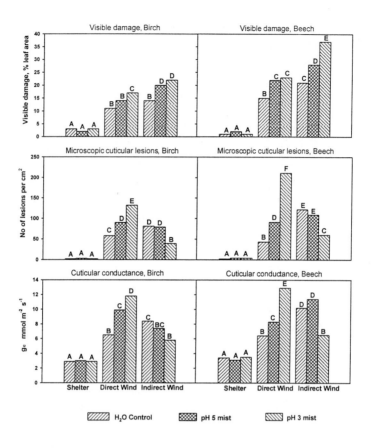

Figure 14   The effects of a combination of acid mist and wind treatment, applied to 3-year-old birch (a, c, e) and beech (b d, f) plants, on visible leaf damage (a, b), the numbers of microscopic cuticular lesions (c, d) and cuticular conductance (e, f). Different letters above each column indicate differences significant at <P = 0.05.

here. Firstly, the collapse of epidermal cells (Figs. 7 to 11) may render the cuticle less susceptible to penetration by wind-borne particles, since turgid structures are probably more readily penetrated by ballistic objects than flaccid ones. Furthermore, dead cells may become hydraulically isolated by the deposition of wound reaction products, and may thus have a lower relative water content than intact cells. The death, hydraulic isolation and consequent dehydration of entire blocks of tissue, which may range in size from microscopic single mesophyll domains to substantial fractions of the original leaf area, may thus account for the observed reductions in g_c when these are expressed on a leaf area basis.

The results presented here suggest that there are significant interactions between mist pH and wind action in inducing leaf damage. They emphasise the importance of control over wind exposure when conducting experiments on the effects of acid mist on plant structure and functions. In interpreting the effects of defined levels of acid mist exposure to stands of natural or crop plants the prevailing wind exposure at a site, and the type of mutual interaction between plants, must also be taken into account.

The physiological impact of additional pathways for the uptake of pollutants in both the gaseous and liquid phases will be reported in full elsewhere. One of the most important effects was a reduction in the rate of photosynthesis, even larger than that found by Eamus and Fowler (1990) in leaves of red spruce exposed to acid mist. It is likely that other responses to atmospheric pollution, including the well-established reduction in winter hardiness (Brown *et al.*, 1987; Fowler *et al.*, 1989; Cape *et al.*, 1991) will likewise be exacerbated by any decline in the integrity of the cuticle brought about by wind.

Acknowledgements

This study was funded by Natural Environment Research Council grant no. GR3/7175. Technical assistance provided by John Findlay and Morna Drysdale is gratefully acknowledged. Grateful thanks is also extended to the Forestry Commission for help in siting and constructing the plant enclosures at Dunslair Heights.

References

Adams MB, Caporn SJM, and Hutchinson TC (1990) Crystal occurrence and wax disruption on leaf surfaces treated with simulated acid rain. New Phytol 114: 147-158

Baker EA, Hunt GM (1986) Erosion of waxes from leaf surfaces by simulated rain. New Phytol 102: 161-173

Brown KA, Roberts TM, and Blank LW (1987) Interaction between ozone and cold sensitivity in Norway spruce: a factor contributing to the forest decline in Central Europe? New Phytol 105: 149-155

Cape JN, Leith ID, Fowlr, D, Murray MB, Sheppard LJ, Eamus D, and Wilson RHF (1991) Sulphate and ammonium in mist impair the frost hardening of red spruce seedlings. New Phytol 118: 119-126

Eamus D, Fowler D (1990) Photosynthetic and stomatal conductance responses to acid mist of red spruce seedlings. Plant, Cell Environ 13: 349-357

Eamus D, Leith I, and Fowler D (1989) Water relations of red spruce seedlings treated with acid mist. Tree Physiol 5: 387-397

Fowler D, Cape JN, Deans JD, Leith ID, Murray MB, Smith RI, Sheppard LJ, and Unsworth MH (1989) Effects of acid mist on the frost hardiness of red spruce seedlings. New Phytol 113: 321-335

Grace J (1974) The effect of wind on grasses. I. Cuticular and stomatal transpiration. J Exp Bot. 25: 542-551

Grace J, Russell GR (1977) The effect of wind on grasses. III. Influence of continuous drought or wind on the anatomy and water relations in *Festuca arundinacea*, Schreb. J Exp Bot 28: 268-278

Grace J, Unsworth MH (1988) Climate and microclimate of the uplands. *In* Usher MB, Thompson DBA, (eds) *E*cological change in the uplands. Blackwell Scientific Publications, Oxford, *pp* 137-150

Hoad SP, Jeffree CE, and Grace J (1992) Effects of wind and abrasion on cuticular integrity in *Fagus sylvatica* L. and consequences for transfer of pollutants through leaf surfaces. Agric Ecosystems Environ 42: 275-289

Leith ID, Murray MB, Sheppard LJ, Cape JN, Deans JD, Smith RI, and Fowler D (1989) Visible foliar injury of red spruce seedlings subjected to simulated acid mist. New Phytol 113: 313-320

Jeffree CE, Read ND (1991) Ambient- and low-temperature scanning electron microscopy. *In* Hall JL, Hawes CR, (eds) Electron Microscopy of Plant Cells. Academic Press, London. Chapter 8, *pp* 313-413

Jeffree CE, van Gardingen PR (1993) A portable cryo-storage system for low-temperature scanning electron microscopy, suitable for international transport of cryo specimens. J Microsc 172: 63-69

MacKerron DKL (1976) Wind damage to the surface of strawberry leaves. Ann Bot 40: 351-354

Mayeux HS, Jordan WR (1987) Rainfall removes epicuticular waxes from *Isocoma* leaves. Bot Gaz 148: 420-425

Percy KE, Baker EA (1987) Effects of simulated acid rain on production, morphology and composition of epicuticular wax and on cuticular membrane development. New Phytol 107: 577-589

Pearcy RW, Schulze E-D, and Zimmerman R (1989) Measurement of transpiration and leaf conductance. *In* Pearcy RW, Ehleringer JR, Mooney HA, Rundel PW (eds) Plant physiological ecology, field methods and instrumentation. Chapman & Hall, London. *pp* 137-160

Pitcairn CER, Jeffree CE, and Grace J (1986) The influence of polishing and abrasion on the diffusive conductance of the leaf surface of *Festuca arundinacea* (Schreb.) Plant, Cell Environ 9: 191-196

Thompson, JR (1974) The effect of wind on grasses. 2. Mechanical damage in *Festuca arundinacea* (Schreb.). J Exp Bot 25: 117-122

van Gardingen PR, Jeffree CE, and Grace J (1989) Variation in stomatal aperture in leaves of *Avena fatua* L. observed by low-temperature scanning electron microscopy. Plant, Cell Environ 12: 887-898

van Gardingen PR, Grace J, and Jeffree CE (1991) Abrasive damage by wind to the needle surfaces of *Pinus sylvestris* L. and *Picea sitchensis* (Bong.) Carr. Plant, Cell Environ 14: 185-194

van Gardingen PR, Grace J (1992) Vapour Pressure deficit response of cuticular conductance in intact leaves of *Fagus sylvatica* L. J Exp Bot 43: 1293-1299

Werkman BR (1993) Effects of acid mist, ozone and wind on Norway Spruce. Ph.D. Thesis, Univ. Edinburgh

Wilson J (1978) Some physiological responses of *Acer pseudoplatanus* to wind at different levels of soil water and the anatomical features of abrasive wind damage. Ph.D. Thesis, Univ. Edinburgh

Wilson J (1980) Macroscopic features of wind damage to leaves in *Acer pseudoplatanus* L. and its relationship with season, leaf age, and wind speed. Ann Bot 46: 303-311

Wilson J (1984) Microscopic features of wind damage to leaves of *Acer pseudoplatanus* L. Ann Bot 53: 73-82

Measurements and Modelling of Ozone Deposition to Wet Foliage

JD Fuentes, G den Hartog, HH Neumann, and TJ Gillespie[1]
Atmospheric Environment Service
4905 Dufferin Street
Downsview, Ontario M3H 5T4 Canada

Abstract

In humid regions, foliage can remain wet for up to 50% of the time during the growing season. Foliage surface wetness, caused by either condensation or rain, can alter the ability of vegetation to remove gaseous pollutants from the lower atmosphere. The chemistry of the solution that eventually develops while leaves remain wet can potentially modify the properties of leaf cuticles. Data from controlled and field experiments will be presented to demonstrate that significant amounts of ozone can be deposited onto wet plant leaves. Depending on plant species, foliage wetness can enhance ozone deposition. The enhanced ozone deposition while leaves remain wet is primarily controlled by the chemistry of the solution resting on leaves. The increases in ozone deposition are measured when foliage is wet with either rain or dew water. Waxy leaves experience only small ozone deposition while wet with either dew or rain water. A one-dimensional model is used to investigate the contribution of dew to ozone deposition to a deciduous forest canopy. The model is based on the tenet that the deposition can be determined from the ratio of the chemical concentration gradient and the sum of physical, chemical, and biological resistances to the diffusion along the source-to-sink pathway. The model is tested to include periods when the forest is either wet with dew or free of foliage wetness. Information from controlled experiments, concerning ozone deposition to wet foliage, is incorporated in the model to determine ozone deposition velocities when the forest canopy remains wet with dew. Modelled and measured ozone deposition onto the forest canopy compare reasonably well.

Introduction

Ozone deposition to terrestrial environments represents a major component of tropospheric ozone depletion. Vegetation readily takes up ozone from the surrounding air, especially during the daytime when leaf stomata are normally open. Ozone deposition to vegetation is a two-step process. First, atmospheric turbulent diffusion transports ozone from the surrounding air to the vicinity of leaf surfaces. Second, foliage properties (leaf size, stomatal aperture and state of plant physiology) determine the final step in the transfer and uptake mechanism. Ozone is immediately consumed upon arrival at the cell wall of stomatal cavities (Amiro and Gillespie, 1985; Laisk *et al.*, 1989).

---

[1]Department of Land Resource Science, University of Guelph, Guelph, Ontario N1G 2W1, Canada

NATO ASI Series, Vol. G 36
Air Pollutants and the Leaf Cuticle
Edited by K. E. Percy et al.
© Springer-Verlag Berlin Heidelberg 1994

Several field studies have provided measurements of ozone deposition to different vegetated landscapes (Enders *et al.*, 1992; den Hartog *et al.*, 1987; den Hartog and Neumann, 1994; Droppo, 1985; Hicks *et al.*, 1987; Leuning *et al.*, 1979; Grantz *et al.*, 1993; Meyers and Baldocchi, 1988; Wesely *et al.*, 1978, 1983). Most studies have been conducted during brief periods of the growing season while the underlying surface remained free of moisture. The ozone sink strength offered by wet foliage is not well known, although foliage can remain wet for a considerable time during the growing season (Hicks, 1986; Fuentes *et al.*, 1992). The chemistry of the solution that eventually develops while leaves remain wet can potentially modify the properties of leaf cuticles. Foliage surface wetness may alter the deposition process (Wesely *et al.*, 1990). For readily soluble gases, such as sulphur dioxide, field studies demonstrate that deposition is enhanced when foliage (Fowler and Unsworth, 1979; Schuepp, 1989) and other non-foliage elements (*i.e.*, bark, litter) (Padro *et al.*, 1993) stay wet. For less soluble gases, such as ozone, the deposition information is limited and the reported data are not consistent for wetness on all vegetation types (Fuentes *et al.*, 1993; Grantz *et al.*, 1993). This paper provides a summary of ozone deposition data obtained from field and controlled experiments, with emphasis on deposition while foliage is wet with either dew or rain water. A one-dimensional single layer model is used to demonstrate that, depending on the type of plant canopies, deposition can be significantly underestimated if models do not consider the effect of foliage wetness.

Field Experiments

Ozone concentration, ozone deposition velocity (V_d) and ozone flux (F_{O3}) for four dissimilar surface types are included to illustrate the effectiveness with which ozone is deposited to terrestrial surfaces. Data (Figure 1) are biased towards fair weather conditions. Data for the leafed deciduous forest were obtained at 33 m above ground at Borden, Ontario in late July through August 1988. The deciduous forest was 18 m tall and of mixed composition, primarily trembling aspen, red maple, white ash, big-tooth aspen, and black cherry. The leaf area index (LAI) of the fully leafed forest was 5.1 (Neumann *et al.*, 1989). Data for the leafless deciduous forest were also obtained at Borden in late March through April 1990. Data for the wetlands were obtained 18 m above ground at Lake Kinosheo, Hudson Bay in late June through July 1990. The underlying surface was covered by lichen bogs and small conifer shrubs. Data for the vineyard in the San Joaquin Valley, California, were measured at 9 m above the ground during July 1991. The vineyard was planted in rows spaced 3 m apart and oriented east-west and had a LAI of 3.4 (Grantz *et al.*, 1993). The field ozone fluxes were measured using the eddy correlation technique. The ozone fluxes were directed downward toward the underlying surface. Details on theory of measurements, sensor requirements and gas analyzer calibration protocols are provided elsewhere (den Hartog and Neumann, 1994; Fuentes *et al.*, 1992).

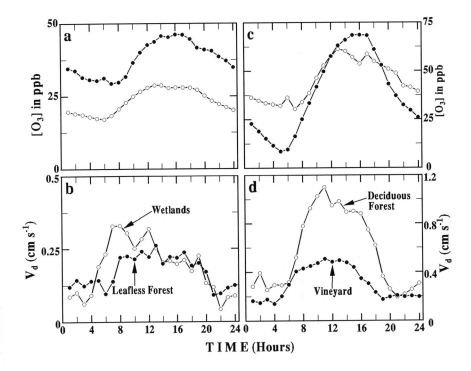

Figure 1   Diurnal variation of ozone concentration ([O3]) and deposition velocity (Vd) for a leafless and leafed forest, wetlands and a vineyard. The wetlands data (○) were measured at 18 m above ground during late June throughout July 1990 (Lake Kinisheo, Hudson Bay). The leafed (□) and leafless (●) forest data were obtained at 33 m above ground in late July throughout August 1988 and late March throughout April 1990, respectively (Camp Borden, Ontario). The vineyard data (■) were measured at 9 m above ground in July 1991 (San Joaquin Valley, California).

Ozone deposition to vegetated surfaces

Average ozone deposition data are presented to illustrate prevailing diurnal variations and typical magnitudes of deposition rates onto four distinct vegetation surfaces (Figure 1). The deposition velocity (V_d = ratio of ozone flux to ozone concentration) is used to indicate ozone deposition rates. The ozone deposition onto the four chosen surfaces exhibited a diurnal variation with highest and lowest values about midday and nighttime, respectively (Figure 1b and 1d). Highest ozone deposition usually occurs when atmospheric mixing and physiological activity of vegetation (if present) are greatest (Fowler *et al.*, 1989). The midday peak deposition rates occurred even when ozone concentrations attained maximum values several hours later (at approximately 16 h, Figures 1a and 1c).

The ozone concentration at the wetlands site exhibited small diurnal variation, with peak values around 25 parts per billion (ppb) while V_d attained maximum values of 0.35 cm s^{-1}. The V_d measured at the leafless forest site reached peak values of approximately 0.25 cm s^{-1}. The V_d values for the deciduous forest exhibited a well defined diurnal variation, with peak values of 1.1 cm s^{-1} measured around noon time. The ozone concentration at the Borden site during the summer was appreciably greater than the one recorded during the early spring. The nighttime ozone concentration at this forest site, on average, remained quite high (> 25 ppb). This is typical of rural environments having little nitric oxide to scavenge ozone during spring and summer time. Despite relatively higher ozone concentrations at the vineyard site, the V_d reached peak values of 0.40 cm s^{-1}. The V_d to the leafed deciduous forest was considerably greater than V_d for the other surfaces, which was possible because of the efficient turbulent transfer from the free air to the deposition substrate and larger leaf area (den Hartog and Neumann, 1994; Fuentes *et al.*, 1992).

Ozone deposition onto wet canopies

Depending on the type of vegetation, some ozone deposition (F_{O3}) can occur while plant canopies remain wet with either dew or rain water (Figures 2 and 3). Data included in Figure 2 were obtained over a mixed deciduous forest in Camp Borden. For the data presented in Figures 2a and 2b, dew onset started ~2230 h the previous day and the canopy remained wet until the dew completely evaporated by 1200 h. Dew took a long time to evaporate because of low solar radiation levels and overcast conditions observed during the morning hours (data not shown). Considerable ozone deposition was measured during the nighttime (from 0100 to 0600 h), when leaf stomata were presumably closed. The ozone deposition measured during nighttime conditions was likely controlled by mechanisms other than leaf stomatal behaviour. Because most leaves were covered with dew (both sides) during 0200-0800 h (Figure 2b), it is likely that ozone was taken up by the water solution on foliage.

Figure 2d shows F_{O3} data after the forest canopy became wet with rain at approximately 0300 h and stayed wet until 1030 h. In contrast with dew, only the adaxial leaf surfaces of deciduous trees were normally wetted with rain. The F_{O3} measurements began at 0830 h. The O_3 concentration steadily increased during the morning and gradually declined during the afternoon (Figure 2c). The F_{O3} increased during the morning hours, reaching peak values around 1000 h (Figure 2d), just before all water on leaves had evaporated. Since the largest F_{O3} occurred early in the day (near 0930 h), when some stomata were still covered with intercepted raindrops and solar radiation was not yet sufficiently strong to completely open uncovered stomata (principally on the abaxial leaf surface), it is believed that some ozone was taken up by the leaf surface water.

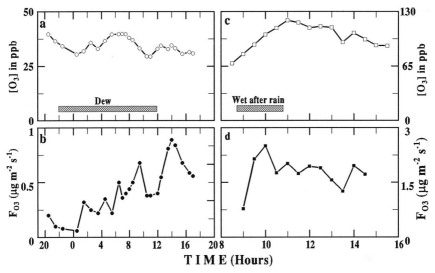

Figure 2   Ozone concentration ([O_3], open symbols) and ozone flux (F_{O3}) onto a deciduous forest wet with dew (●) and wet following rain (■).

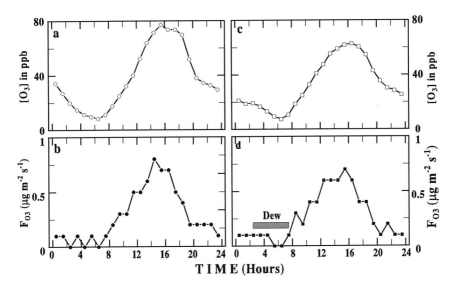

Figure 3   Ozone concentration ([O_3], open symbols) and ozone flux (F_{O3}) onto a vineyard during a day without dew (●) and during a day with dew on foliage (■).

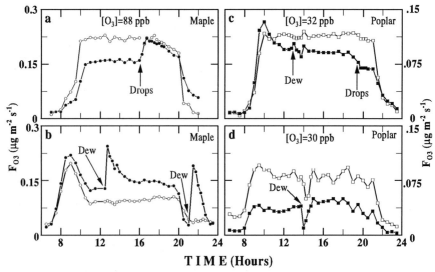

Figure 4   Ozone flux (F_{O3}) onto red maple leaves (circles) sprayed with a) drops and b) dew, c) poplar leaves (squares) sprayed with dew and drops (open symbols denote control leaves), d) abaxial (□) and adaxial (■) surfaces of a poplar leaf whose adaxial surface was wetted with dew.

The ozone deposition to a wet vineyard was not as pronounced as the deposition to the wet deciduous forest (Figure 4). Data during a day without dew (Figure 3b) and day with dew (Figure 3d) showed similar F_{O3} variations. For both days, the F_{O3} values were small during the nighttime, and in some instances the F_{O3} reached values close to zero (0100-0700 h). For the day with dew (Figure 3d), the canopy remained wet between 0330 and 0730 h. The small F_{O3} values during the wet period likely occurred because of the low ozone concentration (Figure 4c) and poor atmospheric mixing during the night. It is also possible that the wet grape foliage represented a poor ozone sink.

Controlled experiments

Data on ozone uptake by individual leaves of hypostomatous red maple (*Acer rubrum*) and amphistomatous hybrid poplar (*Populus deltoides trichocarpa*) are included to help explain the deposition patterns onto wet foliage observed in the field measurements. The photosynthetically active radiation levels during the ozone fumigation experiments were approximately 400 µE $m^{-2}s^{-1}$. Leaves were exposed to the ozone levels shown in the figures. Individual leaves, still attached to the trees, were enclosed in spherical glass cuvettes. The leaf ozone uptake (F_{O3}) was determined using the mass balance approach. Two wetness situations were artificially created. Water droplets were placed on adaxial leaf surfaces to simulate raindrops. Dew was simulated by spraying double-distilled water (pH $\approx$ 6.0) on leaves with an air brush. Further details on ozone fumigation and experimental procedures are provided by Fuentes *et al.* (1994).

Ozone deposition to individual leaves

There was some difference in ozone uptake among leaves and between tree species (Figure 4). The F_{O3} increased substantially immediately after simulated raindrops or dew were placed on maple leaves (Figures 1a and 1b). For the experimental run of Figure 4a, 2 mL of distilled water in the form of drops was placed on the adaxial leaf surface at 1615 h. The F_{O3} gradually increased soon after water spraying and slowly declined as the water evaporated. Because red maple leaves are hypostomatous, the water on the adaxial surface did not cover any stomatal pores. Therefore, the gas exchange of red maple leaves through stomata was unhindered by the water drops.

Water was sprayed to simulate dew on both maple leaf surfaces during light (1215 h) and dark (2115 h) periods (Figure 4b). The F_{O3} abruptly increased soon after water spraying and thereafter gradually declined as water evaporated. During the latter stage of water evaporation, only some isolated droplets were observed on the leaf surface. The fact that F_{O3} substantially increased when leaf surfaces were wet in the dark indicated that mechanisms in addition to stomatal behaviour likely contributed to enhanced ozone deposition onto wet maple leaves.

The effect of foliage wetness on O_3 deposition onto whole poplar leaves was different to that of red maple leaves when the adaxial side of a leaf was artificially wetted with first dew (1300 h) and then drops (2000 h, Figure 4c). Only very small changes in the O_3 deposition were detected after wetting the leaf. The F_{O3} slightly decreased immediately after the dew was sprayed on the leaf, but returned to essentially the same F_{O3} levels after the water had evaporated (Figure 4c). The water placed on the adaxial leaf surface in both wetting events covered some stomatal pores which undoubtedly obstructed the gas exchange between stomata and air.

The gas exchange of individual poplar leaf surfaces was monitored using split cuvettes to investigate whether reduced gas exchange due to water covering the surface of whole leaves could be compensated by increased gas exchange by the abaxial leaf side. In general, the F_{O3} values for the abaxial leaf surface were considerably greater than those for the adaxial side (Figure 4d). This follows the differences in stomatal distribution on adaxial and abaxial surfaces, the abaxial surface having higher stomatal density (data not shown). Results gathered from a leaf with dew sprayed on its adaxial surface at 1400 h indicated that the F_{O3} onto both the adaxial and abaxial surfaces declined soon after water spraying (Figure 4d). The F_{O3} onto the wet surface became nearly zero soon after water spraying, indicating that stomata were blocked and the leaf water was a poor ozone sink. The F_{O3} onto both leaf surfaces gradually increased as water evaporated, and attained nearly the same magnitude as was measured prior to water spraying. The reduced fluxes on the abaxial surface after the leaf became wet may have resulted from stomatal closure due to sudden leaf cooling after water spraying. Similar flux patterns were obtained when the adaxial leaf surface became wet with drops (data not shown).

Modelling ozone deposition to a deciduous forest canopy

A one-dimensional, resistance analogue model was used to examine the influence of foliage surface wetness on ozone deposition to a deciduous forest canopy. The model has been fully described by Baldocchi et al. (1987), Chameides (1987), Monteith and Unsworth (1990), Padro et al. (1991) and Wesely (1989). The theory is briefly reviewed to illustrate the modifications made to the model.

Model theory

This model assumes that the forest canopy represents a "big leaf" and that the deposition (F_{O3}) can be determined from the ratio of the gas concentration gradient (d_c) to the total resistance R_t) to the diffusion along the source-to-sink pathway (equation [1], Monteith and Unsworth, 1990). If the ozone concentration at the deposition substrate s (χ_s) is assumed to be zero, which for vegetation is a reasonable assumption (Amiro and Gillespie, 1985; Laisk et al., 1989), then the ozone concentration measured at a height $z(\chi_z)$ and R_t define F_{O3}. The reciprocal of R_t has velocity units (cm s^{-1}) and is referred to as the deposition velocity (V_d).

$$F_\chi = \frac{d\chi}{R_t} = \frac{\chi_z - \chi_s}{R_t} = \chi_z V_d \tag{1}$$

R_t represents the catena of the physical, chemical and biological resistances to mass transfer between z and s (Figure 4), and is given by [2].

$$R_t = R_a + R_b + R_c \tag{2}$$

R_a is the aerodynamic resistance to mass or energy transfer exerted by the turbulent internal boundary layer between z and the underlying surface characterised by a displacement height (d) and a roughness length (z_o). R_b is the boundary layer resistance of canopy elements and involves the transfer of mass across the quasilaminar sublayers that envelop surface elements. R_c is the bulk canopy resistance to gas exchange by canopy elements and incorporates deposition to stomata, leaf cuticles, bark, and surface water.

The R_a is a function of wind speed, atmospheric stability and underlying surface properties and can be determined from

$$R_a = \frac{Ln\left(\frac{z-d}{z_{om}}\right) - \psi_m(\zeta)}{u_* \, k}$$

[3]

where u_* is the friction velocity (m s^{-1}), k is von Karman's constant (0.4), d is canopy zero plane displacement (m), z_{om} is canopy roughness length (m) for momentum and $\psi_m(\zeta)$ is the diabatic stability correction for momentum transfer and is given by Paulson (1970). The u_* is defined as

$$u_* = \left[\frac{\tau}{\rho}\right]^{1/2}$$

[4]

τ is the measured momentum flux (N m^{-2}) and ρ is the air density (kg m^{-3}).

An R_b expression proposed by Wesely and Hicks (1977) and Hicks et al. (1987) was used

$$R_b = \frac{2}{ku_*}\left[\frac{Sc}{Pr}\right]^{2/3}$$

[5]

where Sc is the schmidt number (Sc = u/D_χ, where υ is the kinematic viscosity (cm^2 s^{-1}) of air and D_χ is the molecular diffusivity (cm^2 s^{-1}) of the gas (χ) under study), and Pr is the Prandtl number (Pr = υ/κ, where κ is the thermal diffusivity (cm^2 s^{-1})).

The R_c is the parallel sum of canopy stomatal (R_s) resistance, the cuticular resistance (R_{cut}) of dry leaves, the resistance of wet leaves (R_w) and a residual resistance (R_r) that accounts for the transfer to bark, litter and other non-foliage canopy elements([6]).

$$\frac{1}{R_c} = \frac{1}{R_s} + \frac{1}{R_{cut}} + \frac{1}{R_w} + \frac{1}{R_r}$$

[6]

R_s depends on physiological and environmental conditions, canopy leaf area and gas diffusivity. During the daytime, R_s for water vapour (R_{sv}) was estimated from measurements of latent heat fluxes in combination with the Penman-Monteith equation (Monteith and Unsworth, 1990). The R_s to ozone transfer (R_{sO3}) was then determined by multiplying R_{sv} by the ratio of the diffusivities of water vapour and ozone ($R_{sO3} = [D_v/D_{O3}]R_{sv}$). This calculation typically results in reasonable estimates for R_{sO3} only if the source distribution for water vapour is nearly the same as the sink distribution for ozone (Finnigan and Raupach, 1987).

R_{cut} was obtained from measurements taken on individual leaves of red maple and poplar in controlled experiments. Red maple and poplar leaves exhibited similar r_{cut} magnitudes and, therefore, an average r_{cut} value is used here (r_{cut} = 22 s cm^{-1}). Upper case symbols are used to denote canopy resistances and lower case symbols are used for corresponding quantities expressed as an individual leaf basis. R_{cut} for the forest canopy was obtained from [7]

$$R_{cut} = \frac{r_{cut}}{LAI} \qquad [7]$$

LAI had a value of 5.1 for the Borden forest (Neumann *et al.*, 1989).

R_t was assigned a value of 10 s cm^{-1}, following Wesely (1989). Equations [1] to [7] enable the calculation of V_d for a canopy free of surface wetness. When foliage was wet it was necessary to introduce R_w to account for the mass transfer of gaseous molecules to drops resting on foliage. If the canopy was partly wet, the deposition took place on both wet and unwet portions of foliage. The resistance offered by unwet foliage was that of leaf cuticles and can be expressed as (Padro *et al.*, 1991)

$$R_{cut} = \frac{r_{cut}}{LAI\,(1 - C_{Wet})} \qquad [8]$$

The R_w was taken as

$$R_w = \frac{r_w}{LAI\,C_{Wet}} \qquad [9]$$

C_{wet} is the canopy wetness obtained from measurements using sensors (Gillespie and Kidd, 1978) deployed at four levels within the forest canopy. The C_{wet} was $0 < C_{wet} < 1$, C_{wet} being 1 when the whole canopy was wet. The r_w was calculated from controlled experiments. The resistances for both red maple (r_{wm}) and poplar (r_{wo}) wet leaves were obtained from ozone deposition measured when water collected from leaves was placed on glass plates and exposed to known ozone concentrations. These resistances were then extrapolated to the forest canopy, taking into account the composition of the forest sand in which red maple represented 1.3 of the total LAI of 5.1 (Neumann *et al.*, 1989).

Two scenarios were considered when the canopy was wet. First, it was assumed that ozone deposition to wet foliage was inhibited. In this instance the canopy resistance was controlled by R_t and R_{cut} of the dry portions of foliage. Second, ozone deposition was assumed to take place and remain constant while foliage remained wet. Thus, R_w was taken as the sum of individual resistances (in parallel) of the tree species with distinct ozone sink strengths [10].

$$\frac{1}{R_W} = C_{wet}\left(\frac{LAI_m}{r_{wm}} + \frac{LAI_o}{r_{wo}}\right) \qquad [10]$$

LAI_m and LAI_o are the leaf area indices of red maple and other tree species (aspens, white ash, and black cherry, respectively). It was assumed that the ozone sink offered by wet foliage of tree species other than maple behaved similarly to poplar leaves (as represented by r_{wo}).

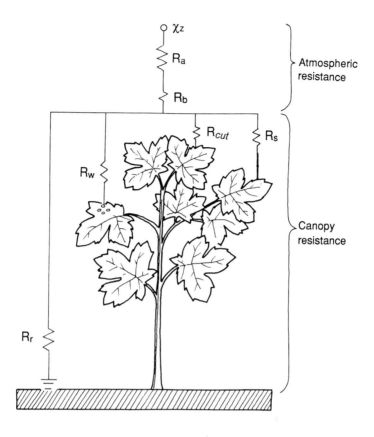

Figure 5   Electrical analogue of pathway resistances to the transfer of ozone to a maple forest canopy (see text for explanation of symbols).

Model results

The first scenario of the model was tested using data obtained over a deciduous forest to estimate V_d. Only results dealing with the wet forest canopy are included (for the Borden forest, the model estimates reasonable V_d values during free-wetness periods (den Hartog and Neumann, 1994; Fuentes *et al.*, 1994)). The V_d data were grouped and averaged for wet periods. Ozone deposition occurred only to canopy elements other than foliage when all surface leaf area was covered with water. The only resistances acting on the transfer process were R_a, R_b and R_t. The agreement

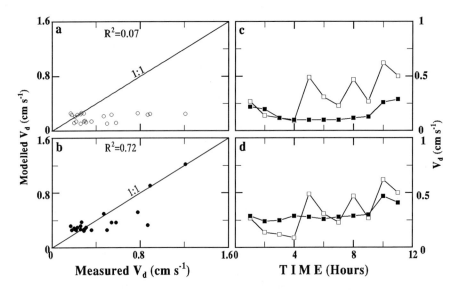

Figure 6   Measured and modelled ozone deposition velocity (V_d) when a) canopy was wet
with dew and no ozone deposition to wet foliage (○), b) canopy was wet with dew
but modelled ozone deposition occurred on wet foliage (●). Measured (□) and
modelled (■) V_d versus time after dew onset c) with no modelled ozone deposition
and d) with modelled ozone deposition allowed.

between measured and modelled V_d values was poor (Figure 6a) when ozone deposition was
inhibited because of foliage surface wetness.

The effect of allowing some ozone deposition onto wet foliage improved the agreement between
measured and modelled V_d (compare Figures 6a with 6b). This implies that the transfer resistance
provided by wet foliage of this deciduous forest canopy affected the deposition process under
the conditions examined. The good ozone sink provided by the maple fraction of the canopy
accounts for much of the ozone uptake but these results indicate that even for wet foliage with
a relatively poor sink for ozone, such as the aspen leaves, there would be some deposition. The
transfer resistance provided by wet leaves of species such as aspen trees had nearly the same
magnitude as the cuticular resistance (*i.e.*, r_{wo} similar to r_{cut}, Table 1). Because the forest in this
case was assumed to predominate with tree species whose foliage exhibited poor ozone uptake
while wet, the modelled V_d values did not increase as much as found in controlled experiments
with red maple leaves alone.

Table 1 Parameters used for estimating the ozone deposition velocity to a deciduous forest

Parameter	Value used
Flux measurement height	33.2 m
Canopy height	18.0 m
Zero plant displacement	11.5 m
Surface roughness length	2.3 m
Canopy leaf area index	5.1
Leaf area index of red maple	1.3
Leaf area index of other trees	3.8
Leaf cuticular resistance	22.0 s cm^{-1}
Maple wet leaf resistance	6.5 s cm^{-1}
Poplar wet leaf resistance	19.1 s cm^{-1}

More detailed model output, for a period when the forest canopy stayed wet with dew for several hours, is presented in Figures 6c and 6d. The time (on the X axis) refers to hours after the onset of dew. This period occurred during the night when leaf stomata were likely closed and inactive. Dew was not evaporating at fast rates as ascertained from C_{wet} measurements. The same two scenarios as those described above were modelled for this period (Figures 6c and 6d). The V_d was increasingly underestimated with time compared with measured values when ozone deposition to wet foliage was inhibited. Immediately after the onset of dew, the modelled and measured V_d compared reasonably well. The leaves at that time were partly covered with dew and so most ozone was assumed to be taken up by leaf cuticles and other canopy elements. The agreement between modelled and measured V_d was not as good as dew progressively accumulated on leaves (Figures 6c and 6d). The modelled V_d remained fairly constant whereas measured V_d changed with time. For the second scenario, the modelled and measured V_d values exhibited similar average trends (Figure 6d).

Conclusions

Experimental evidence from both eddy flux field studies and cuvette experiments in the laboratory indicates that appreciable ozone deposition can occur to wet foliage. This observation is contrary to expectations based solely on the relative insolubility of ozone in pure water. Cuvette studies showed that the effect of wetness on foliar uptake of ozone was strongly dependent on tree species. For example, red maple leaf wetting with either dew or drops enhanced ozone uptake. Poplar leaf wetting reduced but did not completely inhibit ozone uptake. Laboratory experiments revealed that the enhanced ozone deposition onto wet maple leaves was largely controlled by the chemistry of the solution which eventually developed while leaves stayed wet. Measurements in a temperate deciduous forest have shown that leaves are frequently wet, particularly at night and throughout the morning hours. Modelling of ozone deposition to such forest canopies can be improved by allowing for the species-dependent effects of leaf wetness.

Acknowledgements

The authors wish to acknowledge the excellent assistance with the field studies provided by Mr. John Deary of Atmospheric Environment Service. Financial support from the Natural Science and Engineering Research Council and the Atmospheric Environment Service of Environment Canada is also gratefully acknowledged.

References

Amiro BD, Gillespie TJ (1985) Leaf conductance response of *Phaseolus vulgaris* to ozone flux density. Atmospheric Environ 19: 807-810

Baldocchi DD, Hicks BB, Camara P (1987) A canopy stomatal resistance model for gaseous deposition to vegetated surfaces. Atmospheric Environ 21: 91-101

Chameides WL (1987) Acid dew and the role of chemistry in the dry deposition of reactive gases to wetted surfaces. J Geophys Res 92: 11895-11908

den Hartog G, Neumann HH, King KM (1987) Measurements of ozone, sulphur dioxide and carbon dioxide fluxes to a deciduous forest. *In* Preprint volume of the 18th Conference on Agricultural and Forest Meteorology, and 8th Conference on Biometeorology and Aerobiology, September 14-18, 1987 American Meteorological Society, Boston, MA *pp* 206-209

den Hartog G, Neumann HH (1994) Surface conductances for water vapor and ozone for four dissimilar surface types as determined using measured eddy fluxes and the Penman-Monteith model. J Geophys Res *In review*

Droppo JM (1985) Concurrent measurements of ozone dry deposition using eddy correlation and profile methods. J Geophys Res 90: 2111-2118

Enders G, Dlugi R, Steinbrecher R, Clement B, Daiber R, Eijk JV, Gab S, Haziza M, Helas G, Hermann U, Kessel M, Kesselmeier J, Kotzias D, Kourtidis K, Kurth HH, McMillen RT, Roider G, Schurmann W, Teichmann U, Torres L (1992) Biosphere/atmosphere interactions: integrated research in an European coniferous forest ecosystem. Atmospheric Environ 26: 171-189

Finnigan JJ, Raupach MR (1987) Transfer processes in plant canopies. *In* Zeiger E, Farquhar GD, Cowan IR (*eds*) Stomatal function. Stanford University Press, Stanford CA *pp* 385-429

Fowler D, Unsworth MH (1979) Turbulent transfer of sulphur dioxide to a wheat crop. Q J Royal Met Soc 195: 767-783

Fowler D, Cape JN, Unsworth MH (1989) Deposition of atmospheric pollutants on forests. Phil Trans R Soc Lond 324B: 247-265

Fuentes JD, Gillespie TJ, Bunce NJ (1994) Effects of foliage surface wetness on the deposition of ozone to red maple and poplar leaves. Water Air Soil Pollut *In press*

Fuentes JD, Gillespie TJ, den Hartog G, Neumann HH (1992) Ozone deposition onto a deciduous forest during dry and wet conditions. Agric For Met 62: 1-18

Gillespie TJ, Kidd GE (1978) Sensing duration of leaf moisture retention using electrical impedance grids. Can J Plant Sci 58: 179-187

Grantz DA, Massman WJ, Pederson JR, Delaney A, Oncley S, den Hartog G, Neumann HH, Shaw RH, Zhang X (1993) Measurements of surface wetness during the California ozone deposition experiment: effect of leaf wetness and stomatal conductance on ozone deposition. *In* Regional photochemical measurement and modeling studies, San Diego CA (Abstract) Air and Waste Management Association, Pittsburg PA

Hicks BB (1986) Measuring dry deposition: a re-assessment of the state of the art. Water Air Soil Pollut 30: 75-90

Hicks BB, Baldocchi DD, Meyers TP, Hosker RP, Matt DR (1987) A preliminary multiple resistance routine for deriving dry deposition velocities from measured quantities. Water Air Soil Pollut 36: 311-330

Laisk A, Kull O, Moldau H (1989) Ozone concentration in leaf intercellular spaces is close to zero. Planta 90: 1163-1167

Leuning R, Neumann HH, Thurtell GW (1979) Ozone uptake by corn (*Zea mays* L): a general approach. Agric For Met 20: 115-135

Meyers TP, Baldocchi DD (1988) A comparison of models deriving dry deposition fluxes of O_3 and SO_2 to a forest canopy. Tellus 40B: 270-284

Monteith JL, Unsworth MH (1990) Principles of environmental physics. Second edition, Arnold Press, London *pp* 291

Neumann HH, den Hartog G, Shaw RH (1989) Leaf area measurements based on hemispheric photographs and leaf-litter collection in a deciduous forest during autumn leaf-fall. Agric For Met 45: 325-345

Padro J, den Hartog G, Neumann HH (1991) An investigation of the ADOM dry deposition module using summertime O_3 measurements above a deciduous forest. Atmospheric Environ 25: 1689-1704

Padro J, Neumann HH, den Hartog G (1993) Dry deposition velocity estimates of SO_2 from models and measurements over a deciduous forest in winter. Water Air Soil Pollut 68: 325-339

Paulson CA (1970) The mathematical representation of wind speed and temperature profiles in the unstable atmospheric surface layer. J Appl Clim 9: 857-861

Schuepp PH (1989) Microstructure, density and wetness effects on dry deposition to foliage. Agric For Met 47: 179-198

Wesely ML, Hicks BB (1977) Some factors that affect the deposition rates of sulfur dioxide and similar gases in vegetation. J Air Poll Control Assoc 21: 1110-1116

Wesely ML, Eastman JA, Cook DR, Hicks BB (1978) Daytime variations of ozone eddy fluxes to maize. Boundary-Layer Met 15: 361-373

Wesely ML, Cook DR, Hart RL (1983) Fluxes of gases and particles above a deciduous forest in wintertime. Boundary-Layer Met 27: 237-255

Wesely ML (1989) Parameterization of surface resistances to gaseous dry deposition in regional-scale numerical models. Atmospheric Environ 23: 1293-1304

Wesely ML, Sisterson DL, Jastrow JD (1990) Observations of the chemical properties of dew on vegetation that affect the dry deposition of SO_2. J Geophys Res 95: 7501-7514

SECTION III - EFFECTS AND BIOMONITORING

The Effect of Age, Canopy Position and Elevation on Foliar Wettability of *Picea rubens* and *Abies balsamea*: Implications for Pollutant-Induced Epicuticular Wax Degradation

Richard L. Boyce
Environmental Studies Program
Dartmouth College
Hanover, NH 03755-3577 USA

Abstract

The epicuticular wax layer is the outermost layer of the cuticular barrier between the atmosphere and the plant interior. A number of air pollutants can degrade this wax layer, increasing interactions between the plant and atmospheric deposition and thereby inducing stress. However, a number of natural factors also influence the development and degradation of epicuticular wax in evergreen tree species, and any changes induced by air pollution will be superimposed upon these natural variations. Using the contact angle method, the wettability of red spruce (*Picea rubens* Sarg.) and balsam fir (*Abies balsamea* (L.) Mill.) foliage in subalpine regions of the northeastern U.S. was determined. In both species, foliar wettability increased as the foliage aged. Wettability also increased with increasing elevation in both species. Foliage from the bottom of the canopy was more wettable than foliage from the top. Fir foliage was generally less wettable than spruce foliage, particularly the younger age classes. These results indicate that spruce, due to its greater wettability, may be more greatly affected by pollutant-induced epicuticular wax degradation. For the same reason, older conifer foliage, foliage near the bottom of the canopy and foliage at higher elevations may all be more likely to be affected by epicuticular wax degradation caused by air pollutants.

Introduction

The epicuticular wax layer is the outermost part of the cuticular barrier that protects leaf interiors (Martin and Juniper 1970). Because evergreen conifers retain foliage for several years, it is vital that the integrity of this barrier be maintained over a long time period if interactions between foliage and the atmosphere are to be controlled. However, a number of air pollutants have been shown to degrade epicuticular wax and/or increase wettability in conifers, including sulfur dioxide, ozone and acid deposition (Cape, 1983; Barnes *et al.*, 1988; Cape *et al.*, 1989; Jagels *et al.*, 1989; Mengel *et al.*, 1989; Barnes and Brown, 1990; Percy *et al.*, 1990, 1992, 1993; Turunen and Huttunen, 1990, 1991). The resulting increased interaction between the plant and the atmosphere has been found to induce stress (reviewed in Turunen and Huttunen, 1990).

One difficulty in assessing the effect of air pollutants on epicuticular wax or wettability is that they are superimposed on changes caused by natural factors, such as age. For example, foliar

NATO ASI Series, Vol. G 36
Air Pollutants and the Leaf Cuticle
Edited by K. E. Percy et al.
© Springer-Verlag Berlin Heidelberg 1994

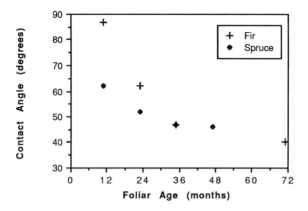

Figure 1. Contact angles of fir and spruce foliage collected from Camels Hump, Vermont, May 1987. Each point is the mean contact angle of 12 needles in each foliar age class. From Boyce *et al.*, 1991.

wettability is known to increase with age; Cape (1983) found that SO_2 exposure increased this rate of change in Scots pine (*Pinus sylvestris* L.). Thus, these natural changes in wax structure and wettability must be quantified before observed changes are attributed to air pollution. I show here how age, elevation and canopy position (height) affected the wettability of red spruce (*Picea rubens* Sarg.) and balsam fir (*Abies balsamea* (L.) Mill.) foliage.

Materials and methods

Detailed descriptions of the site and analyses are given in Boyce *et al.* (1991). Spruce and fir were sampled at three sites in the northeastern U.S.: Camels Hump, Vermont (44°19' N, 72°53' W), Mt. Moosilauke, New Hampshire (44°1' N, 71°51' W) and Mt. Washington, New Hampshire (44°16' N, 71°18' W). The effect of age and species was determined at all sites; elevation effects were determined at Mt. Moosilauke and canopy position effects at Mt. Washington. Wettability was quantified with contact angle measurements, using the method described in Boyce and Berlyn (1988). Contact angles were fit by nonlinear regression to a three-parameter model (Cape 1983): $\theta(t) = \theta_1 + \theta_2 e^{-kt}$, where $\theta(t)$ = contact angle (°) as a function of the foliar age (t) in months, θ_1 = asymptotic value (°), *i.e.*, the angle approached as t→∞, θ_2 = difference between initial and asymptotic contact angles, and k = first-order rate constant (month^{-1}) for the decrease in contact angle with foliar age. Each of these three factors was expanded to incorporate the effects of factors other than age, *e.g.*, $\theta_1 = \mu_1 + \alpha_1 I + \beta_1 H + \gamma_1 E$, where μ_1 = the value of the parameter for spruce at a reference canopy height and elevation, α_1 = the deviation of the value for fir from that of spruce, I = dimensionless coefficient equal to zero for spruce or unity for fir, β_1 = coefficient for the effect of position within the canopy, H = a parameterized measure of position within the canopy (*i.e.*, $0 \le H \le 1$), γ_1 = coefficient for the effect of elevation, and E = a parameterized measure of elevation (*i.e.*, $0 \le E \le 1$). Further details are given in Boyce *et al.* (1991).

The surfaces of randomly selected spruce and fir needles collected from the top of the canopy at the Mt. Washington site were examined with a scanning electron microscope (Boyce *et al.*, 1991), using the procedure of DeLucia and Berlyn (1984).

Results and discussion

Both spruce and fir contact angles decreased exponentially with age. Fir always had higher initial contact angles (was less wettable) than spruce; usually fir had larger final contact angles, although not in every case (Fig. 1). The erosion of epicuticular wax was responsible for the decrease in contact angles and increase in wettability; scanning electron micrographs showed that the fine structure of the stomatal wax plugs rapidly disappeared and became amorphous, and interstomatal wax also eroded and disappeared (Fig. 3-4 in Boyce *et al.*, 1991). Since surfaces with smooth microtextures are more wettable than rough surfaces (Holloway, 1970), the foliar surface becomes more wettable with foliar age. An initially larger amount of wax, particularly in the interstomatal regions, was observed in fir (Boyce *et al.*, 1991), which probably accounted for fir's larger contact angles.

Contact angles in both species also decreased with increasing elevation (Fig. 2). Canopy position also had an effect (Fig. 3). Foliage at the top of the canopy had the largest contact angles, while that collected from the bottom had the lowest. Both of these differences are probably due to photosynthate limitations caused by a shorter growing season at higher elevations and decreased light levels at lower canopy positions. A summary of the effects of the natural factors examined on contact angles of spruce and fir foliage may be given as: $\theta = (\mu_1 + \alpha_1 I + \beta_1 H + \gamma_1 E) + (\mu_2 + \alpha_2 I + \beta_2 H) \exp[-(\mu_3 + \alpha_3) t]$, where the italicized terms were not consistently present at all sites or sampling dates. Changes in elevation and canopy position changed contact angles of all foliar age classes and of both species, and the differences between fir and spruce contact angles was usually largest for the youngest foliar age classes. Neither elevation nor canopy position affected the rate constant, and in most cases there was no species effect, either. These differences in wettability imply that spruce foliage should be more likely to interact with pollutants than fir foliage. In both species, older foliage, foliage lower in the canopy and foliage at higher elevations may interact more strongly with air pollutants.

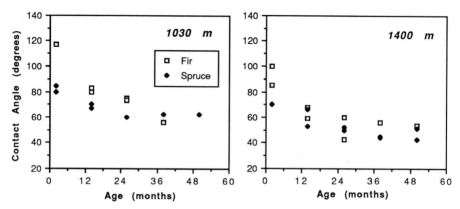

Figure 2. Contact angles of fir and spruce foliage collected from a low-elevation (1030 m) and high-elevation (1400 m) site on Mt. Moosilauke, New Hampshire. Each point is the mean of measurements made on six needles in each foliar age class for each tree. Data from Boyce *et al.* (1991).

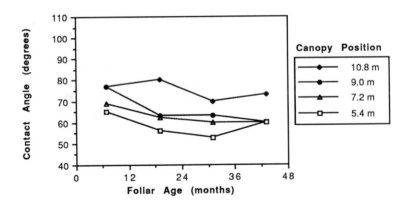

Figure 3. Contact angles of foliage from one spruce tree on Mt. Washington, New Hampshire, collected in January 1988 from heights ranging from the top (10.8 m) to the bottom (5.4 m) of the canopy. Each point is the mean of measurements made on 12 needles in each foliar age class. Data are from Boyce *et al.* (1991).

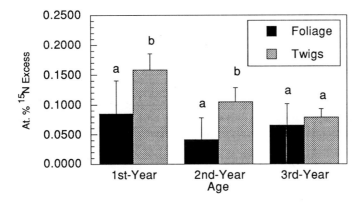

Figure 4. Mean atom % ^{15}N excess and one standard error (n=5) of spruce 1st-year, 2nd-year and 3rd-year+older foliage and twigs for tree branches treated with labeled ammonium applied to the branch. Means considered significantly different by Tukey's test (P < 0.05) are indicated by different letters. A comparison of foliage and twigs showed that 1st- and 2nd-year twigs treated with canopy applications of labeled ammonium had larger ^{15}N atom % excesses than foliage, but older twigs and foliage had similar levels (P < 0.05; Tukey's test). Data from Boyce *et al.* (unpublished).

However, pollution interactions with twig bark (Katz *et al.*, 1989) may be as or more important than interactions across leaf or needle cuticles. We have found greater uptake of ammonium ions by red spruce twigs than by foliage (Fig. 4). Changes in foliar wettability and the resulting changes on air pollution-cuticle interactions are clearly important, but in some cases they may be less important to the whole plant than other interactions.

References

Barnes JD, Brown KA (1990) The influence of ozone and acid mist on the amount and wettability of the surface waxes in Norway spruce [*Picea abies* (L.) Karst.]. New Phytol 114: 531-535

Barnes JD, Davison AW, Booth TA (1988) Ozone accelerates structural degradation of epicuticular wax on Norway spruce needles. New Phytol 110: 309-318

Boyce RL, Berlyn GP (1988) Measuring the contact angle of water droplets on foliar surfaces. Can J Bot 66: 2599-2602

Boyce RL, McCune DC, Berlyn GP (1991) A comparison of foliar wettability of red spruce and balsam fir growing at high elevation. New Phytol 117: 543-555

Cape JN (1983) Contact angles of water droplets on needles of Scots pine (*Pinus sylvestris*) growing in polluted atmospheres. New Phytol 93: 293-299

Cape JN, Patterson IS, Wolfenden J (1989) Regional variation in surface properties of Norway spruce and Scots pine needles in relation to forest decline. Environ Pollut 58: 325-342

Holloway PJ (1970) Surface factors affecting the wetting of leaves. Pestic Sci 1: 156-163

Jagels R, Carlisle J, Cunningham R, Serreze S, Tsai P (1989) Impact of acid fog and ozone on coastal red spruce. Water Air Soil Pollut 48: 193-208

Katz C, Oren R, Schulze E-D, Millburn JA (1989) Uptake of water and solutes through twigs of *Picea abies* (L.) Karst. Trees 3: 33-37

Martin JT, Juniper BE (1970) The cuticles of plants. Edward Arnold London

Mengel K, Hogrebe AMR, Esch A (1989) Effect of acidic fog on needle surface and water relations of *Picea abies*. Physiol Plant 75: 201-207

Percy KE, Jensen KF, McQuattie CJ (1992) Effects of ozone and acidic fog on red spruce needle epicuticular wax production, chemical composition, cuticular membrane ultrastructure and needle wettability. New Phytol 122: 71-80

Percy KE, Krause CR, Jensen, KF (1990) Effects of ozone and acidic fog on red spruce needle epicuticular wax ultrastructure. Can J For Res 20: 117-120

Percy KE, Jagels R, Marden S, McLaughlin CK, Carlisle J (1993) Quantity, chemistry, and wettability of epicuticular waxes on needles of red spruce along a fog-acidity gradient. Can J For Res 23: 1472-1479

Turunen M, Huttunen S (1990) A review of the response of epicuticular wax of conifer needles to air pollution. J Environ Qual 19: 35-45

Turunen M, Huttunen S (1991) Effect of simulated acid rain on the epicuticular wax of Scots pine needles under northerly conditions. Can J Bot 69: 412-419

Effect of Elevation and Foliar Age on Maximum Leaf Resistance to Water Vapor Diffusion in Conifers of the Central Rocky Mountains, U.S.A.

Julian L. Hadley and William K. Smith[1]
Harvard Forest
P.O. Box 68
Petersham, MA 01366
U.S.A.

Abstract

Development of cuticular resistance to water vapor diffusion ($r_c$wv) was measured in wind-protected shoots of Engelmann spruce (*Picea engelmannii*) and subalpine fir (*Abies lasiocarpa*) along the entire elevation gradient of these species in the central Rocky Mountains. Increases in $r_c$wv of new shoots occurred primarily during August. Maximum $r_c$wv was lower at high elevation, particularly in krummholz growth forms, as had been observed in other species. Highest mean rcwv (340 ks m^{-1}) occurred in Engelmann spruce at the lowest elevation (2700 m). At relatively high elevation, erect wind-protected trees showed a slight decline in mean $r_c$wv during September. At lower elevations, this decline did not occur during autumn, but a comparison of different age classes of foliage showed that in open-growth trees, second-year foliage had about 40% lower mean rcwv compared to new foliage sampled in October. Third- and fourth-year foliage did not show any statistically significant additional decline in $r_c$wv. The results could be explained by a superficial wax layer responsible for maximal $r_c$wv, which is produced in trees at low elevation exposed to full sun, but lost during the first fall or winter after the foliage is produced. This superficial wax layer of new foliage also appears to reduce foliar wettability. Loss of this wax or failure to produce it, particularly in wind-exposed trees at high elevations, may simultaneously increase diffusion of water vapor and other gases, and potential adsorption or absorption of solutes by cuticles in older age classes of conifer foliage.

Introduction

A high resistance to diffusion of water vapor through plant leaf surfaces is crucial in preventing lethal dehydration, especially when soil moisture is inadequate or water flow to leaves is blocked. Water can be immobilized by freezing of vascular tissue and soil in winter (Zimmermann 1964, Tranquillini 1979, Sakai and Larcher 1987), and cavitation can interrupt xylem flow during either summer or winter (Tyree and Sperry 1989). Maximum diffusion resistance to water vapor (r^v_{max}) may also correlate with maximum diffusion resistance for other polar molecules in the vapor phase, thus allowing an estimate of leaf surface resistance to penetration of pollutant gases such as SO_2 and NO_2 when stomata are closed.

---

[1]Department of Botany, University of Wyoming, Laramie, WY 82070, U.S.A.

NATO ASI Series, Vol. G 36
Air Pollutants and the Leaf Cuticle
Edited by K. E. Percy et al.
© Springer-Verlag Berlin Heidelberg 1994

In many species, r^v_{max} has been estimated by measuring the decline in mass of an isolated leaf or shoot per unit time, after a nearly constant rate of change in mass has been achieved, indicating that stomata are closed. Changes in mass due to respiration during dehydration are usually assumed to be negligible relative to the mass efflux of water. Stomatal transpiration is also commonly ignored after stomatal closure due to dehydration, and cuticular transpiration resistance is assumed to equal r^v_{max}, calculated as the ratio of the leaf-to-air water vapor concentration or pressure gradient, divided by the rate of change in mass due to dehydration. However, water vapor may diffuse even through "closed" stomata, so the term "maximum transpiration resistance" or r^v_{max}, is more accurate in describing resistance values obtained by this technique.

Maximum transpiration resistance of conifers has been calculated by dehydrating shoots, needles or needle fasicles (Sowell *et al.* 1982, Hadley and Smith 1986, 1990, Herrick and Friedland 1991). In montane and subalpine conifers, r^v_{max} of current-year foliage is usually lower at high elevation, especially near alpine treeline (Tranquillini 1979, Sowell *et al.* 1982, DeLucia and Berlyn 1984). However, there is little information on r^v_{max} of older foliage, even though in some coniferous species, foliage is retained for 10 or more years (Schoettle and Smith 1991, Hadley *et al.* 1993).

This study was designed to examine the interactive effects of elevation and foliage age on r^v_{max} in two conifers of the central Rocky Mountains, Engelmann spruce (*Picea engelmannii* Parry) and subalpine fir (*Abies lasiocarpa* Nutt.). These species occur from lower timberline to alpine treeline where they occur as krummholz forms. Earlier studies (Hadley and Smith 1983, 1986) examined the effects of wind on r^v_{max}, so shoots selected for this study were relatively wind-protected, either by topography or canopy structure.

Methods and materials

Picea engelmannii and *Abies lasiocarpa* were sampled at 11 sites (*Picea*) and six sites (*Abies*) at 2.68 km to 3.40 km above sea level between July and October 1985. At each site, a single randomly selected shoot was cut from the north and south side of each of six saplings or krummholz mats. Erect trees occurred up to 3.29 km elevation in wind-protected sites, and krummholz mats at wind-exposed locations from 3.15 to 3.40 km elevation. In addition to open-grown saplings, understory saplings at 3.1 to 3.2 km elevation were sampled. Three-year-old branch tips were collected in early October, at six sites for *Picea* and four sites for *Abies*, to measure r^v_{max} of older foliage. North- and south-facing shoots showed no significant difference in r^v_{max} for any age class or site for either species; therefore, these shoots were grouped together in further analysis of the data.

Shoots or branch tips were transported to the laboratory in plastic bags held over ice. Shoot bases (or both ends of a growth increment for older shoots) were sealed with paraffin to prevent water loss, and the shoot bases were placed in styrofoam holders under low-level fluorescent illumination (<10 μmoles $m^{-2} s^{-1}$ photosynthetically active radiation). Air circulation at 2 m/s eliminated any significant aerodynamic resistance to water vapor flux. Shoots were weighed every 4 to 24 h depending on the rate of dehydration, and temperature and relative humidity of the air were continuously monitored by a hygrothermograph. After needle abscission began, shoots were dried at 70°C for 72 h before the mass of needles and stem were determined to the nearest 0.001 g. Needle surface area-to-dry mass ratio was determined on a subset of needles from each site using a glass bead technique (Thompson and Leyton 1971). Individual needles spanning the range of needle sizes for each site and date were used to calculate a regression of individual needle dry mass to surface area-to-dry mass ratio. This regression was then used to estimate needle area for each shoot, for which the average individual needle dry mass was also determined. Transpiration resistance (r^{wv}) for whole shoots was calculated as the ratio of leaf-to-air water vapor concentration gradient (assuming water vapor saturation within leaves) to the mass flux through the total needle surface area. Average r^{wv} over a water content range of 90 to 70% of the initial (field) water content was used as the estimate of r^{v}_{max}. The calculated value of r^{wv} did not change significantly over this water content range, except for a slight average increase attributable to shoot dehydration and declining water potential. Nearly constant r^{wv} was taken as an indication that stomata had reached maximum closure.

Results

In *Picea engelmannii*, r^{v}_{max} of new foliage was very low in mid-July (3 to 5 weeks after bud-break) and remained low in early August except in the lowest-elevation trees. During August and September, r^{v}_{max} increased in low and very high-elevation foliage, although r^{v}_{max} was stable or declined during September at most sites between 3.1 and 3.29 km elevation (Fig. 1a-c). In *Abies lasiocarpa*, r^{v}_{max} increased at most sites during late July and August, but then declined except at one krummholz mat site (Fig. 1d-f).

In October, r^{v}_{max} of current-year foliage was higher than r^{v}_{max} of older foliage at elevations up to 3.17 km for open-grown *Picea*, and at all elevations for open-grown *Abies*. There was no significant difference between foliage 1 to 3 years old, except in *Abies* at the lowest elevation (Fig. 2b). All growth forms of *Picea* showed a decline in r^{v}_{max} of current year foliage between 3.1 and 3.3 km elevation, resulting in no significant difference between current-year and older foliage at higher elevations (Fig. 3). Average maximum diffusion resistance of current-year foliage in October was higher in *Picea* than in *Abies* at the lowest and highest elevations. *Abies*

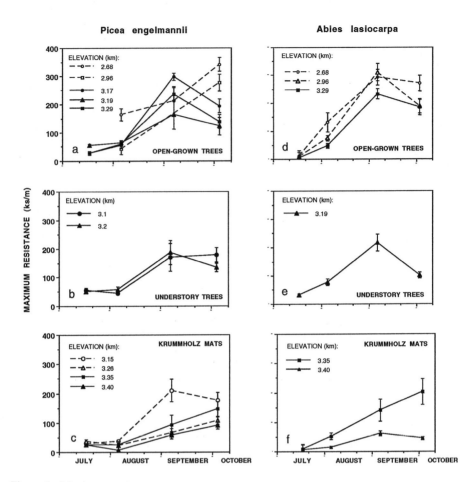

Figure 1   Maximum resistance to water vapor diffusion for current-year foliage of *Picea engelmannii* (a-c) and *Abies lasiocarpa* (d-f) from mid-July through early October 1985. Bars indicate standard errors of means for a total of 12 shoots from six trees or krummholz mats for each date and site.

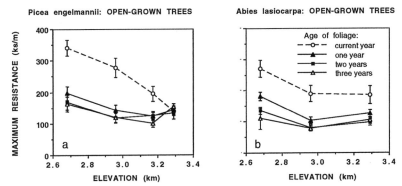

Figure 2   Maximum resistance to water vapor diffusion for different foliar age classes of open-grown trees of *Picea engelmannii* (a) and *Abies lasiocarpa* (b), measured in October 1985. Bars are standard errors of means for a total of 12 shoots of each age class from six trees or krummholz mats at each site.

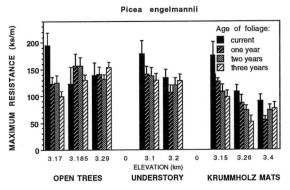

Figure 3   Maximum resistance to water vapor diffusion for different elevations and growth forms of *Picea engelmannii* between 3.1 and 3.4 km elevation. Bars indicate standard errors of means as described for Figure 2.

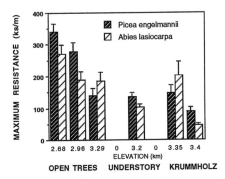

Figure 4   Maximum resistance to water vapor diffusion for mature current-year foliage of *Picea engelmannii* versus *Abies lasiocarpa*, measured in early October 1985. Bars indicate standard errors of means as described for Figure 1.

had higher average r^v_{max} at some intermediate elevations (Fig. 4), but the mean r^v_{max} for *Abies* was not significantly higher (p ≤ 0.05, Student's t-test) at any elevation.

Discussion

In general, r^v_{max} increased more slowly and reached a lower peak value in high-elevation trees, and particularly in krummholz mats, when compared to low-elevation open-grown trees. This is consistent with slower development of cuticles, thinner cuticles, and lower r^v_{max} at the end of the growing season for high-elevation trees (Tranquillini 1979, Sowell *et al.* 1982). The decline in r^v_{max} during September at two sites (3.17 and 3.29 km) may have been due to loss of cuticular surface wax from already mature cuticles. It was visually apparent that there was less epicuticular wax, particularly epistomatal wax, on older foliage at all sites.

The large difference in r^v_{max} between current and 1- to 3-year-old foliage at relatively low elevations was consistent with visible loss of surface wax, and suggests that superficial waxes, either epistomatal or otherwise, contributed substantially to the high r^v_{max} values achieved by low-elevation trees. Trees or krummholz mats at very high elevation (above 3.1 to 3.3 km) apparently did not produce these superficial waxes in sufficient quantity to give current-year foliage a higher r^v_{max} than older foliage. The lack of significant differences in r^v_{max} between 1- and 3-year-old foliage (except for *Abies lasiocarpa* at one site) indicates that another component of r^v_{max} is determined by elements of the cuticle that are relatively resistant to erosion or degradation. The slower decay of r^v_{max} of older needles relative to current foliage at low elevation could be a result of either structural or chemical differences between residual cuticular waxes and waxes lost during the first year, or both. The cuticular components responsible for the residual r^v_{max} of older needles appear to be chloroform-soluble, since a 10-s treatment with $CHCl_3$ increased minimum water vapor conductance (or decreased r^v_{max}) by a factor of approximately 100 in these species (Hadley and Smith 1990).

The decline in r^v_{max} with elevation (for current-year foliage) and the decline in r^v_{max} during the first year following shoot maturation at relatively low elevation shows an inverse pattern to the increase in foliar wettability with elevation and age described for *Picea rubens* and *Abies balsamea* by Boyce *et al.* (1991). Although Boyce *et al.* described increases in foliar wettability (apparently due to degradation or erosion of surface waxes) as a continuous function rather than a change over the first year followed by a lack of significant change, they did observe that in most cases the greatest annual difference in contact angle (θ) for surface water droplets was between current-year foliage and foliage approximately 1 year old. They also observed changes in foliar wettability with elevation in all age classes of foliage, whereas we observed significant changes in r^v_{max} with elevation only in current-year foliage and (in *Picea engelmannii*) 1-year-old foliage. Nevertheless, there were opposite elevational and temporal changes in wettability versus r^v_{max}, at least for leaf surfaces up to 1 year old, in the study by Boyce $et\ al.$ compared to this study. This suggests that loss of the same epicuticular waxes could result in both increased foliar wettability and decreased r^v_{max} with increasing age or elevation.[2]

It is not known whether r^v_{max} correlates with resistance of the leaf surface to penetration of aqueous solutes. If so, the results indicate that with increasing elevation, current-year foliage in *Picea engelmannii* and *Abies lasiocarpa* may allow greater diffusion of solutes out of the leaf interior to precipitation in leaf surfaces, as well as diffusion of solutes in precipitation into leaves, depending on the concentration gradient. Similarly, increasing leaf age for trees at relatively low elevation could allow for greater uptake or leaching of solutes for older compared to current-year foliage. Increasing leaf surface wettability with increased leaf age or elevation, as observed by Boyce $et\ al.$ (1991) would accentuate these trends in uptake or leaching of solutes, by allowing larger quantities of precipitation to remain on older or higher-elevation leaf surfaces. The effects of leaf wettability on retention of precipitation on leaf surfaces may be complicated by shoot structure, with more densely-packed foliage trapping more water between leaf surfaces (Brewer $et\ al.$ 1991). However, needle packing has been shown to increase with elevation in montane and subalpine conifers (Smith $et\ al.$ 1991), and this would reinforce the positive effect of greater foliar wettability on water retention by high-elevation foliage.

In closing, it must be noted that the effects of foliar age observed in this study are only approximations of true aging, because the current- and 1- to 3-year-old shoots were produced in different years. Baig and Tranquillini (1976) showed that near the upper timberline, r^v_{max} of mature current-year foliage may vary from year to year, depending on the growing-season climate, and thus the difference (or lack of difference at high elevation) which we observed between current and older foliage would not necessarily be observed if the study were done in a different year. However, the relatively small differences in r^v_{max} between 1- and 3-year-old foliage suggest that variation in growing season conditions did not have a large long-term effect on r^v_{max} for these three age classes of foliage.

Acknowledgements

This work was supported by grants from the U.S. National Science Foundation (BSR 8200742) and U.S. Department of Agriculture (86 CRCR-1-2061).

---

[2]See DeLucia and Berlyn (1984) for an example of the latter in *Abies balsamea*.

References

Baig MN, Tranquillini W (1976) Studies on upper timberline: morphology and anatomy of Norway spruce (*Picea abies*) and stone pine (*Pinus cembra*) needles from various habitat conditions. Can J Bot 54: 1622-1632

Boyce RL, McCune DC, Berlyn GP (1991) A comparison of foliar wettability of red spruce and balsam fir growing at high and low elevation. New Phytol 117: 543-555

Brewer, CA, Smith WK, Vogelmann TM (1991) Functional interactions between leaf trichomes, leaf wettability, and the optical properties of water droplets. Plant Cell Envir 14: 955-962

DeLucia EH, Berlyn GP (1984) The effect of increasing elevation on leaf cuticle thickness and cuticular transpiration in balsam fir. Can J Bot 62: 2423-2431

Hadley JL, Smith WK (1983) Influence of wind exposure on needle desiccation and mortality for timberline conifers in Wyoming, USA. Arct Alp Res 15: 127-135

Hadley JL, Smith WK (1986) Wind effects on needles of timberline conifers: Seasonal influence on mortality. Ecology 67: 12-19

Hadley JL, Smith WK (1990) Influence of leaf surface wax and the leaf area to water content ratio on cuticular transpiration in western conifers, U.S.A. Can J For Res 21: 269-272

Hadley JL, Amundson RG, Laurence JL, Kohut RJ (1993) Red spruce bud mortality at Whiteface Mountain, New York. Can J Bot 71: 827-833

Herrick GT, Friedland AJ (1991) Winter desiccation and injury of subalpine red spruce. Tree Physiol 8: 23-36

Sakai A, Larcher W (1987) Frost survival of plants. Springer-Verlag 321 *pp*

Schoettle AW, Smith WK (1991) Interrelation between shoot characteristics and solar irradiance in the crown of *Pinus contorta* ssp. *latifolia*. Tree Physiol 9: 245-254

Smith WK, Schoettle AW, Cui M (1991) Importance of leaf area measurement to the interpretation of gas exchange parameters of complex shoots. Tree Physiol 8: 121-127

Sowell JB, Koutnik DL, Lansing AJ (1982) Cuticular transpiration of white-bark pine (*Pinus albicaulis*) within a Sierra Nevadan timberline ecotone, U.S.A. Arct Alp Res 14: 97-103

Thompson FB, Leyton L (1971) Method for measuring the surface area of complex shoots. Nature 229: 572

Tranquillini W (1979) Physiological ecology of the alpine timberline. Springer-Verlag 137 pp.

Tyree MJ, Sperry JS (1989) Vulnerability of xylem to cavitation and embolism. Annu Rev Plant Phys Mol Bio 40: 19-38

Zimmermann MH (1964) Effect of low temperature on the ascent of sap in trees. Plant Physiol 39: 568-572

The Effects of Pine (*Pinus sylvestris* L.) Needle Surface Wax Layer Structure on Water Loss and Uptake of $^{14}CO_2$ and $^{35}SO_2$

S. Godzik and T. Staszewski
Institute for Ecology of Industrial Areas
Katowice, Poland

Abstract

The surfaces of current and one-year-old pine (Pinus sylvestris L.) needles from areas of different air pollution levels were examined using SEM + EDAX. It was found that abrasion of needle surfaces (using a fine hairbrush), thus destroying the wax layer structure, led to an increase in water loss and a decrease in the uptake rate of $^{14}CO_2$. This phenomenon was restricted to current-year needles.

Labelling needles with $^{35}SO_2$ to obtain information on distribution of sulphur taken up between particular needle compartments revealed that particulate matter accumulated on the needle surface contributing from 6 to 15% and from 13 to 24% to the total uptake of $^{35}SO_2$ by needles of shoots taken from control and polluted areas, respectively. Dust contributed from 10 to 30% of $^{35}SO_2$ deposits on needle surfaces. Sulphur compounds were neither soluble nor removable with water. Generally, a significantly higher amount of sulphur was bound to waxes and particulate matter than to needle tissue. There was no evidence of sulphur leaching following needle washin with water.

X-ray fluorescence analysis of pine needle surfaces under SEM has shown some differences between both the area of the needle (stomata region and next to it) and the sampling sites. On the basis of the parameters tested, the protective role of the wax layer with regard to dust accumulation is discussed.

Introduction

Like many other plant species, the needles of *Pinus sylvestris* are covered by a structured wax layer. The natural function of this layer is at present not very well known, but there are suggestions that it may be important in influencing gas exchange and diminishing the effect of UV, among other things (Martin and Juniper, 1970; Clark and Lister, 1975).

The plant surface, and tree foliage in particular, has an additional function; it is where air pollutants, both gaseous and particulate, are first deposited. Some meteorological phenomena, *e.g.*, rainfall, wind, and abscision of foliage bring these deposited pollutants to the soil. Quantities of pollutants supplied to the environment under a plant canopy may be several times larger than those deposited on bare soil.

The aim of this paper is to present results of investigations on the role of the structure of the wax layer of needles on water loss (non-stomatal transpiration), $^{14}CO_2$ and $^{35}SO_2$ uptake.

NATO ASI Series, Vol. G 36
Air Pollutants and the Leaf Cuticle
Edited by K. E. Percy et al.
© Springer-Verlag Berlin Heidelberg 1994

Materials and methods

Shoots of Scots pine (*Pinus sylvestris* L.) with needles of different age classes were taken from trees of the same age, at the same height, and exposure, in an area with high air pollution levels (Zabrze — Upper Silesian Industrial Region) and in a rural (Notec Primaeval Forest — West Poland) — control site.

Depending on size, two or three shoots from each site were taken for labelling with $^{35}SO_2$ or $^{14}CO_2$. The methods of handling and labelling have been described elsewhere (Godzik, 1976; Staszewski *et al.*, 1992). Carbon dioxide uptake was investigated using samples from the rural area only.

In experiments with $^{35}SO_2$, 50 needles of each age were removed from each shoot after labelling. The needles were washed with 20 mL of distilled water for 20 minutes using an ultrasonic bath. After drying, the same procedure was repeated with chloroform. The needles were then dried and weighed. The solutions obtained were filtered through micropore filters.

All components were examined for radioactivity. A gas flow counter with anticoincidence was used for determining radioactivity. At least 10,000 counts were collected for each needle sample. The uptake of sulphur dioxide was calculated from radioactivity measurements and expressed as cpm g^{-1}(dw) of needles. A preliminary test was carried out to establish the duration and type of solvents for removing absorbed ^{35}S. Needles were washed with distilled water. The water samples for radioactivity were taken after 1, 2, 10, 30, and 60 min, then the needles were dried and the same procedure was repeated with two other solvents — chloroform and methanol.

A hairbrush was used to destroy the structural form of the epicuticular wax layer on 100 needles of each age class, and a gravimetric method was used to determine water loss. Particles of feldspar and coal dust, below 10 μm in size, were deposited on surfaces in an experimental treatment. Measurements were carried out between 18 and 24 h after treatment. Results are mean values of at least three series of experiments. Water loss was determined for needles from the reference site only.

A subset of needles was taken for SEM investigation. Both adaxial and abaxial needle surfaces were examined using a JEOl Model U3 SEM.

Results and discussion

There were no distinct differences in wax structure on needles from reference sites, and those described previously (Martin and Juniper, 1970; Hanover and Reicosky, 1971; Grill, 1973). Needle samples from the polluted area showed a significant alteration of wax structure and, in addition, large numbers of deposited particles of different sizes (Figures 1-6). It can be concluded that the wax structure weathering rates were from two to four times faster in samples from the polluted area compared to the control site. Brushing the needles effectively destroyed wax structure on current-year needles.

Results of water loss (non-stomatal transpiration) measurements, calculated for the time between the second and fifth hour of the experiment, are presented in Figure 7. Removing the wax crystals by brushing resulted in a twofold increase in water loss in the current-year needles and a 1.7-fold increase in the older needles. A very good relationship for water loss between treated and non-treated samples in different experiments was found. Results obtained in these experiments are from 1.5 to 3 times higher than those cited by Zelawski (1967). The reason is not yet known. Deposition of coal and feldspar dust had no additional effect on the needle water regime (Figure 7). Removal of wax by a very short treatment with chloroform increased the water loss up to 52-60 $mg^1 g^{-1}$ (fresh weight) h^{-1}, and was not dependant upon needle age.

Results suggest the crucial role of wax in controlling the water regime of the needle. The wax structure, however, is of importance, too. Under normal (field) conditions, alteration of the wax layer structure is a natural process. Physical processes responsible for structural alteration seem to be of importance in limiting the control of water loss from needles. Additional deposition of dust has no further effect on the water regime of pine needles (Figure 7). An increase in transpiration of oak leaves from air-polluted sites was reported by Ricks and Williams (1974). An increase in water loss via the adaxial surface of *Aesculus hippocastanum* has also been reported (Godzik and Piskornik, 1966). Such comparisons are of limited value, however, because horse-chestnut leaves have no structural wax layer. It has been found, however, that in this case the surface structure of the epidermal cells at the adaxial surface was significantly modified (Godzik & Sassen, 1978; Godzik and Halbwachs, 1986).

A large decrease in $^{14}CO_2$ uptake was found in brushed current-year needles (Figure 8) compared to the control (Figure 8). The 1-year-old needles showed a smaller response. Deposition of feldspar and coal dust had an additional effect, depending on needle age (Figure 8). The reason for the different response of needles to coal and feldspar dust is not known, but one may speculate about the alteration of needle optical characteristics (Clark and Lister, 1975), and of changes in the aerodynamical resistance caused by changes in the wax structure in (or over) the antechamber area.

The uptake of $^{35}SO_2$ by needles from the polluted area (Zabrze) was twice as great as uptake by needles from the control site (C). Uptake was greater for current-year needles than for 1-year-old needles (Figure 9). A comparison of the sum of radioactive sulphur compounds extracted by water and taken up by dust with the amount of radioactive compounds bound to needle tissue showed a preference for the former. The amount of sulphur bound to needle tissue ranged from

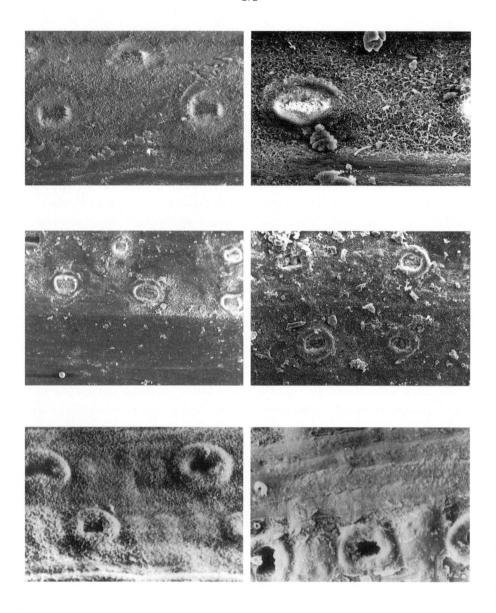

Figure 1   Current-year needle from rural area (X 1350)
Figure 2   1-year-old needle from rural area (X 2025)
Figure 3   Current-year needle from industrial area (X 600)
Figure 4   1-year-old needle from industrial area (X 800)
Figure 5   Current-year needle (unbrushed) (X 1100)
Figure 6   Current-year needle (brushed) (X 1100)

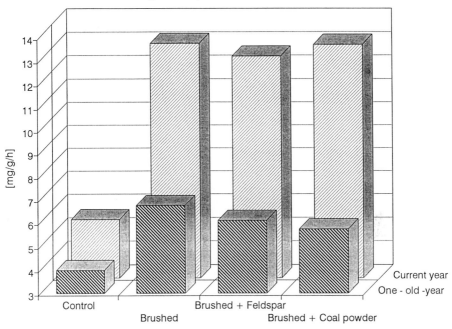

Figure 7.

13 to 41% of the total amount of sulphur taken up, and needles from the control site took up more than needles from the polluted area. Depending on needle origin, accumulated particulate matter on the surface contributed from 6 to 15% or from 13 to 17% of the total uptake of $^{35}SO_2$ by needles from control and polluted areas, respectively.

The contribution of dust to the deposition of ^{35}S compounds localized on the needle surface ranged from 10 to 30% (Figure 9). These values correspond only to the fraction of $^{35}SO_2$ chemically bound to dust, forming slightly soluble salts. It may be assumed that the contribution of dust deposited on the needle surface to the total uptake of $^{35}SO_2$ is higher because of the soluble salts formed as a result of reaction with the gas, as well as absorption of SO_2 on active sites of the dust. Both of these sulphur sinks are removed by washing with water and chloroform, together with sulphur compounds adsorbed on the wax layer. Dust is not only the primary barrier to the deposition of gas pollutants on plant surfaces but is a "competitor" for the uptake of SO_2

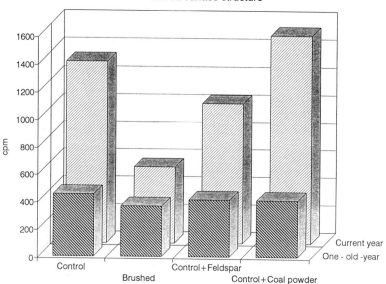

Figure 8.

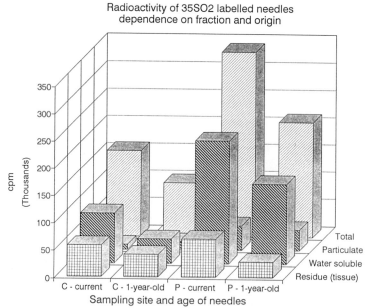

Figure 9.

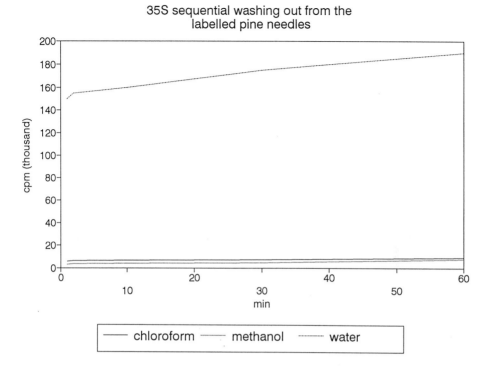

Figure 10.

with the plant surface. The selective removal of sulphur compounds from needle surfaces by using three different solvents exploited differences in surface tension, reflecting different degrees of penetration into the needle surface. Ninety-five percent of sulphur compounds were removed by washing with water, despite water's surface tension. The majority of radioactive compounds was removed during the first minutes of the washing procedure (Figure 10).

Conclusions

1. Water loss (non stomatal transpiration) due to mechanical destruction of wax structure increases by a similar proportion in both current- and previous-year needles.

2. The uptake of $^{14}CO_2$ by current-year needles declines markedly after mechanical destruction of the wax structure. No such effect has been found for the previous year's needles.

3. Deposition of coal dust and feldspar on treated needles influenced the $^{14}CO_2$ uptake in different ways. An increase was found for the current-year needles with deposited coal dust. No effect was found for feldspar-treated needles nor for needles from the previous year.

4. The sorptive characteristics of the needle surface for SO_2 changed as a result of alterations in wax structure and the properties and quantity of dust deposited on it.

5. No leaching was observed for needles labelled with $^{35}SO_2$ and washed with water and other solvents. Only surface $^{35}SO_2$ was removed.

References

Clark JB, Lister GR 1975 Photosynthetic action spectra of trees. II. The relationship of cuticle structure to the visible and ultraviolet spectral properties of needles from four coniferous species. Plant Physiol 55: 407-413

Godzik S, Piskornik Z 1966 Transpiration of *Aesculus hippocastanum* L. leaves from areas of various air pollution. Bull Acad Pol Sci 14: 181-184

Godzik S 1976 Poblerani $^{35}SO_2$ z powietrza i rozmieszczenie ^{35}S u niektórych gatunków drzew. Badania porównawcze. Prace is Studia, PAN, 16

Godzik S, Sassen MMA 1978 A scanning electron microscope examination of *Aesculus hippocastanum* L. leaves from control air polluted areas. Environ Pollut 17: 13-18

Godzik S, Halbwachs G 1986 Structural alterations of *Aesculus hippocastanum* L. leaf surface by air pollutants. Z Pflanzenkrank Pflanzensch 93 (6): 590-594

Grill D 1973 A scanning electron microscope study on leaves of some *Pinaceae, Cupressaceae,* and *Taxaceae*. Microscope 29: 348-358

Hanover JW, Reicosky DA 1971 Surface wax deposit on foliage of *Picea pungens* and other conifers. Amer J Bot 58: 681-687

Martin JT, Juniper BE 1970 The cuticles of plants. Edward Arnold. Edinburgh

Ricks GR, Williams RJH 1974 Effects of atmospheric pollution on deciduous woodland. 2. Effects of particulate matter upon stomatal diffusion resistance in leaves of *Quercus petrea* (Matuschka) Leibl. Environ Pollut 6: 87-109

Staszewski T, Godzik S, Poborski S 1992 Repeated labelling of Scots pine (*Pinus silvestris* L.) shoots with $^{35}SO_2$. Archiwum Ochrony Srodowiska 2: 163-169

Zelawski W 1967 Wymlana gazowa i bilans wodny igliwia [in:] Bialobok S, Zelawski W Zarys lizjologii sosny zwyczajnej 33-93 PWN Poznan 1967

Effects of Acid Mist on Needle Surface and Water Status of *Picea abies*

Andreas Esch and Konrad Mengel
Institute of Plant Nutrition
Justus-Liebig-University of Gieen
Südanlage 6
35390 Giessen

Abstract

In various experiments carried out under controlled conditions in the greenhouse, we have shown that acid mist (pH 2.7-3.0) application affected the cuticle of spruce trees and led to a decomposition and melting of epicuticular waxes. Trees with such an affected cuticle had the same transpiration rate as control trees if abundant soil water was available. When soil water was low, however, trees with an affected cuticle transpired significantly more water than control trees. This effect was particularly evident at noon, when control trees showed virtually no transpiration in contrast to affected trees.

In a further set of experiments, in the spring, we tested the effect of frozen soil on the water status of young spruce trees that had been exposed to acid mist the preceding autumn. These affected trees , during periods of sunshine, had significantly lower water potential than the control trees. This investigation demonstrates that acid mist affects the water status of spruce trees. Because acid mist is common in the area near Frankfurt, we argue that decline symptoms in this area, including cuticle damage, are caused mainly by acid mist.

Introduction

Forest decline in central Europe has been of public concern since 1980. Since then, much scientific work has been carried out in various research fields, with the aim of resolving the ever-worsening situation. Investigations over the last decade have shown that no single cause of forest decline can be found to explain the observed damages. However, a variety of correlations exists among several factors, depending on the location, the forest type, the management, and environmental factors (Forschungsbeirat Waldschäden/Luftverunreinigungen, 1989).

Central to most investigations is the direct effect of air pollution on plants (Bell, 1986; Lichtenthaler, 1984). In various experiments, carried out under controlled conditions in the greenhouse, Mengel *et al.* (1989) have shown that application of acid mist, consisting of SO_2 and NO_x in a pH-range of 2.7 - 3.0, affected the cuticle of spruce trees. The same result was observed by Magel and Ziegler (1986), who exposed young spruce trees to the atmospheric conditions of a natural forest. Given the major role of the cuticle in regulating transpiration at the interface between the plant and the atmosphere, a change in the integrity of epicuticular waxes could lead to uncontrolled water loss. Therefore, the following experiments were focused on the question of whether plants pretreated with acid mist showed a reduced ability to retain their water.

NATO ASI Series, Vol. G 36
Air Pollutants and the Leaf Cuticle
Edited by K. E. Percy et al.
© Springer-Verlag Berlin Heidelberg 1994

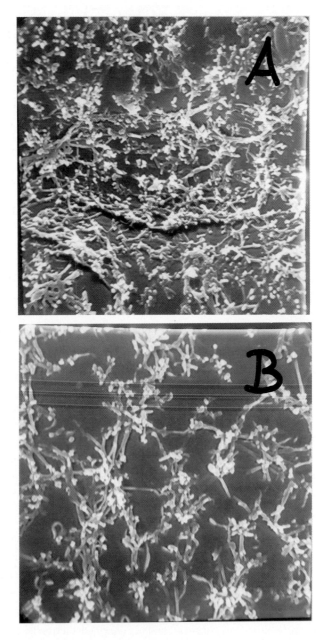

Figure 1 Scanning electron micrographs of the structure of epicuticular waxes of current-year Norway spruce needles. A: After application of control mist (pH 5.0). B: After application of acid mist (pH 3.0).

Materials and methods

The experiments were carried out with four 5-year-old trees of *Picea abies* (L.) Karst.

Two different treatments of mist, an acid mist of pH 3.0 and a control mist of pH 5.0, were simulated in a greenhouse under field conditions. The mist was produced with fine nozzles and applied for 2 min, three times a week, over a period of 10 weeks. The soil was covered by a plastic foil in order to protect it from the mist solution.

After the mist application, the structure of current-year epicuticular wax layer was observed using a scanning electron microscope (SEM).

Cuticular transpiration was measured as water loss of excised twigs under the dry conditions of a desiccator containing silica gel. This controlled testing lasted for 48 h.

Further measurements of transpiration rates and xylem water potential were carried out under the influence of two different types of climatic stress. Aside from water stress in summer, we were interested in the effect of frost stress in winter. Replicating winter conditions in Central Europe, we tested the effect of frost-shock and frost-hardening, while reducing the temperature in the climate chamber more or less quickly to -15°C.

The third frost event simulated is described in literature as frost-drought and occurs under improved sun-light conditions in spring which lead to a warming of the upper plant part and an increase in transpiration. At the same time, water uptake from the soil is still poor or completely blocked by frost. According to Larcher (1985) this typical frost event can be compared with normal drought situations in soil because in both cases water loss is higher than water uptake.

Transpiration rates under water stress conditions in summer were measured gravimetrically, whereas for the later studies of transpiration rates during winter we used a porometer. The different types of transpiration, stomatal, and non stomatal, were confirmed with microscopic observations, depending on the infiltration of dye to classify the stomatal opening width. For measuring the xylem water potential, the pressure bomb technique was applied according to Scholander (1965).

Results

In Figure 1A, the electron micrograph reflects the epicuticular wax layer of the control needles (pH 5.0) with a regular, dense stand of small wax threads all over the cuticle. This situation represents a compact structure with barely visible lesions. In Figure 1B, it is evident that acid mist led to a detrimental influence on the epicuticular wax layer, with a melted appearance among

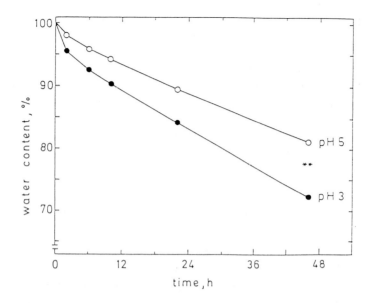

Figure 2   Water content of current-year excised twigs (*Picea abies*) under the dry atmospheric conditions of a desiccator over a drying period of 48 h after the twigs had been pre-treated with acid mist of pH 3.0 (closed symbols) and control mist of pH 5.0 (open symbols). Each point represents the mean of 10 replicates. **, $P < 0.01$. (*From Mengel et al., 1989.*)

individual wax formations. This change in wax structure resulted in the appearance of lesions having no wax-cover.

Figure 2 shows the pattern of water loss of excised twigs exposed to the dry conditions in a desiccator. The rates of water loss clearly reflect that, especially at the end of the experimental period, the water loss of the acid mist-treated twigs was significantly higher, compared to the control treatment.

Furthermore, the figure shows different rates of water loss depending on stomatal and non-stomatal transpiration. Stomatal transpiration took place at the beginning of testing immediately after cutting the twigs, with a steep decrease in water content. These steep initial rates of water loss were different for both mist treatments. After 2 h desiccation, rates of water loss followed a less steep pattern and the linear lines obtained presumably reflect cuticular transpiration at closed stomata.

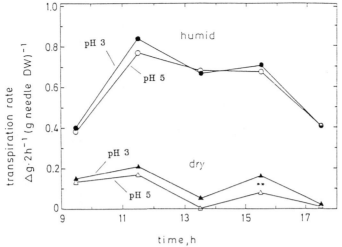

Figure 3   Transpiration rates of *Picea abies* over 1 day (25 August 1987) under humid and dry
conditions of the soil after the trees had been pretreated with acid mist of pH 3,0
(closed symbols) and with control mist of pH 5,0 (open symbols). Each point represents the mean of ten replicates. **, P < 0,01. (*From Mengel et al., 1989.*)

The transpiration rates of *Picea abies* in Figure 3 were not influenced by the pretreatment with
acid mist if the water supply of the trees was sufficient during summer time. Under dry conditions
represented at the bottom of the figure we found lower transpiration rates. There was a clear trend
showing that trees that had been treated with acid mist had higher transpiration rates than the
control. The difference in transpiration between the treatments was significant at the afternnoon
measurement (1530 h). At noon (1330 h), we found zero transpiration of the control trees,
indicating a closure of the stomata, while the acid mist treatment showed a distinct water loss.

Xylem water potential of *Picea abies* was measured throughout a summer day, while the trees
were well supplied with water (Fig. 4). The upper part of the figure shows the pattern of air
temperature and air moisture of a typical summer day. At the bottom of the figure, the course of
water potential is depicted, clearly indicating that, except for the situation at night and in the late
evening, the twigs of the acid mist treatment (pH 3.0) had lower water potentials than those of
the control mist (pH 5.0). For the period from noon until 7 p.m. the differences were significant
in the range of 0.1 to 0.2 MPa.

The transpiration rates of the different frost-treated trees (Fig. 5) showed an immediate reduction
of transpiration level to the zero level. During the subsequent test period, a recovery took place
that differed for the various frost treatments. The transpiration rates of the frost-shocked trees
increased to a level of half of the rates before frost. The frost-adapted trees, however, increased

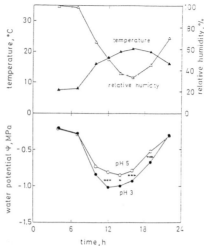

Figure 4   Top: Course of temperature (closed symbols) and relative humidity(open symbols) of air during 7 August 1987. Bottom: Changes in the xylem water potential of *Picea abies* during 7 August 1987 under humid conditions of the soil after the trees had been pretreated with mist of pH 3.0 and control mist of pH 5.0. The points at 4, 7 and 22 h represent the mean of ten replicates and the other points represent the mean of five replicates each. *, P < 0.05, ***, P < 0.001. (*From Mengel et al., 1989.*)

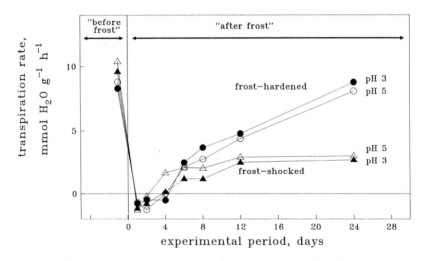

Figure 5   Transpiration rates of different frost-treated *Picea abies* (frost-shock, frost-adaptation) after the trees had been pretreated with acid mist of pH 3.0 (closed symbols) and control mist of pH 5.0 (open symbols). Each point represents the mean of ten replicates.

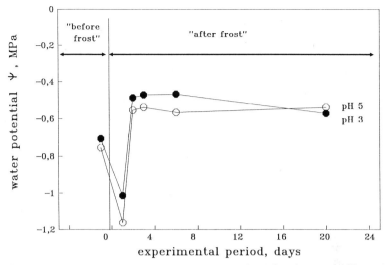

Figure 6   Xylem water potential of frost-shocked *Picea abies* after the trees had been pre-
reated with acid mist of pH 3.0 (closed symbols) and control mist of pH 5.0 (open
symbols). Each point representing the mean of five replicates.

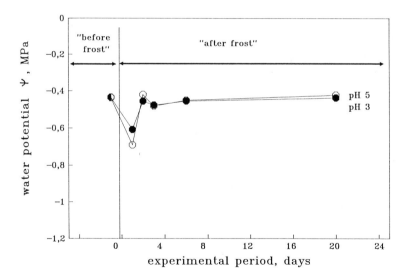

Figure 7   Xylem water potential of frost-hardened *Picea abies* after the trees had been pretreated with acid mist of pH 3.0 (closed symbols) and control mist of pH 5.0 (open
symbols). Each point representing the mean of five replicates.

their transpiration rates continously until, at the end of the experimental period, the same transpiration level was attained as before the frost event.

Xylem water potentials of the various frost-treated plants shown in Figures 6 and 7 reflected a tendency similar to the transpiration rates in Figure 5. There was a sharp decline of the water potential directly after frost with a recovery almost to the same levels as before frost, after the second day. The decline in water potential was greater after the frost shock frost-adapted trees. These responses of the trees in water potential and transpiration were not influenced by the pretreatment with acid mist.

Figure 8 shows the transpiration rates under frost-drought as tested under field conditions. There was a total reduction of transpiration rates independent of the different mist treatments during the whole period of frost-drought. In comparison, the unfrozen soil conditions raised transpiration rates up to 25 mmol H_2O g^{-1} h^{-1}, but with also no major difference between the pH-treatments.

From the data in Table 1 it is clear that frost-drought resulted in a remarkable decrease in the needle water potential, and this decline in water potential was significantly greater in the needles pretreated with acid mist than in the control needles.

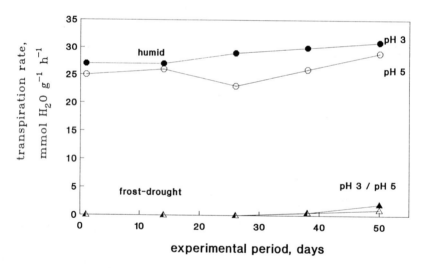

Figure 8   Transpiration rates of *Picea abies* under frost-drought and humid conditions of the soil after the trees had been pretreated with acid mist of pH 3.0 (closed symbols) and control mist of pH 5.0 (open symbols). Each point represents the mean of ten replicates.

Table 1 Xylem water potential of *Picea abies* (on 31 March 1993, at 12 h) under frost-drought and humid conditions of the soil after the trees had been pretreated with acid mist of pH 3.0 and control mist of pH 5.0. Each term represents the mean of five replicates. [***], $P < 0.001$.

Water Potential, MPa

experimental day: March 31, 1993 at 12 h

	pH 3		pH 5
frost-drought	-2.26	***	-1.49
	***		***
humid	-0.61		-0.60

Discussion

The results obtained in our recent study confirm our assumption that the degradation of the epicuticular waxes of current-year needles caused by acid mist impairs the water retention capability and, especially, enhances water loss by non-stomatal transpiration. This result, raised cuticular transpiration, corresponds well with Godzik and Piskornik (1966), who found that leaves from a polluted area dried faster than those taken from an unpolluted area. Although, in this study, surfaces that lacked stomata showed the same pattern of water loss as those with stomata it seems more likely that a change in cuticular conductance was responsible for the water losses in the polluted area.

The effect of uncontrolled water losses in our study was evident under dry conditions, like the situation in the desiccator or the situations under summer and winter drought. It is clear that these water losses, when there is no water uptake, will have a dramatic effect on the whole water status of a tree, such that the situation will last for a longer period.

Therefore, these results concur with field observations in and after years of drought (Rehfuess 1985).

However, given humid soil conditions, considering transpiration rates and xylem water potential in summer, results show that the water status of the trees is only affected for a short period throughout the day, here at noon. At this time, a lower water diffusion resistance of the trees pretreated with acid mist could be observed compared to the control trees, because the water potential of the acid-treated trees was significantly lower (Fig. 4), while the corresponding transpiration rates (Fig. 3) were not influenced. Normally one would expect a decline in transpiration rates with a decrease in water potential.

In the evening and overnight, when the demand on the water status became low, the water situation was always normalized. The same result could be found after frost-shock and frost-adaptation in winter. There the recovery of the water potential was fully obtained after the frost event, when the soil started to thaw and water uptake could take place.

A change in epicuticular wax structure is, therefore, not directly lethal. The situation can last for years, with no serious effect on tree life, depending on the humid conditions throughout the year.

Duration of the cuticular damage depends on the level of the plant's metabolism. As shown with the simulation of frost-drought in spring, the change in wax structure lasted for months, beginning in summer with the mist application until the following spring period and was not repaired over the winter, the level of metabolism being low.

References

Bell JNB (1986) Effects of acid deposition on crops and forests. Experentia 42: 363-371

Forschungsbeirat Waldschäden/Luftverunreinigungen (1989) Dritter Bericht, November 1989

Godzik S, Piskornik Z (1966) Transpiration of *Aesculus hippocastanum* L. leaves from areas of various kinds of air pollution. Bull Acad Pol Sci 14: 49-61

Larcher W (1985) Kälte und Frost *In* Die nicht parasitären Krankheiten, 5 Teil, Paul Parey

Lichtenthaler HK (1984) Luftschadstoffe als Auslöser des Baumsterbens. Naturw. Rdsch. 37: 271-277

Magel E, Ziegler H (1986) Einfluss von Ozon und saurem Nebel auf die Struktur der stomatären Wachspropfen in den Nadeln von *Picea abies* (L) Karst Forstw Cbl 105: 234-238

Mengel K, Hogrebe AMR, Esch A (1989) Effect of acidic fog on needle surface and water relations of *Picea abies*. Physiol Plant 75: 201-207

Scholander PF, Hammel HT, Bradstreet EC, Hemmingsen EA (1965) Sap pressure in vascular plants. Science 148: 339-346

Effect of High Dose SO_2 and Ethylene Exposure on the Structure of Epicuticular Wax of *Picea pungens*

James Patrie and Virginia Berg[1]
Department of Biology
University of Northern Iowa
Cedar Falls, IA 50614-0421
U.S.A.

Abstract

Conifers in polluted air generally exhibit accelerated degradation of epicuticular wax, but it is not clear whether the change is due to direct exposure to the pollutant or some other mechanism. Needles from blue spruce (*Picea pungens*) were exposed to sulfur dioxide or ethylene gas at 0 to 10,000 microliters per liter for 2 to 196 h; samples were examined by scanning electron microscopy. Neither gas caused changes in the wax crystals, although late in the growing season a fungal infestation was associated with degradation of wax structures. This supports hypotheses explaining accelerated epicuticular wax degradation by indirect effects of exposure to air pollutants.

Introduction

The leaf cuticle presents a barrier that limits exchanges between plants and the environment. The properties and integrity of this extracellular membrane are critical in protecting leaf tissue from fatal water loss, from excess leaching during episodes of precipitation, and from penetration of deleterious substances, such as acid precipitation (Cape, 1988). The barrier is not a perfect one, however, as these substances do pass through the cuticle, even if slowly (MacFarlane and Berry, 1974; Dryer *et al.*, 1981; Tyree *et al.*, 1990; Hauser *et al.*, 1993). Some cuticles, including those of many conifers, have fine tubular epicuticular wax structures on top of, and fused to, the continuous wax layer covering the leaves (Reicosky and Hanover, 1976). This wax holds droplets of liquid above the surface, preventing wetting of the leaf (Martin and Juniper, 1970). When the epicuticular waxes are degraded, presenting a smoother surface, contact angles between aqueous liquids and the surface decrease, resulting in drops more spread out, with an increased area of contact between the liquid and the leaf.

Due to natural weathering processes, as conifer needles age, the individual wax tubes fuse, reducing the hydrophobic effect of the wax tubes (Cape, 1983; Huttunen and Laine, 1983). The impact of rain and particulates, and contact with snow and other vegetation, promote this process (Baker and Hunt, 1986; Mayeux and Jordon, 1987). Some scanning electron microscope (SEM)

---

[1]Corresponding author.

NATO ASI Series, Vol. G 36
Air Pollutants and the Leaf Cuticle
Edited by K. E. Percy et al.
© Springer-Verlag Berlin Heidelberg 1994

studies of epicuticular waxes of conifer needles indicate that the fusion of epicuticular wax tubes is accelerated when the tubes are exposed to high levels of air pollutants (Huttunen and Laine, 1983; Cape, 1983; Riding and Percy, 1985; Crossley and Fowler, 1986). Other studies, however, have demonstrated individual trees with relatively intact wax despite air pollutant exposure (Grill et al., 1987). Thus, it is possible that changes in the wax are largely a consequence of changes within the leaves, rather than a direct response to the atmospheric environment. Indeed, there is considerable uncertainty as to how SO_2 might accelerate the natural aging process of the wax. The epicuticular wax on conifer needles is composed of relatively non-polar substances such as long-chain secondary alcohols (Cape, 1986), which should strongly absorb lipophilic substances from the atmosphere.

Structural alterations might occur directly, as a result of SO_2 dissolving in the wax. Alternately, SO_2 might affect the wax tubes indirectly, by means of some response by the plant, either a modification of the nature or amount of wax produced, or synthesis of additional compounds that could in turn interact with the wax. Ethylene synthesized by plants under stress (Peiser and Yang, 1979; Kimmerer and Kozlowski, 1981) might ultimately cause structural alterations by dissolution of the gas in the wax. Other metabolic changes involving carbon balance might also be involved (Grill et al., 1987). Experiments involving long-term exposure of living tissue cannot distinguish between internal and external sources of modification of the wax tubes.

When wax structure is altered by air pollutants, directly or indirectly, there may be an increase in the exchange of substances through the cuticle due to increased wettability of the surface (Cape, 1983, 1988). This has the possibility of altering the integrity of the cuticle itself (Smalley et al., 1993), as well as injuring the underlying cells. In addition, the cuticle provides an ideal site to look for early evidence of air pollutant exposure, as it has a large surface area and is constantly exposed to ambient conditions, even over a span of years for evergreen leaves (Huttunen and Laine, 1983).

The objectives of this study were 1) to determine whether short-term exposure to high levels of SO_2 or ethylene altered the structure of the epicuticular wax on needles of blue spruce (*Picea pungens*), and 2) to compare any observed experimentally-induced epicuticular wax degradation with that seen in the field.

Methods

From June through November, current-year needles were removed from the south side of a blue spruce tree located in Cedar Falls, IA, U.S.A., at about 1.5 m height. Previous SEM studies had shown the epicuticular wax on these needles to be relatively uniform. Needles were removed by grasping them at the base with forceps, and they were placed in 2.5-mL glass vials so that only the tips and bases contacted the surfaces of the vials. Using a gas syringe (Precision Sampling, Baton Rouge, LA), SO_2 (Aldrich, Milwaukee, WI) or ethylene (Aldrich) was injected into a teflon gas bag (Fisher, Pittsburgh, PA). Filtered air was added with a syringe to dilute the gas to the desired concentration, and the contents of the sampling bag were thoroughly mixed. For each sample, the SO_2 or ethylene mixture was then injected into a sealed vial containing a fresh spruce needle. Filtered air was injected for control samples. All tubes were submerged in a 25°C water bath for the duration of each treatment. Doses are given in Table 1.

Needles were removed from the vials immediately following exposure and were transferred to a desiccator containing a drying agent ($CaCl_2$). Following dehydration for 24 h, the needles were mounted on aluminum stubs and sputter coated (Technic, Hummer 5) with gold. Specimens were examined at magnifications from 100 to 3000x using a Hitachi 570 SEM at 20 KV. The appearances of the surface waxes of treated and control samples were compared to assess structural alterations to the epicuticular wax.

Table 1   Gas concentrations (SO_2 or ethylene) and duration of exposure for needles of *Picea pungens*.

Concentration ($\mu L\ L^{-1}$)	Duration (h)					
	2	8	24	36	48	196
0	X	X	X	X	X	X
10			X	X	X	X
100		X	X	X	X	X
1000	X	X	X	X	X	X
10,000	X	X	X	X	X	X

Results

Needles exposed to SO_2 at concentrations from 10 to 10,000 $\mu L\ L^{-1}$ exhibited chlorosis, sometimes combined with necrosis, particularly at the higher doses. However, SEM comparisons of the epicuticular wax indicated that neither the concentration of SO_2 nor the duration of exposure altered the morphology of the epicuticular wax compared to that of controls (Figs. 1, 2). Neither the concentration of ethylene nor the duration of exposure appeared to cause changes in the morphology of the epicuticular wax (Fig. 3), compared to control specimens. During early August, fungal hyphae were observed on the needle surfaces (Fig. 4). From August through late November, as the fungus infestation proliferated on the needle surfaces, the morphology of the epicuticular wax was progressively altered, with the greatest change observed immediately adjacent to the hyphae (Fig. 5).

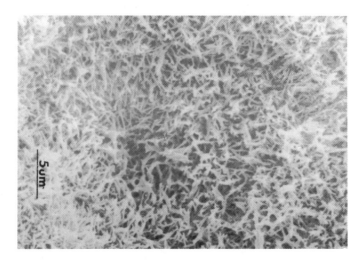

Figure 1   Needle surface of *Picea pungens* treated with filtered air and incubated for 24 h at 25°C (control).

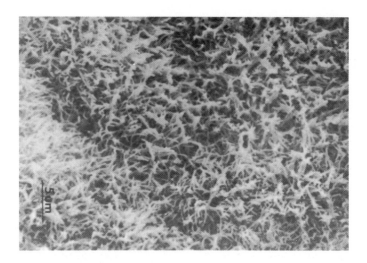

Figure 2   Needle surface of *Picea pungens* treated with 10,000 μL L^{-1} SO$_2$ and incubated for 196 h at 25°C. No degradation of the wax tubes was apparent.

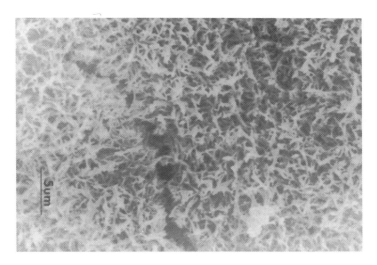

Figure 3   Needle surface of *Picea pungens* treated with 10,000 μL L^{-1} ethylene and incubated for 196 h at 25˚C. No degradation of the wax tubes was apparent.

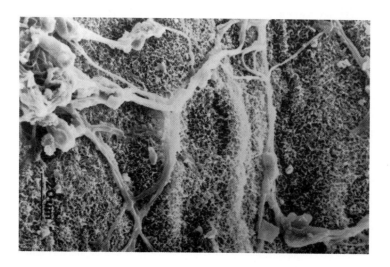

Figure 4   Needle surface of *Picea pungens* sampled in November, when the fungus had proliferated on the needle surface.

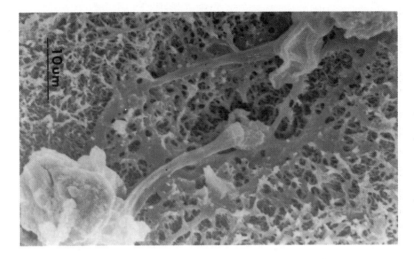

Figure 5 Needle surface of *Picea pungens* sampled in November. The wax in contact with the fungal hyphae has been totally degraded.

Discussion

The lack of alteration of the epicuticular wax observed in this study was similar to the results of Riding and Percy (1985) in a study of epicuticular wax on jack pine (*Pinus banksiana*) needles exposed to SO_2 at 2.65 µL L^{-1} for 10 weeks. There may be differences in the susceptibility of epicuticular waxes to structural alterations when exposed to air pollutants (Turunen and Huttunen, 1990). This may indicate that SO_2 is not directly responsible for the observed structural alterations of epicuticular wax on conifer needles exposed to SO_2. In addition, the positive correlation between healthier trees and relatively intact epicuticular wax supports the idea that the condition of the wax in part reflects metabolic vigor, rather than direct exposure to pollutants (Grill *et al.*, 1987, individual variation in spruce; Chiu *et al.*, 1992, fertilized and unfertilized Douglas fir). Similarly, as no unusual structural alterations to the epicuticular wax were observed following exposure to very high doses of ethylene (10 to 10,000 µL L^{-1} for periods from 2 h to 7 d), stress-induced ethylene is also unlikely to account for the naturally occurring degradation of epicuticular wax in the field.

There is considerable uncertainty as to the mechanisms by which the natural aging process of epicuticular wax on conifer needles take place. The wax tubes may represent a thermodynamically unstable form of the principle chemical constituent, 10-nonacosanol (M. Reiderer, Univ. of Kaiserslautern, pers. comm.). Changes in the conformation of the waxes may be hastened by physical factors such as abrasion by wind, rain, snow or contact with leaves (Baker and Hunt, 1986; Hadley and Smith, 1986). However, the results presented here do not eliminate the possibility that SO_2 or ethylene dissolved in epicuticular wax could increase susceptibility to these physical factors.

In the study presented here, the epicuticular wax progressively deteriorated as the fungus proliferated. The pronounced degradation of the wax in the immediate vicinity of the fungal hyphae suggests the production of a lipophilic substance by the fungus, which may be using the epicuticular wax as a carbon source. As these fungi were not evident on the smooth wax surface of older (second year) needles, it is apparent that examining foliage throughout the year (and across a number of years) is critical if the causes of wax degradation are to be known. In addition, it reinforces the idea that indirect responses involving microflora or insects may complicate the picture (Turunen and Huttunen, 1990).

Thus it can be seen that acute exposures to SO_2 or ethylene alone cannot account for the degradation of epicuticular wax observed in the field in polluted and unpolluted environments. The accelerated degradation observed in most trees in areas of high air pollution is thus less likely to be caused by direct damage from these gases than by combinations of internal and external factors, including both physical and biological entities.

References

Baker EA, Hunt GM (1986) Erosion of waxes from leaf surfaces by simulated rain. New Phytol 102: 161-173

Cape JN (1983) Contact angles of water droplets on needles of Scots pine (*Pinus sylvestris*) growing in polluted atmospheres. New Phytol 93: 293-299

Cape JN (1986) Effects of air pollution on the chemistry of surface waxes of Scots pine. Water Air Soil Poll 31: 393-399

Cape JN (1988) Chemical interactions between cloud droplets and trees. *In* Acid deposition at high elevation sites. Kluwer Academic Publishers, *pp* 639-649

Chiu ST, Anton LH, Ewers FW, Hammerschmidt R, Pregitzer KS (1992) Effects of fertilization on epicuticular wax morphology of needle leaves of Douglas fir, *Pseudotsuga menziesii*. Amer J Bot 79: 149-154

Crossley A, Fowler D (1986) The weathering of Scots pine epicuticular wax in polluted and clean air. New Phytol 103: 207-218

Dryer CA, Seymour V, Cleland RE (1981) Low proton conductance of plant cuticles and its relevance to the acid-growth theory. Plant Physiol 68: 664-667

Grill D, Pfeifhofer H, Halbwachs G, Waltinger H (1987) Investigation on epicuticular waxes of differently damaged spruce needles. European J Forest Path 17: 246-255

Hadley JL, Smith WK (1986) Wind effects on needles of timberline conifers: Seasonal influence on mortality. Ecology 67: 12-19

Hauser HD, Walters KD, Berg VS (1993) Patterns of effective permeability of leaf cuticles to acids. Plant Physiol 101: 251-257

Huttunen S, Laine K (1983) Effects of air-borne pollutants on the surface wax structure of *Pinus sylvestris* needles. Ann Bot Fennici 20: 79-86

Kimmerer TW, Kozlowski TT (1981) Ethylene, ethane, acetaldehyde, and ethanol production by plants under stress. Plant Physiol 69: 840-847

MacFarlane JC, Berry WL (1974) Cation penetration through isolated leaf cuticles. Plant Physiol 53: 723-727

Martin J, Juniper B (1970) The cuticles of plants. St. Martin's Press, New York

Mayeux HS, Jordon WR (1987) Rainfall removes epicuticular waxes from Isocoma leaves. Bot Gaz 148: 420-425

Peiser D, Yang SF (1979) Ethylene and ethane production from sulfur dioxide injured plants. Plant Physiol 63: 142-145

Reicosky DA, Hanover JW (1976) Seasonal changes in leaf surface waxes of *Picea pungens*. Amer J Bot 63: 449-456

Riding RT, Percy KE (1985) Effects of SO_2 and other air pollutants on the morphology of epicuticular waxes on needles of *Pinus strobus* and *Pinus banksiana*. New Phytol 99: 555-563

Smalley SJ, Hauser HD, Berg VS (1993) Effect of cations on effective permeability of leaf cuticles to sulfuric acid. Plant Physiol 103: 251-256

Turunen M, Huttunen S (1990) A review of the response of epicuticular wax of conifer needles to air pollution. J Environ Qual 19: 35-45

Tyree MT, Tabor CA, Wescott CR (1990) Movement of cations through cuticles of *Citrus aurantium* and *Acer saccharum*. Plant Physiol 94: 120-128

Preliminary Observations on the Influence of Increasing Atmospheric CO_2 Levels on Cuticular Waxes of Spruce Needles

Bärbel Prügel and Georges Lognay[1]
Laboratoire de la Pollution atmosphérique
INRA-CRF, F-54280 Champenoux (France)

Abstract

The impact of elevated levels of CO_2 on the cuticular waxes of Norway and Sitka spruce needles was investigated. The trees were fumigated in open-top chambers and samples were taken at four different stations in Europe. The total wax weight was determined after chloroform extraction and the amount of 10-nonacosanol, 4,10- and 5,10 nonacosandiol and seven fatty acids was quantified by capillary gas chromatography. Wax weight decreased for higher CO_2 levels, whereas there was a tendency to increase for 10-nonacosanol and fatty acids. As regards the diols, no effect wasobserved.

Introduction

The increasing levels of atmospheric CO_2 and the related increase in mean global temperature, the so-called "greenhouse effect", have been widely discussed. The application of high CO_2 levels in greenhouses is a commonly used technique to increase the harvest yield of vegetables like tomatoes; however, very little is known about the impact of CO_2 on long-living organisms such as trees or whole ecosystems like forests. It has been observed that high CO_2 levels lead to an increase in the growth of young trees and, at the cell level, to modifications of the activity of some enzymes such as RubisCO (Ribulose-bisphosphate-Carboxylase-Oxygenase) (Jarvis, 1989).

Considering such changes in plant physiology, modifications in leaf wax biosynthesis might occur as well. As the atmosphere-leaf interface, cuticular waxes have important protective functions. Changes in wax chemistry might lead to alterations of leaf surface properties. Such modifications have already been shown for air pollution in general and some specific pollutants like acid deposition (Cape, 1983; Percy and Baker, 1990; Barnes and Brown, 1990); nevertheless, to the authors' knowledge, the effect of increasing CO_2 levels has not yet been investigated.

Hence, the principal objective of this work was to find out if increased CO_2 levels modify the wax chemistry. In a preliminary step, the impact of CO_2 on the total wax weight as well as the quantity of some important wax components was examined.

---

[1]U.E.R. Chimie générale et organique, Faculté des Sciences agronomiques, B-5030 Gembloux (Belgium)

NATO ASI Series, Vol. G 36
Air Pollutants and the Leaf Cuticle
Edited by K. E. Percy et al.
© Springer-Verlag Berlin Heidelberg 1994

Material and methods

Norway spruce [*Picea abies* (L.) Karst.] and Sitka spruce [*Picea sitchensis* (Bong.) Carr.] were chosen as plant material. CO_2 fumigation was carried out using an open-top chamber (OTC) technique. In collaboration with three other research groups, four OTC sample sites were available, each representing a different environmental situation for the trees.

The Sitka spruce samples were provided by Dr. Maureen Murray and Dr. Neil Cape of the Institute of Terrestrial Ecology (Scotland). Pot-planted and fertilized trees inside the OTC's were exposed to 350 ppm and 700 ppm CO_2. The experiment was carried out in three replications at an open field site.

Norway spruce samples were taken mainly in Vielsalm, the experimental site of the Faculté des Sciences Agronomiques of Gembloux (Belgium) under the direction of Dr. Eric Laitat. Here, the trees were exposed to 300 ppm, 525 ppm and 700 ppm CO_2. For each CO_2 level, a non-filtered air OTC (NFA) as well as a charcoal-filtered air OTC (FA) was available. Additionally, there was a non-chambered control (control plot without OTC) for each of the experiments. The whole station was situated in a forest clearing and the trees were planted directly in the forest soil without any fertilization.

The second *Picea abies* site, maintained by the Air Pollution Laboratory under the direction of Dr. Jean-Pierre Garrec, was situated in the Massif Central (France). At this ancient volcanic site, CO_2 is naturally emitted from the soil and the ambient CO_2 level is higher (about 380 ppm) than at the other sites. One experimental unit was built up here, consisting of an ambient air-OTC, a 700 ppm-OTC and a non-chambered control. The trees were planted directly in the surrounding old pasture and were not shadowed by other plants.

The last experimental site was situated in one of the greenhouses of the INRA-CRF in Champenoux and directed by Dr. Jean-Marc Guehl. Inside this greenhouse, two CO_2 tunnels, respectively at 350 and 700 ppm CO_2, and a greenhouse-control plot outside the tunnels were installed. The Norway spruce trees were planted in pots and fertilized.

The Scottish and Belgian samples were collected during the winters of 1991/1992 and 1992/1993. All other samples were available only in the winter 1992/1993.

For each treatment, current-year needles were taken from three individuals and pooled in equal proportions to give two or three samples of about 1 g needle fresh weight. This procedure allows a sampling of several individuals even if there is only a very small sample amount per tree available.

For analysis, each pooled sample was extracted with chloroform. Quantitative analyses were performed by means of a GC-FID; qualitative analyses were carried out using a GC-MS. Analytical details will be published elsewhere.

Apart from the total wax weight, the following wax components were quantified in this first step of data analysis : 10-nonacosanol, 4,10- and 5,10-nonacosandiol (in the following called total diols) and seven even-numbered fatty acids ranging from 14 to 26 carbons as chain length (here called total acids). Natural variability as well as the influence of the applied technique and the analytic variability have been taken into account. Additionally, for one experimental site, the combined effects of CO_2 and natural ozone were investigated.

Results and discussion

Natural variability

As concerns natural variability, the results for chamberless controls were compared separately according to the different sites, years, and examined parameters.

The results for the total wax amount and the quantity of 10-nonacosanol are shown in Figure 1. The bars represent the standard deviation for the three replications of the non-chambered controls at the Belgian site (corresponding to a total of nine measurements); for the other two sites, there was only one control without chamber; therefore, only the mean value of three measurements is presented.

The most obvious result was, that there were great variations between the different sites for each parameter, but that the variability between the replications is rather limited. This was also valid for the diols and the acids (Figure 2), where we notice that natural variability depends on the parameter examined; it is very small for the diols (variation coefficient : 0.6%) and highest for the acids (variation coefficient: 15%).

Chamber effect

To consider the chamber effect, the results for the controls without chambers have to be compared to those for the controls with OTCs. As expected, a chamber effect existed, but a clear effect could be noticed only for total wax weight. Inside the chambers, wax weight was increased for all sites except the greenhouse. As wax amount is also dependent on light conditions (Tevini and Steinmuller, 1987), the greenhouse results may tentatively be explained by the reduced light in this installation.

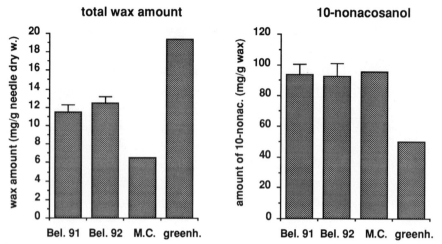

Figure 1   Mean values for controls without chambers for the total wax amount and the amount of 10-nonacosanol.

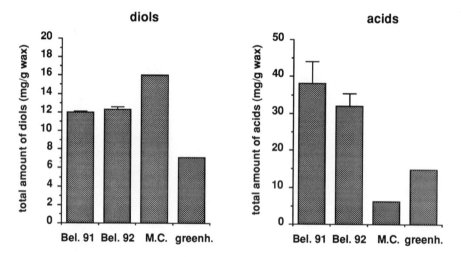

Figure 2   Mean values of the amount of total diols and total acids for controls without chamber.

<u>CO_2effect</u>

To consider the CO_2 effect, the chambered controls were compared to the CO_2 treatments; for the Belgian site, the non-filtered air CO_2 treatment was used.

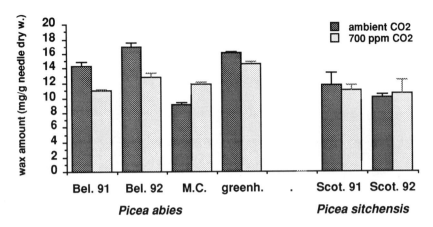

Figure 3   Total wax amount for needles of all sites.

The results for all sites are presented separately for each parameter. For the Scottish samples, the standard deviation bars correspond to a variability within the same experiment; for all other sites, they represent the variability of the three samples taken inside of the same chamber. So, these bars represent the total variability of all the manipulations undertaken, *i.e.*, sampling procedure, gravimetric extraction and chromatographic measurements.

When considering the impact of CO_2 in the following, one should always be aware of the fact that, except for the Scottish site, no replications were available.

Wax weight
A decrease in the total wax amount (Figure 3) can be observed for the CO_2-treated samples of the Belgian site and the greenhouse samples; there was no significant difference for Scottish needles. Nevertheless, there was an increase in the wax amount for the Massif Central site. Here, the CO_2-injection began only a few days before bud break because of some technical problems. As wax biosynthesis begins while the leaves are still inside the buds, this might explain the different result.

10-nonacosanol
The 10-nonacosanol quantity (Figure 4) increased for the Belgian site and for both of the studied years, but there was no effect for the other sites.

Total diols
When looking at the results for diols (Figure 5), one of the differences between the two spruce

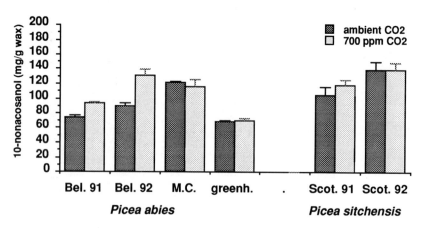

Figure 4   Total amount of 10-nonacosanol for needle wax of all sites,

waxes becomes obvious. In Sitka spruce waxes, diols constitute one of the main wax components (Percy and Baker, 1990) and are generally much more abundant than in Norway spruce waxes. For both species, 4,10-nonacosane diol was the most abundant isomer.

The two species reacted similarly to increased CO_2 levels. The slight tendency towards an increase is almost certainly not important enough to be considered as an increasing effect, especially when considering the probable variability between replications.

Total acids

Important variations in the quantity of acids for the different sites are shown in Figure 6. These variations were already observed for the controls without chamber. In most cases, *Picea abies* waxes contained higher amounts of fatty acids than *Picea sitchensis* waxes. According to our results, docosanoic acid was the principal component.

The Belgian sample, as well as the 1992 samples from Scotland, showed increased amounts of acids.

Combined CO_2-ozone effects

For the Belgian site "charcoal-filtered" treatments were available. As the applied filters mainly limited the ozone input to about a maximum of 10-20 ppb ozone, an evaluation of the effect of CO_2 combined with the naturally occurring ozone pollution could be obtained. At this site, mean ozone concentrations of 30-45 ppb with ozone peaks up to 180 ppb occur in general twice a year during approximately 3 weeks; the annual average (17 ppb O_3) is relatively low. Other monitored

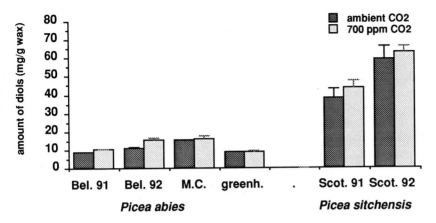

Figure 5   Total amount of diols for needle wax of all sites.

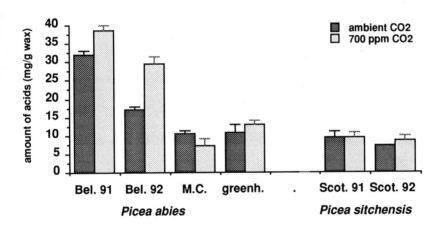

Figure 6   Total amount of acids for needle wax of all sites.

air pollutants, such as SO_2, NO_2 and NO, show very low levels close to the detection limit of the instruments.

The results for each pair of OTCs at the same CO_2 level, one with non-filtered air (NFA), the other one with filtered air (FA), were compared. The results gathered for the three Belgian CO_2 treatments (ambient CO_2, 525 and 700 ppm CO_2) are presented schematically in Figure 7.

		wax amount	10-nonacosanol	diols	acids
Bel. 91	amb. CO2	NFA > FA	NFA ~ FA	NFA ~ FA	NFA < FA
	525 ppm	NFA ~ FA	NFA > FA	NFA > FA	NFA ~ FA
	700 ppm	NFA < FA	NFA > FA	NFA > FA	NFA > FA
Bel. 92	amb. CO2	NFA > FA	NFA < FA	NFA < FA	NFA ~ FA
	525 ppm	NFA ~ FA	NFA ~ FA	NFA > FA	NFA > FA
	700 ppm	NFA < FA	NFA > FA	NFA > FA	NFA > FA

Figure 7   Effect of non-filtered- and filtered air treatment on all examined parameters.

In nearly all cases, the same tendencies can be noticed for both years. For the ambient CO_2 treatment, total wax weight is higher for the NFA treatment than for the FA treatment; for 525 ppm and 700 ppm CO_2, the inverse result can be observed.

When looking at the results for the wax components, the ambient CO_2 treatment again shows the inverse result of the two elevated CO_2 treatments, but this time the FA treatment shows higher results for ambient CO_2 and the NFA treatment for the elevated CO_2 levels.

These results seem quite interesting, even if no explication for this phenomenon can be given as yet. However, our observations are in line with the results of McQuattie (*this volume*). She noticed modifications to cuticular membrane ultrastructure for plants that were exposed to a combined CO_2/ozone treatment in comparison to those that were exposed to CO_2 or ozone only.

Conclusion

In considering the results described above, several conclusions can be outlined.

Concerning natural variability, we noticed a great variation for the quantitative data between the different sites for all of the examined parameters. Hence, they cannot be compared directly; however, the comparison of the observed tendencies is possible.

Natural variability also depends on the parameter examined, but for each one of them it is less important than the variations found for the CO_2 treatments. That means that we can interpret the results in terms of "real" CO_2 effects.

Analytical variability is in general much lower than natural variability; thus, the applied analytical methods can be considered as adapted to the studied problems.

As expected, an effect of the OTC technique can be noticed showing a clear tendency of an increase of total wax weight for the trees inside the OTC's in comparison to those from the outside control plots.

As regards the CO_2 treatment, we often observe similar tendencies for the different sites, although the environmental conditions for the trees were rather different at each site.

Also, no clear distinction between the responses of the two spruce species can be made. The response to elevated CO_2 levels varies with the examined parameter. In summary, total wax amount decreases, the amounts of 10-nonacosanol and acids show a tendency to increase and for the diols no effect can be noticed.

Another interesting point is the possible interaction of elevated CO_2 levels and ozone, which has to be examined more closely.

The data available in the frame of this study give some indications for the impact of increasing CO_2 levels on spruce waxes. More complete conclusions could be drawn provided that further studies with a sufficient number of replications are performed.

Acknowledgements

The authors are indebted to Dr. Maureen Murray and Dr. Neil Cape from the Institute of Terrestrial Ecology, Penicuik (Scotland), Dr. Eric Laitat from the Faculté des Sciences Agronomiques of Gembloux (Belgium), and Dr. Jean-Marc Guehl from the Institut national de Recherches agronomiques, Nancy (France) for having given us the chance to sample plants from their CO_2 experiments.

B. P. gratefully acknowledges the European Communities for financial support.

References

Barnes J, Brown KA (1990) The influence of ozone and acid mist on the amount and wettability of the surface waxes in Norway spruce [*Picea abies* (L.) Karst.]. New Phytol 114: 531-535

Cape JN (1983) Contact angles of water droplets on needles of Scots pine (*Pinus sylvestris*) growing in polluted atmospheres. New Phytol 93: 293-299

Jarvis PG (1989) Atmospheric carbon dioxide and forests. Phil Trans R Soc Lond 324: 369-392

Percy KE, Baker EA (1990) Effects of simulated acid rain on epicuticular wax production, morphology, chemical composition and on cuticular membrane thickness in two clones of Sitka spruce [*Picea sitchensis* (Bong.) Carr.]. New Phytol 116: 79-87

Tevini M, Steinmüller D (1987) Influence of light, UV-B radiation and herbicides on wax biosynthesis of Cucumber seedlings. J Plant Physiol 131: 111-121

Effects of Ozone Exposures on Epicuticular Wax of Ponderosa Pine Needles

Andrzej Bytnerowicz and Minna Turunen[1]
USDA Forest Service
Pacific Southwest Research Station
4955 Canyon Crest Drive
Riverside, CA 92507, USA

Abstract

Two-year-old ponderosa pine (*Pinus ponderosa* L.) seedlings were exposed during the 1989 and 1990 growing seasons to ozone in open-top chambers placed in a forested location at Shirley Meadow, Greenhorn Mountain Range, Sierra Nevada. The ozone treatments were as follows: charcoal-filtered air (CF); charcoal-filtered air with addition of ambient concentrations of ozone (CF + O_3); and charcoal-filtered air with addition of doubled concentrations of ozone (CF + 2 x O_3). Ozone effects on ponderosa pine seedlings progressed and accumulated over two seasons of exposure. Throughout the first season, increased visible injury and accelerated senescence of the foliage were noted. Subsequently, during the second season of ozone exposure, various physiological and biochemical changes in the foliage took place. All these changes led to reduced growth and biomass of the seedlings. Epistomatal waxes of needles from the CA + 2 x O_3 treatment had an occluded appearance. This phenomenon may be caused by earlier phenological development of needles from the high-ozone treatments and disturbed development and synthesis of waxes. It may also be caused by chemical degradation of waxes by exposures to high ozone concentrations.

Introduction

Ozone is the only air pollutant that has proved to be clearly phytotoxic at ambient levels in some forests of the western United States. One of the best known examples of ozone phytotoxicity is the decreased growth, reduced foliar retention and visible injury of ponderosa and Jeffrey pine (*Pinus ponderosa* and *P. jeffreyi*) in the San Bernardino Mountains as an effect of more than 30 years of exposure (Miller *et al.*, 1963, 1986). Elevated ozone concentrations have been correlated with reduced radial growth of Jeffrey pine (Peterson *et al.*, 1987), and foliar injury to ponderosa and Jeffrey pine on the western slopes of the Sierra Nevada (Duriscoe and Stolte, 1989).

In order to understand mechanisms leading to chronic injury symptoms, several controlled studies on the effects of ozone on growth and physiology of western conifer seedlings have been conducted recently (Bytnerowicz *et al.*, 1990; Temple *et al.*, 1992; Beyers *et al.*, 1992). Little, however, is known about the effects of ozone on the cuticular waxes of western conifers (Bytnerowicz and Grulke, 1992). It has been demonstrated that an accelerated fusion of wax

[1]University of Lapland, Arctic Centre, P.O. Box 122, 96101 Rovaniemi, Finland

NATO ASI Series, Vol. G 36
Air Pollutants and the Leaf Cuticle
Edited by K. E. Percy et al.
© Springer-Verlag Berlin Heidelberg 1994

tubes in the stomatal areas of the needle surfaces is a common characteristic of the effects of air pollution and acidic precipitation on conifers (Huttunen and Laine, 1983; Turunen and Huttunen, 1991). The specificity of the symptoms in the wax structure to different air pollutants is limited. Natural variability, even within similar-aged trees of the same provenance, and complexity of environmental factors affecting wax tubes, restrict the use of epicuticular waxes as an early indicator of air pollution effects (Turunen and Huttunen, 1990). In a study on the effects of ambient levels of photochemical smog on seedlings of four pine species in the San Gabriel Mountains of southern California, small cracks on needle surfaces and deep stomatal cavities were determined for *P. coulteri* needles from the ambient-air treatment. In the same study some smoothing of young wax tubes of *P. sylvestris* needles in the ambient-air compared with the clean-air treatment was also seen (Bytnerowicz *et al.*, 1989).

This paper presents information on changes in epicuticular waxes of ponderosa pine seedlings exposed to ozone in the Sierra Nevada location. Most of the exposure effects on the seedlings (growth, visual injury development, physiological, biochemical and chemical changes) have been described elsewhere (Bytnerowicz *et al.*, 1991; Bytnerowicz and Grulke, 1992). However, some of the growth and physiological data will be used here to explain the origin of the observed changes in epicuticular waxes and to discuss their possible consequences.

Methods

Site location

The study was performed at Shirley Meadow, on the eastern slope of the Greenhorn Range of the Sequoia National Forest, southern Sierra Nevada. The site was located 1950 m above sea level at $35^{\circ}42$'N and $118^{\circ}33$'W, about 50 km NE of Bakersfield, California.

Air pollution exposures

Pine seedlings were exposed to air pollution in open-top chambers designed for plant studies (Heagle *et al.*, 1973). A shade cloth reducing light intensity to about 55% was installed on the tops and sides of the chambers.

The air pollution treatments in open-top chambers were as follows:

- charcoal-filtered air (CF)
- charcoal-filtered air containing ambient ozone concentrations (CF + O3)
- charcoal-filtered air containing 2 x ambient concentration of ozone (CF + 2 x O3)

Each pollution treatment chamber was duplicated. Ozone was produced with a Griffin ozonizer by exposing oxygen to UV light and delivered to the open-top chambers through Teflon tubing.

One Dasibi Model 1003 AH instrument was used for monitoring ambient concentrations of ozone. Its readings were sent to the ISAAC-Apple II+ data acquisition system, which translated ozone ambient concentrations values into a voltage signal. Changes in the voltage signal controlled production of ozone by the Griffin ozonizer. Samples of air were taken by a Scanivalve system from the chambers and sent to a second Dasibi ozone monitor. Pollutant concentrations at each chamber were monitored every hour. During the first year, the ozone exposures started on June 5, 1989 and continued until October 17, 1989. During the second season, the exposures started on May 9, 1990 and lasted until October 20, 1990. Between the two seasons of exposures the seedlings were removed from the chambers and stored in forest near the experimental site.

Plant material

Two-year-old seedlings from the Greenhorn Range stock (1650 m elevation) were planted in February 1989 in 6-L pulp pots filled with native soil collected in the Greenhorn Range from a typical ponderosa pine stand. The seedlings were watered with deionized water as needed (typically once a week).

SEM evaluation of epicuticular waxes

At the final harvest in October 1990, single fascicles of the current growth (1990) needles were collected from ten individual seedlings in every chamber. The needles were about 5 months old at the time of the collection. The needle samples were air dried and shipped to the Department of Botany, University of Oulu, Finland, for the SEM evaluation of surface changes. Three 1-cm long segments were cut from the middle section of selected needles, mounted on brass stubs with double stick tape, and sputtered with Au-Pd (80:20%, 45 nm) at 11.2 nm min^{-1}, 2.5 kV, and 20 mA (Polaron E5100). The samples were examined with an SEM (JEOL JSM-6400) at 12 kV with an exposure of 45 s. The epistomatal wax structures were classified visually from SEM micrographs of magnifications 100X, 400X, and 2000X as follows:

class I	-	well developed and preserved
class II	-	slightly eroded or melted
class III	-	heavily eroded or melted

Occurrences of three classes of wax at different ozone regimes were calculated and presented as percentages.

Measurements of new needle development

At the beginning of the second season (May 9, 1990), development of new needles was evaluated. Percentages of needles on each tree assigned to four different categories (stages of development) was determined. The categories were assigned as follows:

stage 1 - needles not developed

stage 2 - developing needles mm long

stage 3 - developing needles 2 mm and 10mm

stage 4 - developing needles 10 mm

Measurements of stomatal conductance

Measurements of stomatal conductance of water vapor of the current growth (1990) needles were made using a portable photosynthesis system (LI-COR 6200). The 0.25-L leaf cuvette was used, with a total sampling time per seedling of 60 s representing the average of ten 6-s long measurements. Results are expressed on a total needle surface area basis.

Statistical analysis

Statistical analysis of data was performed using analysis of variance for plot means. For occurrence of wax classes and new needle development statistical analysis was performed after the arcsin transformation of data. Significance of ozone treatments and significance of contrasts between the individual treatments were determined.

Results and discussion

The monthly 24-h average concentrations of ozone in the CF treatment did not exceed 0.024 ppm during the entire study, nor did the highest 1-h peak values exceed 0.055 ppm. No large differences in ozone concentrations between the individual months and years occurred during the 2 years of the study (Table 1). The diurnal profiles of ozone were similar for most of the months — the lowest concentrations occurred in the morning hours and the highest in the afternoon hours. Concentrations of ozone at the CF + 2 x O_3 were very high, much higher than ever experienced in the Sierra Nevada forests. These levels, however, were lower than concentrations observed in some of the most polluted areas of the San Bernardino Mountains of southern California (Miller *et al.*, 1986).

The appearance of the epicuticular wax on the needles, including edges of the stoma, was generally amorphous with wax tubes occurring only in epistomatal chambers (Figure 1). Occasionally, single wax tubes were found in the interstomatal areas (Figure 2). As a result of the ozone exposure, an increased number of stomata of slightly fused wax tubes (Figure 3), or completely fused appearance with occluded stomatal apertures (Figure 4) was seen. A trend for an increasing occurrence of the occluded stomatal chambers as ozone concentrations grew was seen (Figure 5). Similar changes have been reported for other conifers exposed to ozone such as Norway spruce (*Picea abies* (L.) Karst.) (Barnes *et al.*, 1988) and red spruce (*P. rubens* Sarg.) (Percy *et al.*, 1990).

Table 1   Comparison of ozone concentrations [monthly 24-h averages and 1-h peak values (in parentheses)] between different air pollution regimes (ppm).

| Month | Ozone Regime | | |
| | CF | CF + O_3 | CF + 2 x O_3 |
	1989		
June	0.022 (0.044)	0.036 (0.109)	0.055 (0.219)
July	0.024 (0.033)	0.069 (0.124)	0.130 (0.255)
August	0.022 (0.035)	0.063 (0.105)	0.117 (0.206)
September	0.021 (0.043)	0.053 (0.107)	0.092 (0.200)
October	0.020 (0.043)	0.050 (0.095)	0.087 (0.187)
	1990		
May	0.018 (0.055)	0.051 (0.079)	0.103 (0.163)
June	0.020 (0.031)	0.053 (0.086)	0.122 (0.193)
July	0.021 (0.033)	0.061 (0.090)	0.142 (0.203)
August	0.019 (0.030)	0.056 (0.084)	0.129 (0.221)
September	0.020 (0.031)	0.055 (0.096)	0.129 (0.221)
October	0.020 (0.039)	0.069 (0.122)	0.154 (0.282)

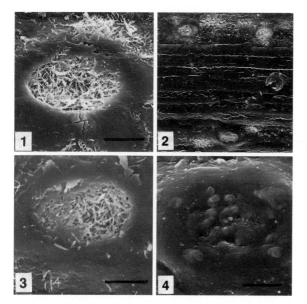

Figure 1   Well-developed and preserved epistomatal wax structure of 5-month-old needles of ponderosa pine seedlings. Wax outside stomatal cavities generally has an amorphous appearance (Class I, CF treatment).

Figure 2   Wax tubes are concentrated inside stomatal cavities; however, single wax tubes can also be found in the interstomatal areas (Class I, CF treatment).

Figure 3   Slightly eroded epistomatal wax structure with part of the stomata occluded by melted wax tubes (Class II, CF + O_3 treatment).

Figure 4   Heavily melted epistomatal wax tubes completely occluding the epistomatal chamber (Class III, CF + 2 x O_3 treatment).

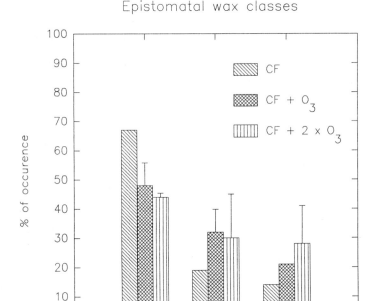

Figure 5   Occurrence of three epistomatal wax stage classes (%) in different ozone treatments.

Two causes of the observed changes in epicuticular wax appearance can be considered. The first cause may be related to disturbed synthesis of waxes. Observations of development of new needles in spring 1990 (following one season of ozone exposures), indicated that the new needles were more developed on the seedlings previously exposed to ozone (Figure 6, Table 2). The enhanced growth of needles under the influence of ozone could affect wax synthesis resulting in abnormal fusion of wax tubes inside stoma. The second cause may be a direct effect of elevated concentrations of ozone and oxidation of epicuticular waxes. It has been postulated that high concentrations of ozone, oxygen free radicals, and some of the organic components of photo-chemical smog may be especially effective in producing changes in aromatic compounds and unsaturated hydrocarbons of the cuticular waxy layer (Mudd *et al.*, 1984; Hewitt *et al.*, 1990). Such effects, expressed as reduced amounts of secondary alcohols, diols, alkyl esters, fatty acids, and hydroxy-fatty acids in red spruce exposed to ozone concentrations as low as 0.07 ppm were reported for red spruce needles (Percy *et al.*, 1992). The increased occurrence of fused wax crystals inside stomatal cavities, and in extreme cases complete occlusion of the stomata, could

Table 2   Results of analysis of variance (p values) for new needle development measured on May 9, 1990 (analysis performed after arcsin transformation).

Parameter	Source of Variation			
	Air pollution treatment	CF vs. CF + O$_3$	CF vs. CF + 2 x O$_3$	CF + O$_3$ vs. CF + 2 x O$_3$
Stage 0	0.005	0.040	0.002	0.008
Stage 1	0.073	0.131	0.033	0.188
Stage 2	0.010	0.308	0.005	0.008
Stage 3	0.465	0.308	0.308	1.000

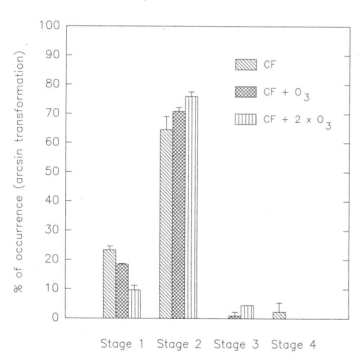

Figure 6   Development of new needles after one season of ozone exposure expressed as treatment means and standard deviations. For each plot mean, 20 measurements were made on individual seedlings.

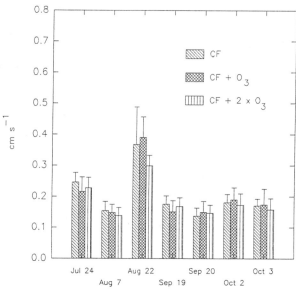

Figure 7   Stomatal conductance of 1990 needles during the 1990 season expressed as treatment means and standard deviations. For each plot means measurements from four individual seedlings were used.

theoretically lead to reduced stomatal conductance of needles. However, such changes did not occur (Figure 7).

The pine seedlings experienced additional changes when exposed to the elevated levels of ozone. First noticeable symptoms were the increased visible injury and accelerated senescence of the needles (observed in the first season of exposure). These changes continued during the second season and were accompanied by reduced stomatal conductance, net photosynthesis, chlorophyll fluorescence, and pigment concentrations of the previous year (1989) needles. At the final harvest, reduced growth and biomass production of the plants exposed to the highest concentrations of ozone were determined (Bytnerowicz et al., 1991).

The observed degradation of epicuticular waxes may have a high importance for water relations of plants (DeLucia and Berlyn, 1984). This may be especially true for mixed coniferous forests of the southwestern United States which often experience long periods of droughts. Damage of plant surfaces, especially lesions or cracks, may also affect resistance of plants to various types of microbiological infections (Turunen and Huttunen, 1990). In addition, damages in epicuticular waxes caused by ozone may affect resistance of pine needles to other air pollutants. Under southern California conditions, this type of ozone damage can modify plant responses to nitric acid vapor present in high concentrations. On the other hand, little is known about the effects of nitric acid vapor exposures on plant cuticles and possible modifications of plant responses to ozone. Changes in the appearance of epicuticular waxes can also influence physical and chemical properties of plant surfaces and change deposition rates of pollutants contained in air, rain, fog, cloud water and dust.

Acknowledgements

The authors thank Phil Dawson, Lynn Morrison, Adam Johnson, Minh Tran and Michelle Held for their excellent technical assistance during the course of the study. The study was sponsored by the California Air Resources Board, contracts No. A733-137, A833-083, and A033-056. Gratitude is expressed to the Institute of Electron Optics of the University of Oulu, where SEM investigations were conducted.

References

Barnes JD, Davison AW, Booth TA (1988) Ozone accelerates structural degradation of epicuticular wax on Norway spruce needles. New Phytol 110: 309-318

Beyers JL, Riechers GH, Temple PJ (1992) Effects of long-term ozone exposure and drought on the photosynthetic capacity of ponderosa pine (*Pinus ponderosa* Laws.). New Phytol 122: 81-90

Bytnerowicz A, Dawson PJ, Morrison CL (1991) Physiological and growth responses of ponderosa pine seedlings to ambient and elevated ozone concentrations in southern Sierra Nevada. 84th Annual Meeting & Exhibition of the Air & Waste Management Association, Vancouver, British Columbia, June 16-21, 1991, Publication No. 91-142.2

Bytnerowicz A, Grulke NE (1992) Physiological effects of air pollutants on western forests. *In* Olson RK, Binkley D, Bohm M (*eds*) The Responses of Western Forests to Air Pollution. Springer-Verlag New York *pp* 183-233

Bytnerowicz A, Olszyk DM, Huttunen S, Takemoto B (1989) Effects of photochemical smog on growth, injury, and gas exchange of pine seedlings. Can J Bot 67: 2175- 2181

Bytnerowicz A, Poth M, Takemoto BK (1990) Effects of photochemical smog and mineral nutrition on ponderosa pine seedlings. Environ Pollut 67: 233-248

DeLucia EH, Berlyn GP (1984) The effects of increasing elevation on leaf cuticle thickness and cuticular transpiration in balsam fir. Can J Bot 62: 2423-2431

Duriscoe DM, Stolte KW (1989) Photochemical oxidant injury to ponderosa (*Pinus ponderosa* Laws.) and Jeffrey pine (*Pinus jeffreyi* Grev. and Balf.) in the National Parks of the Sierra Nevada of California. *In* Effects of Air Pollution on Western Forests. Olson RL, Lefohn AS (*eds*)Air & Waste Management Association, Anaheim, California. *pp* 261- 270

Heagle AS, Body DE, Heck WW (1973) An open-top field chamber to assess the impact of air pollutants on plants. J Environ Qual 2: 365-368

Hewitt CN, Lucas P, Wellburn AR, Fall R (1990) Chemistry of ozone damage to plants. Chemistry & Industry 15: 478-481

Huttunen S, Laine K (1983) Effects of air-borne pollutants on the surface wax structure of *Pinus sylvestris* needles. Ann Bot Fennici 20: 79-86.

Miller PR, Parmeter JR, Jr, Taylor OC, Cardiff EA (1963) Ozone injury to the foliage of *Pinus ponderosa*. Phytopathol 53: 1072-1076

Miller PR, Taylor OC, Poe MP (1986) Spatial variation of summer ozone concentrations in the San Bernardino Mountains. 79th Annual Meeting & Exhibition of the Air Pollution Control Association, Minneapolis, Minnesota, June 22-27, 1986. Publication No. 86-39.2.

Mudd JB, Banerjee SK, Dooley MM, Knight KL (1984) Pollutants and plant cells: effects on membranes. *In* Gaseous Pollutants and Plant Metabolism. Koziol MJ, Whatley FR (*eds*) Butterworth, London. *pp* 105-116

Peterson DL, Arbaugh MJ, Wakefield VA, Miller PR. 1987. Evidence of growth reduction in ozone injured Jeffrey pine (*Pinus jeffreyi* Grev. and Balf.) in Sequoia and Kings Canyon National Parks. J. Air Pollut. Control Assoc 37: 906-912

Percy KE, Jensen KF, McQuattie CJ (1992) Effects of ozone and acidic fog on red spruce needle epicuticular wax production, chemical composition, cuticular membrane ultrastructure and needle wettability. New Phytol 122: 71-80

Percy KE, Krause CR, Jensen KF (1990) Effects of ozone and acidic fog on red spruce needle epicuticular wax ultrastructure. Can J For Res 20: 117-120

Temple PJ, Riechers GH, Miller PR (1992) Foliar injury responses of ponderosa pine seedlings to ozone, wet and dry deposition, and drought. Environ Exper Bot 32: 101- 113

Turunen M, Huttunen S (1990) A review of the response of epicuticular wax of conifer needles to air pollution. J Environ Qual 19: 35-45

Turunen M, Huttunen S (1991) Effects of simulated acid rain on the epicuticular wax of Scots pine needles under northerly conditions. Can J Bot 69:412-419

Observations on the Effects of Acid Rain Treatment on Needle Surfaces of Scots Pine and Norway Spruce Seedlings

Minna Turunen, Satu Huttunen[1] and Jaana Back[1]
Arctic Centre
Univ. of Lapland
P.O. Box 122
SF-96101 Rovaniemi
Finland

Abstract

Scots pine (*Pinus sylvestris* L.) and Norway spruce (*Picea abies* L. Karst.) seedlings were subjected to acid rain treatment at pH 3, pH 4 and pH 7 in a field experiment during 1986-1989. SEM+EDS, TEM, and measurements of wax quantity were used to detect changes in needle surfaces. After 5 weeks at pH 3 and pH 4 acid rain treatment, $CaSO_4$ - crystallites were observed on visibly undamaged pine and spruce needle surfaces. Direct acid rain damage in conjunction with $CaSO_4$ - crystallites was observed only occasionally in wax structures. Two-month-old pine needles had 50% less wax in early August after exposure at pH 3 and pH 4 than water controls. The occurrence of $CaSO_4$ -crystallites on acid rain-treated needle surfaces, and more abundant deposition of Ca oxalate crystallites in the inner walls of epi- and hypodermal cells could be involved with acid rain-induced calcium leaching. Calcium sulphate is probably a result of the disturbed wax and cuticle biosynthesis resulting in undeveloped, permeable cuticles. At the end of experiment, no $CaSO_4$ - crystallites were seen on needle surfaces. Soil analysis revealed an increase in the soluble Ca concentrations at pH 3.

Introduction

The interaction between acid rain and conifer needle cuticles has been investigated in a few controlled environment experiments, and evidence suggests that pH values of less than pH 3-4 can affect cuticular structures (Rinallo *et al.*, 1986; Mengel *et al.*, 1989; Percy *et al.*, 1990; Turunen and Huttunen, 1990, 1991; Hogan, 1992). However, the correlation between the observed structural and chemical changes in needle cuticles and the physiological response (*e.g.*, in water and nutrient economy) has not often been made. The objective of the present investigation was to document the changes in needle surfaces caused by acid rain in pine and spruce seedlings.

---

[1]Dept of Botany, Univ. of Oulu, SF-90570 Oulu, Finland

NATO ASI Series, Vol. G 36
Air Pollutants and the Leaf Cuticle
Edited by K. E. Percy et al.
© Springer-Verlag Berlin Heidelberg 1994

Material and methods

The acid rain experiment was performed during 1986-1989 in Oulu (65° 00'N, 25°30'E) in an urban pine forest using 1- and 2-year-old Scots pine (*Pinus sylvestris* L.) and Norway spruce (*Picea abies* L. Karst.) seedlings (29 provenances). Treatments included pH 3 and pH 4 acid rain, clean water (pH 7) and an untreated, dry control. The acid solutions were made by adding H_2SO_4 and HNO_3 (2:1) to obtain a pH of 3 or 4. The seedlings were treated with sprinklers three times a week (5-10 minutes per event, an amount corresponding to 5 mm of rain each time). The irrigation took place over a total of 451 days from 1986 to 1989: 25 August to 13 October 1986, 11 May to 23 October 1987, 6 June to 17 October 1988 and 17 May to 24 August 1989. For a detailed description of the protocol, see Huttunen *et al.* (1990).

Scanning electron microscope (SEM) investigation of epicuticular wax structures and micro-analysis of particulate deposition on the needle surfaces were performed according to Turunen and Huttunen (1991), and TEM investigation according to Back *et al.* (1993). Quantity of chloroform soluble waxes was determined by a modification of the method of Schuck (1976). The Ca and Mg concentrations from the soil were analyzed by atomic absorption spectropho-tometer.

Results and discussion

No visible foliar symptoms relating directly to the acid rain treatment were observed during the 3-year experiment. First SEM confirmation of effects of acid rain were seen after 5 weeks (10 exposures) treatment at pH 3 and pH 4 acid rain in the end of September, when $CaSO_4$ - crystallites (10-20 m long, 0.5-4 m wide), were observed on the pine and spruce needle surfaces (Figure 1). The occurence of $CaSO_4$ - crystallites was at its maximum in October-November (Huttunen *et al.*, 1990, 1991), when whole needle surfaces were covered with $CaSO_4$ - crystal-lites. Only in a few exceptional cases, were crystallites observed on dry and water control needles.

Pine needles were characterized by an undeveloped wax structure. The wax tubes were short and sparsely distributed leading to unoccluded epistomatal chamber. In conjunction with $CaSO_4$ - crystallites, only occasional direct erosion of epicuticular waxes was observed.

Under TEM, Ca oxalate crystallites were seen in spruce needle epi- and hypodermal cell walls, more abundantly in the inner than outer walls. It was found that the deposits increased in the inner wall due to acid treatment (Figure 2) (Back *et al.*, 1993). Instead of precipitation to oxalate, it is suggested that Ca leached from the external walls of the epidermal cells, or from subsidiary cells, reaching the surface of the needles to form $CaSO_4$ - crystallites. The lack of Ca in the outer

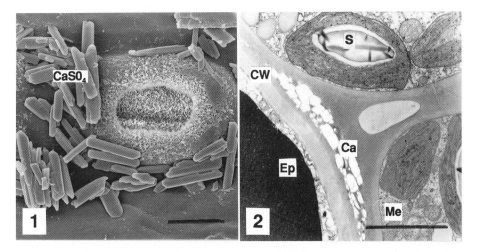

Figure 1 SEM micrograph of CaSO₄-crystallites on current needle surface with undeveloped wax structure of pH 3-treated southern pine after 5 weeks acid rain treatment. Bar 10 μm.

Figure 2 TEM micrograph of mesophyll and epidermal cells from a current spruce needle, after 2 years' treatment with pH 4 acid rain. Abundant Ca-oxalate crystals are seen in the inner wall of epidermal cell. Abbreviations: S= starch, CW= cell wall, Ca= calcium oxalate, Ep= epidermal cell, Me=mesophyll cell. Bar 5 μm.

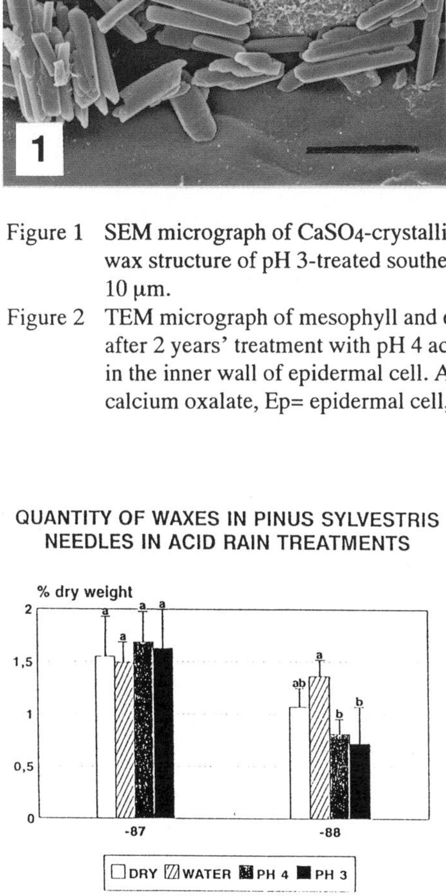

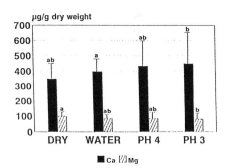

Figure 3 Quantity of chloroform soluble waxes in the two most recent needle age classes of acid rain-treated pine seedlings. Different letters above the columns indicate significant difference at 95% level between the means.

Figure 4 Calcium and magnesium content in the soil of the boxes in the end of the experiment. Different letters above the columns indicate significant difference at 95% level between means.

epidermal wall of seedlings may enhance the permeability of the cuticle for other substances as well, due to loosening of cell wall structures (Fink, 1991; Klumpp and Guderian, 1990).

Evidence exists that Ca and other cations neutralize acidic input on plant surfaces (Musselman, 1988; Steubing *et al.*, 1989). In this investigation, $CaSO_4$ occurrence was most probably a result of a reaction between the calcium leached out of the needle, and sulphur derived from the watering solution. Calcium sulfate crystallites may principally be a consequence of the changed or inadequate wax and cuticle biosynthesis resulting in undeveloped and permeable cuticles and poor stomatal protection, rather than being due directly to acid rain (Huttunen *et al.*, 1989). Wax production was slowest or started latest in pH 3- and pH 4-treated 2-month-old pine needles, which had almost 50% less wax than water controls in early August (Figure 3).

At the end of the 3-year experiment, only a few $CaSO_4$-crystallites could be seen on needle surfaces, possibly because of the Ca-deficiency in the acid rain-treated seedlings. Analysis of soil revealed an increase in the soluble Ca and decrease in Mg concentrations due to pH 3 treatment (Figure 4).

References

Back J, Huttunen S, Kristen U (1993) Carbohydrate distribution and cellular injuries in acid rain and cold-treated spruce needles. Trees (*in press*)

Fink S (1991) Unusual patterns in the distribution of calcium oxalate in spruce needles and their possible relationships to the impact of pollutants. New Phytol 119: 41-51

Hogan GD (1992) Physiological effects of direct impact of acidic deposition on foliage. Agriculture Ecosystems and Environment 42: 307-319

Huttunen S, Reinikainen J, Turunen M (1990) Wintering response of conifers to acid rain in northern conditions. *In* Kauppi P, Kenttämies K, Anttila P (*eds*) Acidification in Finland. Springler Verlag, Berlin, FRG, *pp* 607-635

Huttunen S, Turunen M, Reinikainen J (1989) Studies on Scots pine (*Pinus sylvestris* L.) and Norway spruce (*Picea abies* (L.) Karst.) needle cuticles. Ann Sci For 46(suppl.): 553-556

Huttunen S, Turunen M, Reinikainen J (1991) Scattered $CaSO_4$-crystallites on needle surfaces after simulated acid rain as an indicator of nutrient leaching. Water Air Soil Poll 54: 169-173

Klumpp A, Guderian R (1990) Leaching von Magnesium, Calcium und Kalium aus immissionsbelasteten Nadeln junger Fichten (*Picea abies* (L.) Karst.) Forstwiss Zentralbl 109: 13-39

Mengel K, Hogrebe AMR, Esch A (1989) Effect of acidic fog on needle surface and water relations of *Picea abies*. Physiol Plant 75: 201-207

Musselman RC (1988) Acid neutralizing capacity of leaves exposed to acidic fog. Environ Exp Bot 28: 27-31

Percy KE, Krause CR, Jensen KF (1990) Effects of ozone and acidic fog on red spruce needle epicuticular ultrastructure. Can J For Res 20: 117-120

Rinallo C, Raddi P, diLornardo V (1986) Effects of simulated acid deposition on the surface of Norway spruce and silver fir needles. Eur J For Path 16: 440-446

Schuck HJ (1976) Quantitative Variation der Wachsauflage und der cuticularen Kohlenwasserstoffe bei *Picea abies*-Nadeln. Flora 165: 303-314

Steubing L, Fangmeier A, Roth R, Frankenfeld M (1989) Effect of SO_2, NO_2, and O_3 on population development and morphological and physiological parameters of native herb layer species in a beech forest. Environ Poll 58: 281-302

Turunen M, Huttunen S (1990) A review of the response of epicuticular wax of conifer needles to air pollution. J Environ Qual 19(2): 35-45

Turunen M, Huttunen S (1991) Effect of simulated acid rain on epicuticular wax of Scots pine needles under northerly conditions. Can J Bot 69: 412-419

Problems in Interpreting Effects of Air Pollutants on Spruce Epicuticular Waxes

Edith Bermadinger-Stabentheiner
Institute of Plant Physiology
Karl-Franzens-University of Graz
Schubertstraße 51
A-8010 Graz
Austria

Abstract

Spruce needles are covered with rod-like crystals, which also fill the antechambers of the stomata with a dense meshwork. The scanning electron microscope (SEM) is a very useful for studying epicuticular wax structures; with no intricate or laborious preparation, it is possible to obtain valuable information about the needle surface. Because the epicuticular wax layer forms a barrier between the plant and its environment, all influences that reach the surface from outside impact on this layer and, therefore, changes in epicuticular wax structure serve as diagnostic criteria for damage caused by air pollutants. This pollution influence begins as fusion of wax rods at the tips and results finally in total loss of the crystalline structure.

Despite the simplicity of SEM investigations, alterations (artefacts) can occur to wax structures that may be confused with alterations caused by air pollutants (*i.e.*, a too dense layer of twigs and needles, or careless handling with tweezers, results in mechanical damage that often influences the entire surface). Overheating occurring during transport or preparation and/or incorrect storage also produce artefacts.

If the occurrence of such artefacts is taken into consideration, several contradictory interpretations of effects of air pollutants on epicuticular waxes can be explained.

Introduction

The epicuticular wax layer on plant leaves is interposed between the plant and its environment and is one of the first targets of all influences that reach the surface from the outside. The antechamber wax of spruce, a dense but porous meshwork, is an important factor in gas exchange processes (Jeffree *et al.*, 1971). Alterations to this meshwork, therefore, will influence the mechanisms of transpiration and photosynthesis (Sauter and Voss, 1986; Bermadinger and Grill, 1987). Injured wax structures favour needle infestation by parasites (Elstner and Osswald, 1984), and a structurally or chemically altered surface may influence the uptake of pollutants.

Since the beginning of the early 1970s, changes in the epicuticular wax structures, above all others in conifers, have served as diagnostic criteria for damage caused by pollutants (*e.g.*, Grill, 1973; Bermadinger *et al.*, 1987, 1988a, b; Turunen and Huttunen, 1990). However, since the

NATO ASI Series, Vol. G 36
Air Pollutants and the Leaf Cuticle
Edited by K. E. Percy et al.
© Springer-Verlag Berlin Heidelberg 1994

epicuticular wax structures are not exclusively affected by pollutants, but also by other natural or artificial influences, an assignment to a specific cause of damage is sometimes very difficult.

This paper deals with several alterations to epicuticular wax structures of spruce caused by natural aging and pollutants, but also by other influences that are not connected with pollution effects.

Materials and Methods

Air-dried needles [*Picea abies* (L.)Karst.] were mounted on aluminium stubs with double-sided tape. After application of a thin coating of gold (sputtering), the samples were studied with a Cambridge Stereoscan Mark II-a or a Leitz AMR-1000 at 20 NS 30 kV, respectively (Grill, 1973; Bermadinger *et al.*, 1987).

"Normal State" (Aging and Pollution Effects)

The surface of spruce needles is covered with tubular wax crystalloids that, especially, fill the antechambers of the sunken stomata with a dense meshwork (Fig. 1). The degree of wax covering the surface within the stomatal rows differs considerably between individual trees, ranging from only some clusters of wax rods on a smooth surface to a dense layer of wax crystals completely covering the surface. With increasing needle age the crystalline structure of the antechamber wax is lost (Bermadinger *et al.*, 1988b).

Many investigations report the influence of several air pollutants leading to a degradation of the structural waxes and an erosion of the surface (*e.g.*, Grill, 1973; Grill *et al.*, 1987; Sauter and Voss, 1986; Bermadinger *et al.*, 1987, 1988a, b; Percy *et al.*, 1990; Turunen and Huttunen, 1990).

The succession of wax alterations, however, is on principle the same for aging and pollution effects. Structural wax degradation is not pollutant-specific (Grill *et al.*, 1992; Bermadinger *et al.*, 1988b).

Alteration of the antechamber waxes always starts with the fusion of the wax rods at their tips (Fig. 2), which causes a dilation of the pores between the wax rods and, in consequence, the stomatal conductance for water vapour of fully open stomatas is increased (Bermadinger and Grill, 1987). As the fusion and the structural degradation of the wax rods continues, the crystalline structure is completely lost and the stomata may be occluded by a flat and solid wax plug (Fig. 3), which distinctly decreases the stomatal conductance for water vapour (Bermadinger and Grill, 1987). This process of degradation is evidently enhanced in areas where "classical" pollutants dominate (*e.g.*, SO_2, acidic depositions, alkaline fine dusts)(Grill *et al.*, 1987; Bermadinger *et al.*, 1988b). In contrast, ozone does not affect the epicuticular wax structures (Bermadinger *et al.*, 1988b; Grill *et al.*, 1989, 1992).

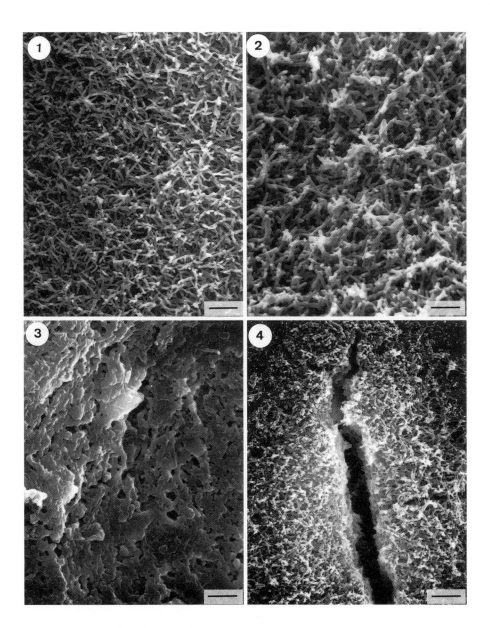

Figure 1   Completely uninfluenced antechamber wax of a young needle; bar = 1,7 μm
Figure 2   Slightly influenced antechamber wax; bar = 1,7 μm
Figure 3   Heavily influenced antechamber wax; bar = 1,7 μm
Figure 4. Fissure in the antechamber wax; bar = 4,2 μm

Fissures in the Antechamber Wax

Due to the incomplete development of the supporting tissues (*e.g.*, sclerenchyma cells) in young needles, shrinkage during the drying process leads to fissures in the antechamber wax (Fig. 4). Such drying artifacts occur on air-dried as well as on freeze-dried needles and can be avoided only by low temperature scanning electron microscopy of fresh material. If such fissures appear considerably increased on older needles, however, this may be an indication of an incomplete development of the supporting tissue and consequently an indirect indication of reduced vitality.

Mechanical influences

The crystalline wax structures are easily damaged by mechanical forces, *e.g.*, a) squashing them to a flat mass, b) melting them due to frictional heat (melting point of spruce waxes: 45-60°C) and c) loss of wax due to abrasion. Consequently, the crystalline structure is destroyed and sometimes mechanically-induced wax degradations are interpreted as pollution effects.

Mechanical damage is easily detected on young needles with a dense wax layer (Fig. 5). The crystalline structure of the wax rods is lost only in distinctly defined areas, while other areas are completely undisturbed. When the crystalline structure is affected to a larger extent, however, the appearance of the mechanically injured waxes resemble that of needles heavily damaged by pollutants (Fig. 6, compare to Fig. 3).

Preparation artifacts can easily be avoided by taking appropriate care during sampling, transport and preparation. However, especially in chamber experiments, close spacing of the trees (to make best use of limited space) and repeated handling (sampling, various measurements during exposure) promote mechanical injury and, for this reason, investigating pollution effects is a delicate task (Bermadinger *et al.*, 1990). Environmental influences, such as wind (impaction of particles on the surface, rubbing together of twigs and needles), snow and ice also can cause mechanical injury to a significant degree (van Gardingen *et al.*, 1991). A careful interpretation with regard to pollution effects, therefore, will be necessary when field studies reveal differently affected wax structures on trees varying in exposure (*e.g.*, exposed to or shielded from wind). Up to now, it has not been known whether pollutants can influence biosynthesis of waxes in such a way that they become more susceptible to mechanical forces.

Melted waxes

Sometimes the antechamber wax may be changed in a way completely different from that mentioned above. Instead of normal antechamber wax there is only an amorphous mass and no crystalline structures can be observed — the wax has been melted (Fig. 7). Sometimes only the wax near the edge of the antechamber is melted while the central part remains unaffected (Fig. 8). As a general characteristic of this phenomenon only the antechamber wax is affected but not the wax of the surrounding needle surface.

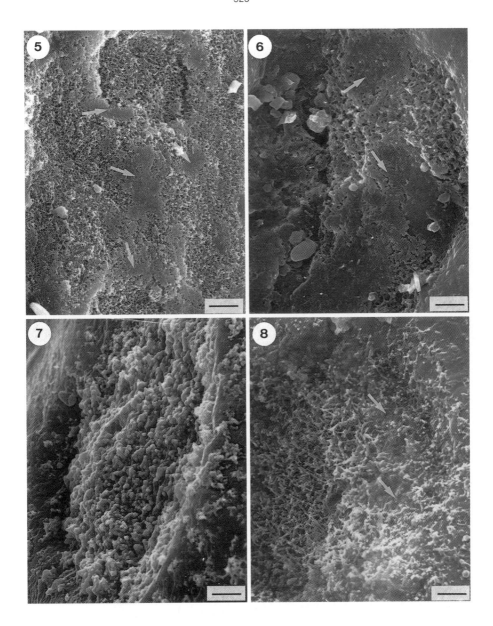

Figure 5   Mechanically injured wax on a young needle (arrows); bar = 8,4 μm
Figure 6   Severe mechanical damage of the antechamber wax; bar = 4,2 μm
Figure 7   Complete antechamber wax is melted; bar = 4,2 μm
Figure 8   Parts of the antechamber wax are melted (arrows); bar = 4,2 μm

These alterations are often observed for needles stored in small air-tight boxes but never occur on needles stored in air-permeable paper bags. Therefore, it is a mere storage artifact. Though not completely cleared up yet it is supposed that water or volatile substances accumulate within the needle during storage. During sputtering or during the investigation with the SEM, the accumulated substances are emitted and destroy the wax structures by melting or dissolving them. The more substances accumulate the more intensive is the wax destruction.

These artifacts can be avoided by storing the needles in air-permeable paper bags or by examining fresh material using low temperature scanning electron microscopy.

Conclusion

Crystalline wax structures are easily altered by various influences and several of these alterations are not the result of pollution effects. By using appropriate care during sampling, storage, preparation and interpretation of the results, a vast quantity of valuable information on the epicuticular wax structures will be obtained.

Acknowledgements

The scanning electron microscopic investigations were performed at the Zentrum für Elektronenmikroskopie, Graz. I am greatly indebted to Dieter Grill for helpful discussion.

References

Bermadinger E, Grill D (1987) Pflanzenphysiologische Untersuchungen im Immissionsgebiet Breitenau. Mitt naturw. Ver Steiermark 117: 73-87

Bermadinger E, Grill D, Golob P (1987) Einfluss von Magnesitstäuben auf Fichtennadelwachse. Phyton (Austria) 27: 15-29

Bermadinger E, Grill D, Golob P (1988a) The different influence of magnesite emissions on the surface of Norway spruce and silver fir. Can J Bot 66: 125-129

Bermadinger E, Grill D, Golob P (1988b) Influence of different air pollutants on the structure of needle wax of spruce (*Picea abies* (L.) Karsten). GeoJournal 17: 289-293

Bermadinger E, Guttenberger H, Grill D (1990) Physiology of Norway spruce. Environ Pollut 68: 319-330

Elstner EF, Osswald DW (1984) Fichtensterben in "Reinluftgebieten": Strukturresistenzverlust. Naturw Rundschau 37: 52-61

Grill D (1973) Rasterelektronenmikroskopische Untersuchungen an SO2-belasteten Fichtennadeln. Phytopath Z 78: 75-80

Grill D, Pfeifhofer H, Halbwachs G, Waltinger H (1987) Investigations on epicuticular waxes of differently damaged spruce needles. Eur J For Path 17: 246-255

Grill D, Guttenberger H, Zellnig G, Bermadinger E (1989) Reactions of plant cells to air pollution. Phyton (Austria) 29: 277-290

Grill D, Zellnig G, Bermadinger-Stabentheiner E, Müller M (1992) Strukturelle Veränderungen in Abhängigkeit verschiedener Luftschadstoffe. Forstw Cbl 112: 2-11

Jeffree CE, Johnson RPC, Jarvis PG (1971) Epicuticular wax in the stomatal antechamber of Sitka spruce and its effects on the diffusion of water vapour and carbon dioxide. Planta (Berl.) 98: 1-10

Percy KE, Krause CR, Jensen KF (1990) Effects of ozone and acidic fog on red spruce needle epicuticular wax ultrastructure. Can J For Res 20: 117-120

Sauter JJ, Voss JU (1986) SEM-observations on the structural degradation of epistomatal waxes in *Picea abies* (L.)Karst. and its possible role in the "Fichtensterben". Eur J For Path 16: 408-423

Turunen M, Huttunen S (1990) A Review of the response of epicuticular wax of conifer needles to air pollution. J Environ Qual 19: 35-45

van Gardingen PR, Grace J, Jeffree CE (1991) Abrasive damage by wind to the needle surface of *Picea sitchensis* (Bong.) Carr. and *Pinus sylvestris* L. Plant, Cell and Environment 14: 185-193

Recent Advances Using Electron Beam Analysis to Detect Cuticular Changes Induced by Air Pollution

Charles R. Krause
United States Department of Agriculture
Agricultural Research Service
Application Technology Research Unit
The Ohio State University/ Ohio Agricultural Research and Development Center
Wooster, Ohio 44691
United States of America

Abstract

Invisble or "hidden injury", terms from the earliest air quality literature, expressed the diagnostician's frustration in identifying abiotic disease symptoms. Direct visualization was not technically possible until the advent of electron beam analysis (EBA) hardware and software. Electron beam analysis, a combination of scanning electron microscopy (SEM), energy dispersive x-ray analysis (EDXA), and computer-controlled image processing (CCIP) is useful for detecting changes in the cuticle and adjacent cells due to common phytotoxicants. Artifacts, caused by improper specimen preparation, inherent in the high vacuum of SEM and use of hydrated plant samples, fill the literature. Unique methodologies are necessary to interpret the minute changes to plant surfaces caused by a variety of environmental stresses such as sulfur dioxide, ozone, acidic deposition, pesticide residues, NACl, *etc*. EBA was used to show: the progression of surface alterations that occur to stomata of hybrid poplar (*Populus* spp.) following exposure to SO_2 and O_3; between SO_2-sensitive and SO_2-tolerant clones of eastern white pine (*Pinus strobus* L.). CCIP was especially useful in determining that acidified rain or mist and O_3 do not physically erode existing epicuticular wax of red spruce (*Picea rubens* Sarg.) as previous literature stated. EBA was used to crrelate field and laboratory data showing similar injury to epistomatal wax of red spruce. Improved field emission micrsoscopy and EDXA that offer increased resolution with little sample preparation can provide opportunities to observe cuticular modifications not previously available.

Introduction

"Invisible" or "hidden injury", terms from the earliest air quality literature, expressed the diagnostician's frustration attempting to identify symptoms to leaf surfaces induced by air pollution (Heck, 1968; Went, 1955). In this paper, air pollution is defined as any gaseous or particulate phytotoxicant (*i.e.*, SO_2, O_3, PAN, NO_X, acid precipitation, particulates, NaCl, pesticides, *etc*.) that causes injury or damage to the tree species (Figure 1). Macroscopic symptoms to leaf surfaces induced by certain air pollutants have been determined in many laboratory studies (Jacobson and Hill, 1970). In the field, gross symptomology can be subjective, confusing or indefinite because of mimicry by other biotic or abiotic factors (Skelly *et al.*, 1988).

NATO ASI Series, Vol. G 36
Air Pollutants and the Leaf Cuticle
Edited by K. E. Percy et al.
© Springer-Verlag Berlin Heidelberg 1994

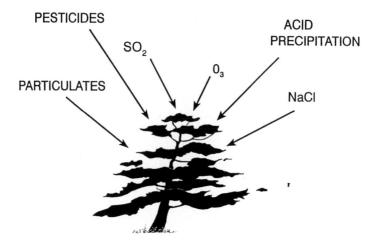

Figure 1   Diagram of air pollution agents that can cause injury to trees.

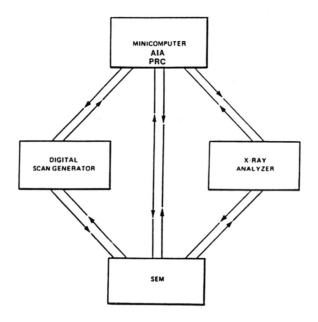

Figure 2   Conceptual diagram of electron beam analysis.

The plant cuticle acts as the main barrier to the entry of air pollutants (Bukovac *et al.*, 1981), while bearing much of their initial insults.

Accurate direct visualization of cuticular injury due to air pollution was not technically possible until the advent of electron beam analysis (EBA) hardware and software (Krause *et al.*, 1983). Electron beam analysis, a combination of scanning electron microscopy (SEM) energy dispersive x-ray analysis (EDXA) and automated image analysis (AIA), allows rapid acquisition of a digitized image in 5-10 seconds (Figure 2).

EBA is useful for detecting changes induced by common phytotoxicants in the cuticle and adjacent cells. In contrast, conventional SEM using thermionic beam emission with livetime photography requiring extended beam exposure to specimens (@100 seconds), can create erroneous results. Artifacts, caused by improper specimen preparation, inherent in the high vacuum of SEM along with the use of dehydrated plant samples and thermionic electron beam damage fill the literature (Crang and Klomparens, 1988; Trimble *et al.*, 1982). Unique method-ologies are necessary to interpret minute changes to plant surfaces caused by a variety of environmental stresses such as sulfur dioxide, ozone, acidic deposition, NaCl, pesticide residues, *etc.* (Krause, 1985).

EBA was used to show the progression of surface alterations that occur to stomatal configurations of hybrid poplar (*Populus* spp.) following exposure to SO_2 and O_3, in combination, but not alone (Krause *et al.*, 1979). Figure 3a shows a "normal" image of a stomata grown in carbon-filtered air, while Figures 3b-c show the gradual cytolysis of the stomatal apparatus over time. In a study conducted near a major industrial area, visualization and characterization of particulate air pollutants on red maple leaves (*Acer rubrum* L.) were studied with SEM and EDXA (Krause, 1983). Figure 4 shows various shaped particles that were characterized by EBA.

Morphological differences in epistomatal wax structures between previously screened SO_2-sen-sitive and SO_2-tolerant clones of eastern white pine (*Pinus strobus* L.) were characterized with SEM (Krause *et al.*, 1983). Continuous epistomatal wax on an SO_2-tolerant needle is shown in Figure 5a and discontinuous split over the epistomatal wax (arrows) of an SO_2-sensitive white pine clone are shown in Figure 5b. EBA was used to detect sulfur within *A. rubrum* leaf chloroplasts exposed to SO_2 (Krause *et al.*, 1988; Figure 6a). Note the x-ray spectrum (Figure 6b) and distribution maps that illustrate locations of magnesium (part of the chlorophyll molecule) and exogenous sulfur (Figure 6c) from SO_2 exposure.

In another study, variations in the sensitivity of *Acer* species induced by SO_2 were characterized using EBA (Krause *et al.*, 1989). In the latter study, five *Acer* species were exposed to either carbon-filtered air or 2.5 ppm SO_2 for 6 h per day for 6 days, then osmium vapor-fixed, mounted, coated with Au and examined with EBA after Krause *et al.* (1983). *Acer saccharum* exhibited

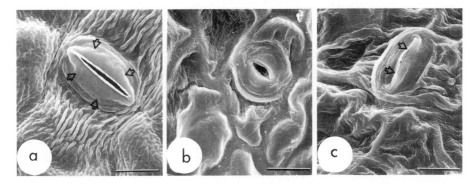

Figure 3   A progression of upper epidermal leaf surface alterations on *Populus* spp. induced by SO$_2$ and O$_3$. **3a**. Unaffected stomatal apparatus (bars =10 microns). **3b**. Leaf stomata exposed to SO$_2$ and O$_3$ showing progressive injury over time until lesion formation (**3c**) occurs.

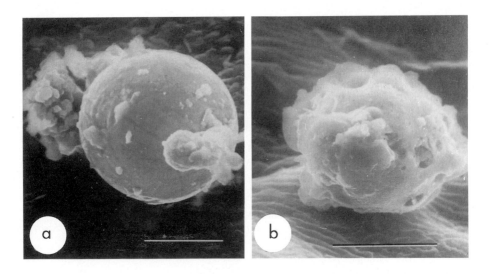

Figure 4   Particles on abaxial lesions of red maple leaves grown in polluted ambient air characterized with EBA by various shapes and chemistry (bar = 5 microns).

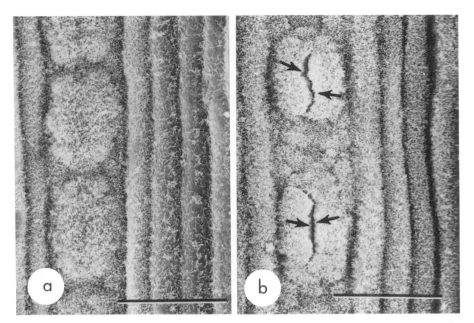

Figure 5   **5a**. SO$_2$-tolerant *Pinus strobus* needle surface with continuous episomatal wax (bars = 10 microns).
5b. Discontinuous epistomatal wax with split (arrows) from SO$_2$-sensitive *P. strobus* needle.

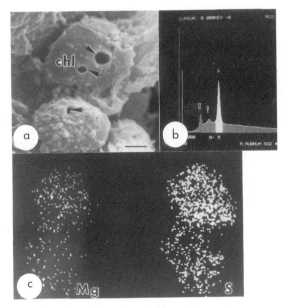

Figure 6   **6a**. *Acer rubrum* leaf chloroplast exposed to SO$_2$. Note holes (arrows, bar = 0.5 microns). **6b**. X-ray
spectrum of chloroplast in Figure 6a showing sulfur. **6c**. X-ray distribution map showing presence
of magnesium and sulfur in the chloroplast.

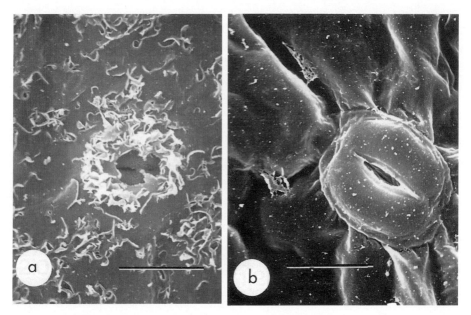

Figure 7   **7a.** *Acer saccharum* leaf surface exposed to SO$_2$ with slight alteration (bars = 5 microns). **7b.** *Acer negundo* leaf surface exposed to SO$_2$ exhibited severe injury.

only slight alterations to epicuticular leaf wax (Figure 7a) when exposed to SO$_2$. Intermediate levels of SO$_2$ injury were noted when *Acer platanoides*, *A. rubrum*, and *Acer saccharinum* were examined with EBA. *Acer negundo* leaves exhibited severe morphological changes in epicuticular wax, cytolysis of epidermal cells and lesion formation (Figure 7b) when exposed to SO$_2$ at the above level. Epicuticular variations described above could relate to SO$_2$-tolerance for use in future screening programs. Disruption of the cuticle and epidermis could predispose affected *Acer* spp. to foliar pathogens or enhance the injurious effects of other abiotic stress factors.

EBA was especially useful in determining that acidified rain or mist and O$_3$ did not physically erode existing epicuticular wax of red spruce (*Picea rubens* Sarg.) as previous literature stated but that it was developmentally altered during synthesis (Figure 8, Percy *et al.*, 1990). EBA was used to compare similar microtopographical symptomology of injury to epistomatal wax of red spruce needles grown under controlled conditions of carbon-filtered air (Figure 9a), severe injury on needles grown in O$_3$ + acid precipitation (Figure 9b) and similar injury (Figure 9c) on needles grown in high ambient O$_3$ + acid precipitation(Krause *et al.* 1991). Red spruce needle injury occurred during epistomatal wax synthesis. Injury to *Pinus* spp. due to road de-icing salt was characterized with EBA (Krause, 1982). When sprayed with distilled water, mounted, Au sputter-coated and examined with EBA, wax tubules appeared regular (Figure 10a). Fused epistomatal wax tubules (Figure 10b) were observed when various *Pinus* spp. were sprayed with 2% NaCl solutions.

Phytotoxicity or chemical "burn" to *A. rubrum* leaves caused by Cu(OH)₂ was described using EBA (Krause, 1985). Marginal chlorosis was characterized, associated with the presence of Cu(OH)₂ particles on necrotic lesions as identified with EBA (Figure 11a-c). Cu was also detected in mesophyll cells using EBA. It was used to characterize and track the fate of fungicide smoke, vinclozolin on *Rhododendron* spp. leaf surfaces (Figure 12a,b, Krause *et al.*, 1986). Vinclozolin particles were found on both leaf surfaces and identified by EDXA based on the presence of Cl. Direct detection of pesticide dispersal with EBA could lead to the reduction of pesticide usage, more efficient crop management practices and improved water quality.

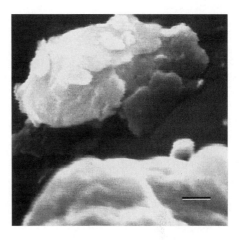

Figure 8   *Picea rubens* epicuticular wax altered during synthesis by O₃ and acid mist (bar = 0.5 micron).

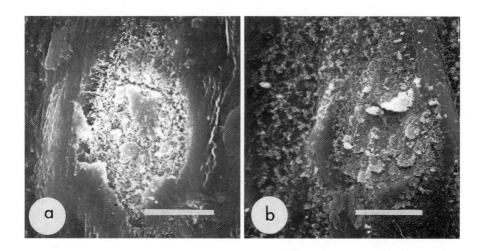

Figure 9   *P. rubens* epistomatal wax. **9a**. Severe injury to epistomatal needle surfaces exposed to acidified rain and O₃, expressed as agglomerated was tubules (bars = 5 microns). **9b**. *P. rubens* needle surface grown in high ambient O₃ and acidified rain with injury similar to spruce grown in the laboratory.

336

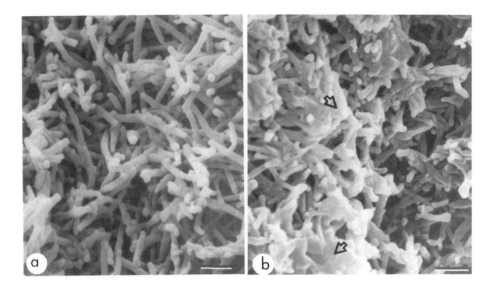

Figure 10   **10a.** Regular epistomatal wax tubules of *Pinus aristata* sprayed with H₂O (bars = 0.5 microns). **10b.** Fused epistomatal wax tubules of *P. aristata* sprayed with 2% NaCl.

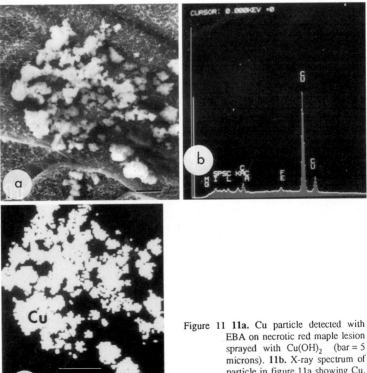

Figure 11 **11a.** Cu particle detected with EBA on necrotic red maple lesion sprayed with Cu(OH)₂ (bar = 5 microns). **11b.** X-ray spectrum of particle in figure 11a showing Cu. **11c.** X-ray distribution map of Cu in the particle.

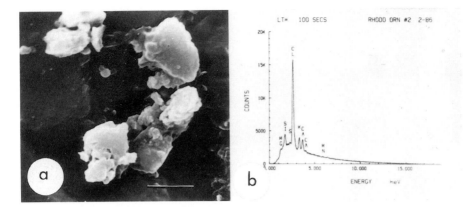

Figure 12   **12a.** Vinclozolin particle of *Rhododendron* spp. leaf surface (bar = 5 microns). **12b.** X-ray spectrum of vinclozolin particle showing Cl peak.

Conventional thermionic scanning electron microscopy (TSEM) has provided increased knowledge about the nature of the plant cuticle and air pollution as cited above. Cryofixation techniques also reduce artifacts when appropriately used (Crang and Klomparens, 1988). A new technology, cold field emission scanning electron microscopy (CFE-SEM) offers the greatest opportunity for improved structural analysis of the cuticle. The electron beam of TSEM is produced by heating a tungsten wire or lanthanum hexaboride tip, which transfers heat into plant samples at high acceleration voltages (20-30 kV), necessary to attain maximum resolution of approximately 70 Angstroms. Such beam corrosion can cause artifacts, often impeding examination of specimens or can lead to misinterpretation of results (Crang and Klomparens, 1988). Conversely, the electron beam emitted by CFE-SEM is electronically extracted from an extremely sharp tip of mono-crystalline tungsten resulting in a fine, relatively cool electron probe producing a resolving power of less than 8 Angstroms at 1 kV. Recent improvements in differential vacuum systems coupled with the cool, fine electron beam allow examination of fresh, hydrated leaf samples without carbon or metal coating procedures. Digitized images can be rapidly archived on video compact disks. High accuracy EDXA can be interfaced with CFE-SEM to complete an improved EBA. Figure 13a shows a fresh, hydrated *Ficus* spp. leaf examined with CEF-SEM at 1 kV. Note stomatal field and droplet residue (bar = 300 microns). Within the above crystal, pyrethroid insecticide crystals, identified with EDXA, are shown in Figure 13b (bar=3 microns). Cryogenic specimen stages further enhance the use of CFE-SEM.

Conclusions

After 30 years of air quality research studying air pollution effects on plants and plant cuticles with electron microscopy (EM), research standards would useful for investigations in light of past research and new technologies. Sample handling and preparation guidelines should be created for deciduous versus coniferous species. Since most pine and spruce needle surface waxes

338

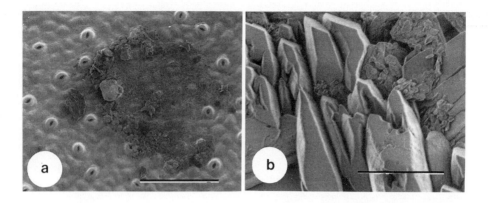

Figure 13   **13a.** Fresh, hydrated uncoated *Ficus* leaf surface examined with a cold field emission scanning electron microscope (CFE-SEM) at 1 kV (bar = 100 microns). **13b.** Pyrethroid insecticide crystals within the lesion in Figure 13a as viewed with CFE-SEM (bar = 3 microns) and identified with EDXA.

are damaged by ethyl alcohol, it should be avoided in EM histological studies of the cuticle. Operational standards for EM investigations of particular groups of plants could be set up according to instrumentation. EM standards used in future research would increase efficiency, promote high quality, comparable air quality research throughout the world in a climate of dwindling resourses.

CFE-SEM and high resolution EDXA offer increased resolution with minimal sample preparation and provide new opportunities to observe cuticular modifications induced by air pollutants or other environmental stresses.

Acknowledgements

The above research was partially supported by grants from the North Central Regional Pesticide Assessment Program (United States Department of Agriculture) and the Horticultural Research Institute, American Association of Nurserymen (Washington, D.C.)

All programs and services of the U.S. Department of Agriculture are offered on a non-discriminatory basis without regard to race, color, national origin, religion, sex, age, marital status, or handicap.

The author of this article is an employee of the Government of the United States of America. The work of this publication is work of the U.S. Government which is not subject to copyright.

References

Bukovac MJ, Rasmussen HP, and Shull VE (1981) The cuticle: surface structure and function. Scanning Electron Microsc III: 213-223

Crang REF, Klomparens KL (*eds*) (1988) Artifacts in biological electron microscopy. Plenum Press, New York

Heck WW (1968) Factors influencing expression of oxidant damage to plants. Ann Rev Phytopathol 6: 165-188

Jacobson JS and Hill AC (*ed*) (1970) A pictorial atlas. Air Pollution Control Assoc, A-1

Krause CR (1980) Scanning electron microscopic detection of injury to hybrid poplar leaves induced by ambient air pollution. Scanning Electron Microsc, III: 591-594

Krause CR (1982) Identification of salt spray injury to *Pinus* spp with SEM. Phytopathology, 72: 382-386

Krause CR (1983) Detection of particulate air pollution injury to red maple leaves with energy dispersive X-ray analysis. Scanning Electron Microsc, III: 1493-1497

Krause CR (1985) Foliar penetration of a fungicide as detected by scanning electron microscopy and energy dispersive X-ray analysis. Scanning Electron Microsc, II: 811-815

Krause CR (1985) Use of electron micoscopy in plant pathology: abiotic diseases. Proc 43rd Annual Meeting Electron Microsc Soc Am, *pp* 628-631

Krause CR, Houston DB (1983) Morphological variation in epicuticular wax of SO_2-sensitive and SO_2-tolerant eastern white pine clones. Phytopathology, 73: 1266-1269

Krause CR, Jensen KF (1979) Surface changes on hybrid poplar leaves exposed to ozone and sulfur dioxide. Scanning Electron Microsc III: 22, 77-80

Krause CR, Powell CC (1986) Deposition and distribution of fungicide smoke particles detected with electron beam analysis. Proc Ann EMSA Meeting, 44: 198-199

Krause CR, Roberts BR, Ichida JI, and Schnipke VM (1989) Variation in the sensitivity of maple species to sulfur dioxide. Phytopathology 79: 1004.

Percy KE, Krause CR, and Jensen KF (1990) New evidence for the direct interaction between air pollutants and the plant cuticle. Can J For Res, 20: 117-120

Skelly JM, Davis DD, Merrill W, Cameron EA, Brown HD, Drummond DB, and Dochinger LS (*eds*) (1988) Diagnosing injury to eastern forest trees. Pennsylvania State Univ, College Park, PA

Trimble JL, Skelly JM, Tolin SA, and Orcutt DM (1982) Chemical and structural characterization of the needle epicuticular wax of two clones of *Pinus strobus* differing in sensitivity to ozone. Phytopathology, 72: 652-656

Went FW (1955) Air pollution. Scientific American 192: 63-72

Physico-Chemical Characteristics of Pine Needle Surfaces Exposed to Different Air Pollution Sources

T Staszewski, S Godzik, P. Poborski
Institute for Ecology of Industrial Areas
Environmental Protection Abatement Centre
6 Kossutha
Katowice 40-832
Poland

Abstract

The properties of pine (*Pinus sylvestris* L.) needle epicuticular waxes and accumulated particulate matter were investigaged. Characteristics of needles of different ages, taken from sites with various levels and patterns of air pollution, were determined by the SEM + EDAX, TEM, labelling with $35SO_2$ technique, and contact angle measurements. The contact angles formed on current-year needles were found to be higher than those on 1-year-old needles. The values of contact angles ranged from 118 and 98° for the control sites to 68 and 43° for the most polluted area for current and 1-year-old needles, respectively. The $35SO_2$ uptake rate by needle surfac es showed the same pattern, except for needles from the vicinity of a cement plant, where needle surfaces were completely covered with dust. The SEM photos revealed gradual changes and the disappearance of fine wax structure with age of needles and air pollution level. Correlations between the analysed factors, as well as effects of surface roughness and chemical composition of particulate matter on the sulphur dioxide uptake rate, are analyzed.

Introduction

The structure of a pine needle's surface is altered by the deposition of large amounts of particulate matter. The physical and chemical characteristics of particulate matter residing on the surface significantly influence the deposition rate of $^{35}SO_2$. One of the parameters related to the deposition rate of gaseous pollutants is surface wettability during rain and fog events (Fowler and Unsworth, 1974; Brimblecombe, 1978; Garsed, 1985). However, wettability does not equate with water volume retained on the needle surface. Barely wettable surfaces of young needles can retain three to five times more water than easily wettable surfaces (Cape and Fowler, 1981). Assuming that young needles with a crystalline structural wax retain more water than needles without this structure, it is reasonable to expect that the value of the contact angle characterizing the quality of the surface structure could be correlated with the amount of SO_2 retained on the surface. Needle surfaces were examined by scanning electron microscopy (SEM) to determine the structural status.

NATO ASI Series, Vol. G 36
Air Pollutants and the Leaf Cuticle
Edited by K. E. Percy et al.
© Springer-Verlag Berlin Heidelberg 1994

Material and methods

Four locations with 70-year-old Scots pine (*Pinus sylvestris* L.) and different levels and patterns of air pollution were selected for needle sampling:

> Control site (Slemien, K.) — rural area in the Beskidy Mountains, relatively low level of air pollution.
>
> Cement plant (Rudniki, R.) — in the vicinity of a cement factory, having poor control of particulate matter emission and high dustfall.
>
> Zinc and lead smelter (Miasteczko Slaskie, M.) — pollution by SO_2 and particulate matter (Upper Silesian Industrial Region).
>
> Urban area (Zabrze, Z.) — pollution by cokery, coal-fired power station, heating station and other sources of both gaseous and non-gaseous air pollutants (Upper Silesian Industrial Region).

Shoots were exposed to $^{35}SO_2$ (0.3 ppm) in a flow-through system (Godzik, 1976; Staszewski *et al.*, 1992). After needle sheaths were removed, needles were washed with water and then with chloroform. The solutions obtained were filtered using a microporous filter to separate particulate matter. Filtrates, particulate matter, and washed needles were examined for radioactivity. A gas flow counter with anticoincidence was used to measure radioactivity in counts per minute (CPM). It was calculated per 1 $g_{d,w}$ and used as a measure of the $^{35}SO_2$ uptake rate.

Before fumigation, 50 needles from each shoot were taken to determine their wettability. Contact angles were measured according to Cape (1983). Also, contact angles formed on waxes extracted from needles from the control site were measured.

Results and discussion

$^{35}SO_2$ uptake depends both on the needles' age and origin. Needles of both age classes from the Rudniki site (R) and current-year needles from the Zabrze site (Z) had the greatest uptake of $^{35}SO_2$ (Figure 1, R1R, R2R and Z1R). $^{35}SO_2$ uptake by current-year and 1-year-old needles from the Rudniki (R) site was almost identical. For the other sites, $^{35}SO_2$ uptake was approximately twice as great for younger needles (Fig. 1, K1R, K2R, Z1R, M1R and M2R). The results agree with those obtained by several other authors (Materna and Kohout, 1969; Materna, 1973; Godzik, 1976; Jensen and Kozlowski, 1975). Needles from Miasteczko (M), the site with the highest level of SO_2 in the air of all the sites compared, had the lowest uptake of $^{35}SO_2$ (Fig. 1, M1R and M2R).

The total amount of sulphur taken up by needles consists of two parts: one part can be extracted from the needle surface with water and chloroform; the other is bound firmly to the needle tissue.

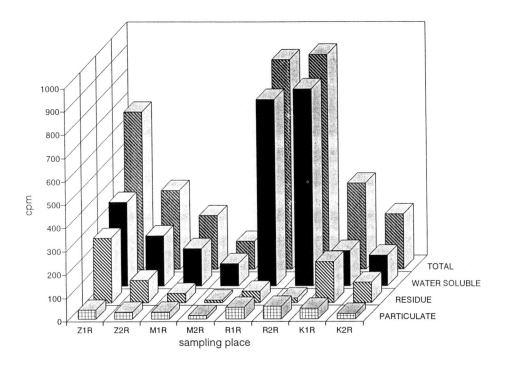

Figure 1   Radioactivity of marked pine needles: dependence on fraction and origin.

A similar pattern of differentiation was found for the surface and total $^{35}SO_2$ uptake, in the order R > Z > K > M. In the case of ^{35}S firmly bound to the needle tissue (residue), the order was the same for young and older needles — Z > K > R > M. The data seem to confirm that particulate matter deposited on the needle surface has an effect on the total uptake of $^{35}SO_2$ (Fig. 1).

More ^{35}S (percent) is localized on the needle surface (the term 'surface' also includes particulate matter deposited on the needle surface) than is firmly bound to the tissue for both needle ages and all sampling sites.

The contribution (percent) of needle surface sulphur to the total pool of sulphur taken up by needles is higher for older needles for all sampling sites (Table 1).

Sulphur accumulates on the waxy surface of needles as a result of absorption. This can be confirmed by removing ^{35}S with water from plants grown and cultivated in greenhouses (thus avoiding particulate matter on the surface) — after labelling with $^{35}SO_2$ (Garsed and Read, 1974; Godzik, 1976).

Table 1   Radioactivity of $^{35}SO_2$ labelled needles. Dependence on fraction and origin

Sampling site and age of needles	Radioactivity [10^3cpm/g_{dw}]						
	Total	Particulate matter (removed with water and chloroform)	%	Water soluble (washed with water from the needle surface)	%	Residue (bound with tissue)	%
Z1R	675.5	40.0	6.0	360.0	53.3	275.0	40.7
Z2R	340.0	30.0	8.8	215.0	63.1	95.0	27.9
M1R	230.0	30.0	13.0	160.0	69.5	40.0	17.5
M2R	120.0	15.0	12.5	95.0	79.2	10.0	8.3
R1R	898.0	50.0	5.6	800.0	89.1	48.0	5.3
R2R	920.0	55.0	6.0	845.0	91.8	20.0	2.2
K1R	370.0	45.0	12.2	150.0	40.5	175.0	47.3
K2R	238.0	23.0	9.7	130.0	34.6	85.0	35.7

1R - current year needles
2R - one-year-old needles

As a result of chemical reaction, $^{35}SO_2$ is firmly bound to dust (probably in the form of weakly soluble salts). The amount of $^{35}SO_2$ bound in this way ranged from 6-13% of the total amount of $^{35}SO_2$ taken up by the needles (Table 1).

The amount of ^{35}S removed from needle's surface suggests that $^{35}SO_2$ is absorbed by deposited particulate, matter forming soluble salts or accumulating on the active polar sites of the surface. This is demonstrated by the fact that the amount of ^{35}S removed is, in all investigated cases (except the 1-year-old needles from M site), higher than that removed from needles from the control site (K), where the amount of surface particulate matter is smallest.

The lower polarity of needle surface waxes from needles sampled in the polluted areas as well as from older ones (Cape, 1983; Percy and Baker, 1988) may be an argument supporting the above assumption. If SO^2 was absorbed only on the waxy surface, the amount of S washed from the needle surface should be highest for the reference site. However, the reverse was found to be true (Fig. 1, K1R, K2R, R1R and R2R).

Similar amounts of ^{35}S were washed from the surface of both age classes of needles sampled in the control area (Fig. 1, K1R and K2R). The small dustfall in this area and the slow process of change is such that structural and chemical composition of wax can be seen as further support for the above mentioned opinion. It should be noted that the absorption capacity of the wax surface decreases together with the age of the needles as a result of being covered by particulate matter and the disappearance of fine structural forms of wax gives an amorphous layer.

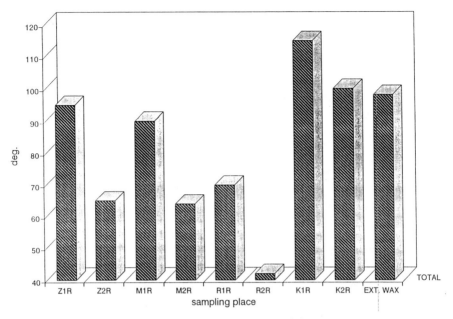

Figure 2   Advancing contact angle depending on needle origin.

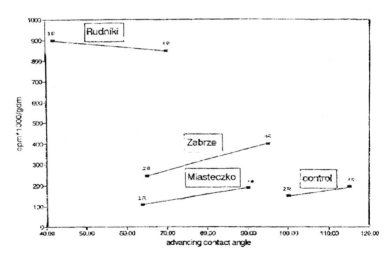

Figure 4   Dependence of surface $^{35}SO_2$ uptake on advancing contact angle.

The values of contact angles formed on the needle surface can be ranked according to their origin as follows: K > Z > M > R (Fig. 2). In all cases, the contact angles formed on current-year needles (1R) were higher than those on 1-year-old needles (2R).

The contact angle values (>90°) obtained for needles from the control site are close to literature data (Martin and Juniper, 1970). The current-year needles from the control site (K) have a well-developed, fine wax structure and little particulate matter was found on the needle surface (Fig. 4). However, erosion of the wax structure of 1-year-old needles was observed (Fig. 5). Despite the small amount of dust deposited on the needle surface, the wax crystalline structure was significantly destroyed, possibly as a result of episodically high concentrations of SO_2 transported from industrial regions. However, other explanations (*e.g.*, effect of climatic conditions) cannot be excluded because we do not know to what extent the disappearance of the fine structure is a specific response to air pollution.

The contact angles formed on current-year and 1-year-old needles from the control site were higher than those formed on wax extracted with chloroform from the surface of current-year needles from this site (Fig. 2, EXT, WAX, K1R and K2R). This reveals the importance of spatial wax structure. The needles from polluted areas were more wettable (less contact angles) than ones from the control area (Fig. 1, Z, M, R). The wettability of particulate matter itself is strongly variable and should to some extent influence the wettability of needle surfaces. It seems that recently deposited matter is of major importance because the particles deposited previously are partially or totally covered (depending, among other things, on their shape and size) in newly produced epicuticular waxes. These two factors determine the surface roughness and free area available for gas sorption. The chemical composition of dust is of importance too because it determines the number of reactive sites for gaseous air pollutants.

Relatively high contact angles (96° ± 9°) were found on the current-year needles from Zabrze (Z). These can be partially explained by the presence of hydrophobic particulate matter (*i.e.*, shoot) adhering firmly to the needle surface and resistant to removal by precipitation (Martin and Juniper, 1970). An increase in surface roughness due to deposited dust may be a further reason for lower wettability. As was pointed out by Schönherr and Bukovac (1972), surface roughness increases contact angles on non-wettable surfaces (>90°) and decreases them on wettable ones (<90°). The wax crystalline structure of current-year needles from Zabrze was well developed only in stomatal hollows and disappeared in their vicinity (Fig. 6). On the surface of both age classes of needles, much particulate matter was observed (Fig. 6, 7). The amorphous dust is probably soot; spherical particles originate from high-temperature processes. In the case of 1-year-old needles, no crystalline wax structure was observed in stomatal hollows (Fig. 7).

The lowest values of contact angles are formed on the needles collected close to the lead and zinc smelter (M) and cement factory (R). Contact angles formed on current-year needles from

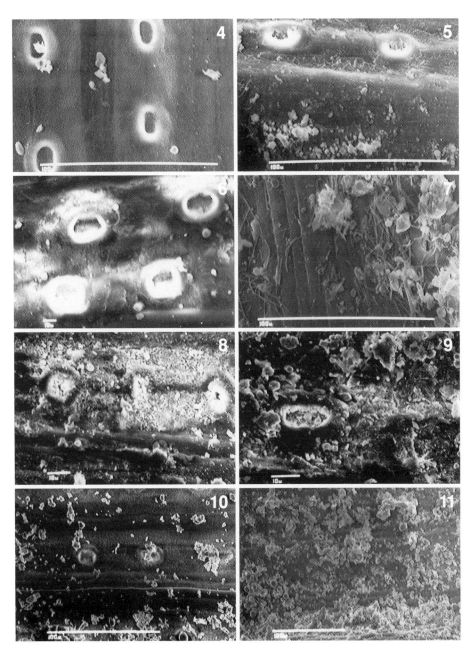

Figure 4   Current-year needle from control site.
Figure 5   1-year-old needle from control site.
Figure 6   Current-year needle from Zabrze.
Figure 7   1-year-old needle from Zabrze.
Figure 8   Current-year needle from Miasteczko Slaskie.
Figure 9   1-year-old needle from Miasteczko Slaskie.
Figure 10   Current-year needle from Rudniki.
Figure 11   1-year-old needle from Rudniki.

(Magnification for all photographs X1100.)

the former (M) are around 90° although the wax structure is highly cooled and much dust has been found on the surface (Fig. 8). In the case of 1-year-old needles, the amount of deposited dust is higher (Fig. 9), accompanied by a significant decrease in contact angle (Fig. 2, M1R and M2R).

The needles of both age classes from (R) (Fig. 2, R1R and R2R) were most easily wetted. Many had contact angles equal to 0, $i.e.$, were totally wetted. Significant amounts of dust were deposited on the surface of current-year needles, although the wax structure was hardly changed (Fig. 10). For 1-year-old needles, the surface coating was totally covered with dust (Fig. 11).

No general simple linear dependence between angle and intensity of $^{35}SO_2$ uptake was obtained (Fig. 3), especially for needles from Rudniki. One reason may be the presence of alkaline hydrophillic dust on the needle surface. In the case of needles from the reference site (with low dust pollution) or from Miasteczko, where part of the dust was calcium sulphate (which does not react with SO_2), a closer relationship was formed between the investigated factors. For needles from Zabrze, the larger slope seems to be the result of specific dust characteristics, particularly dust from the cokery (soot).

Conclusions

1. The particulate matter deposited on needle surfaces protrudes above the primary surface (epidermal tissue) according to the size of the particles or their aggregates. Accordingly, SO_2 reaching the surface by diffusion contacts the particles first then the lower tissue layer coated with wax. Thus, the particulate matter may be a "competitor" for the underlying waxy leaf surface in receiving SO_2.

2. Air pollution (including particulate matter) leads to two opposing processes. On one hand, the crystalline waxes are eroded; on the other, deposition of particulate matter increases the total needle surface area (forming an additional structure) exposed to gaseous air pollutants. These processes may compensate each other, but the important physical and chemical differences between both types of surface structures must be remembered.

3. It has been confirmed that a large proportion of sulphur dioxide deposited to pine needle surfaces can be removed by immersion in water for a short period.

4. Contact angle measurements must be interpreted with care as a measure of needle surface wax destruction, and for monitoring purposes. Physico-chemical properties of particulates deposited to the needle surface significantly affect contact angles.

References

Brimblecombe P (1978) Dew as a sink for SO_2. Tellus 20: 151-157

Cape NJ, Fowler D (1981) Changes in epicuticular wax of *Pinus sylvestris* exposed to polluted air. Silva Fennica 15(4): 457-458

Cape NJ (1983) Contact angles of water droplets or needles of Scots pine (*Pinus sylvestris*) growing in polluted atmospheres. New Phytol 93: 293-299

Fowler D, Unsworth MH (1974) Dry deposition of sulphur dioxide on wheat. Nature 249: 389-390

Garsed SG, Read KJ (1974) The uptake and translocation of $^{35}SO_2$ in soybean (*Gilicine max* var *biloxi*) New Phytol 73: 299-307

Garsed SG (1985) SO_2 uptake and transport. *In* Winner WE, Mooney HA, Goldstein RA Sulfur dioxide and vegetation. Stanford University Press Stanford, California *pp* 75-95

Godzik S (1976) Pobieranie $^{35}SO_2$ powietrza i rozmieszczenie ^{35}S u niektórych gatunków drzcw. Badenia porównawcze. Piaoo i Studia, PAN, 16

Jensen KF, Kozlowski TT (1975) Absorption and translocation of sulfur dioxide by seedlings of four forest-tree species. J Environ Qual 4: 379-382

Martin JT, Juniper BE (1970) The cuticle of plants. Edward Arnold. London

Materna J, Kohout R (1969) Uptake of sulphur dioxide into the leaves of some tree species Communic Inst For Szechosl 6: 39-47

Materna J (1973) Kriterien zur Kennzeihung einer Immissionseinwirkung auf Waldbestande *In* Proc 3rd International Clean Air Congress Dusseldorf *pp* 121-123

Percy KE, Baker EA (1988) Effects of simulated acid rain on leaf wettability, rain retention and uptake of some inorganic ions. New Phytol 108: 75-82

Schönherr J, Bukovac MJ (1972) Penetration of stomata by liquids. Dependence on surface tension, wettability and stomatal morphology. Plant Physiol 49: 813-819

Staszewski T, Godzik S, Poborski S (1992) Repeated labelling of Scots pine (*Pinus silvestris* L.) shoots with $^{35}SO_2$. Archiwum Ochrony todowiska 2: 163-169

A Comparison of Epicuticular Wax of *Pinus sylvestris* Needles from Three Sites in Ireland

Alison Donnelly and Paul Dowding
Environmental Science Unit
Trinity College Dublin
Ireland

Abstract

Three forest stands of *Pinus sylvestris* were chosen for comparison in Ireland. Needles from three year classes were collected. Cuticular transpiration curves showed that the rate of water loss from 1-year-old needles was faster than either 2-year-old or current-year needles at all sites. The amount of epicuticular wax extracted was similar to that reported in the literature. Needle wettability increased with needle age. Amorphous wax coverage was estimated using scanning electron microscopy (SEM) and was found to increase with needle age. Algal cells were noted on needles of all ages at one site and appeared to affect transpiration and microroughness. The presence of fungal hyphae was also noted.

Introduction

It is generally accepted that all higher plants contain a partial or continuous layer of amorphous wax on their aerial surfaces (Baker, 1982). "The physical form of the wax reflects both environment and chemical composition, and may be a good indicator of environmental change" (Cape, 1986). Epicuticular wax is continuously exposed to natural and anthropogenic influences (Turunen and Huttunen, 1990) and should provide an historical record of such influences. The wax may become eroded by a number of mechanisms both mechanical and chemical (Crossley and Fowler, 1986). Epicuticular wax is produced only at leaf expansion, and erosion of this layer, especially from plants that retain their leaves over several years, may cause premature senescence of the leaf (Crossley and Fowler, 1986). The epicuticular wax layer forms a protection which permits conifers to survive under unfavourable conditions, such as temporary drought, high radiation, heat, wind, snow and frost (Gunthardt-Goerg, 1986). Occasionally, as in the case of conifers, wax deposits may be composite. The epicuticular wax of pine and spruce needles have a plate-like layer overlaid by a layer of rod-like waxes (Cape *et al.*, 1989).

Materials and methods

All sites were located on peaty soils, two of which (Glendalough Forest, in the east of Ireland and Kinnitty Forest, in central Ireland) were located in upland areas and one (Ards Forest Park,

NATO ASI Series, Vol. G 36
Air Pollutants and the Leaf Cuticle
Edited by K. E. Percy et al.
© Springer-Verlag Berlin Heidelberg 1994

in northwestern Ireland) in a coastal lowland area. All sites were sampled in December 1992. Three year classes were sampled from five trees from each site, following Cape (1983).

Twenty pine needles from each year class per tree from each site were placed in a pre-weighed Petri dish. The Petri dishes containing the pine needles were placed in air-tight containers with 100% relative humidity overnight to allow the needles to become fully hydrated. The Petri dishes plus the needles were weighed before being placed in an incubator at 20°C. The Petri dishes were weighed at regular intervals for approximately 60 h. The readings were plotted against time in order to draw up cuticular transpiration weight loss curves.

The contact angles were measured according to Cape *et al*, (1989).

Ten needles per year class, per tree, per site were examined by scanning electron microscopy (SEM). The samples were prepared following Crossley and Fowler (1986). The pine needles were mounted on aluminium stubs, five adaxial surface uppermost and five abaxial surface uppermost. The samples were than coated with 200 nm of gold-palladium in an M-Scope SC-500 sputter coater. The samples were viewed by Hitachi S520 SEM. In order to establish amorphous wax stages the images of the pine needles were examined adapting the method proposed by Thijsse and Baas (1990).

Epicuticular wax extraction was performed according to Cape (1983). Needle area was measured using a Delta-T leaf area meter and a conversion factor of 2.8 (Cannell, 1982) to obtain the true surface area. Regression analysis and T-tests were performed on the resulting data.

Results

For all three sites mean relative water content was plotted against time in order to obtain the cuticular transpiration weight loss curves shown in Figures 1, 2 and 3. It is apparent that needles from year class 2 lost water faster at any given time than needles from either year classes 1 or 3. This trend occurred at all three sites. The data also suggest that samples taken from Kinnitty lost water faster than samples taken from either Glendalough or Ards respectively.

In order to establish if the differences between the year classes and the differences between the sites were significant, the natural logarithmic values of the data were fitted to a straight line and subjected to regression analysis. This analyses revealed at 90% significance Kinnitty differed from the other sites.

The average amounts of wax were expressed both on a dry weight basis and as amount per unit surface area (Tables 1a & 1b). A two-way analysis of variance on site and year class revealed significant differences in wax amount between sites, whether amount was expressed in terms of needle dry weight or needle surface area. However, significant differences between year class

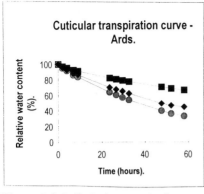
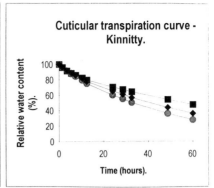

Figures 1 & 2 Cuticular transpiration curve for needles of *Pinus sylvestris* sampled at Ards and Kinnitty. Key to Figures given in Figure 3.

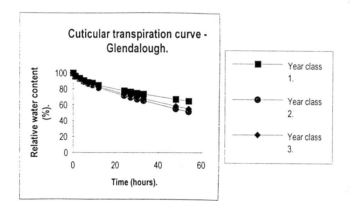

Figure 3 Cuticular transpiration curve for needles of *Pinus sylvestris* sampled at Glendalough.

were only seen for wax % dry weight, where year class 1 had larger proportions of wax than older year classes. There was no significant increase in wax per unit surface area as needles aged.

In all cases the greatest contact angles were recorded from year class 1 samples, indicating a greater degree of microroughness, with a decreasing trend towards samples taken from year class 3. The results show a greater difference in the contact angle between year classes 1 and 2, than between year classes 2 and 3. T-tests revealed that there was no statistical difference between

Table 1   Amounts of surface wax from three year classes of pine needles growing at three
          sites in Ireland: Ard = Ards Forest, Kin = Kiniity, Gle = Glendalough.
          Means followed by the same letter are not significantly different (p > 0.05).

a)   As a proportion of needle dry weight (mg g^{-1})

Site		Year 1	Year 2	Year 3	Mean
Ard	ave	17.2	15.1	15.4	15.8 a
	s.d.	5.0	1.5	0.8	
Kin	ave	15.4	10.2	11.6	12.4 b
	s.d.	2.2	2.0	1.3	
Gle	ave	18.8	15.0	14.8	16.2 a
	s.d.	2.7	9.4	1.2	
Mean		17.1 a	13.4 b	13.8 b	

b)   As a proportion of needle surface area (μg cm^{-2})

Site		Year 1	Year 2	Year 3	Mean
Ard	ave	235	245	231	232 a
	s.d.	5	64	82	
Kin	ave	172	113	147	137 b
	s.d.	47	43	40	
Gle	ave	163	141	187	163 b
	s.d.	28	59	50	
Mean		186 a	166 a	188 a	

year classes from different sites. However, there was a statistical difference at the 95% significance level between year classes 1 and 2 and 1 and 3 at Kinnitty.

Both amorphous and crystalline waxes were observed to varying degrees on all year classes with
the amount of amorphous wax increasing as needles aged. Statistical analysis reveal that there
was no difference between the scores obtained for adaxial and abaxial surfaces. Therefore, the
scores for both surfaces were combined to give an overall score for the particular year class for
the particular site.

There seemed to be a gradual transition with time from stage 1 to stage 5 as regards the wax
morphology (Figure 4). The wax on current-year needles appeared much less eroded, with a
greater percentage cover of crystalline wax, than on needles from either year classes 2 or 3.

Fungal hyphae were observed on very few needles and appeared to be absent from year class 1
samples. The presence of the fungal hyphae may have a dissolving effect on the wax layer (Thijsse
and Baas, 1990).

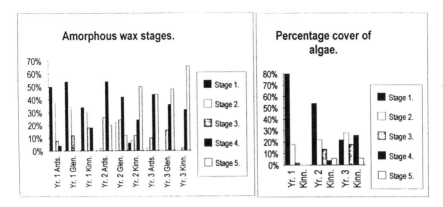

Figure 4   Frequency distribution of amorphous wax stages for three sites and for three year classes. The frequency of stage 1 scorings decreases with the age of the needles while the frequency of stage 5 scorings increases.

Figure 5   Frequency distribution of algal stages for three sites and for three year classes. Stage 1 represents an absence of algal cells and stage 5 represents more than 80% cover of algae. The frequency of stage 1 scorings decrease with age.

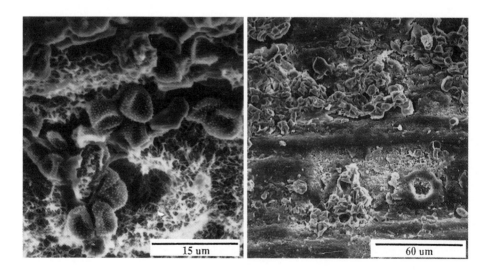

Plate 1   Algal cells obstructing stomata   Plate 2   Algal cells on a 3-year-old needle.

Algal cells were observed on needles sampled at Kinnitty and often blocked the stomata (Plate 1). They were present on all three year classes and often covered large areas of the needle (Plate 2). The presence of these algal cells may possibly be due to exposure to fertiliser dust from surrounding arable land, prolonged humidity or shading.

Discussion

Figures 1 - 3 suggest that under the experimental conditions there was an initial drop in water content followed by a more gradual loss of water. Barnes *et al.* (1990) reported that year class 3 needles lost water faster than year class 2 needles which in turn lost water faster than year class 1 needles. However, this was not the case in the present study, as at all three sites year class 2 needles lost water faster than year class 3 needles. This, in part, may be explained by the weather conditions prevailing during the first 6 months of 1991 before bud break. The average monthly temperatures were slightly lower in the first half of 1991 than for the other two years. There was considerably less rainfall than average and there were fewer hours of sunshine, at all three sites, in May of 1991. These three factors combined may possibly have had an adverse effect on the needles at bud break in the beginning of May, leading to increased rates of cuticular transpiration during the experiment in early 1993.

Needles from the Kinnitty site lost water faster at any given time than needles from the other two sites. This could be due to a combination of factors, including a greater number of frost days per annum at this site and the presence of algal cells which may prevent the stomatal guard cells from closing.

Turunen and Huttunen (1991) reported quantities of wax between 0.93 - 1.14% needle dry weight for present year needles as compared to 1.54 - 1.89% in Ireland. There is clearly more wax on the *Pinus sylvestris* needles in Ireland when compared on a dry weight bases. Cape *et al.* (1989) reported a small decrease in the amounts of wax over time (three year classes were used) when expressed as a percentage of dry weight. The wax yields range from 1.6% of dry weight to 2.5%, with Scottish pine needles consistently yielding the smallest amounts of wax. The range obtained for Ireland was consistent with the European range. Epicuticular wax yields can also be expressed on the bases of surface area. Cape and Fowler (1981) extracted 160 - 200 μgcm^2 epicuticular wax from needles of *Pinus sylvestris* with no decrease with needle age. In the present study the range of extractable wax was recorded to be slightly wider than that reported by Cape and Fowler (1981), ranging between 110 and 240 μgcm^2 with no significant decrease with age.

According to the data presented in this study the contact angle of a water droplet placed on the adaxial surface of needles of *Pinus sylvestris* decreased with needle age, in agreement with the literature. Initially there was a greater decrease represented by a more pronounced difference between year classes 1 and 2 than between year classes 2 and 3. It appeared that the rate of erosion occurred more rapidly once the wax was produced and levelled off as the amorphous stage was reached. Cape *et al.* (1989) reported a decrease in contact angle with needle age after one year's exposure for both Scots pine and Norway spruce; this is consistent with the results recorded by Barnes *et al.* (1990) on Norway spruce and with the results obtained in this study.

As needles aged the most obvious change in morphology, as seen under SEM, was the increasing amount of amorphous wax probably due to natural weathering and exposure. These findings are consistent with the work of Wells and Franich (1977), Crossley and Fowler (1986), Sauter and Voss (1986), Turunen and Huttunen (1991), Thijsse and Baas (1990). It was thought initially that there would be a marked difference between the adaxial and abaxial surfaces of the needles. The abaxial surface is more sheltered and wax deposits were expected to be in better condition, *i.e.*, having a more crystalline structure than the adaxial surface. However, this was not the case and on average both surfaces showed the same percentage cover of amorphous wax. Reports by Sauter and Voss (1986) were contrary to these findings and suggested that the adaxial surface became more heavily eroded. Figure 4 shows a decrease in stage 1 wax with time and an increase in stage 5 waxes.

Fungal hyphae did not invade many of the needles that were investigated during this study and would not seem to play a major role in the overall erosional process of the epicuticular wax. These results are consistent with the results of Turunen and Huttunen (1991) in that fungal hyphae occurred occasionally and had a minor locally eroding effect on the wax structure.

Algal cells were recorded on needles taken from the Kinnitty site only, with increasing amounts as needles aged (Figure 5). The presence of the cells may be the result of shading, prolonged humidity or fertiliser dust from surrounding arable lands. As these cells appeared to block the stomata (Plates 1 and 2) the rate of transpiration may be affected in that water will be lost at a faster rate if the stomata are unable to close properly, which suggests that needles from this site may lose water faster at any given time than the other sites. This may be explained by the higher rates of transpiration observed in Figure 2. The cells may affect the microroughness of the surface which in turn may give a false representation of the contact angle results. The hydrophilic gel surrounding the algal cells could reduce the contact angle. The high scoring of algal cells may account for the lowest contact angle being recorded on year class 3 needles at this site.

Conclusions

The rate of cuticular transpiration was found to be faster for year class 2 needles at all sites, which was probably due to the climatic conditions during the first half of 1991. The needles from the Kinnitty site lost water faster the other two sites, this may be in part due to the colonisation of these needles by algal cells. Pine needles from Ireland yielded similar amounts of extractable wax as their counterparts when expressed on a surface area and dry weight basis. Wettability was found to increase with needle age which is consistent with the literature. There was an increase in the amount of amorphous wax with needle age at all sites due to natural weathering and exposure. Fungal hyphae were present on very few of the samples and did not seem to have a great effect on the wax morphology. Algal cells were recorded on needles from all year classes from the Kinnitty site probably as a result of fertiliser influences, prolonged humidity or shading.

References

Baker, EA (1982) Chemistry and morphology of plant epicuticular waxes *In* The Plant Cuticle. Cutler DF, Alvin KL, Price CE (*eds*) Edward Arnold (publishers) Limited. *pp* 139 - 161

Barnes, JD Eamus, D Davison, AW Ro-Poulsen, H Mortsen, L (1990) Persistent effects of ozone on needle water loss and wettability in Norway Spruce Environ Poll 63: 345-363

Cannell, MCR (1982) World Forest Biomass and Primary Production Data. Academic Press, London. *p* 3

Cape, JN Fowler, D (1981) Changes in epicuticular wax of *Pinus sylvestris* exposed to polluted air. Silva Fennica 15(4): 457-458

Cape, JN (1983) Contact angles of water droplets on needles of Scots Pine growing in polluted atmospheres. New Phytol 93: 293-299

Cape, JN (1986) Effects of air pollution on the chemistry of surface waxes of Scots Pine. Water Air Soil Poll 3: 393-399

Cape JN Paterson, IS Wolfenden, J (1989) Regional variation in the surface properties of Norway Spruce and Scots Pine needles in relation to forest decline. Environ Poll 58: 325-342

Crossley, A Fowler, D (1986) The weathering of Scots Pine epicuticular wax in polluted and clean air. New Phytol 103: 207-218

Guthardt-Goerg, MS (1986) Epicuticular wax of needles of *Pinus cembra*, *Pinus sylvestris* and *Picea abies*. Eur J For Path 16: 400-408

Juniper, BE Jeffree, CE (1983) Plant Surfaces. Edward Arnold Publishers Limited

Sauter, JJ Voss, J-U (1986) SEM observations on the structural degradation of epistomatal waxes in *Picea abies* L. Karst and its possible role in 'Fichtensterben'. Eur J For Path 16: 408-423

Thijsse, G Baas, P (1990) 'Natural' and NH3-induced variation in epicuticular needle wax morphology of *Pseudotsuga menziesii* (Mirb.) Franco. Trees 4: 111-119

Turunen, M Huttunen, S (1990) A review of the response of epicuticular wax of conifer needles to air pollution J Environ Qual 19: 35-45

Turunen, M Huttunen, S (1991) Effects of simulated acid rain on the epicuticular wax of Scots Pine under northerly conditions. Can J Bot 69: 412-419

Wells, LG Franich, RA (1977) Morphology of epicuticular wax on primary needles of *Pinus radiata* seedlings. NZJ Bot 15: 525-529

Characteristics and Geographical Distribution of the Changes in Scots Pine Needle Surfaces in Finnish Lapland and the Kola Peninsula

Minna Turunen, Satu Huttunen[1], Jukka Lamppu[1], and Paivi Huhtala[1]
Arctic Centre
Univ. of Lapland
P.O. Box 122
SF-96101 Rovaniemi
Finland

Abstract

Effects of air pollution and a variety of other environmental factors on physicochemical characteristics of Scots pine (*Pinus sylvestris* L.) needle surfaces were studied in an extensive field investigation, comprising 114 sample plots (356 trees) on transect lines extending from the Nikel and Monchegorsk industrial complexes on the Kola Peninsula, Russia, across Finnish Lapland. Preliminary results from some of the investigated physicochemical parameters are presented in this paper. Condition of epicuticular wax structures, occurrence of particle deposition, fungal hyphae and insect damage on needle surfaces were investigated quantitatively under a scanning electron microscope, and needle wettability was measured in terms of contact angles. The investigated parameters showed great variability in terms of pollution, climate and ecology. Both the epicuticular wax erosion rate and needle wettability changed significantly faster during the first year on pines in Kola Peninsula, Russia (transect 1, extending to Monchegorsk) than on pines in Finland (transects 1,2,3,7). Site dependent effects, *e.g.*, variation in ecological conditions of the sample plot, could be diminished by investigating the rate of change in the physicochemical parameter of pine needle surface during the first year, instead of using absolute values from different needle age classes.

Introduction

The acclimation of conifers to changing environmental factors or stresses involves both short-term physiological response and long-term physiological, structural and morphological modifications. One of the first targets is the needle surface. Observations on physicochemical characteristics of needle surfaces have shown air pollution induced erosion of epicuticular waxes (Huttunen and Laine, 1983), delayed development of cuticles, deformed stomatal complexes, and increased wettability of needle surfaces (Turunen and Huttunen, 1991).

Sulphur and heavy metal pollution emitted by the Monchegorsk and Nikel industrial complexes in the Kola Peninsula, Russia, represent a serious threat to Finnish boreal forest ecosystems. This investigation is a part of the multidisciplinary 5-year (1990-1995) Lapland Forest Damage Project, subproject Stress and Damage Symptoms of Scots pines.

---

[1]Dept. of Botany, Univ. of Oulu, SF-90570 Oulu, Finland

NATO ASI Series, Vol. G 36
Air Pollutants and the Leaf Cuticle
Edited by K. E. Percy et al.
© Springer-Verlag Berlin Heidelberg 1994

Objectives of this investigation are the following: 1) to characterize stress and damage symptoms of Scots pine needle surfaces and their geographical distribution in Finnish Lapland and the Kola Peninsula, and 2) to test the applicability of the changes in physicochemical parameters on pine needle surfaces to ecological monitoring in large field investigations. This paper presents preliminary results from this investigation.

Material and methods

Research area and sampling

Scots pine (*Pinus sylvestris* L.) needle samples were collected from 107 plots in Finland and 7 plots in Russia along transect lines extending from the Nikel and Monchegorsk industrial complexes on the Kola Peninsula across Finnish Lapland. The sample plot system was established by the Lapland Forest Damage Project (Mikkola and Nöjd, 1992) (Figure 1). The plots were situated in a dry heath forest, with pines aged 50-200 years as the dominant tree species. Needle samples were taken from September to November 1990 from a height of 4-6 m on the west and east-facing aspects of the trees.

The area is characterized by varying ecological conditions possessing features of both a continental and a maritime climate, and varying geological patterns. According to Kalela (1961), the research area represents principally the northern boreal coniferous forest zone, but the northernmost parts belong to the northern boreal mountain birch woodland zone. Duration of the growing season (days with mean temperature $>+5°C$) in the research area varies between 115-145 days, and annual precipitation is 500-650 mm (Atlas of Finland, 1987, 1988). The Kola Peninsula is characterized by the fjel chain from Saariselka to Hiipina (1200 m a.s.l.) and Laplanskiej Biosphere Reserve fjels. Largest lakes are Imandra and Lovosero. The mean temperature in January is -8°C on coastal and -13°C in inland sites. In July the mean temperatures are respectively +8°C and + 13°C. Annual precipitation on the Kola Peninsula is about 401 mm. Sudden rapid weather changes are typical.

Air quality measurements have revealed that SO_2 and heavy metal emissions from the Kola Peninsula are episodic. Annual and monthly average values of pollutants are not high, but short-term concentration peaks of SO_2, (hourly averages over 400 gm^{-3}), and particle deposition are characteristic in Finnish Lapland when air arrives from easterly and southerly directions. During northern and western winds, values are close to the detection limit 0.4 gm^{-3} (Virkkula *et al.*, 1992; Tuovinen and Laurila, 1992).

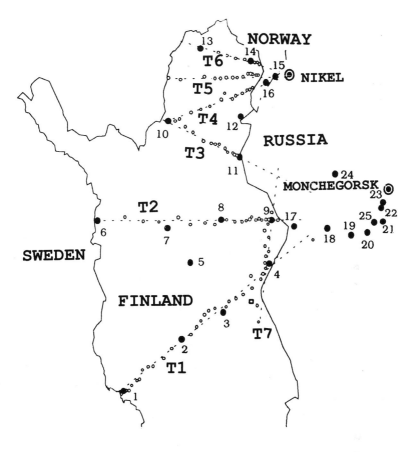

Figure 1   The research area and transect lines with permanent sample plots.

Study parameters

For this investigation 356 pines were investigated (three pines per plot in Finland and five pines per plot in Russia). Visibly undamaged needles from the two most recent needle age classes (c = current, c+1 = 1-year-old needles) were examined under a scanning electron microscope (SEM) at the Institute of Electron Optics of the University of Oulu. Air-dried (room temperature) needle samples were covered with gold-palladium (45 nm) using sputter equipment (Polaron 5100), and photographed (exposure 45 s) under a SEM (JEOL JSM-6400, 12 kV). Needle surfaces were rated according to the following classes (Turunen *et al.*, 1992):

1. *Epicuticular wax structures* (distribution of crystalline waxes in epistomatal area)
Class I   Distribution of crystalline waxes 100 %
Class II Distribution of crystalline waxes 71-100 %
Class III Distribution of crystalline waxes 31-70 %
Class IV Distribution of crystalline waxes 0-30 %
Class V Distribution of crystalline waxes 0 %

2. *Occurrence of particulate deposition*
Class I   No particles inside a 400X micrograph area
Class II 1-5 particles
Class III 5-20 or more particles, but their distribution is less than 25 % of the micro-
          graph area
Class IV More than 20 particles covering over 25 % of the micrograph area

3. *Occurrence of fungal hyphae*
Class I   No fungal hyphae or spores inside a 400X micrograph area
Class II Single spores and/or stumps of fungal hyphae
Class III Numerous spores and/or fungal hyphae, changes in wax structure, holes may
          occur in the cuticle as a consequence of extrusion of hyphae
Class IV 400X micrograph area fully covered with fungal hyphae, wax structures have
          become amorphous, holes may occur in the cuticle

4. *Occurrence of insect damage*
Class I   No signs of insects or their marks
Class II Insects or their remnants (holes in cuticle, eggs, stylet sheets, cases, skins,
          webs), coverage less than 20 % of the 400X micrograph area
Class III Insects or their remnants, coverage over 20 %

Microanalysis of the particulate deposits on the needle surfaces was performed by JEOL JCXA 733 microprobe analyzer equipped with LINK AN10/85 energy dispersive analyzer (EDS). Needle wettability was determined by contact angle measurement using the method of Cape

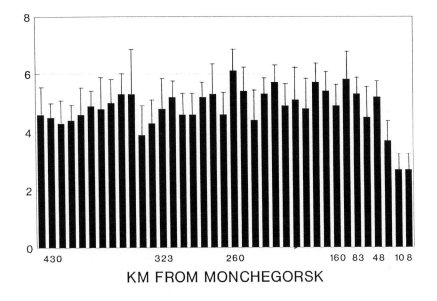

Figure 2   Number of needle age classes in Scots pines on the plots of transect 1.

(1983). Statistical analysis was performed by ANOVA and GLM (General Linear Models, simple regression) tests.

Results

<u>Visible damages</u>

Visible and microscopical parameters, and contact angles showed great variability in terms of the pollution, climate and ecological conditions of the area. Pines growing on plots 8-38 km from the Monchegorsk industrial complex had only 2- to 3-year-old needles left, whereas in Finland the average number of needle age classes was 5-6 (Figure 2). Pine needles around Monchegorsk were characterized by needle tip chlorosis and necrosis. The older the needles, the more evident were the differences between plots (Turunen *et al.*, 1992).

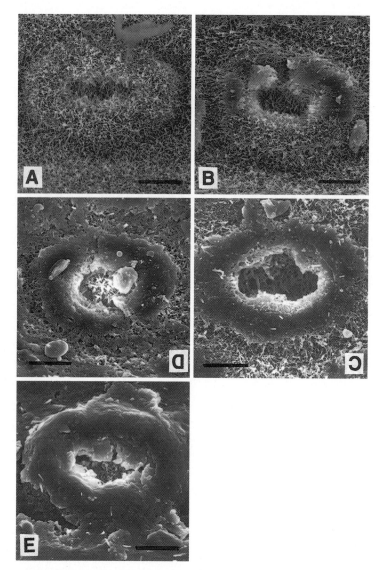

Figure 3a-e SEM micrographs from different stages of epistomatal wax of Scots pine needles from transect 1. A. Class I, current needle, 377 km from Monchegorsk, B. Class II, current needle, 343 km from Monchegorsk, C. Class III, 1-year-old needle, 384 km from Monchegorsk. D. Class IV, 1-year-old needle, 416 km from Monchegorsk, E. Class V, 1-year-old needle, 280 km from Monchegorsk. See the classification from material and methods. Bar-length 10 μm.

Microscopical parameters

Quantitative evaluation of needle surfaces was performed under SEM (Turunen *et al.*, 1992). Figure 3 presents micrographs of different classes of epistomatal wax structures from transect 1. One-year-old pine needles exhibited significantly (F=31.87, p=0.0001, df=1) more degraded epicuticular wax structure (expressed as a mean class value) than current needles. The mean

Table 1   Statistical differences in physicochemical parameters measured from the plots in Finland (transects 1,2,3,7) and Russia (transect 1). GLM-test (df=84).

Parameter	Needle age class	Finland x (std)	Russia x (std)	F	p
Stage of waxes[1]	c	2.1 (0.4)	1.6 (0.2)	16.30	0.0001
	c+1	3.2 (0.4)	3.0 (0.6)	0.74	0.3913
Wax erosion index	(c+1)-c	1.0 (0.3)	1.4 (0.7)	8.77	0.0040
Fungal hyphae[1]	c	1.4 (0.2)	1.3 (0.1)	1.59	0.2104
	c+1	1.5 (0.2)	1.5 (0.2)	0.01	0.9337
Insect damage[1]	c	1.0 (0.1)	1.0 (0.0)	0.83	0.3657
	c+1	1.0 (0.1)	1.0 (0.0)	0.78	0.3794
Particles[1]	c	2.1 (0.2)	2.1 (0.1)	0.00	0.9981
	c+1	2.3 (0.2)	2.6 (0.1)	11.75	0.0009
Deformed stomatal complexes[2]	c	1.3 (0.8)	1.4 (0.9)	0.09	0.7667
	c+1	0.9 (0.7)	0.5 (0.2)	3.04	0.0849
Contact angles	c	75.7 (6.1)	85.2 (1.4)	16.35	0.0001
	c+1	71.7 (6.1)	76.6 (3.5)	4.60	0.0349
Needle wettability index	c-(c+1)	4.2 (1.9)	8.6 (2.9)	32.59	0.0001

[1] mean class value, [2] sum of four types of deformed stomatal complexes (Turunen and Huttunen, 1991)

distribution of crystalline waxes in epistomatal area of current needles was 71-100 %, whereas in 1-year-old needles it was reduced to 31-70 %.

The condition of epicuticular wax structures of current pine needles in Kola Peninsula (transect 1) was better than in Finland (transect 1,2,3,7) (Table 1), although the pines were strongly characterized by necrotic needle tips (Turunen et al., 1992). The phenomena may be explained by the acute damage physiology of the pines near the industrial plants, age of the pines, and climatic and soil factors within the area.

To diminish the site-dependent variation, the wax erosion index ((c+1)-c) was calculated to describe the erosion rate during the first year of needle growth. The epicuticular wax erosion rate during one year was faster in Kola Peninsula than in Finland (F=8.77, p=0.0040, df=84), being quicker the closer the industrial sources were. Eight km south-west from Monchegorsk, the first year's rate of deterioration of waxes was two and a half classes per year, whereas in Finland the mean deterioration rate was about one class per year (Figure 4, Table 1).

The amount of particle deposition, and fungal spores and hyphae increased slightly as the needles aged. Surfaces of 1-year-old needles in the immediate vicinity of Monchegorsk had more particles than needles in Finnish plots, and the elemental composition of particles was characterized by Fe, Ni, Cu and S (Turunen et al., 1992).

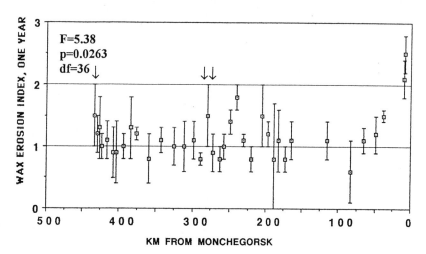

Figure 4   Wax erosion indexes on the plots of transect 1. Wax erosion index describes the change in the stage of epicuticular wax structure during the first year (difference in the mean wax class between c+1 and c needles). ↓= steel mill, ↓↓ =pulp mill.In Finland the values are means of three pines per plot, and in Russia, means of five pines per plot.

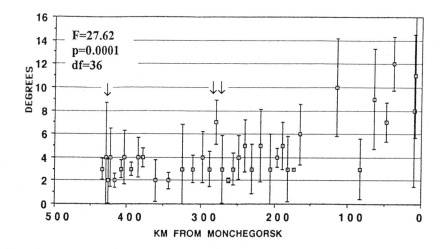

Figure 5   Needle wettability indexes on the plots of transect 1. Needle wettability index describes the change in the contact angles during the first year (difference in the contact angles between c and c+1 needles). ↓ =steel mill, ↓↓ =pulp mill. In Finland the values are means of three pines per plot, and in Russia means of five pines per plot.

Needle wettability

Contact angles on needle surfaces varied from 61 to 88 degrees and were lower for 1-year-old needles than for current needles (F=21.77, p=0.0001, df=1). Contact angles measured from adaxial and abaxial sides of the needles correlated very well in both needle age classes. For current needles, y=10.2+0.879x, r^2=0.92, and for 1-year-old needles, y=7.94+0.883x, r^2=0.89.

There was a good relationship between the contact angles and the mean wax class, as the condition of epicuticular wax structures explained 85% of the variation in contact angles in Kola Peninsula (y=93.3+5.53x, r^2=0.85). However, the distribution of crystalline waxes alone does not explain the needle wettability which is also determined by the wax chemistry (predominantly by the presence of 10-nonacosanol in wax tubes), or by particulate deposition (Cape, 1983; Percy *et al.*, 1993).

The change in needle wettability over one year (needle wettability index, c-(c+1)) was significantly greater, and showed a steeper gradient with higher standard deviations in Kola Peninsula when compared to that in Finland (F=32.59, p=0.0001, df=84). The mean increase in contact angle over one year was 9° in Kola Peninsula, whereas in Finland (transect 1,2,3,7) the mean increase was 4° (Figure 5, Table 1). When Kola Peninsula plots are exluded from transect 1, neither the wettability index nor the wax erosion index showed an increasing gradient towards pollution sources on transect 1 in Finland. Some evidence was found for the effects of local emission sources (steel mill, pulp mill) and populated areas on these parameters (Figure 4,5).

Discussion

Erosion rate was significantly faster and needle wettability change greater during the first year of needle growth, and showed a large increase in Kola Peninsula when compared to that in Finland. However, when Kola Peninsula plots were excluded, no gradient in the effects on transect 1 in Finland could be observed, although evidence was found for the effect of local emission sources and populated regions. In this investigation, the rate of change during the first needle year in two physicochemical parameters of needle surfaces proved to be better indicator of SO_2 and heavy metal pollution than absolute values from different needle age classes.

According to several field investigations and experimental exposures to pollutants, the condition of epicuticular wax structures of polluted conifer needles has generally deteriorated (see Turunen and Huttunen, 1990), and needle wettability increased (Cape, 1983; Cape *et al.*, 1989; Turunen and Huttunen, 1991; Percy *et al.*, 1993). There may be several reasons for higher contact angles and better wax classes in current pine needles in the Kola Peninsula, when compared to needles in Finland. Firstly, the pines are younger in Kola Peninsula, and their response may have been different. The wax synthesis of the current needles may have been changed so that the pines near the industrial sources try to protect the elongating needles by producing more crystalline-type waxes. Raitio (1992) observed higher nitrogen, phosphorous and potassium concentrations in the pine needles near Monchegorsk which might have been caused by the younger age of the trees and the smaller number of needle age classes.

The main reason for higher needle wettability, and wide distribution of crystalline waxes on needle surfaces in Kola Peninsula may be, however, the climate (fogs, rains) and even the changed microclimate of polluted areas near the emission source. A wide range of natural environmental factors (light intensity, photoperiod, temperature, water stress, nutrient status) influence the development and degradation of plant surfaces (*e.g.*, Cape and Percy, 1993). Percy *et al.* (1993) observed that the trees exposed to the greatest amount of fog had the largest wax deposits and greatest amounts of secondary alcohols and alkyl esters. In Kola Peninsula, there is no grazing pressure by reindeer and, especially in the plots near the border, the ground lichen cover (*Cladina* sp.) is 10-15 cm thicker than in Finland. By accumulating air pollutants and changing the microclimate of the soil, thick lichen cover in the ground could provide protection for the soil and pine roots.

In large field studies, simultaneous evaluation of site and other environmental factors influencing needle surface is difficult. These preliminary results will be further evaluated along with other study parameters and ecological factors.

References

Atlas of Finland (1987) Appendix 131 Climate, National Board of Survey, Geographical Society of Finland 31 *p*

Atlas of Finland (1988) Appendix 141-143 Biogeography, nature conservation, Geographical Society of Finland 32 *p*

Cape JN (1983) Contact angles of water droplets on needles of Scots pine (*Pinus sylvestris*) growing in polluted atmospheres. New Phytol 93: 293-299

Cape JN, Paterson IS, Wolfenden J (1989) Regional variation in surface properties of Norway spruce and Scots pine needles in relation to forest decline. Environ Pollut 58: 325-342

Cape JN, Percy KE (1993) Environmental influences on the development of spruce needle cuticles. New Phytol 125: 787-799.

Huttunen S, Laine K (1983) Effects of air-borne pollutants on the surface wax structure of *Pinus sylvestris* needles. Ann Bot Fenn 20: 79-86

Kalela A (1961) Waldvegetationszonen Finnlands und ihre klimatische Paralleltypen. Archs Soc Fenn "Vanamo" 16 suppl: 65-83

Mikkola K, Nöjd P (1992) Itä-Lapin metsävaurioprojektin koealajarjestelmä. Abstract: Sampling method in the Lapland Forest Damage Project. *In* Kauhanen H, Varmola M (*eds*) Itä-Lapin metsävaurioprojektin väliraportti. The Lapland Forest Damage Project. Interim report. Metsäntutkimuslaitoksen tiedonantoja 413: 13-17

Percy KE, Jagels R, Marden S, McLaughlin CK, Carlisle J (1993) Quantity, chemistry, and wettability of epicuticular waxes on needles of red spruce along a fog-acidity gradient. Can J For Res 23: 1472-1479

Raitio H (1992) The foliar chemical composition of Scots pines in Finnish Lapland and on the Kola Peninsula. *In* Tikkanen E, Varmola M, Katermaa T (*eds*) Symposium on the state of the environment and environmental monitoring in northern Fennoscandia and the Kola Peninsula. Oct 6-8 1992. Arctic Centre Publications 4: 226-231

Tuovinen JP, Laurila T (1992) Key aspects of sulphur pollution in northernmost Europe. *In* Tikkanen E, Varmola M, Katermaa T (*eds*) Symposium on the state of the environment and environmental monitoring in northern Fennoscandia and the Kola Peninsula. Oct 6-8 1992 Arctic Centre Publications 4: 37-40

Turunen M, Huttunen S (1990) A Review of the response of epicuticular wax of conifer needles to air pollution J Environ Qual 19: 35-45

Turunen M, Huttunen S (1991) Effect of simulated acid rain on the epicuticular wax of Scots pine needles under northerly conditions. Can J Bot 69: 412-419

Turunen M, Huttunen S, Back J, Koponen J, Huhtala P (1992) Needle damage in the Scots pines of Lapland and the Kola Peninsula *In* Tikkanen E, Varmola M, Katermaa T (*eds*) Symposium on the state of the environment and environmental monitoring in northern Fennoscandia and the Kola Peninsula. Oct 6-8 1992 Arctic Centre Publications 4: 235-239

Virkkula A, Mäkinen M, Hillamo R (1992) Atmospheric concentrations of aerosols and gaseous pollutants in the Finnish Arctic *In* Tikkanen E, Varmola M, Katermaa T (*eds*) Symposium on the state of the environment and environmental monitoring in northern Fennoscandia and the Kola Peninsula. Oct 6-8 1992 Arctic Centre Publications 4: 43-45

Forest Health Monitoring by the Canadian Forest Service: Now and the Future

J. Peter Hall
Science and Sustainable Development Directorate
Canadian Forest Service - HQ
Natural Resources Canada
351, blvd St-Joseph, Hull, Québec, Canada K1A 1G5

Abstract

In 1984, the Canadian Forest Service initiated a national forest health monitoring program, the Acid Rain National Early Warning System (ARNEWS), to monitor the health of the forest and determine the effects of acid rain and regional air pollutants on the forest. Monitoring is done by personnel of the Forest Insect and Disease Survey, who are experienced in the evaluation of forest health. They assess trees in permanent sample plots for forest damage and identify the causes. Causes of tree mortality are also determined. If damage is found for which no apparent cause is evident, research is initiated to determine the source of the damage.

To date, ARNEWS has reported on the health of 18 conifer and 9 hardwood species from across Canada, including areas known to receive some of the highest levels of atmospheric pollution in Canada. Results indicate that there is no large-scale decline in the health of our forests and, where pollution-like symptoms were observed, they could usually be accounted for by natural factors. Tree mortality in these natural stands is also normal.

However, the monitoring system depends on being able to recognize damage and to determine the cause. The more easily this can be done, the more efficacious is the system. As our researchers assess the trees, they need to know what all type of damage looks like since many pollution symptoms are easily confused with natural effects. The research done on leaf cuticles should help expand this knowledge base.

Introduction

Canada's forests are a valuable economic and sociological resource whose sustainability is essential to our well-being. To ensure sustainability forest managers need to know if forests are healthy and, if they are not, what is causing the problem? Concerns about forest health in the face of environmental change led the Canadian Forest Service to establish the Acid Rain National Early Warning System (ARNEWS) in 1984. There have been few forest declines in Canada and little evidence that pollutants in high concentrations are affecting the forest. Stands showing classic effects of pollutants occur around strong point sources of heavy metals, fluorides, sulfates and nitrates.

It is primarily the hardwood/mixedwood forests in southern Canada that are exposed to poten-tially damaging levels of pollution. These forests cover 15 million ha and are some of the most

NATO ASI Series, Vol. G 36
Air Pollutants and the Leaf Cuticle
Edited by K. E. Percy et al.
© Springer-Verlag Berlin Heidelberg 1994

productive in the country and the most heavily used and so have raised the most concern. They are exposed to levels of sulfate deposition (20 kg/ha/yr) known to cause damage to aquatic systems.

Biological systems respond to a complex of environmental factors rather than to a single factor such as 'air pollution'. Other stresses affect forests, with such large impacts that subtle responses such as pollution are lost in the 'noise' of the data. Consequently, monitoring biological responses to pollutant deposition in the field, is very difficult. An alternative approach to monitoring was to assess the state of the health of the forest, using a common set of measurements taken on permanent sample plots established by the Forest Insect and Disease Survey (FIDS) of the Canadian Forest Service. FIDS has provided an annual national overview of forest conditions in their survey of the 220 million hectares of productive forest for nearly 60 years.

This national biomonitoring network was designed to detect early signs of the effects of acid rain on Canada's forests to enable action to be taken to forestall anticipated damage.

Objectives

The objectives of ARNEWS are to detect damage to forest trees and soils caused by air pollutants by identifying the damage sustained by Canadian forests that is not attributable to natural causes or management practices, and to monitor over the long term, vegetation and soils to detect changes attributable to acid deposition and other pollutants in representative forest ecosystems.

ARNEWS consists of about 150 permanent sample plots, mostly in eastern Canada where pollution levels are highest. Attempts were made to monitor and assess commercially important forest types in each province.

Most ARNEWS plots are located in semi-mature, natural forests, where the number of trees would normally be expected to decline at 1-2% annually from competition as the stand matures. Mortality in excess of this is a result of natural factors such as insect or disease damage, drought or windstorms, *etc.* If severe enough, mortality can also result from pollution damage.

Methods

Several types of measurements are made:

- Descriptive measurements include slope, aspect and forest cover type.
- At 5-year intervals, growth, crown structure and density, and chemical composition of foliage and soil are measured.
- Annual measurements are made on tree condition, defoliation, and the presence of

DETAILED TREE MEASUREMENTS

A. *One+ assessments/growing season*
1. Acid rain symptoms
2. Insect and disease conditions
3. Seed production (optional)

B. *Annual assessments*
1. Tree mortality
2. Tree condition
3. Acid rain symptoms

C. *Every 5 years*
1. Radial growth
2. Vertical growth
3. Crown structure and density
4. Foliage nutrients
5. Soil chemistry

Tree condition classification for conifers

01 = Healthy and no defoliation.
02 = Healthy and only current defoliation.
03 = Current and some older foliage damaged, total defoliation less than 25%.
04 = 26–50% total defoliation.
05 = 51–75% total defoliation.
06 = 76–90% total defoliation.
07 = More than 90% total defoliation.

Tree condition classification for hardwoods

01 = Normal healthy tree.
02 = Foliage thin, off-colour, particularly in the upper crown,no bare twigs or branches.
03 = Dead twigs present but no dead branches. Dead twigs occur at the ends of the branches, usually in the top of the crown about 0.5 to 1.0 m from the edge of the crown. In this and subsequent categories the foliage is usually, but not necessarily, weak.
04 = Dead branches present on up to 25% of the crown.
05 = Dead branches present on up to 50% of the crown.
06 = More than 50% of the crown is dead but some living branches still present on the tree.
07 = More than 50% of the crown is dead. No living branches present except small adventitious ones, usually at the base of the crown or on the stem.

insects and diseases. Insects and diseases are surveyed at various times of the year to detect all major forest pests.

The trees in the plots are assessed visually; sampling and detailed measurements requiring hand-held branch samples are made on off-plot trees to ensure that trees in the plot are not disturbed. Insects and diseases are identified and their levels of damage are determined.

The health of the tree crown in conifers is assessed as the percentage of foliage missing, for whatever reason, from the 'normal' foliage complement of the tree. This takes into account the natural loss of needles as a twig matures. The retention of needles by conifers is measured as the percentage of a full complement for each age-class on the branch. The crown condition classification in hardwoods integrates foliage loss with the proportion of dead twigs and branches in the crown.

The strategy of the ARNEWS program is to detect early signs of damage to forests by determining the causes of the damage, and to monitor the long-term changes in vegetation and soils. Because the symptoms of air pollution damage are not highly specific, they frequently resemble damage from other causes. The critical part of the whole process is the detection of damage symptoms and determination of the causes. The experience of FIDS field technicians trained to distinguish these symptoms from abnormal climatic conditions, nutrient deficiencies, and the effects of insects and diseases is crucial in the separation of the effects of normal forest damage from those of air pollution. The ability of FIDS to call on a cadre of forest health specialists further enhances the reliability of the system.

Tree mortality, tree condition, and the type and degree of foliar damage, including any symptoms of air pollution are reported annually. Possible symptoms of air pollution are compared with known symptoms of emission toxicity on vegetation.

Many trees assessed as part of ARNEWS have been stressed by weather conditions, insects, diseases, and other natural processes in forest ecosystems. Individual trees are altered by stress and so become susceptible to insect and disease organisms that attack and may kill them. Usually forest ecosystems are not permanently damaged and recover to a state resembling their original condition. It is usually the interaction of several abiotic and biotic factors that produces an unhealthy forest, rather than the effect of a single factor. It is in this context that ARNEWS data are interpreted.

Conclusions

Results to date show that mortality was generally in the normal range of 1-2% and was attributed to identifiable stresses. In 1992, of over 8500 trees assessed, mortality was 1.22%; among conifers, 1.33% and among hardwoods, 0.81%. When mortality figures were exceeded, causes of mortality were apparent. There appears to be no evidence of large-scale decline in the health of Canadian forests. Little evidence was found of damage caused by pollution, apart from the damage on birch in southern New Brunswick.

During the past decade, higher mortality rates of jack pine, balsam fir, white and yellow birch, and trembling aspen were attributed to drought, frost, windstorms, winter storms, root rots, spruce budworm, and other defoliators. Insects caused defoliation on most species in all regions, the greatest damage occurring on conifers in the Maritimes. Mortality in both conifers and hardwoods occurred in Ontario from drought and blowdown. Trees were weakened by decay, and weakened trees were invaded by Armillaria (*Armillaria* spp.) root rot and other secondary organisms. Drought continues to play an important role the health of white birch and sugar maple.

In the Maritime provinces, ozone damage-like symptoms have been observed on white spruce, black spruce, balsam fir, yellow birch, sugar maple, red maple, and white birch. These symptoms were needle flecking, chlorosis, and marginal discoloration. The damage on white birch has been duplicated by exposing birch seedlings to ambient levels of ozone and observing similar symptoms.

Observations in 1992 suggest that drought, which in previous years played a major role in tree health, has largely disappeared as a cause of deterioration as rainfall levels approached or exceeded normal amounts. There has been some recovery from the effects of spruce budworm damage on balsam fir and from pear thrips on sugar maple. The leaf browning and dieback damage on white birch along the Bay of Fundy has abated. The healthier trees are showing some recovery and the more heavily damaged ones continue to deteriorate.

The conclusions from ARNEWS are supported by results from other surveys in the FIDS system, enhancing the credibility of the results.

An early warning system to detect and monitor conditions remains an essential part of our commitment to the sustainability of Canada's forests.

References

Bormann FH (1985) Air pollution stresses on forests. Bioscience 35(7): 434-441
D'Eon SP, Power JM 919890 The Acid Rain National Early Warning System (ARNEWS) plot network. Forestry Canada, Petawawa Natl. For. Inst., Chalk River, Ont. Inf. Rep. PI-X-91 119 *p*
Fraser GA (1989) Acid rain control: Potential commercial forestry benefits to Canada. Forestry Canada, Ottawa, Ont Inf Rep E-X-42. 31 *p*

Garner JHB, Pagano T, and Cowling E (1989) An evaluation of the role of ozone, acid deposition and other airborne pollutants in the forests of eastern North America. USDA For Serv Southeast For Expt Sta, Asheville, NC, Gen Tech Rep SE-59. 172 *p*

Hall JP (1991) ARNEWS Annual Report 1990. Forestry Canada, Ottawa, Ont, Inf Rep ST-X-1. 17 *p*

Hall JP (1993) Acid Rain National Early Warning System (ARNEWS) Annual Report 1992. Forestry Canada, Ottawa, Ont, Inf Rep ST-X-71. *in press*

Hall JP, Addison PA (1991) Response to air pollution: ARNEWS assesses the health of Canada's forests. Forestry Canada, Ottawa, Ont, Inf Rep DPC-X-34. 13 *p*

Hall JP, Pendrel B (1992) ARNEWS Annual Report. (1991) For Can, Sci and Sustainable Devel Dir, Ottawa, Ontario. Inf Rep ST-X-5

Magasi LP (1988) Acid rain national early warning system: Manual on plot establishment and monitoring. Can For Ser, Ottawa, Ont, Inf Rep DPC-X-25

Magasi LP (1989) White birch deterioration in the Bay of Fundy region, New Brunswick 1979-1988, Forestry Canada - Maritimes Region, Fredericton, NB, Inf Rep M-X-177

Malhotra SS, Blauel RA (1980) Diagnosis of air pollutant and natural stress symptoms on forest vegetation in western Canada. Can For Serv, North For Res Centre, Edmonton, Alta, Inf Rep NOR-X-228. 84 p

Manion PD (1981) Tree disease concepts. Prentice-Hall Inc, Englewood Cliffs, NJ

National Acid Precipitation Assessment Program (NAPAP) (nd) Diagnosing injury to eastern forest trees. NAPAP Forest Responses Program, Vegetation Survey Research Cooperative, USDA, USFS 122 *p*

SECTION IV - RAPPORTEURS' REPORTS

SESSION 1
Chairperson: J.N. Cape (U.K.)
Rapporteur: S. Godzik (Poland)

Compared to the importance of stomata in the uptake of trace gases, the role of the non-stomatal part was rather underestimated.

Topics presented and discussed during this session covered three separate fields:

1. Current state of knowledge on the plant cuticle.
2. Deposition processes - both modelling and measurements.
3. Effects of deposited trace gases and elevated UV-B radiation on the cuticle.

A general conclusion concerning the first question is that our present fundamental knowledge about the biosynthesis, chemical composition, and structure of the plant cuticle was gained in the 1960s and '70s. No major progress has been made since then. An exception is the identification of cutan in 1986, a non-saponifiable component of the plant cuticle (in a narrower sense).

When modelling deposition of air pollutants (trace gases) to plants, two groups of parameters, at least, have been underestimated:

a. chemical properties of air pollutants (trace gases);
b. physico-chemical properties of the plant surface.

Examples of data presented during this session are:

- 90% of nitric acid vapours are deposited to the cuticle, even when stomata are open;
- a higher proportion of N^{15} is deposited to twigs than leaves, when NH_4NO_3 was applied.

Another important question is the level of biological organisation, which should be used as a basis for modelling. Scaling up to the canopy level and scaling down to the chemical level from the leaf, as a basis, seems to be an appropriate proposal.

Minor changes in spruce needle wax composition have been found after ozone exposure of clonal material and mature trees. There was similar variability of clonal material and mature trees (from a stand) in response to treatments and the physical environment (based on analysis of wax chemical composition). Both these conclusions are of great importance from a theoretical and practical point of view. It remains, however, to be determined if a similar patter of response is of more general value, or is restricted to wax chemical composition only. Experiments carried out with elevated UV-B intensity have shown that an increase of 20% above the present-day level may induce direct effects (necrotic leaf injuries) in more sensitive species.

NATO ASI Series, Vol. G 36
Air Pollutants and the Leaf Cuticle
Edited by K. E. Percy et al.
© Springer-Verlag Berlin Heidelberg 1994

Data presented later at this workshop provided additional arguments for the importance of the leaf surface, for both the interaction between pollutants, and the sites of direct effects on plants.

SESSION 2
Chairperson: M. Riederer (Germany)
Rapporteur: M. Turunen (Finland)

Gerhard Kerstiens (University of Lancaster, UK) gave an overview of studies on transport rates of gases across isolated cuticles. Some of the key questions of his research are: Why are some cuticles more permeable than others? Can gas uptake through cuticles be predicted well? and Do air pollutants affect water permeability of cuticles? It was found that long-term exposure to a wide range of air pollutants generally did not have any effect on water permeability of different broadleaved tree species. Effects on water permeability were restricted to visibly damaged leaves or to experiments where the general growing conditions were unfavorable to plants. Mel Tyree (United States Forest Service, USA) talked about the transfer of ions across the cuticle and the electropotential differences. It is not yet clear, if the main leaching pathway of nutrient cations involves transcuticular permeation. Mel Tyree's recent work on ion transport in isolated cuticles promises to provide answers for the mechanism and rate of ion permeation in cuticles.

Two presentations reported and discussed the effects of open-top chamber fumigations with gaseous air pollutants, predominantly CO_2, on characteristics of leaf surfaces. Barbel Prugel's (Institut nationale de la Recherche agronomique, France) preliminary results indicated that the total quantity of waxes decreased, and the amount of acids and 10-nonacosanol increased in spruce needle waxes after CO_2 treatment. There also seemed to exist effects of CO_2 + other pollutants, but no explanation could be made yet. Carolyn McQuattie (United States Forest Service, USA) reported preliminary results in cuticular membrane ultrastructure of yellow poplar and white pine seedlings from an experiment with O_3 and CO_2 treatments. In yellow poplar, the thinnest membranes were found in leaves from 2 X ambient O_3 treatment, but no differences in membrane thickness were observed in white pine.

There is not much evidence on the relationship between the structural or chemical changes in leaf cuticles and the physiological response of the plant. Chris Jeffree (University of Edinburgh, UK) reported that exposing beech leaves to wind damage increases the uptake of (^{35}S) sulphate compared with beech leaves grown in sheltered locations. Stefan Godzik (Institute for Ecology of Industrial Areas, Poland) had a presentation on the effects of Scots pine wax structure on water loss and uptake of $^{14}CO_2$ and $^{35}SO_2$. It was found that abrasion of current needle surfaces destroying the wax structure led to increase in water loss and decrease in the uptake of $^{14}CO_2$.

SESSION 3
Chairperson: P.J. Holloway (U.K.)
Rapporteur: A. Donnelly (Ireland)

The main topics discussed were the effects of air pollutants (mainly, ozone and acid mist) on epicuticular wax chemical composition, structural morphology, and water status.

As regards chemical composition, there was evidence of a direct pollutant interaction with epicuticular wax biosynthesis. There was less variation in chemical constituents within provenances than between species and also there was evidence of wax recrystallisation on needles exposed to ozone and acid deposits of pH 1 and 3.

With regard to the effects of air pollutants on epicuticular wax structural morphology, research has been mostly concentrated on conifers, other evergreens, and broadleaved trees. The effects are more species specific than pollutant specific. Acid deposits may cause biosynthetic disturbances and accumulation of lipids in mesophyll cells. Effects can be caused by exposures of different time lengths, for example, after a few days or after a few weeks. To avoid difficulties in the interpretation of results, methods should be kept as simple as possible, for example, by using air-dried, untouched samples.

There were no visible symptoms related to acid rain treatment found at pH 3 or 4. However, after 5 weeks, occasional gypsum crystals were observed which occurred in greatest numbers during October-November. The gypsum crystals probably resulted from calcium being leached out of the needle and reacting with sulphates from acid rain or disturbed wax biosynthesis. TEM revealed calcium oxalate crystals in the cell wall or attached to the cell wall of spruce needles. After this particular presentation, a discussion took place regarding the origin of the calcium. One school of thought was that it was transported by dust or aerosols from the surrounding environment and the other was that it originated from within the needle.

Acid mist of pH 3 resulted in a degradation of the epicuticular wax impairing the water retention capacity of the needle and enhancing the water loss by non-stomatal transpiration. Under water stress conditions, such as drought conditions in summer or frost drought conditions in spring the water status situation becomes more severe leading to highly increased water losses of the trees pretreated with acid mist, while a recovery of the water status by water uptake is not possible. Air pollution predisposes trees to disease and, when combined with drought conditions, may result in the death of the tree.

Ponderosa pine showed changes in various physiological and chemical parameters and a decrease in growth with clean air and ozone treatment. Changes, *i.e.*, increased degradation of epicuticular waxes can be caused by a direct effect of ozone and disturbed development and synthesis of plant waxes.

SESSION 4
Chairperson: G. E. Taylor (U.S.A.)
Rapporteur: A. Bytnerowicz (U.S.A.)

The main points of the four papers presented at the sessions are as follows:

R. Jagels (keynote paper) — droplet contact angle (DCA) techniques provide an integrated assessment of physical and chemical characteristics of the epicuticular wax layer. However, since environmental and temporal factors modify biophysical features of epicuticular wax and affect DCA measurements, standardization of the method is needed before being widely used.

M. Riederer (keynote paper) — permeability of organic pollutants through plant cuticles differs among plant species and can be predicted from lipophilicities. Microscopically rough surfaces of conifer needles enhance the scavenging and uptake of organic pollutants from precipitation. Various factors (*e.g.*, surfactants, organic vapor) affect the permeability of the cuticular transport barrier. UVB radiation may lead to altered chemical composition of cuticular waxes by initiating the photo-oxidation of aldehydes. Optically pure S-nonacosan-10-ol is the constituent of epicuticular tubules in conifers. Tubes and plates, the metastable modifications of this compound, occur in equilibrium.

J. L. Hadley (voluntary paper) — cuticular resistance to water loss of conifers decreased with time and increased with elevation. This is related to loss of wax and increased wettability. Observed changes allow for better penetration of pollutants from clouds and fog into foliage of trees at high elevations. This may partially explain high susceptibility of conifers to acidic deposition in high mountains.

E. Paoletti (voluntary paper) — synthetic surfactants, such as ABS, increase susceptibility of trees to acidic deposition. Differences in damage of cuticular waxes between species and provenances of trees were determined. Presence of other substances deposited on foliage (sea salt, pollen, dust) affects responses of trees to acidic deposition and ABS. No clear relationship between morphological features of leaves and wax structure and degree of sensitivity to air pollutants was found.

SESSION 5
Chairperson: Richard Jagels (U.S.A.)
Rapporteur: B. Prügel (France)

The main topics were the cuticular characteristics of plant surfaces in terms of detection or mapping of plant stresses.

Another important point was the notion of "critical levels".

Additionally, a model for reasonable monitoring of forest health, as used by Natural Ressources Canada, was presented.

There was general agreement that three phases, the gas, the lipid, and the liquid phase, are implicated in all events taking place on plant surfaces.

Changes in surface properties for plants exposed to different pollution climates were investigated in field studies, as well as the effects of some specific pollutants (ethylene, SO_2 and ozone) in laboratory-experiments.

In most of the cases, exposure to specific pollutants did not lead to important structural changes of surfaces (except for extreme doses). These findings provide more evidence for the theory that changes on plant surfaces are mostly due to modifications in the metabolic pathway and not to direct interactions of the pollutants and the surface.

Attention was drawn to three points that must be respected for future research :

- the influence of the pollutants themselves on the surface properties (*e.g.*, roughness)
- the importance of organic pollutants (effect of softening)
- the impact of the microflora such as fungi on surface structures (melting effects of hyphae)

All these factors have to be taken into account when using surface characteristics such as contact angles for mapping or detection of plant stress.

All authors agreed that the results depend very strongly on the species investigated, the sample site, and the sampling period.

Finally, it is important to be aware of the "critical levels" for each pollutant and to carry out experimental studies on this basis, in order to initiate and help political decision-making.

SESSION 6
Chairperson: M.S. Gunthardt-Goerg (Switzerland)
Rapporteur: J.D. Barnes (U.K.)

Conclusions & recommendations for future work

1. Modern techniques have enabled advances to be made in our understanding of the chemistry of plant waxes and cutin. However, what is known constitutes only a beginning. Many gaps remain in our knowledge of the underlying biochemistry; enzymology, regulation of synthesis, and even the biosynthetic pathways. Furthermore, we know very little about the way in which wax is transported to, and deposited at, its extracellular location.

2. Isolated astomatous cuticular membranes provide a useful research tool to probe the effects of various environmental factors on the permeability of the cuticle to water and ions. However, great care needs to be exercised during the isolation process in order to ensure optimization; even a small amount of residual polysaccharide may significantly alter the properties of "isolated" cuticles. Scanning electron micrographs of inner cuticle surfaces indicate that the efficiency of the enzymatic digestion process is influenced by a number of factors.

3. Measured electrical potentials across isolated cuticles are positive, indicating greater permeability of the cuticle to cations. There is an urgent need to establish whether accelerated rates of cation leaching under the influence of various wet- and dry-deposited pollutants are of sufficient magnitude to result in significant changes in leaf/needle mineral composition.

4. The scanning electron microscope (SEM) provides a convenient means of studying epicuticular wax structure. However, artifacts can easily be introduced during the preparation of leaf material for conventional SEM investigation that can be confused with alterations in wax structure induced by air pollutants. In order to minimize confusion, there are two recommendations for future research: 1) when conventional SEM techniques are employed, plant material should be sampled and prepared in accordance with standardized guidelines; 2) wherever possible, studies of wax structure should take advantage of recent advances in SEM technology, employing cryopreservation and cryovisualization techniques.

5. New analytical techniques such as pyrolysis-gas chromatography/mass spectrometry (Py GC/MS) and direct pyrolysis-mass spectrometry (Py-MS) should be explored along with pattern recognition techniques/principal component analysis in an effort to improve the resolution of current GC-MS methodology.

6. The cuticle obviously plays a role in the interaction between the plant and other biotic and abiotic factors. However, we have a poor understanding of the way in which changes in the leaf cuticle influence plant response to a range of environmental factors and vice versa. One of the main aims of future research must be to fill this gap in our knowledge. Not only to

provide information about the biological significance of environmentally induced changes in the surface waxes, but also to aid the interpretation of certain measurements, *i.e.*, wettability. The most exciting advances are likely to be made in this area by those undertaking interdisciplinary research.

7. Collaboration should be instigated in order to fathom the molecular events involved in the response of the cuticle to environmental stress. This may allow common responses to be identified and enable some general predictions to be made regarding plant response. The technology is available to make substantial progress in this field, but there is a strong need for a multidisciplinary type of approach.

RECOMMENDATIONS BY PARTICIPANTS

The summary discussion delved into several areas but focused particularly on: 1) a concren about the scientific methods being used in cuticular wax research which, in turn, led to suggestions for possible standardization of some procedures; 2) a recognition of the vast array of air pollutants presently identified and the mostly unidentified interactions between these pollutants and plant cuticular waxes; and 3) a general discussion of the ecophysiology of plant leaf surfaces. Some further discussion followed on terminology.

Methodology

The concerns about methodology were targeted to sample collection, preparation, and aspects of measurement. It was recognized that the handling of leaves collected in the field was key to achieving consistent and reproducible results for scanning electron microscopy (SEM), droplet contact angle measurements or chemical analysis. The general consensus was that droplet contact angles should be meashred within 1-3 h of leaf collection; which often means field measurement. If storage is necessary, liquid nitrogen cryostorage was proposed. Leaves transported need to be protected from mechanical abrasion and, if not cryostored, then procedures should be instituted to maintain leaves in a turgid state and to prevent microbial growth or other biological deterioration.

Cryostorage was also recommended for leaf material to be examined in the SEM, with similar caveats about handling. Fixation methods for SEM were discussed but the consensus seemed to be that chemically fixed material was less desirable than fresh or cryostored material. Predryed leaves (i.e., conifer needles) were judged likely to have more artifacts (extrusion of wax plugs, wax cracking) than fresh or cryostored material. Fresh leaves in a humid environment could develop problems with fungal growth that might be misinterpreted as natural epiflora. Full disclosure of methods used should be included in journal articles.

A discussion of the analysis of leaf surfaces, whether by droplet-contact angle measurements or by microscopy, led to a closer examination of the variability of leaf surfaces. Depending upon the nature of the research, an investigator might want to examine only "pristine" idealized leaf surfaces (or surrogates) or might want to develop a survey of "real" leaves in the field, including such "artifacts" as microflora and fauna, natural mechanical erosion, etc. Likely a full range of studies is needed ranging from isolated cuticles to field-collected leaves from stressed sites.

It was recognized that inadvertent sampling distortion could be introduced if protocols for season of collection, and even time of day of collection, were not standardized. Degrees of wax synthesis or erosion or leaf turgor could all be affected by these time variables.

Pollutants

In the arena of pollutant effects, discussion went beyond the well-studied pollutants like ozon, SO_2, and acidic fog or rain and focused on the interactions between these and other pollutants, such as salts, surfactants, PAN's, HNO_3, and UV-B radiation. Particularly singled out were all forms of organic molecules, both those that might dissolve in aqueous solutions on leaf surfaces and those that might react with surface waxes or migrate through the cuticle.

Further research should focus on separating direct effects on cuticular waxes from indirect effects (physiological/biochemical changes in leaf interior that may lead to changes in surface waxes). It was recognized that physical processes are often neglected, such as kinetic and thermodynamic phase changes. The physical parameters involved in droplet contact angle measurements also need to be better understood and methods adopted to maximize repeatability.

Ecophysiology of leaf surface

It was recognized that we have an incomplete understanding of the role of various cuticular wax structures. The function of some structures may be multiple (control of moisture loss, reflection of specific wavelengths of light, barrier to insect predation). It was proposed that some structures may be redundant or vestigial, serving no real function at present. Within this range of possibilities, the effects of pollutants on surface structre could range from no biological effect to life endangering. The effect may be greater for plants stressed by other factors or for plants growing in particular habitats. More controlled experiments are needed to move from speculation to documented effects.

Terminology

Several terms were cited as ones that were vague or had different meanings to different researchers. Sometimes different terms were used to describe the same phenomena. The most troubling were;

Transpiration - does the researcher mean total leaf transpiration (i.e., stomatal and cuticular water loss) or is the term being used in the more restricted sense to cover only cuticular transport. Several participants agreed that we need to distinguish between 1) water loss through the undamaged cuticle (cuticular transport), and 2) water loss through damaged stomata, which do not close properly, or through mechanically damaged cuticle or surface wax.

Epicuticular Wax - does this mean only the surface was easily stripped of with chloroform or other solvent; or does it include intracuticular waxes. Some argued that the latter should be described as surface wax or total leaf wax. Operationally, a distinction perhaps could be made between extractable wax (using a particular solvent) versus location of wax, structurally, on the leaf.

Crystalline - leaf waxes generally described as crystalline usually mean those with a tubular form, but the term is vague in usage.

Erosion - the absence of wax structures on a leaf can be a consequence of: 1) mechanical abrasion which leads to wax loss; 2) a shift from one form to another with no net loss (e.g., nonacosanol transition from tube to amorphous forms); 3) the lack of synthesis of the structures. Distinguishing among these processes in mature leaves is often difficult.

Conclusions

The group felt it was important to improve communication between researchers in order to coordinate efforts, avoid duplicative research, and work toward resolving some of the issues raised above. An Internet communication network was proposed and was greeted with unanimous approval. Future meetings of the group were also proposed.

LIST OF PARTICIPANTS FROM NATO COUNTRIES

ARW NO.:   930609

TITLE: Air Pollutants and the Leaf Cuticle

DIRECTOR: Dr. K.E. Percy **LOCATION:** Fredericton, Canada **DATES:** 04-08.10.93

1.   KEY SPEAKERS

Canada

Dr. K.E. Percy
Canadian Forest Service - Maritimes
Natural Resources Canada
P. O. Box 4000
Fredericton, N.B.
Canada E3B 5P7

France

Dr. J.-P. Garrec
INRA - Centre de Recherches
  Forestières
Laboratoire d'étude de la Pollution
  Atmosphérique
54280 Champenoux
Siechamps
France

Germany

Dr. M. Riederer
Physiologische Okologie
Universitat Kaiserslautern
Postfach 30 49
D-67653 Kaiserslautern
Germany

Dr. H.-R. Schulten
Fachhochschule Fresenius
Department of Trace Analysis
Dambachtal 20
D-6200 Wiesbaden
Germany

United Kingdom

Dr. J.N. Cape
Institute of Terrestrial Ecology
Bush Estate
Penicuick
Midlothian EH26 0QB
UK

Dr. P. J. Holloway
Long Ashton Research Station
Long Ashton
Bristol BS18 9AF
UK

Dr. G. Kersteins
Division of Biological Sciences
University of Lancaster
Lancaster LA1 4YQ
UK

United States

Dr. R. Jagels
Department of Forest Biology
University of Maine
Orono, Maine
USA 04469

Dr. T.D. Scherbatskoy
Department of Botany
University of Vermont
Burlington, Vermont
USA 05405

United States (cont'd)

Dr. G. E. Taylor
Desert Research Institute
University of Nevada
P. O. Box 60220
Reno, Nevada
USA 89506-0220

Dr. M.T. Tyree
USDA Forest Service
Northeastern Forest Experiment Station
P. O. Box 968
Burlington, Vermont
USA 05402

2. OTHER PARTICIPANTS

Canada

Dr. J.D. Fuentes
Atmospheric Environment Service
Environment Canada
4905 Dufferin Street
Downsview, Ontario
Canada M3H 5T4

Dr. L.W. Carlson
Director,
Forest Health
Natural Resources Canada
351 St. Joseph Blvd
Hull, Québec
Canada K1A 1G5

Dr. T. Brydges
Atmospheric Environment Service
Environment Canada
4905 Dufferin Street
Toronto, Ontario
Canada M3H 5T4

Dr. R.T. Riding
Department of Biology
University of New Brunswick
Bag Service 45111
Fredericton, N.B.
Canada E3B 5A3

United Kingdom

Dr. J.D. Barnes
Department of Agricultural and
Environmental Science
The University
Newcastle-Upon-Tyne NEI 7RU
UK

Dr. C.E. Jeffree
Department of Botany
University of Edinburgh
The King's Building
West Mains Road
Edinburg EH9 3JH
UK

France

Dr. B. Prügel
INRA, Centre de Recherches
 forestières
Laboratoire d'étude de la Pollution
 atmosphérique
Champenoux
54280 Siechamps, France

Italy

Dr. E. Paoletti
Centro di Studio delle
 Specie legnose montane
Plazzale delle Cascine 28
50144 Firenze, Italy

Spain

Dr. A. Heredia
Departmento Bioquimica y Biologia
  Molecular
Universidad de Malaga
25071 Malaga
Spain

United States

Dr. V. Berg
Department of Biology
University of Northern Iowa
Cedar Falls, Iowa
USA 50614

Dr. R.L. Boyce
Environmental Studies Program
Dartmouth College
6182 Murdough Centre
Room 324
Hanover, N.H.
USA 03755-3577

Dr. Andrzej Bytnerowicz
USDA Forest Service
PSW Station
4955 Canyon Crest Drive
Riverside, CA
USA 92507

Germany

Dr. A. Esch
Institute of Plant Nutrition
University of Giessen
Sudanlage 6
6300 Giessen
Germany

Dr. C.R. Krause
USDA-ARS
OARC-OSU
Selby Hall
Wooster, Ohio
USA 44691

Dr. C.J. McQuattie
USDA-Forest Service
Northeastern Forest Experiment Station
359 Main Road
Delaware, Ohio
USA   43015

Dr. J.L. Hadley
Harvard University
Harvard Forest
P.O. Box 68
Petersham, Mass.
USA 01366-0068

LIST OF PARTICIPANTS FROM NON NATO COUNTRIES

1. KEY SPEAKERS

Finland

Dr. S. Huttunen
Department of Botany
University of Oulu
Oulu
SF 90570
Finland

2. OTHER PARTICIPANTS

Austria

Dr. E. Bermadinger-Stabentheiner
Institute fur Pflanzenphysiologie
Schubertstrasse 51
A-8010 Graz
Austria

Finland

Dr. M. Turunen
Arctic Centre
University of Lapland
P.O. Box 122
SF-96101 Rovaniemi
Finland

Switzerland

Dr. M.S. Gunthardt-Goerg
Swiss Federal Institute of Forestry
   Research
Zucherstrasse 111
CH-9803 Birmensdorf
Switzerland

Ireland

Ms. A. Donelly
Department of Botany
Trinity College
Dublin 2
Ireland

Poland

Dr. S. Godzik
Institute for Ecology of Industrial Areas
Environmental Protection Abatement
   Centre
6 Kossutha
Katowice 40-832
Poland

NATO ASI Series G

NATO ASI Series G

DATE DUE